IACOB BOHME[...]
Gebohren zu altseyde Gesto[...]
burg. Anno 1575. Anno [...]

Wenn Peter Juden Fischt, der Weber Wirbt die Heyden
Begint der Schuster Ietz sie bey derseits zu Weyden
Weil er die Heylige Schrifft mit der Natur verfaßt
Doch ist er eine last die Amasias haßt.

Boehme

An Intellectual Biography
of the Seventeenth-Century Philosopher and Mystic

Andrew Weeks

STATE UNIVERSITY OF NEW YORK PRESS

The cover design employs a detail from the first published map of Upper Lusatia (1495), composed by Bartholomäus Scultetus, mayor of Görlitz during Boehme's lifetime. The map, as well as the illustrations from early German and Dutch editions of Boehme's works, were provided courtesy of the Upper Lusatian Library of Sciences in Görlitz.

Published by
State University of New York Press, Albany

© 1991   State University of New York

All rights reserved

Printed in the United States of America

No part of this book may be used or reproduced
in any manner whatsoever without written permission
except in the case of brief quotations embodied in
critical articles and reviews.

For information, address State University of New York
Press, State University Plaza, Albany, N.Y. 12246

Production by Ruth East
Marketing by Fran Keneston

Library of Congress Cataloging-in-Publication Data

Weeks, Andrew.
    Boehme : an intellectual biography of the seventeenth-century philosopher and mystic / Andrew Weeks.
        p. cm.
    Includes bibliographical references and index.
    ISBN 0-7914-0596-6 (acid free) . —ISBN 0-7914-0597-4 (pbk. : acid free)
    1. Böhme, Jakob, 1575–1624. 2. Mystics—Germany (East)—Görlitz--Biography. 3. Mysticism—Germany—History—17th century.
I. Title.
BV5095.B7W423   1991
230'.044'092—dc20
[B]   90-37130
                                                                           CIP

10 9 8 7 6 5 4 3 2 1

To the librarians and archivists of Bloomington, Indiana; Görlitz, East Germany; Middlebury, Vermont; Urbana, Illinois; Vienna, Austria; and Wolfenbüttel, West Germany—whose intelligent and unstinting help was an invaluable source of assistance in my researches.

Contents

Preface		xi
Introduction		1
1	Upper Lusatia	13
2	The Genesis of Boehme's Vision	35
3	The Twofold *Aurora*	61
4	The Three Worlds	93
5	The Fire-World	127
6	The Mirror of Darkness	157
7	The Will to Revelation	185
8	Boehme's Last Year	209
Notes		221
Bibliography		247
Index		257

PREFACE

Few writers are remembered more by their legend and less by the content of their writings than Jacob Boehme. Few have been rediscovered as often. And few have been marked by such contradictory cachets: as the humble soul and God-taught theosophist, and as the "fanatical" heretic and blasphemer; the illuminate outside of time, and the philosopher in advance of his time; harbinger of enlightenment, and vanguard of German chauvinism; devious charlatan, and forthright muddle-head. No common ground has been found for reconciling these contradictory images.

What this study attempts is therefore not a balance but a new presentation, based on the premise that the writings are virtually all we can know of the man. Like any writer, Boehme wrote in a particular time and place; he wrote for readers who understood and encouraged his efforts. Much can be gained by interpreting his work with reference to the environment in which and for which it arose.

Those who have heard of Boehme, who lived from 1575 until 1624, may not associate him with the period in which Shakespeare, Descartes, Cervantes, Kepler, or Wallenstein lived. As a rule, he is either allocated to the timeless category reserved for the mystics of all ages and cultures, or detemporalized as the prescient forerunner of more modern developments in literature, art, and philosophy. Numerous studies have been written placing his illuminism in the context of a German or universal mysticism. His doctrines have been compiled and interpreted by theologians and philosophers; his existence registered by literary historians and ethnographers. However, there is no basic study in English or German of the kind that examines his writings work by work and relates them to his life and times, in order to survey and, where necessary, revise his standing in intellectual history. This book, as an introductory portrait and intellectual biography of Jacob Boehme, is intended to fill that gap.

For their kind assistance in reading my work and offering many helpful suggestions, I would like to express my gratitude to Prof. Willis Barnstone (Bloomington, Indiana), Mr. William Dickey (Urbana, Illinois), Ms. Janet Meek (Bloomington, Indiana), Prof. Heinz Strotzka (Salzburg, Austria), Ms. Alice Wang (Bloomington, Indiana), and, last but not least, my mother, Mary Weeks. I would also like to thank the Faculty Research Committee of Middlebury College for a modest grant which covered my initial expenses in compiling research materials.

Introduction

The Seminal Mystery and Its Consequences

In the year 1600, a twenty-five year old Lutheran German shoemaker in the Upper Lusatian provincial city of Görlitz experienced a sudden inner transformation. For some time, the shoemaker had been afflicted with severe melancholy. A man of intense and troubled piety, he had come to feel depressed at the very sight of nature. He was oppressed by the heavens, which he took to be an impenetrable blue vault, hundreds or thousands of miles away. He was disturbed by the sun, stars, clouds, rain, and snow that filled "the great depths of the world." He was distressed by the mixture of good and evil that he found not only in all living creatures, but even in stones, wood, earth, and the elements. He had heard of new astronomical measurements and of the discovery of rich lands in the New World; but these advances only deepened his melancholy. The measurements proved that the deity was inaccessibly remote, while the discovered lands of the New World indicated that God favored the "Barbaric Peoples" more than the pious ones. Entertaining "heathenish thoughts," the shoemaker feared for his soul.

The immediate stimulus of his inner experience may not have seemed significant enough to write about. His later friend, the nobleman Abraham von Franckenberg, gave an account that was to become legendary. Surprised by a gleam, presumably of sunlight, in a tin or pewter vessel, the shoemaker began to imagine that he was seeing into the secret heart of nature, into a concealed divine world. Intent upon clearing his mind of this "phantasy," perhaps so that he could resume his shoemaking labors, the young man went out-of-doors. Since the city was small, he could easily pass through a nearby gate and into the green countryside. There, according to Franckenberg, the rapt cobbler continued to see all the more powerfully into the secret "center of nature." Forms, lines, and colors now bore some new meaning for him. In his own account, the strongest emotional effect associated with the experience was his sense of having been embraced by divine love: as if life had been resurrected from death, he recalled twelve years afterward.[1]

The shoemaker later mentioned that his experience had lasted no more than "a quarter of an hour." Only his friend related the gleam of light and the walk through the gate into a green world. Neither of them claimed that voices were heard, or any phenomenon sighted which surpassed the ordinary course of events. Nevertheless, something spectacular clearly did take place at the outset of Jacob Boehme's new path of life; for he was ultimately transformed into a speculative mystic and philosopher whose influence endured for centuries.

Looking back in 1621, he wrote that, after his brief seminal experience, he had begun by attempting to study and formulate its significance. These first efforts resulted in a long, unfinished book to which he gave the title *Morgenröthe im Aufgang*, or *Rising Dawn*—a work which he and his supporters later called *Aurora*. Twelve years elapsed before this *Memorial* of his illumination of 1600 was near completion. The shoemaker then lent the manuscript to a visitor, a nobleman interested in religious questions. The manuscript was copied and circulated. When a copy came into the hands of the chief pastor of Görlitz, the city's ministers and magistrates reacted by subjecting the author to hostile questioning, censuring him and forcing him to agree to write no more.

For several years Boehme kept his word and remained silent. Then, at the urging of those who had seen his first manuscript, he again took up the pen. He started his second book around the beginning of 1618, on the eve of the Thirty Years' War. Nearly two years went by before the work was finished; but it was followed by an unceasing stream of writings. During the first years of the war, which soon devastated the whole region, his writings were copied and circulated by hand within a rapidly expanding circle of readers. By his death in 1624, the author's reputation was already established in several areas of North Germany.

After his death, Boehme's fame soon spread abroad: first to Holland, and then in successive waves to England, France, Russia, and even America. His writings influenced German Baroque poets, as well as dissenters and intellectuals of seventeenth-century England. His reputation waned during the eighteenth century, only to be revived before the century ended. During this second epoch of his reception, his books provided inspiration to poets, including Blake, Tieck, and Novalis. In general, the German Romantics revered him as a forerunner of their movement. More remarkable still, the autodidactic author was praised by the German philosophers Baader, Schelling, Hegel, and Schopenhauer—a trend culminating in Hegel's characterization of the shoemaker as the thinker in whom philosophy had first come into its own in Germany: "the first German philosopher."[2]

This brief account of the career and influence of the man who called himself the *Philosophus der Einfältigen* ("philosopher of the simple folk") and the *Philosophus Teutonicus* is intended to suggest both the incontrovertible facts and the layers of legend which impede a fresh biographical approach to Boehme. The questions to be confronted in this study include the problem posed by his illumination, the enigma of his meaning and role as a "prophet," and the problematic relationship of common experience to the content of his writings. What is at issue in these questions is whether Boehme should be read critically, like other writers, or set apart as an "illuminate" who can only be accepted or rejected wholesale.

The miracle of Boehme's "illumination" of 1600 claims no verification beyond his writings. Mircea Eliade has discussed many accounts of "experiences of the mystical light."[3] In the case of Boehme, one can cite no reports of supernatural visions, no brilliant flashes of light, no voices from the other world, and no ensuing powers of healing. He himself asserted little more than that the essentials of his vision as a mystical writer had come to him during his brief experience—an assertion that is rather more modest than the claims of many other mystics. His interpreters can be divided into those who have emphasized his illumination, and those who have not. The former have cited his remarkably prodigious output, the latter the evolving content of his writings.[4] In either instance, the understanding of Boehme's illumination determined what was read and given consideration in the immense and repetitive corpus of his work.

I will suggest that Boehme's illumination, though surely a singularly transforming and inspiring experience, should not be thought of as fundamentally distinct from other processes of inspiration. The notion that his writings were records of ecstatic visions not only contributes almost nothing to their interpretation, it is detrimental to our understanding of the writer in the cultural context of his times. We know that in Boehme's age, inspiration often came by way of a divine flash. Descartes and Pascal are thought to have been profoundly inspired by sudden experiences of conversion or illumination. But who would be inclined to interpret their respective complete works as mere memoranda of instantaneous and passively received intuitions? Repeatedly, the scholarly literature on Boehme demonstrates that his classification as an "illuminist" has prejudiced the manner in which he is read. Our hypothesis that his inspiration was intellectual in nature should have the opposite effect of focusing attention in categories of analysis which are seldom applied to his writings.

The prophetic element in Boehme's writings has likewise been exaggerated and misconstrued: exaggerated by being considered in isolation of an environment in which prophetic sentiments were widespread, and misconstrued by being taken with reference to specific historical events, of which Boehme had no foreknowledge. Eberhard Pältz and Ernst Benz have contributed much to the discussion of Boehme's status as a prophet—Benz, by distinguishing the original significance of the term within church history and by making the case for a kind of prophecy concerned less with the foreknowledge of events than with a profound religious message.[5] Benz firmly places Boehme in the Protestant tradition and calls attention to later Protestants who were affected by his writings. But the argument by tradition also encounters grave difficulties. It should suffice to consider the two most important later German Baroque poets who were to acknowledge Boehme's influence on their lives: Johannes Scheffler (Angelus Silesius) and Quirinus Kuhlmann. Inspired to convert to Catholicism, Scheffler entered the priesthood and zealously championed the Counter-Reformation in Silesia.[6] Reading his Boehme very differently, Kuhlmann proclaimed a radical Protestant millenarianism in his poetry and demonstrated his sincerity in life, incurring a grim martyrdom by fire in a Moscow street. A lesser-known German Protestant named Johann Jakob Spaeth is said to have converted to Judaism under the influence of Boehme's writings.[7] The message of the Protestant prophet was thus anything but unequivocal. Similar ambiguities prevail with respect to his influence as a prescient "philosopher." Though Boehme's varied impact on posterity is of considerable interest in itself, it offers us no clear point of departure for the interpretation of his writings.

The obfuscations of "illumination," "prophecy," and "prescience" are complemented by—and have often been linked with—nationalistic interpretations of the *Philosophus Teutonicus*. It is well known that Luther associated the cause of the Reformation with that of the German nation. Boehme, the conscious heir to Luther's Reformation, offers surprisingly scant evidence of a comparable attachment. Even his famous defenses of the German language—justified with reference to his mystical "language of nature"—are universalistic in spirit.[8] The mystical *Natursprache* is the forgotten language of all humankind. In the context of his work, the phrases, *teutsch wissen, teutsch davon reden*, or *teutsch genug schreyben*, mean: to know, to speak, and to write—"in plain English."[9] The *Philosophus Teutonicus* is the *Philosophus der Einfältigen*: the philosopher of the simple folk. Common experience, albeit of a distinct and distant kind, is the better key to his meaning. Certainly Boehme is as quintessentially *German* as

Goethe or Nietzsche, but his image and meaning have also been no less distorted than theirs by the stereotypes of German culture.

The Irreducible Ambiguities of Boehme's Work

The record of Boehme's reception is a sequence of verdicts: hereticized or vindicated in the seventeenth century, shunned by the Enlightenment, rehabilitated by the Romantics, Boehme in this century has been reclaimed as a cultural nationalist by national-minded Germans, as a Lutheran by Lutheran church historians, and as a fund of universal myths by Jungians or New Age enthusiasts. Even granting that no interpretation can be free of period bias, the little-read and syncretic nature of his writing makes it an especially sensitive litmus for absorbing interpretive points of view.

The traditional tendency to filter the particular contents of Boehme's writings through general definitions of "mysticism," "German mysticism," "nature mysticism," "nature philosophy," or "theosophy" can best be counteracted by proceeding from the historical context, to the contents of his works. Because of the ambiguities of his writings, it is counterproductive to begin with general definitions that allocate him to a special category and distort the bonds which connect him to his times. His illumination took place in a period of competition between rival theologies, philosophies, and cosmologies, when there were more things in heaven and earth than a school philosophy might dream of. The relationship of heaven and earth was itself under dispute. In 1600, empires, nations, and religions were pitted against one another. The forces of the Counter-Reformation were slowly gathering against a bitterly divided Protestant world. In 1600, Bruno, an early heliocentrist, was burned at the stake in Rome. Kepler arrived in Prague. William Gilbert, another early heliocentrist, published his treatise, *On the Lodestone*. Microscopes and telescopes were not yet available. Not only things invisibly small or inaccessibly remote, but even the internal workings of organic life were still obscure in 1600. Several years would elapse before Harvey would complete his studies of arterial circulation, of animal generation, and of embryonic development. The universe of Aristotle, Ptolemy, and Galen was losing its power to convince, but the outline of the new universe was as uncertain as the charts of the North American continent—which was known but as yet devoid of European settlements in 1600. At the same time, the unknown was not a mere *terra incognita* for the shoemaker and his contemporaries. Philosophers and scientists even speculated about life on other planets. Boehme's speculative mysticism was in no small measure an imaginative voyage of exploration, fired by faith and intellectual curiosity.

In order to comprehend Boehme's philosophical mysticism as thought and as writing, it is necessary to proceed from his real premises: by reconstructing the questions and problems to which his symbols and concepts provided answers which were meaningful to his own contemporaries, if not to us. The complexity of his speculative mysticism was not called into being simply by the needs of Protestants for a religion of immediacy—a need which would have been ill-served by his long and difficult treatises. Nor was his work adapted to fill the need for a new scientific-philosophical understanding of the world. Although his work inspired numerous poets, he had no self-awareness as a poet.

Nothing can be gained by subsuming Boehme exhaustively under the headings of the philosopher or the mystic. The discussions of mysticism organized by Steven Katz have established that there is no simple way of characterizing the interrelations of mysticism, religious tradition, and philosophy.[10] Boehme was a writer and thinker whose themes are not only mystical but also—at least in the broadest sense of the term—philosophical. The hidden God, the order and intelligibility of the world, and the life of nature and the soul occupy him as aspects of a single question. Few if any of his striking visionary symbols—neither the "seven source-spirits," nor "the wheel of essences," nor the "Celestial Virgin Sophia"—were spontaneous inspirations. Yet his ecstatic mode of writing is indisputably visionary.

Boehme's argumentation is premised on doctrinal beliefs, on articles of faith concerning the Trinity, the sacraments, and grace. Through a process of reflection and imagination, the cobbler elaborated these pious articles of faith into something no longer identical with his premises: a body of thought which could stand on its own, demonstrating its merits to the poets and philosophers of later, more secularized, times. The relationship of doctrinal faith to speculative thought is of significance for the approach of this study.

Even the most distinguished study of "the philosophy of Boehme," the book of that title by the French historian of ideas Alexandre Koyré, treats the role of doctrinal questions as no more than a ballast, naively retained by an early philosopher—rather than as a precise guide to the premises and goals of the Baroque thinker. Yet if one underestimates Boehme's doctrinal concerns, the term philosophy becomes misleading in itself, with the result that his thinking appears as an epigonal "pansophic" eclecticism, as in the interpretation of Will-Erich Peuckert's *Pansophia*.[11] Hans Grunsky's *Jacob Böhme* likewise disregards the doctrinal point of departure—yet maintains that the shoemaker developed a full-blown "philosophical system," employing more than *fifty* philosophical terms and expressing a lucid philosophy received in a series of philosophical intuitions. The thesis of the spontaneous inspiration safeguards the coherence of the work but tends to obfuscate the diversity of its sources.

It should be abundantly evident that an author whose first three books alone add up to more than 1200 pages can scarcely have been motivated exclusively by a fifteen-minute inspiration. The illumination of the year 1600 is an important theme, but it is hardly the complete content of his writings. The concepts and images of his work evolve, even while conforming to underlying patterns. The conditions of his period and region affected his speculative mysticism. His mind was engaged by new theories of nature, and by issues from confessional quarrels which now appear abstruse to most believers. In an age of intolerance, the shoemaker sought grounds for reconciling conflicting beliefs. He registered the hostilities of the Thirty Years' War as it spread into his native region. In this respect, he was closer to the common life of his times than were the contemporaneous poets and theologians, who largely ignored the impact of these events on the life of the people.[12] Boehme's mysticism is as much bound up with the historical and intellectual currents of his own period and place as are the motives of those religious painters whose portrayals of Biblical scenes reveal the artists' subjective worlds, including their notions of space, time, and meaning.

We therefore stand to profit considerably by acknowledging Boehme's proximate sources of inspiration. This is not intended to discourage comparisons of his mysticism with that of earlier or of more distant religions. Much has been learned by juxtaposing his speculative constructs with those of Neoplatonism and by comparing him with Eastern mystics and Kabbalistic authors. If his mysticism can be likened to a *dialect*, then its origins lie in certain predecessor "languages" (notably those of Gnosticism and Neoplatonism). The structures of Boehme's mysticism resemble those of other mystical systems. However, like any set of symbols, his speculative vision was also molded by a specific time, place, culture, and character. The consideration of his symbolism in its own setting and idiom will take precedence here over comparisons with other systems of thought and intuition.

Similar strictures are applicable to sympathizing presentations of "mystical awareness": the latter is sometimes defended as a valid alternative to scientific intellection (a defense that implicitly admonishes us against raising any suggestion that the vision of the mystic is conditioned by his objective ignorance). However, even if mystical truth is indeed as true as scientific truth, the vision of the artisan—who confidently measures the heavens with his naked eye and reasons from the analogies of the human body to the corpus of the world—still remains far removed from the perceptions of those who strain to grasp his meaning in a later century. In considering Boehme's obscure and unfamiliar notions, we would only be led down blind alleys by postulating a cosmic consciousness, an ineffable experience, or a primitive mythopoetic thinking.

As to the method of analysis, I have chosen not to introduce demanding theoretical digressions. At the risk of seeming unsophisticated, the exposition will strive to maintain a clear demarcation between its own inadequacies and the inherent difficulties of its subject. In the interest of a sustained narrative-biographical development, I have relegated much of my documentation and discussion of sources to the endnotes. In interpreting Boehme for the reader, I will attempt to bring his notions and, through them, their author to life. This is surely an appropriate task for a biographer, but it is also one which ought to entail no denial of the weaknesses and contradictions of his subject.

In addition to his advanced heliocentrism and his apparent anticipation of certain later philosophical trends, his writings also present us with an array of irrational notions which cannot be ignored. The congruence of his thought rests on what modern philosophical analysis might call "category errors." Time is in eternity, eternity in time. What is eternal appears as if it were born and transformed. Conversely, the processes of history and causality are superseded by figural metaphors for eternal patterns of being. The mystic not only opens up the door to new insights; he also truncates reality and introduces supernatural, numinous presences into its midst. Experience is pervaded by the two eternal realms of good and evil, of light and darkness. How are the two worlds coordinated in our world? If time mirrors eternity, how can a temporal reflection of eternity approach its resolution? If history is an incessant back-and-forth struggle between the realms of good and evil, how does it happen that our world is not altogether overshadowed by the two eternal ones? Ernst Cassirer has argued that the dual hierarchies of Pseudo-Dionysius resembled the dual feudal hierarchies of church and state.[13] How, we may inquire, does Boehme's dual, yet threefold, world-totality refer to his historical experience? Even his handful of references to apparitions deserve more attention than they have been accorded. His ghosts are more than immaterial wraiths of the deceased; they are embodiments of a past which, though buried and half-forgotten, still wreaks immense havoc in the present. These and other details can provide clues to the referential experience of the writer.

Scholars intent upon absolving Boehme of all stains of obscurantism have taken widest umbrage at the wondrous occurrences reported in Franckenberg's biography—unnecessarily, since the biographer's miracles require no supernatural explanation. In relating his "report," Franckenberg rather guardedly submits his providential interpretations. His anecdotes therefore in no way impinge upon the content of Boehme's writings. It is surely worth bearing in mind that Franckenberg's accounts are from the hand of a man who knew his subject for several years. Instead of disassociating Boehme from this first-hand report, one can learn more by considering the implications which are conveyed together with the biographer's intimations of foreshadowed marvels.

This applies especially to the legendary anecdote that has given the greatest offense. Once, writes Franckenberg, the child Jacob, while tending cattle with the other village boys, absented himself around noon, wandered onto a mountainside, and discovered a cavernous treasure trove, hidden away between great red stones and luxuriating vegetation. The boy Jacob fled from the site in terror. Returning later with his companions, they were unable to relocate the site of the cache. The biographer speculates that this occurrence prefigured Boehme's later discovery of a divine secret treasure of "Natural Wisdom."

In order to cleanse Boehme of the odium of occultism, some critics have been at pains to present the biographer's account as an improbable invention. The mountain (*die Landeskrone*, outside Görlitz) is said to have been too remote from any pasturage used by the peasants from Jacob's home village. (But what if only the less decisive details about herding were incorrect?) This weak refutation is hardly worth the bother, since Franckenberg himself makes no pretense that the wondrous *Bütte mit Gelde* was the font of his friend's knowledge. (The matter would be very different if he had claimed that the child had discovered the man's wisdom inscribed on golden tablets, or if Boehme himself had written any such tale in order to bolster his own reputation.) Whether the child Jacob really discovered a hidden cache of money, or whether the aging mystic, in conversation with his credulous younger admirer, talked his way into this pretty tale, is less significant than the remaining details of the anecdote, which I will take up in the discussion of Boehme's Lusatian surroundings. Why should the boy Jacob have fled in terror upon finding a hidden treasure? Why does the biographer mention various other legendary sites of concealed treasures in the region, undercutting his own assertion that *this* treasure was special and providential?

If more attention is accorded to such details, Boehme's writings can reveal traces of bygone issues, places, perils, and hopes. Although no significant new biographical information is likely to be discovered after the archival researches of Fechner, Jecht, Heimbach, and Lemper,[14] the available information about Boehme's era and region has scarcely been brought to bear on the analysis of his writings. Ernst Troeltsch long ago demonstrated that mystical cults and religious movements are part of the real social experience of their adherents, an insight which has been reconfirmed in such recent studies as Emmanuel Le Roy Ladurie's *Montaillou*, Carlo Ginzburg's *The Cheese and the Worms*, and Frances A. Yates's *The Rosicrucian Enlightenment*.[15] However, heretofore these lessons have not been applied to the illuminate of Görlitz. A less fanciful image of this plebeian intellectual of the Baroque Age needs to be disentangled from the trappings of cobbler's paraphernalia and arcane folklore framing his legendary figure, and then recontextualized in the Middle European* setting in which he lived and wrote.

---

*In preference to the geographical "Central Europe," I will use the term "Middle Europe" in order to allude to the historical conditions of a region in which the boundaries of language area, nation, confession, and ideology have often been more fluid than in the West of Europe.

1 Upper Lusatia

An engraving from an early Dutch edition of Boehme's works shows him writing at his workbench amidst the tools of his trade. The floor is littered with a fold of uncut leather, scraps, and a pattern-cut piece for a shoe. This, together with the fact that he is wearing a heavy apron, announces that a simple shoemaker has momentarily paused in his accustomed labors. The quill is gripped in a firm artisan's hand. An hourglass on the bench measures the fleeting minutes stolen from his handicraft.[1]

It is certainly not impossible that Boehme wrote his first book like this. His writing has certain artisanlike qualities. Despite the sublimity of his themes and the originality of his verbal innovations, his first endeavors at extended composition were ponderous and mechanical. Patterns of Biblical sequence are taken over and maintained, even when they run counter to his developing train of thought. Refractory cogitations come up repeatedly, as if he were hammering out his ideas from a verbal material, widening, altering, and shaping them.

The engraving also strikingly emphasizes the isolation of the shoemaker-mystic. The shadowy walls of his workroom lock out the exterior world. Dramatically, the light from an unseen high window falls upon the writer's intense countenance and touches his manuscript. The angle formed by this light from above with his downward gaze suggests that his writing reflects an invisible source. The dim milieu of scattered objects is on hand merely to contrast with the luminous transfer. The image has a strong graphic appeal—precisely because it sums up the Jacob Boehme legend.

Another facet of this same legend is the anachronism of many German studies: the designation of Boehme as a "Silesian mystic." Görlitz and Eastern Lusatia were incorporated into a Prussian-administered Silesia only between 1815 and 1945. In his scant remarks touching on his home region and its neighbor to the east, Boehme consistently mentioned Silesia (*Schlesien*) as a distinct neighboring territory. When he stated his "country" by name, it was Lusatia (*die Lausitz*), never Silesia.[2] Silesia, from Caspar Schwenckfeld to Angelus Silesius, was the terrain of Eastern German mysticism. By overlooking a seemingly minor detail of historical accuracy, scholars absorbed the Lusatian writer into the nimbus of the nearby territory. Displacing the man also shifted the perspective on his work toward otherworldliness.

Lusatia and Silesia shared much in common as northern crown lands of the Kingdom of Bohemia, but there were also significant religious and political differences, especially in Boehme's time. These differences should not be glossed over in the interest of consolidating German literary landscapes.

Two Centuries of Religious Upheaval

Situated between Bohemia to the south, Silesia to the east, Brandenburg to the north, and the lands of Saxony and Meissen to the west, Lusatia was a characteristic Middle European territory, rocked by the fall of dynasties and the upsurge of new religious movements. For two centuries, in intervals of about fifty years, its mixed Slavic and German populace suffered the reverberations from shifting centers of power and changing doctrines of faith. For even longer than that, the small territories of the Margravates of Upper and Lower Lusatia had been handed or wrenched from one dominion to another. The two Lusatias had already been ruled by the Holy Roman Empire, Poland, and Brandenburg before they became Bohemian crown lands in the fourteenth century.

In the course of passing between dominions, the cities of Upper Lusatia acquired a degree of territorial cohesion which was cemented by the League of Six Cities, (*der Sechsstädtebund*), founded in 1346. By the end of the fifteenth century *das Land der Sechsstädte* had become an alternate name for Upper Lusatia.[3] Prominent in the federation were the city of Bautzen (which is now the center of the Slavic Sorb minority of East Germany) and, about one day's journey east of Bautzen, Görlitz on the Neisse. History is eschatology in Boehme's writings, not chronicle. He mentions no specific events of the past—not even of the religious strife which lay within the living memory of his older contemporaries. In the allegorical preface of his first book, even the Reformation appears as one episodic altercation in the incessant battle of truth against falsehood. However, this lack of historical perspective is in itself revealing of the circumstances of a region over which waves of order and discord rolled seemingly without end. The prefatory allegory obliquely recalls a time of "war and stormwinds" between the allegorized adulteration of the truth by Rome and the revival of truth by the Reformation (I 11/49). In Middle Europe, the great period of war and turmoil prior to Luther was the era of the Hussite Wars in the fifteenth century—a period which was not forgotten by Boehme's contemporaries. One of them, the Humanist Mayor Scultetus of Görlitz, even undertook to reconstruct a chronicle of his city during the years of the Hussite Wars.

In 1415, Jan Hus, the leader of the Czech Reformation which preceded Luther's by a hundred years, was burned at the stake at the Council of Constance. The followers of Hus rebelled against the pope and their Catholic king. Their religious and national uprising began in earnest in 1419 with the first "Defenestration of Prague." Marching beneath the banner of the chalice (signifying the Utraquist demand for Communion in both kinds), the Hussites defeated the Imperial armies and invaded the surrounding German territories. The Upper Lusatian League of Six Cities remained staunchly loyal to Rome and to the expelled King Sigismund of Bohemia. When the victorious armies of Hussites and Taborites marched north toward Brandenburg and the Baltic Sea, Lusatia and Silesia lay in their path. The stalwart League of Six marshaled its burgher forces and hired mercenaries to resist the invaders.

During this distant age of "war and stormwinds," Lusatia had fallen into a state of violent lawlessness. Feuding nobles and "outlaw knights" (*Raubritter*) declared war on towns, raiding and burning their outlying villages and terrorizing the roads and countryside. The outlaw knights lived on, not only in legend:[4] their progeny continued to terrorize the townspeople. Noble bandits and marauding criminals still imperiled the main road through Upper Lusatia in the middle of the sixteenth century.[5]

The fabled memory of the outlaw knights reverberates in Boehme's most persistent metaphor for the power of evil. From the first fragment to the last voluminous tome, Lucifer inhabits a figurative "outlaw castle," a *Raubschloß*. In a treatise on melancholy, the satanic robber knight descends upon his victims under cover of darkness, invading their melancholy imaginations and convincing them that they are challenged by the just wrath of God. These characteristic metaphors for the *Anfechtung* or trial of the spirit provide clues to the background of the mysterious treasure from Boehme's childhood and of his characteristic fear of violence and disorder.

During the fifteenth century, the burghers of the League responded to the *Raubritter* by carrying out military expeditions against the outlaw bastions and executing the defeated nobles. One of the most destructive of these strongholds stood on the promontory of *die Landeskrone* overlooking the city walls of Görlitz.[6] In 1422, the combined League forces stormed, conquered, and razed the fortifications, delivering a stinging blow to a class enemy who, if granted the opportunity, knew how to retaliate viciously. The summit of the *Landeskrone* became one of the legendary sites of an outlaw treasure trove said to lie beneath the ruins of a *Raubschloß*.[7]

The Lusatians, who continued to suffer the excesses of their violence-prone gentry, expressed their fears in numerous legends, songs, and superstitions. A confused mixture of mortal terror at the thought of retribution, and of guilt at the prospect of being tempted with illicit wealth, must have invaded the imagination of the boy Jacob on the legendary summit of the *Landeskrone*. In *Aurora*, the fallen Prince Lucifer is a lawless vassal who becomes inflamed by pride. When he attempts to usurp the highest place within the divine order, his vain fury ignites a corrupting fire in nature. After a successful counterassault by Prince Michael, the fury of the usurping host is contained and hemmed in. The forces of good in this world can only ward off satanic incursions by maintaining constant vigilance. The devil still dwells in the darkness between the moon and the earth, favoring deep caves and places of stony desolation (I 370/25.20).

However, there is a curious ambiguity in Boehme's metaphors for evil, an ambiguity characteristic of the divided longings for order and freedom, experienced by the mystic and by his fellows. In one and the same tract, the devil may appear both as a fallen prince, an enemy of the rightful order, and in a second guise: as an executioner or, lower still, as the mere lackey of the judge or executioner, as the *Henkersknecht* or *Büttel-Knecht*, who leads the condemned to the scaffold. In Upper Lusatia, as elsewhere, the executioner was thought to exercise a dishonorable, though necessary, profession. Even in the view of the mystic, human evil called for the punishing sword of justice. However, Upper Lusatia had also known numerous executions of a kind understandably feared by Boehme and his fellow Protestants in a region in which Protestantism was threatened: executions of heretics.

Aside from the *Raubritter*, a second pattern had been set by the violence of the fifteenth century. During the Hussite Wars, the Upper Lusatian cities not only defended themselves against the invaders— who are referred to in the annals simply as *die Ketzer*, "the heretics"— the burghers also acted against certain Lusatians who were accused of collaborating with the heretical foreigners. Everywhere—writes the historian Jecht—even in Görlitz and Bautzen, these heretical sympathizers and traitors were ferreted out: the merest suspicion resulted in torture and execution. Jecht, a man of National Liberal inclinations, was obviously perturbed by the record of these persecutions. He offers makeshift explanations: Terror drove people to treason. The townspeople were rebelling against the harsh rule of their urban governments. Hussite spies were recruiting agents. Old personal scores were being settled. Conspicuously, Jecht fails to consider two possibilities: that the accused heretics may have been Upper Lusatian Sorbs; and that the heretics, whether Sorbs or Germans, may actually have been true converts to the Hussite creed. The Sorbic population was located mainly in the countryside.[8] Significantly, Jecht stresses that the "heretics" were not only in the villages, but even in the cities.[9] It would stand to reason that the alleged *Ketzer*, who were accused of aiding and informing the invaders, were those in the populace whose Slavic tongue enabled them to communicate with the invaders. An exceptional urban heretic was the city council member of Bautzen named Peter Preischwitz, a Germanicized Slavic name. Preischwitz had been active in the defense of his city. Accused of shooting messages tied to his arrows to the besieging Hussites, he was cruelly disemboweled and beheaded for treason. A legend in Bautzen identified one of the stones in the city gate with his impaled head.[10]

Beyond this, why should the possibility be excluded that the victims, whether Sorbs or Germans, were converts to the Hussite faith? The Hussite banner and creed were not hard to decipher. If the Lusatians, Germans and Sorbs alike, in later times stood ready to sacrifice themselves for the sake of various religious causes, some of them may have done so even earlier as Utraquists.

What is certain is that, in the centuries that followed, the Lusatians suffered repeatedly because of conflicts between power and faith. In the aftermath of the Hussite Wars, a subsequent generation in Lusatia found itself in the peculiar dilemma of having to choose between loyalty to an acknowledged king and fidelity to a no less devoutly acknowledged pope. In 1467, Poděbrad, the new Bohemian king whom the Six Cities solemnly accepted as their ruler, was excommunicated as a heretic by the pope. Upper Lusatia was plunged into confused warfare between the Poděbradian loyalists and the forces loyal to pope and emperor. Reluctantly, the Six Cities disengaged themselves from their king. And, again, Görlitz witnessed persecutions, as its heretics were exiled, tortured, and executed.[11] These events were also chronicled by Mayor Scultetus during Boehme's time.[12] Even unchronicled, the pattern of a persecution brought on by the uncoordinated relations of political and religious allegiance can only have been well known to all, since it in fact recurred in ever more dire variants, right down to the fateful replay of the Defenestration of Prague at the outset of the Thirty Years' War.

A century after the Hussite invasions of the 1420s, and a half century after the crisis of the Poděbradian turmoil, Lusatia was again unsettled, this time by the Lutheran Reformation. Its centers of influence were in the Saxon domains that lay to the west of the League of Six Cities. The patrician leadership of the Lusatian cities responded coolly to the new Reformation. The city councillors were resolved to remain loyal to the old faith. Johann Hass, a city scribe who became a tyrannical mayor of Görlitz, even threatened to eradicate all heretical elements.[13]

The advent of the Reformation in Upper Lusatia conformed to the pattern in other German provincial regions. It was a popular movement, supported from below. It was accompanied and at times overshadowed by the struggles of the local guildsmen against the ruling patrician oligarchy. But, all in all, the Reformation was carried out with more caution and restraint than in other areas, where peasant uprisings and iconoclastic riots took place. The Reformation in Lusatia was implemented haltingly and without the aid of an inspiring local leader like those who led the movement in other regions.[14] An unimportant Catholic priest named Franz Rotbart was responsible for the church reform in Görlitz.

Rotbart did not arrive as a reformer in Görlitz, but as the new parish priest, whose docility had made him acceptable to the orthodox city fathers. Rotbart at first kept his sympathies to himself, performing the mass, and even allowing the papal ban of Martin Luther to be nailed to his church door in February of the year 1521.[15] Later in the same year, one of the recurrent plague epidemics reached Görlitz. The epidemic undermined the unpopular Catholic doctrine of salvation by good works. In the name of the citizenry, and expending the wealth of their city, the patrician oligarchy had performed "good works" by building and outfitting churches and shrines. Plague epidemics delivered a powerful rebuttal to all such *Werkheiligkeit*. The wealthier burghers, including most members of the city council, fled their city in order to escape from the plague. The priest Rotbart remained in his parish and preached the Evangelical message of Luther to an aroused congregation. The new message of justification by faith alone provided solace to his stricken parishioners.[16]

This marked the beginning of the reform in Görlitz. Several years passed before it was established. The city council drove Rotbart from his parish, but later allowed him to return. The situation was complicated by the fact that the weavers' guild was preparing an insurrection against the patricians, and this was complicated further by a disastrous fire that broke out before the guild could act. The weavers were demanding a role in city government as well as the acceptance of the Lutheran reform. The council stood firm against their political demands, but allowed Rotbart to be installed as the Lutheran pastor of Görlitz.[17] In 1527, when the revolutionary conspiracy of the guildsmen was at last quelled, its leaders were beheaded and quartered. A stone beside the door of the house where they had plotted was engraved with initials signifying: "the Door of the Traitors' Mob." The stone still marks the *Verrätergasse*, the "Street of Traitors," in Görlitz.[18] Pastor Rotbart's difficulties continued: he married the daughter of an influential weaver and was once again hounded out of Görlitz by the zealous Mayor Hass. Philipp Melanchthon intervened from Wittenberg but could not save Rotbart's pastoral position. In Görlitz, Catholic recidivism marred the transition to Evangelical Protestantism.[19]

In 1526, just as the burghers of Görlitz were recovering from their great fire and growing accustomed to receiving the Holy Communion or *Abendmahl* in both forms from Pastor Rotbart, their new sovereign, King Louis II of Bohemia and Hungary, was undertaking a momentous military expedition against the Turks who had recently captured Belgrade. In August 1526, the twenty-year old monarch led a gallant Hungarian army across the Danube at Mohács in southern Hungary in order to engage the vastly superior forces of Süleyman the Magnificent. In the ensuing debacle, the childless king drowned in a Danubian swamp. The Crown of Bohemia went to his brother-in-law, Ferdinand I of Austria: the Lusatians embarked upon the Reformation beneath Habsburg sovereignty.

In 1547, the Habsburg emperor defeated the Protestant Schmalkaldic League at Mühlberg in Saxony-Anhalt. By this time, the burghers of Görlitz were confirmed Protestants. As in the Poděbradian conflict of the preceding century, the city councils were again torn between loyalty to their sovereign and fidelity to their religious faith.[20] Because of these hesitations, the Land of the Six Cities was convicted, along with other Protestant cities of the region, of withholding support from their lawful sovereign in his just war against the German Protestant states. The Upper Lusatian delegates were humiliated and imprisoned in Prague. The *Pönfall* imposed severe political and economic sanctions which put an end to the age of urban autonomy and prosperity. Inadvertantly, however, the *Pönfall* also drew the Upper Lusatian estates together. Burghers and nobles alike suffered a loss of autonomy under the oppressive government of the Imperial *Landvogt*. Both estates had reason to rejoice when the acute threat of complete subjugation had passed them by.[21]

An extended interim of relative peace and calm set in. There was even an incidental benefit of the *Pönfall* in that the tighter central controls imposed by the emperor eliminated the blight of the aristocratic highway robbers.[22] Workable relations with the Imperial government were restored after 1559.[23] Perhaps as a palliative against rebellion, the Lusatians were left more or less unmolested in their confessional practices. Lutheranism remained the measure of burgher independence, not the standard of rebellion, in Görlitz. The dream of peacefully reconciling order with freedom could retain its credibility.

Protestant Internecine Conflicts toward 1600

Born in 1575, Boehme inherited a Lutheran culture which was firmly established—albeit against perilous odds and within an environment in which confessional, social, and political affairs were entangled so as to vex him and his fellows. The situation in Lusatia was an anomaly by the norms of the day. The standard of the time was *cuius regio, eius religio*: the subjects had to conform to the religion of their territorial rulers. The Margravates of Upper and Lower Lusatia functioned as "republics of the estates" (*Ständerepubliken*). They had no territorial ruler, his role being filled by the *Landvogt*, the governor appointed by the emperor to administer a crown land. In Protestant Bohemia, Lutherans or Utraquists were tolerated; and this toleration was formalized by the Letter of Majesty in 1609. *De facto*, the religious autonomy of the Lusatians was also respected. However, unlike the Bohemians, they were not successful in their attempts to obtain a Letter of Majesty formalizing this state of affairs.

Since they had no Lutheran territorial ruler, they also had no *Consistorium*, no official church administration. The *Summus Episcopus* in Upper Lusatia was an administrator appointed by the Roman Catholic bishop of Meissen. This Catholic deacon, Johann Leisentritt of Bautzen, installed the Lutheran pastors in office and acted as the highest arbiter in disputes over church law.[24] There was also a residual Catholic population in Lusatia, mainly in Bautzen, where the church was a *Simultankirche*. (Catholic and Lutheran altars stood at opposite ends; and the church served the two confessions in alternating shifts.)

The absence of a territorial church *Consistorium* reinforced the longstanding subordination of the local clergy to the local city council—a state of affairs which sometimes provided more latitude to doctrinal individualists. Precariously enough, then, the Upper Lusatians actually enjoyed a modest degree of *de facto* pluralism precisely because their status as Protestants ruled by a Catholic sovereign hung in the balance. To be sure, the Catholic threat was always on the horizon, evinced by assaults on Protestant peoples from Holland to Hungary. Yet during Boehme's formative years, the Counter-Reformation was either upstaged by other disputes closer to home, or overshadowed by the elusive prospects of confessional harmony.

Unfortunately, the situation in the whole region passed from crisis to crisis. The Reformation of the sixteenth century had pitted Protestant Germans against the Roman Catholic pope and the Holy Roman Emperor. In midcentury, the first round of religious warfare ended in 1555 with the Peace of Augsburg. The Religious Peace allowed only for a Protestant denomination which followed the unchanged version (*Invariata*) of the Augsburg Confession with its strictly worded doctrine of Christ's real presence in the Eucharist. This excluded the Calvinists and any other sects or doctrines deviating from orthodox Lutheranism or Catholicism.

This also excluded the Anabaptists, who had already fallen victim to frightful persecutions during and after the Peasant Wars. Though there were no significant peasant uprisings in Lusatia, the Anabaptist movement did spread in the 1540s to the rural folk just east of Görlitz. Cruel persecution obliterated their congregation.[25] However, reports of wandering Anabaptist preachers in the countryside in nearby Silesia suggest that the Anabaptist threat of religious and social rebellion could not have been discounted altogether even during Boehme's lifetime.[26]

Around Görlitz, the situation was further complicated by the presence of three aristocratic families interrelated by marriage, which either were, or had been, affiliated with the teachings of Caspar Schwenckfeld. Schwenckfeld was an early Silesian leader of the Reformation who incurred Luther's condemnation by shunning the Lutheran doctrines and hierarchy. Rejecting what they viewed as unspiritual and hypocritical, Schwenckfeld and his followers took issue with the Lutheran understanding of the Eucharist and abstained from Communion. After a final dispute in 1540, Luther declared Schwenckfeld a religious outlaw and had him barred from Silesia.[27] His adherents persisted among the Silesian gentry and peasantry in the form of conventicles. A scion of one of these Schwenckfeldian families near Görlitz, Carl von Ender, later became Boehme's chief patron within the gentry.

Unlike the communalist Hutterites in Moravia, the landowning Schwenckfeldians could hardly have been interested in abolishing private property. An intriguing explanation for their social motivations has been advanced by Lemper.[28] The Schwenckfeldians in general rejected the Lutheran centralized church hierarchy, which consisted of the old parishes, governed by the new territorial *Consistoria*. The opponents of this hierarchical church called it *die Steinkirche* or *die Mauerkirche*, the "church of stone" or "walled church"—epithets also used by Boehme. By stressing spiritual brotherhood, the Schwenckfeldian conventicles had the effect of bolstering the community of the aristocratic landowner with his laborers. For the Schwenckfeldian landowners around Görlitz, this spiritual brotherhood filled an important social need. As members of a recent nobility which had acquired its lands when former church properties held by the city council were sold to pay the fines of the *Pönfall*, the Schwenckfeldian landowners employed agricultural laborers: men without long ties of subservience, in some cases Protestant refugees from Bohemia, who had artisanal skills and independent doctrinal opinions. The landowners themselves were of burgher origin. They were better educated than the older Lusatian gentry, and they were not molded by the old spirit of rivalry and revenge. Some held offices in the Imperial service. As a class, they had a strong interest in confessional alternatives of a conciliatory nature.

In midcentury, the Lutheran pastors of Görlitz carried out a campaign against the Schwenckfeldian families. In 1544, one of the Schwenckfeldians exercised his autonomy as lord of the estate of Leopoldshain by appointing an uneducated cobbler from Görlitz to preach in the village church. With the weapons at its disposal, the clergy of Görlitz fought back, refusing church burial to deceased members of the noble families who had rejected church Communion. With some success, the aristocrats appealed to the city council and, in one instance, even to the Catholic emperor; but the pastors maintained their authority. The protracted feud embittered both sides. A pastor who had been forced by the city council to bury a noble woman insulted her family in his sermon. Her husband then engraved on her tombstone the words: "The Pharisees (*Schriftgelehrten*) damned Christ to Hell." In order to secure the religious peace so essential to the survival of their city, the council finally threatened the Schwenckfeldians with exile, forcing them to lay aside their grievances and forbidding the local printing of Schwenckfeldian literature.[29]

Toward the end of the century, these internal conflicts were overshadowed by supraterritorial religious tensions. As in the past, tiny Lusatia ran afoul of the dynastic shifts and changing doctrines in the neighboring centers of power. The new conflict stemmed from the controversies that divided the major Protestant confessions. The Calvinists, who had been effectively excluded from the Religious Peace, began gaining ground on their Lutheran opponents. The Calvinists objected to the laxity of Lutheran observances. They regarded the Lutheran Communion as a form of "idolatry," ridiculing the doctrine of ubiquity which held that the flesh and blood of Christ were consubstantially present in the bread and wine of Communion. Apart from their reasons of conscience, the German advocates of the

Calvinistic reforms, known as the "Second Reformation," also had reasons of state:

> Characteristic of Germany was that the change, or attempted change, from the Lutheran to the Reformed faith was imposed by fiat of the ruler.... The Second Reformation was also accompanied by a reorientation to a more aggressive and international stance in foreign policy, and therefore ultimately, towards 1600, by a change in defence arrangements under the influence of the militia schemes of the House of Nassau.[30]

When so inclined, the Protestant territorial rulers could convert and impose Calvinistic practices. In the nearby territories of Saxony-Anhalt, Electoral Saxony, and Brandenburg, attempts were made to introduce religious reforms by official decree; this resulted in popular upheavals of a common folk that still clung passionately to the old beliefs, resisting the imposition of the new practices from above. Several Silesian duchies were pledged by their territorial rulers to Calvinism in 1609 and 1616.[31]

In this spirit, *Aurora* also rejects the eucharistic doctrine of "Calvinus." However, for Boehme, the real culprit was neither the prince, nor even the follower of Calvin's teachings. By far the gravest offense—responsible for all the religious troubles and conflicts of the age—arises from the class of theologians, philosophers, lawyers, and scholarly know-it-alls: their disputes are presented as interminable, and as being ever at the point of escalating from insults and recriminations of "heresy," to blows, bloodshed, murder, *autos da fé*, warfare, and desolation.

In the last few decades of the sixteenth century, the increasingly strident Lutheran professors and churchmen of Saxony condemned the deviations of "Philippism" and "Crypto-Calvinism." The fact that the former used Melanchthon's name to designate the furtive betrayal of the Lutheran faith is characteristic of the undertow of doctrinal conformism during the second half of the sixteenth century. The Humanistic fellow reformer and successor to Martin Luther, Philipp Melanchthon, was blamed by the orthodox Lutheran churchmen for having compromised Luther's true creed in order to appease the Calvinists. Melanchthon had changed the eucharistic words of institution to "*cum* pane" in the *Variata* of the Augsburg Confession. This change was denounced by orthodox Lutherans as a betrayal of the true doctrine of real presence. Seeberg's *History of Doctrines*, a work of the late nineteenth century, summarizes the background of the Philippist controversy with reference to Melanchthon:

The great Reformer had two souls, one of which was orthodox Lutheran and the other Humanistic. The heirs of Humanism had since 1574 been branded as Crypto-Calvinists and regarded with suspicion, and they were also the supporters of the positions in which Melanchthon differed from Luther. Some of them, influenced in part by the adoption of the Formula of Concord, went over to Calvinism.[32]

After Melanchthon's death in 1560, the Philippists and "Crypto-Calvinists" were in and out of favor in Saxony, depending on the inclinations of successive Saxon princes. Elector Prince August, favoring orthodoxy, commissioned the Book of Concord, published in 1580, in order to codify the acceptable creed. Under threat of dismissal, the Lutheran pastors of Saxony were required to affirm their adherence to the Formula of Concord. One who signed but secretly continued to write heretical works was the mystical Pastor Valentin Weigel—who had connections in Görlitz. During this period of repression, Caspar Peucer, a Wittenberg professor and son-in-law of Melanchthon, was sentenced to life imprisonment as a Crypto-Calvinist. A Bautzener by birth, Peucer whiled away the time during his eleven years in prison by composing a lengthy Latin poem in praise of his native Upper Lusatia, "Idyllium in Patria."[33]

Peucer's fortunes improved, along with those of the pro-Calvinist faction in Saxony, when August's successor, Elector Christian I, pulled Saxony back toward the opposite side in the Lutheran-Calvinist quarrel. The new elector's energetic adviser, Nikolaus Krell, set about reforming Saxony, thereby modifying its religious practices in the interest of the Second Reformation.[34] Pastors were no longer required to sign the Formula of Concord. Pro-Calvinist professors came to prominence at the universities. Unfortunately, this new trend hardly promised a triumph of free opinion. An incidental consequence of the change was the abrupt termination in 1588 of Giordano Bruno's happy stay in Wittenberg. The pro-Calvinists did not hold power for long. After the early death of Christian I in 1591, his successor, Christian II, reverted to the Book of Concord; and the Lutheran faction came back with a vengeance. An English visitor in Dresden reported that the houses of the Calvinists were assaulted by student-led mobs: "My eyes and eares were witnesses what threatnings, what reproaches, what violent abuses the Lutherans cast upon the Calvinists preferring the Papists yea Turks before them...."[35] The prolonged denouement to the Crypto-Calvinist repression was Krell's legally dubious imprisonment and execution on charges of high treason—after a trial that lasted ten years and involved the collusion of the

Catholic emperor's government in Prague.³⁶ The suppression of Crypto-Calvinism in Electoral Saxony also had consequences for the small neighboring territory. Acting in concert with the Imperial authorities in Prague, the Saxon church officials prepared public inquests in order to enforce the Book of Concord in Upper Lusatia. Many among the older generation of Lusatian pastors and scholars had been educated in Wittenberg under the milder aegis of Melanchthon.³⁷ They naturally leaned toward Philippism, and refused to see the doctrines of their former teacher as heretical. There were also Crypto-Calvinists, or at least people open to Calvinistic ideas, notably at the *Gymnasium*. When its rector, Ludovicus, died, Calvinist books were found among his effects. Abraham Scultetus (a Silesian graduate of the Görlitz *Gymnasium* who later became the notorious Calvinist court chaplain to the king of rebel Bohemia) praised Ludovicus as an enlightened Philippist, and his old school for having breached numerous aristocratic houses in the manner of a "Trojan horse."³⁸

When Peucer was released from prison in 1586, he sought his patriotic *Idyllium* in Bautzen. When the second wave of Calvinist or Crypto-Calvinist pastors and officials was expelled from Saxony in 1591, they were cordially received in Upper Lusatia.³⁹ This augmented the suspicions of the orthodox. A commission of inquiry was convened in Bautzen. Rumors circulated concerning military intervention, either by the emperor or by the Saxons acting on his behalf.⁴⁰ However, the proceedings were soon interrupted by distant events. The Turks were gaining ground against the Empire in Hungary so that a united home front was needed for raising taxes and recruits.

Around the year 1600, the crisis again intensified. As in the previous war, Upper Lusatian support for the imperial war effort proved inadequate. Compensatory war taxes were levied, less punitive ones than in the *Pönfall*, but still burdensome.⁴¹ The propaganda of Emperor Rudolf II portrayed the dire threat of a new Turkish advance north toward Brandenburg—along the old Hussite invasion route.⁴²

In 1601, the inquest into the alleged Upper Lusatian Crypto-Calvinist circles was resumed in Bautzen. The new Elector Prince of Saxony made the Formula of Concord again binding, at the same time confirming the death sentence of Nikolaus Krell. According to Gottfried Arnold, Krell's execution was attended by a chorus of orthodox Lutheran preachers, who clamored that the condemned man was responsible for the perdition of infant souls. (Because of his reforms, the words of exorcism had not been invoked regularly at christenings.) The prayers of the condemned man on the scaffold were greeted by derisive laughter; the executioner congratulated himself on a "Calvinist blow."⁴³ The entire ugly affair was much publicized in the region.

It could only have been observed with the keenest interest in Upper Lusatia. In the same year, 1601, Martin Moller, chief pastor of Görlitz, was accused of Crypto-Calvinism by the Wittenberg professor, Salomon Gessner. There followed a public controversy, conducted by means of published accusations and rebuttals. Official hearings were held in Bautzen in 1602. Teachers and clergymen from Görlitz attended and reported back. The controversy was never formally resolved: it came to an end because Gessner died in 1605 and Moller in 1606.[44]

Against this background, one can better evaluate the consistent features of Boehme's seemingly contradictory attitudes toward doctrine and authority. Like the common folk in much of Protestant Germany, he maintained his adherence to the Lutheran understanding of the Eucharist. The popular nature of this loyalty was no doubt part of his self-conception as *Philosophus der Einfältigen* (I 256/18.80)—but it was only one part. The philosopher of the simple folk was also open to numerous ideas, influences, and doctrines, and willing to subject even the word of Scripture to critical scrutiny.[45] His rejection of the sole authority of Scripture was accompanied by an assertive anti-authoritarianism: "Listen, if it is not proper for me to ask questions, then it is not proper that you judge me..." (I 326/22.43). This was no mere personal defense. It was expanded into an anticlerical warning against violence, in anticipation of the future and, very probably, in remembrance of the past: "Oh blind human beings, desist from quarreling. Do not shed innocent blood, and do not lay waste on this account to land and cities in accordance with the devil's will..." (I 327/22.45).

Heretical Pluralism in Görlitz

Upper Lusatia looked back on a long history of "war and stormwinds," on centuries of religious and political stirrings, risings, and repressions. Görlitz itself was a breeding ground of heterodox theories and doctrines. From the beginning, the writings of the shoemaker reflect this diversity of ideas and beliefs. He labors over them. He attacks and defends them, and searches for a common ground of synthesis. He endeavors to reconcile his faith in the Bible with the findings of science and scholarship, and to reconcile his Lutheran articles of faith with the spiritual equality of "Jews, Turks, and heathens." The results are often contradictory; but even in its contradictions, his thought becomes implicated in the speculative openness of a kind of philosophy. The author of *Aurora* is a rural peasant turned burgher, suspicious of, but hardly less fascinated by, the diverse culture of his adopted city.

Among its population of not quite ten thousand, Görlitz supported a surprising number and variety of writers, publicists, and speculative truthseekers. Many of the currents of Renaissance and Reformation culture had accumulated in this backwater corner of Middle Europe.

Bartolomäus Scultetus dominated the intellectual life of his city. During Boehme's formative years in Görlitz, Scultetus was the mayor. He was a renowned mathematician and scholar who had written and published on a wide variety of topics. Born in 1540, Scultetus embodied the most cosmopolitan aspects of his city's Humanistic age. He had studied at Leipzig and Wittenberg, at the latter university before the death of Melanchthon. Despite his promise as a scholar, Scultetus had failed to obtain a position at the universty. Returning to his home city in 1570, he taught at the *Gymnasium*, served as a judge and city council member, and finally as mayor, until his death in 1614.[46] From his student days, he knew the Danish astronomer Tycho Brahe and continued a correspondence with him. Through Brahe, Scultetus also made the acquaintance of Johannes Kepler, who visited Görlitz in 1607. Kepler recruited a local youth in Görlitz to copy the *Astronomia Nova*.[47]

Scultetus's universal interests also brought him into contact with men of other confessions. He met with Rabbi Jehudah Löw on two occasions. When the illustrious scholar and Kabbalist paused in Görlitz in transit to Prague, he conversed with Scultetus who took the opportunity to solicit instruction on the calculation of the Jewish calendar and possibly also on kabbalistic questions.[48] Scultetus was consulted by the Jesuit scholar and papal delegate Possevino in order to discuss the modalities for carrying out the calendar reform of 1582.[49] Thanks to the good offices of the Mayor, this papal reform which caused turmoil elsewhere came into effect without delay or incident in Protestant Lusatia (although the Lutheran sermons scheduled for the obliterated calendar days had to be preached in shifts, and the League City Zittau directed anxious inquiries to Görlitz).

As mayor, Scultetus continued his projects of astronomical measurement, cartography, the construction of calendars, and the compilation of Biblical and historical chronologies, of the lives of Christ and the Disciples, and of the heroic deeds of the past in Görlitz. (To the Humanist, time was mathematical and chronological, but certainly not secular.) Scultetus was not alone in the pursuit of his varied interests. Others in Görlitz followed the developments of the new astronomy and dabbled in the study of comets.[50] Scultetus and Peucer, who visited Görlitz soon after being released from prison, understood astronomy as a theoretical and practical, prognostic science. Both men probably continued to adhere to the modified geocentric cosmology of Tycho Brahe.[51]

Judging by the titles of their publications (*Lusatia, Hortus Lusatiae, Idyllium in patria*), the Humanists were united in their local patriotism. Humanist scholarship was also represented by the influential professors at the *Gymnasium*, who authored books of a learned nature. Buchholzer, the city scribe, was the son of a famous scholar and pastor. The son continued the work of his father by finishing their chronicle of world history from the Creation to 1580, a terminal date suggesting that Abraham and Gottfried Buchholzer remained orthodox in their Lutheranism.

However, the chief pastors of Görlitz were Philippists—by some standards even Crypto-Calvinists. This applies as much to the shoemaker's longstanding enemy, Gregor Richter, as to the latter's precursor, the mystically inclined Martin Moller. Both pastors were mentally active, writing and publishing books.

Recent scholarship has pointed to the lack of evidence to support the time-honored claim that Boehme's enemy, Richter, was a narrow, orthodox Lutheran; and that Moller was Richter's benevolent counterpart, the spiritual patron who launched the young shoemaker into his theosophical speculation.[52] Nevertheless, the circumstantial evidence continues to suggest that Moller's early pastoral tenure and person could only have been more congenial to the shoemaker than Richter's. Gregor Richter was an accomplished scholar. He was not closed to new scientific ideas, but he preferred to write in Latin, an abomination to the shoemaker who knew only German. Moller translated Latin texts and published popular works in German. Thematically as well, the publications of the aging, blind Pastor Moller must have been more congenial. Moller's German *Meditationes sanctorum Patrum* was a devotional collection of sayings, prayers, and verses, inspired by the works of Augustine, Bernhard, Tauler, and others. Printed in Görlitz in 1584, it had gone through numerous reprintings by 1600. A skilled translator, Moller had rendered the Latin hymn *Dies Irae* in a manner that was impressive, as well as indicative of widespread sentiments. His verses bespoke the final "day of wrath," the "signs and wonders" of the age, and the daily perils of war, inflation, pestilence, fire, and great suffering in "these last, onerous times."[53] One of Moller's titles anticipated that of Boehme's ultimate large book: *Mysterium Magnum*.

Scultetus's circle of association was the singing club called the *Convivium Musicum*. Most of its members were locally born professionals or nobles, about his own age. Most were university educated, frequently at the University of Wittenberg.[54] Members of the Schwenckfeldian nobility belonged, as did Pastor Richter. Had the cobbler tried to gain access to the *Convivium Musicum*, he would have been rejected on several counts. The author of *Aurora* is a man profoundly pained and insulted by his exclusion from the circles of the educated—whose knowledge he alternately admires and despises.

Threatened from without, as in 1601, the leading citizens of Görlitz were capable of closing ranks to defend their city vis-à-vis the Imperial officials or the Saxon church authorities. Considered from within, and judged by the standards of the orthodox, Görlitz presented a diverse panorama of potential heresies. The alleged secret Calvinism of the pastors and Humanist professors was only one hue in the spectrum.

The tradition of alchemy preceded the Reformation and the influence of Paracelsus. As early as 1500, a man named Georg Goer, a tradesman or communal employee, had corresponded with another alchemist in Mainz. Goer had claimed to work by day and to pursue his esoteric interests by night. The fact that he was preoccupied with a *sal indicum* makes it appear probable that his alchemical research was aimed at developing dyes for the thriving textile industry of Görlitz (a purpose nearly as venerable as the art of gold-making). Goer knew at least the titles or rubrics of the alchemistic writings of Raymond Lull, Geber (Jabir), Avicenna, and the Pseudo-Aquinas. Goer also cited the term or title *Turba Philosophorum*. In Boehme's writings, *Turba* and *turbiren* are frequently used to signify a kind of vortex of thought at the outer limits of the knowable. Another work of Pseudo-Aquinas, though it is not mentioned by Goer, is called *Aurora consurgens*—the Latin equivalent of Boehme's first manuscript title. An additional notion, which is again quite important in *Aurora*, is expressed in Goer's view that, "in the number of the seven days all things are conceived."[55] The existence of a forerunner like Goer lends a strong resonance to Boehme's intimations of a store of *popular* knowledge, more ancient than that of the new science.

In Boehme's time, the medical doctors of Görlitz were mainly adherents of Paracelsian medicine. Already in 1570, a Paracelsian heresy had caused a stir of controversy. A book was printed in Görlitz denouncing the "unheard-of blasphemies and lies which Paracelsus spewed out against God, His Word, and the laudable art of medicine, in the books of the *Philosophia ad Athenienses*."[56] (I will argue in chapter seven that this work contains a probable prototype for both the title and concept of Boehme's *Mysterium Magnum*.) Because of such accusations, the alchemistic physicians of the city were summoned to the *Rathaus* for questioning, to determine if they belonged to an heretical *Secta Paracelsi*.[57] The summons and interrogation were presumably mere formalities, since the medical men had a friend with influence in the city hall.

One of the Paracelsian physicians was a man named Conrad Scheer. When Scheer died in 1615, a chronicler in the city hall archive noted that during forty years in Görlitz "the old Conrad" had never once been observed attending church, and no one even knew what he believed in.[58] Whether Scheer was a disgruntled Christian, a secret Jew, or a freethinker, the fact that he could maintain his independence suggests something about the latitude of nonconformity in a city of under 10,000.

A second member of this group is even more intriguing. His name was Abraham Behem. In 1579, when Jacob Boehme was only four, Abraham Behem—Scultetus's brother-in-law—corresponded with the heretical Valentin Weigel. At the time, Weigel's reputation as a mystic was known only to a few colleagues or correspondents. His writings did not circulate in print until 1609. The name *Behem* is an orthographic variation of *Boehme*. The name with its variants was too common in the region to establish any kinship. Whether they were related or not, Abraham clearly anticipated a number of Jacob's mystical tropes. If the shoemaker had a single important mentor, it was this mysterious figure who had previously proffered his theories to Weigel.

Another important contributor to the underground culture of Görlitz was a man, younger than Behem, but older than Boehme: Dr. Balthasar Walter. By origin a Silesian, Walter's wife was from Görlitz. He visited the city before the turn of the century, but it was only after 1612 that he is known to have formed his close friendship with Boehme. Walter was remarkable for his readiness to undertake journeys, immense for the time, in pursuit of his unusual goals. In the last years of the sixteenth century, he traveled to the Near East. Franckenberg records that Walter's journey led him to "Araby, Syria, and Egypt," and served the purpose of his research into the wisdom of "Kabbalah, magic, alchemy."[59] Later, in 1619 or 1620, Walter is said to have sojourned with Boehme for three months, conferring with him at great length. The biographer also alludes to an apparent clash of personalities between the "Mosaically" severe Walter and the gentler Boehme (X 14–15). The wandering *medicus* died in Paris after having done much to spread his friend's fame abroad.

Lastly, Scultetus himself was implicated in the same kind of questionable pursuits. The mayor was an official Humanist and an unofficial Paracelsian. The writings of Paracelsus were being collected and edited in Görlitz, and Scultetus himself worked on a treatise concerning the plague—a work which accounted for the spread of epidemics by theorizing about the magic powers of pregnant women left to die of the disease, a notion certainly not far removed from the mentality of witchcraft.[60]

Around 1600, witchcraft hysteria was approaching its zenith in Germany. Persecutions occurred in Electoral Saxony, Electoral Brandenburg, Moravia, and, probably, Silesia.[61] In Germany, the confessional border areas were prone to the worst persecutions.[62] Though Upper Lusatia was just such an area, Görlitz and the other League Cities were apparently spared the terrors of witchhunts.

Several factors which fomented the persecutions elsewhere were missing in Lusatia. There was no local church orthodoxy backed up by princely power and preaching the fundamental rift between the elect and the damned. The prevailing philosophy of Melanchthonian Aristotelianism conceded the "synergistic" freedom of the will. On the Protestant side, the Calvinist and Lutheran orthodoxies, both of which saw the will as bound, were more conducive to the supposition that Satanic wickedness is incorrigible and everpresent within the world. For the most part, the clergy in Görlitz lacked both the compelling incentive and the authority to galvanize the people against alleged witches in their midst.

All of this notwithstanding, Humanistic enlightenment and burgher independence surely provide only a *partial* answer to the question why there were no witchcraft persecutions in Görlitz. Not long after the Paracelsian controversy of 1570, the beliefs and practices of "white magic" had begun to attract the elite of the city. What would have caused alarm elsewhere aroused curiosity in Görlitz. This shows, for example, in Scultetus's interest in nature. Meticulously and credulously, he noted observations of events—real and phantasmagorical. Grain has fallen from the sky like raindrops—in sufficient quantities to be carried to market. A giant meteor has crashed to earth—roaring like an artillery barrage.[63] The miraculous and supernatural exists, but comes in good and evil variants. With his customary attention to detail, the mayor even made note of having enlisted the services of a wise woman to conjure away the dysentery of his son, dryly recording that the treatment proved successful.[64] Boehme was not relapsing into rural backwardness in recognizing the existence of both "good witches and whores of magic" (II 225/16.25).

However, even without witchcraft hysteria, there were enough dismal superstitions and cruel punishments in Görlitz.

Darkness and Light in Upper Lusatia

The assumption that Boehme was inspired by a universal experience of light, shared equally by all mystics but unknown to nonmystics, disregards the important fact that the "light" and "illumination" of his usage are opposed to a more specifically characterized "darkness." If not the light, then the surrounding darkness is a vast repository of experiences shared with his fellows. Huizinga argued in *The Waning of the Middle Ages* that fifteenth-century Europe knew extreme contrasts of darkness and light, winter and summer, and punishment and mercy. In Boehme's writings, these contrasts are no less harsh. His mystical notion of darkness is identified with *Ängstlichkeit*: "fearfulness." Darkness is a natural and societal reign of terror.

Harsh class justice was either the rule of the time, or at least a matter of very recent memory—as the memorial stone in the Street of Traitors suggests. Between 1567 and 1577, no less than fifty executions or corporal punishments were recorded in Görlitz. They included twenty-three beheadings (some for minor theft), six hangings, two quarterings, and two "aggravated death penalties" (involving torture and mutilation).[65] The frequency of these executions apparently slackened under the mayoralty of Scultetus; for in 1606, the executioners' guild protested of a work shortage.[66] Class justice was still the rule. Most of the executed criminals were either peasants or artisans. Between 1591 and 1600, the Görlitz city council repeatedly appealed to the Imperial authorities to intervene against the disorderly and occasionally murderous conduct of the nobles who made a sport of terrorizing Görlitz by firing their weapons in the city streets. Duelists and felonious aristocrats were punitively sent to fight in the Turkish Wars in Hungary. With the *Pönfall*, Görlitz had lost its jurisdiction over the nobles. This removed a source of conflict between city and country but also weakened the rule of burgher justice, loosening the reins on an unruly class enemy.[67]

"Darkness" in Boehme's writings is not a momentarily conditioned absence of light. It is a world unto itself, infested with spirits and ghosts. By night, a certain "Juncker Hans" is said to gallop from heaven into hell and death (I 348/23.74). An Upper Lusatian legend recorded in the nineteenth century recounts that the ghost of a *Junker Hans* was caught in a sack by a village fiddler, who then wasted away and died of fright. *Junker Hans* is a characteristic folk legend of a feudal past.[68] Boehme's ghosts are said to visit houses, fields, and churches and to entreat the living (III *Dreyfaches Leben* 244/12.24). Ghosts wander, clothed in the fiery form of their last earthly existence (II 306/19.23). Are they the outlawed noblemen who were decked out in red robes before they were hanged from the highest gallows in Görlitz, or the spirits of heretics who were burned at the stake?[69] In his treatise on the "four complexions," Boehme wrote that people are afraid of the dark, not out of concern for their flesh, but out of fear for their souls (IV 244/90). Even before it is defined, the "soul" is adumbrated by darkness. The devil and the elements are implicated in darkness, since it was Satan's uprising against God that extinguished the light of a once translucent world. The same rebellion gave rise both to the clump of matter which is the element and to the black depths of space (I 356/24.14). Even the stars occupy a combat zone between darkness and light (I 292/20. 50ff.). The elements are never neutral, not even in their everyday condition. The first chapter of *Aurora* describes an innate reaction within the element of water. The reaction results in "flying pestilence and sudden death" (I 28/1.22).

In the summer of 1585, a great plague epidemic descended upon Görlitz. Scultetus kept detailed records describing the progress of the epidemic which killed off nearly a fourth of the city's population before being halted by cold weather. He recorded the following harbinger of the plague: on the warm July night that preceded the first instances of the plague, an evil vaporous "stench and foul taste" wafted up mysteriously in the streets of Görlitz.[70] One wonders if the smell came from the dead epidemic-bearing rats. Or did the city's gutters, privies, and tanneries stink with a will of their own? Boehme's writings associate the devil not only with the darkness of violence and anger; a further trademark is his hellish stench, which is like the smell of a sewer or cesspool (*Cloaca*). Of the same mind, Luther, in arguing that our world is the battleground for the kingdoms of Christ and Satan, observed that the common folk knew and feared this duality of existence, acknowledging its reality in their constant prayers and proverbs.[71]

Nature, in the vision of the most lyrical of nature mystics, is full of violence, stench, pain, death, ugliness, wicked creature cannibalism, and beastly incest. "This corrupted world" is infested with, "vipers and snakes... with all sorts of vermin, of worms, toads, flies, lice, and fleas. And hence also lightning, thundering, flashing, and hail..." (I 218/15.66). Yet, incongruously, nature also presents a spectacle of perfect harmony, love, joy, and beauty. The variety of a field of wildflowers allegorizes the peaceable kingdom in which freedom flourishes amidst plurality. The beautiful and harmonious diversities of the plant kingdom convey the utopian designs of Paradise.

The two irreconcilable aspects of a good and an evil nature evolve into two interpenetrating eternal worlds, the light-world and the dark-world. The moral-philosophical nucleus of Boehme's thought consists of his realization that good and evil are not simply inextricably bound up together in all things. They are the mutually conditioning, opposing powers, without which the world could not have arisen and could not go on recreating and revitalizing itself in time.

Aurora is written from the perspective of the man from the country. This accounts for its unique vitality and charm among all his writings. The *Philosophus der Einfältigen* requires no academies or learned treatises in order to see by what Paracelsus called "the light of nature." The tone and style of his book impart this same point of view. His symbolic language intimates colorful fragments of village life. *Aurora*'s leitmotival supernatural dawn and eschatological marriage (based on Matt. 22, 25) are epitomized as a nocturnal peasant wedding feast with music by a village fiddler and dancing for all who are not lame from gout and come appropriately attired, in angelic garments, with their lamps properly lighted and adorned. (The same author condemns all dancing and frivolity which are associated with urban mores.) *Aurora*'s exhortations, invectives, and evocations of bliss can hardly be in imitation of the sermons of academically trained pastors; in tone, they owe more to folk sermonizing. The reader is addressed as a "half-dead angel"; and consoled: "So, you, child-of-man, don't be so fearful..." (I 270/19.38). The devil is subjected to baits and taunts: "Listen, Lucifer! Whose fault is it that you're a devil?" (I 174/13.48). There are interior dialogs: "Dear fellow, tell me, why was the devil expelled?... Guess Fritz! With what—what sort of power did he have? Now say what you know! If nothing, then be still and listen..." (I 274/19.60). Words are sounded out to reveal their hidden meanings in the Adamic "language of nature." The exposition incorporates rhymed ditties. The continuing creation which expands on Genesis appears to offer the scenarios for vivid folk fairy tales.

The author of *Aurora* is sufficiently sure of himself to ridicule peasants and scholars in a single diatribe. The learned seekers after the key to nature are compared to a peasant who looks for his horse and does not notice that he is mounted on it (I 323/22.17). But although the peasant is already a stock type whose mind is closed to whatever cannot be taken in hand, the author still stands on his peasant common sense. This is evident in the tone of his most essential reflections concerning the old and renewed controversy over the Creation *ex nihilo*:

> ...but it makes me wonder that with so many excellent men, not one has been found who could describe the true ground; all the more, since the same God has been from eternity who is now. For where there is Nothing, nothing arises. Everything must have a root; otherwise nothing can grow... (I 273/19.55–56).

Gradually, in tract after tract, these seemingly naive speculations are worked into an immense, ramified edifice of beliefs, intuitions, symbols, and ideas.

2 The Genesis of Boehme's Vision

Before 1600

From the common life of his surroundings, the Upper Lusatian peasant and cobbler knew the tensions of order and freedom, anger and mercy, darkness and light. As a mystic, he also recognized peculiar configurations of "outer" and "inner" worlds and of time and eternity. In order to make sense of these relationships, it is necessary to take a closer look at Boehme's circumstances, reconstructing them from historical records, from Franckenberg's brief anecdotal account, and from his own limited references to his life.

Little is known about Boehme's first twenty-five years. He was born the fourth of five children in 1575 in Alt-Seidenberg, a village near Görlitz but affiliated with a minor town that was not one of the Six Cities. Franckenberg calls it "a former market spot about one and a half miles from Görlitz in the direction of the mountains," that is, southeast, near the border with Bohemia (X 6–7). His parents, Jacob and Ursula, were prosperous and free Lutheran peasants. His schooling was elementary, though sound for reading and writing in the vernacular. We can assume that it was his parents who made the decision to send him to school and they who committed him to learn the shoemaker's craft. Perhaps they were motivated, as Franckenberg says, out of a kind esteem for his "fine, good, and spiritual nature" (X 8.6). This would hardly have precluded the sensible economic deliberation of securing an artisanal livelihood for a younger son. Jacob the Elder was a deacon of the church as well as a *Gerichtsschöppe* or lay jurist. Franckenberg states that the young Jacob was drawn to church sermons (X 8). From early childhood on, the voice of paternal authority was reinforced by the solemnity of the oath and the sermon: by the voice of the law and the voice of grace.

Childhood is a lost Paradise and Fatherland in the symbolic language of the mystical writer.[1] The Prodigal Son longs to return to the

Father. The Father exists to bring forth the Son. All experience is an ABC-tutelage for eternity.[2] But there is also a second set of mystical symbols, with an angry Father, a rebellious son, and a world of fleshly lusts, demonified by references to violence and incest. Neither set of symbols can be interpreted without considering Boehme's language and beliefs.

The context of his language and beliefs contains its own tensions and ambivalences with respect to authority. One of the most prevalent of these involves what he terms the "historical faith." The historical faith accepts hearsay evidence, goes by the literal word of Scripture, and orients itself toward events in the past.[3] The nonhistorical faith—it is implicitly evident—looks to the eternal and discovers the meaning of Gospel events in immediate experience, in the soul and life of the believer. If the historical faith is complacent in its opinion that Christ died for our sins, and if it just as complacently accepts the chronological account of the Creation from Genesis, the nonhistorical faith emphasizes the Prolog of John, with its eternal "Word" and "light," present "in the beginning," even before time began as recounted in Genesis.[4] Eternity is the dimension of divine perfection and the source of the inner certainty of the heart. The purer light of eternity shines "within," just as it fills the world beyond the external darkness of the created world in time. Without the irradiating power of eternity, the created world would be frozen in death and darkness.

Corresponding roughly to Luther's distinction between *fides historica* and *fides fiducialis*, Boehme's usage is more visionary than analytical. One might say that the historical faith resides in a world firmly anchored in time and caulked tight against eternity, while the higher, nonhistorical, mystical faith recognizes that time is awash in and saturated with eternal forces, so that everything in time is ordered by the transcendent power of eternity. Given the limits of human imagination and the constraints of everyday life, one can assume that most of those around the young Boehme, like most believers in any age, gave credence to an historical faith, so that his gradual rejection of it, in stages which we cannot reconstruct, resulted in conflicts for the child, youth, and young man. The pious, imaginative son may well have experienced tensions in his relationship with the paternal peasant, church elder, and lay jurist—the authority figure for whom the word meant law. In Boehme's writings, there is an opposition between the binding voice of the law and the freer and more meditative voice of grace: a conflict reflected in the tension between the narrative and symbolic elements in the language of the writer.

1. The author is most narrational in attempting to resolve the question of how evil came into being and of how man fell from grace.

The explanation of evil presupposes the actions of an individual who commits deeds and bears a personal responsibility for them. This context is therefore not only historical; it is also legalistic. *Aurora* employs a great many legal terms and subtly applies jurisprudential modes of thinking to the problem of the fall from grace, as for example: *Natur-Recht*, "natural right" (154/12.51); *sein väterlich Erbe verloren... Macht zu enterben* "lost his paternal inheritance... power to disinherit" (154/12.54); *weltliche Rechte* "secular rights" (154/12. 55); *bei Poen ewiger Feindschaft* "on pain of eternal enmity" (176/13.76); *Rechtsprecher...Malefitz-Recht* "legal speaker... criminal law" (189/14.2); *Citation ...Hie ladet euch der Geist unseres Königreichs...soll das Recht vollführet werden* "Citation... the spirit of our kingdom summons you... justice shall be carried out" (197/14.50); *Juristen...leget eure Antwort ein, ob ihrs Recht könnt erhalten...soll condemniret werden als ein Verderber und Feind GOttes* "jurists... deliver your reply, whether you shall be proven in the right... shall be condemned as a spoiler and enemy of God" (206/14. 108); *Der arme Mensch ist nicht aus seinem vorsätzlichen Willen gefallen...* "The poor human being did not fall because of an intentional will" (227/16.70); *behielt sein Recht für sich* "kept his right" (233/16.70)... *zur ewigen Gefängnis verurtheilet* "condemned to eternal imprisonment" (235/16.89). Lucifer and Adam cannot be exculpated by the claim that theirs was an unfree birth rooted in a creation *ex nihilo*. They were free and answerable to God because they were created from the very being of God.

2. This sequential and quasi-legal perspective, stressing deeds, accountability, and guilt, is balanced from the beginning by a symbolic visualization of the objects of belief. Here, the free meditation upon the sermon takes precedence over the binding performance of the oath. The church sermons attended by young Jacob apparently echoed Luther's (which were printed, distributed, and read from many Lutheran pulpits[5]). According to Bornkamm, Boehme actually derived his knowledge of Lutheran doctrine from homiletic sources.[6] Although this may go too far, much of Boehme's symbolic imagery does stem from the Lutheran sermon.

Although Luther rejected mystical "enthusiasm," his sermons liberally extracted visionary symbols from nature and Scripture. The sacramental miracle elicits a symbolic language of magic and rebirth. The bread and wine truly and really are the flesh and blood of Christ. If this seems inconceivable, it is hardly more so than daily existence itself: no more wondrous than the miracle by which plant life emerges from dead sand and stone, nor more baffling than the phenomenon of verbal communication. It is no more miraculous than the psychic unity of sensation throughout the entire body, nor more inexplicable than the eye's dispersal of its seeing among the many visual objects taken in by a single glance.[7] The blossoms of spring are the metaphorical harbingers of the Kingdom of God. The wrath of God, symbolized by darkness, contrasts with the brightness of joy, and with the light in the sky in the time of Christ's birth. Spiritual darkness contrasts with the flame and fire kindled in the believer by faith, and with the gleaming, sunlike bodies of the redeemed souls in the world to come. If, in Luther's "A Sermon on Preparing to Die," the sudden pain besetting a woman in labor is a fitting metaphor for the crisis preceding spiritual rebirth, then human death and resurrection are a kind of cosmic birth in which the soul ascends through the narrow, dark womb of this world into the bright world lying beyond the visible firmament. Comparable symbolic images, of darkness and light, flowers, the magic of sight and speech, the corporeal unity of sensation, the birth pangs of the spirit, and the vision of spiritual rebirth as a penetration of the closed firmament, are echoed in Boehme's visionary language.

3. Despite his figures of speech, Luther in midcareer was an implacable enemy of *Geisterei und Schwärmerei*, of Spiritualism and Enthusiasm, as, no doubt, were many Lutherans of Boehme's own day. The further step beyond the historical faith leads to the faith of Protestant Spiritualists like Sebastian Franck, Caspar Schwenckfeld, and Valentin Weigel. According to Troeltsch, the Spiritualistic faith (which he considers the prototype of later Quakerism) is typified by a preoccupation with the "spirit" and *logos* of the fourth Gospel, as against the "letter," "law," and "historical" being of Christ. Although Troeltsch was contrasting the Spiritualist with the Baptist, his typology is nonetheless useful in that it calls attention to certain features of Boehme's mysticism. The Spiritualist rejects formal church organization, tends toward individualism, emphasizes a "millenium of the spirit," above the literal Second Coming, and stresses the "baptism of the spirit," rather than adult baptism. The "spirit, its freedom and inner movement" are decisive for Spiritualism. However, Troeltsch also notes that Boehme's Spiritualism differs from this general type by faithfully retaining the sacraments.[8] If, instead of the Baptist, the comparison is drawn to the orthodox Lutheran, the Spiritualist type is distinguished by a change-about in the concept of conversion. For Luther, the believer receives the word "from hearing" and is affected as if by an external force. For Schwenckfeld or Weigel, the Holy Spirit, acting inside of the believer, proceeds outward, disclosing the meaning of the Scriptural letter. The "inner word" and "spirit" overshadows the external "letter" in matters of faith.[9]

Boehme could have arrived at his Spiritualism through Pastor

Moller, through the Schwenckfeldian nobles, or through the Paracelsian physicians, whose number included Abraham Behem (the man who had corresponded with Weigel in 1579). Behem's allegorical interpretation of Genesis 1:6–7 (separation of waters above and below the firmament) demonstrates his concern with spiritual baptism and mystical rebirth. Behem identified the waters above the firmament with the crystalline seas of the Apocalypse. What lies beyond the closed firmament is the purer "upper spiritual waters" presided over by a "Heavenly Virgin." This suprasensible region is the domain of the "New Birth": of the celestial reborn human. The Spirit of God hovers over the dark face of the waters in the first verses of Genesis. To Behem, characteristically, these were the pure spirit-waters.[10] The historical trope was thus turned into something like a schematic representation of the created visible cosmos within the invisible womb of eternity.

The letter of 1579 clearly anticipates many of Boehme's own notions. The "Celestial Eve" foreshadows his Celestial Virgin of Divine Wisdom. The epistle also provides a gloss on Boehme's use of the term "birth" to designate a kind of Neoplatonic sphere of emanation, or at one point even to describe the power which holds a spinning earth together (I 290/20.43–44). However, in itself, Behem's understanding of the separation of the waters above and below the firmament could only have *entrenched* the dualism which Boehme's thinking aimed to surmount. In order to bear fruit in *Aurora*, the Schwenckfeldian-Behemian dualism had to be combined with the theories of alchemy, astrology, and astronomy, with the Hermetic wisdom of the Emerald Table (which taught that "what is above is also below"), and with an astronomy that was progressing toward the conclusion that the celestial and earthly realms lay within a single, homogeneous field of forces. Anticipating this synthesis, Boehme envisaged common spirit-forces operating in the world above and the world below. This then established the common denominator of the transcendent world with our created one.

In the perspective that resulted, the world beyond the visible firmament became the "inner birth," while the much baser visible world was called the "outer birth." The inner birth or "eternal nature" secured permanence and stability. The "internal" spirit realm encompassed and pervaded the external realm of transience and death. We can only conjecture as to when and how this inversion of the usual meaning of "outer" and "inner" was effected in Boehme's thinking. It was consonant with the mysticism of his age, yet also surpassed it, inverting the structure of the natural cosmos, and at the same time reorienting the soul of the contemplative believer.

The information imparted by Franckenberg is sketchy, though rather suggestive. After his schooling, which took place in his village or in the adjacent town of Seidenberg, Jacob accepted an apprenticeship of three years. This was followed by journeyman years, during which he wandered beyond his home area. He was a sixteen-year old journeyman when the Saxon Elector, Christian I, died and the persecution of Crypto-Calvinists began anew.

According to Franckenberg, an early illumination was visited upon the journeyman. Troubled by the conflicts over doctrine, he is said to have prayed and meditated until he was graced with a divine light of contemplation and joy, a "Holy Sabbath," which is said to have remained upon him for seven days (X 8–9). Certain scholars have questioned the report, pointing to the formulistic appearance of a transported state that lasted for precisely seven days. But such objections are based on the assumption that the duration of such an event is a matter of passive psychological affectation. If the Holy Sabbath lasted for seven days, this was precisely how long it was supposed to last. Franckenberg himself asserts openly and unequivocally that the youth played an active role in inducing his transported state. The causes of Jacob's distress, the numerological determination of his graced state, and his method of achieving serenity accord with the subsequent attitudes of the mystical author.

Not the state of contemplative serenity itself but rather an event which, so Franckenberg tells us, *preceded* it, provides us with a more individualized impression of the young Boehme. After stating that this first illumination was brought on by prayer and meditation, and occasioned by distress over the "school disputes of religion" (*Schul-Gezänke der Religion*), the biographer reports on a providential encounter. Obviously it occurred even earlier, since it was experienced by the "apprentice" (*Lehr-Junge*). As an apprentice in his master's shop, the boy Jacob was sought out by a memorable figure: a man whose clothing was indeed plain, but whose appearance was "fine and honorable" (X 9ff.). The visitor insisted on buying a pair of shoes. Now, it so happened that at the moment neither the master nor his wife was in the house. The apprentice replied that he could not sell shoes in their absence. When the stranger kept insisting, Jacob named an excessive price. The ploy failed. Overcharged, the remarkable customer paid, took the shoes, and went his way.

So far, the behavior of the stranger does not tax belief. Only the fact of young Jacob's discomfiture seems odd. Perhaps we can surmise the reasons for his embarrassment. Just as in the the earlier episode involving the discovery of the cache of money on the *Landeskrone*, young Jacob was terrified at the prospect of receiving what did not belong to him, most especially if further illicit gain was involved. (With respect to the treasure trove, Franckenberg added that sometime later an "artist," that is, an alchemist, seized the treasure; but since a curse was upon it, the finder came to a bad end.) Now, it seems unlikely that the master of the shop objected to selling his shoes for good money. Either Jacob was expected to make the sale, but forbidden to do so by guild rules, or he did not know the fair price. Or he knew his master's prices to be unfair. (The master, we soon learn, was an evil, impious, and angry man.) In naming the prohibitive price, Jacob therefore was attempting to placate two masters: the master of the shop and the master of his conscience. For his part, the "fine and honorable" stranger appears to have willingly allowed himself to be overcharged, perhaps in recognition of the palpable dilemma and evident good will of this sincere lad.

The man went out. Outside, he halted and summoned Boehme by name: *Jacob, komme heraus*! Frightened upon hearing his name, the guilt-stricken apprentice obeyed the summons and ran out into the street. With sparkling eyes, the stranger seized Jacob's right hand, prophesied a great future for the small-sized boy, foretold for him a transformation that would amaze "the world," and counselled him to remain pious and read the Bible as a source of consolation in coming tribulations.

The man departed. Jacob took his words to heart, and very soon their providential message was fulfilled in the spiritual summons and Holy Sabbath induced by prayer and meditation. The prophesied persecutions also came to pass when the apprentice was fired and turned out of house for daring to take exception to his master's impious speech (X 9–10).

Nothing here need strain the belief of even the wariest of sceptics: neither that the visitor should have known the name of Jacob, nor that his knowing it should have startled the apprentice (who must have felt that his actions had been exposed to the scrutiny of an omniscient adult world). Nor is it surprising that the stranger should have meant well by him, nor even that he should have performed his gesture of a prophetic laying on of hands. (Franckenberg recounts how the older Boehme once singled out the daughter of a noble patron and pronounced oracular blessings upon her.) Even the pronouncement that "the world" would some day be amazed at Jacob's transformation hardly implies that the world meant the whole wide world. Franckenberg might have come up with more impressive miracles than this if his purpose had merely been to enhance the aura of his friend.

But perhaps the biographer also wanted to tell us something else. Franckenberg was profoundly impressed by the fact that so many like-minded spirits, including himself, had succeeded in joining together as a kind of secret informal brotherhood. The unknown customer was an early candidate for this secret brotherhood, a man like the Paracelsian physicians. Perhaps it was even Abraham Behem, Jacob's secret mentor and near-namesake. In any event, Franckenberg's anecdotes poignantly portray an ambience polarized by bitter disputes, obsessed with righteous conduct, and haunted by spiritual eccentrics, surreptitiously seeking others to share and carry on their fervent longings for better days to come. In the time of the Crypto-Calvinist purges, deviants and dissenters were under suspicion. Moreover, the Lusatians were a people whose bane was the necessity of serving two masters simultaneously. The incident at the shoeshop is providential in that it suggests an early *personal* conflict between inner and external authority.

The furtiveness of the poor, but "fine and honorable," well-wisher foreshadows Boehme's initiation into the half-clandestine circles of Görlitz. Though there is no report of his initiation as such, his first writings provide oblique references to the intellectual apprenticeship of the God-taught shoemaker. He has read the books of "many high masters." He knows the excitement of witnessing or hearing about secret procedures for enhancing precious ores, for transforming poisons into cures, and for selecting the medicinal herbs which grow wild in meadows. The angry Father of Boehme's mystical Trinity need not have been his flesh and blood parent: wrath and punishments characterized the patriarchal stringency of the prevailing order. By contrast, the inner world of grace and light corresponds to the more democratic circles into which the young man gained entry in Görlitz.

In 1592, the nineteen-year old shoemaker finished his journeyman years and arrived in Görlitz. From Boehme's hand-dating of his *Aurora* manuscript, from his references to twelve years having elapsed between his seminal experience and his successful composition (I 266/19.14; *cf.* ep. 12.10), and from Franckenberg's reference (X 10), we can safely conclude that it was at the turn of the century, just after his personal and professional station had become established, that the great illumination recounted by the biographer took place. Unfortunately, we know nothing about the young man's earliest years in the city. In April 1599, he acquired the rights of a burgher and at the same time purchased a cobbler's shop. In May 1599, he married Katharina Kuntzschmann, a butcher's daughter. (Franckenberg relates only that the couple was harmonious unto death.) In August 1599, they bought their first house. Their first child, christened Jacob, came into the world in January 1600, no doubt to the great relief of the father, since the year 1599 witnessed new occurrences of plague. A second son, born in 1602, may have died in another plague epidemic. Two other sons were born in 1603 and 1611. During the interval between 1600 and 1612, while at work on *Aurora*, Boehme was both a shoemaker and a bold member of his guild who participated in its efforts to break the rival tanners' prerogative to supply leather. After 1612, he gave up shoemaking and engaged in small-scale commerce.

Though it was near the village of Alt-Seidenberg, the cosmopolitan commercial center of Görlitz stood worlds apart from the rustic piety of village life. The clash between a lost world of childlike innocence and a perturbing urban milieu is suggested by images of an erstwhile pastoral idyll: there, the little children once danced rondels and wove wreaths of May flowers—in stark contrast to the hostile atmosphere of the city, where the rich wring wealth like sweat from the poor and the poor intone songs of protest and rebellion. In the present age, when one greets another (*Gott grüsse dich*...), one's quaking heart rhymes: God help me! (...*ja hitte dich!*) (*Urschriften* I 121–22/12.69).

One could flesh out the void in Boehme's biography for the interval after his arrival in Görlitz by speculating about the effect of various occurrences which are recorded in the diaries of Scultetus or in the annals of his city. One could hypothesize about the death of Abraham Behem in 1599, the return of Balthasar Walter in the same year, the birth of Boehme's first child in January 1600, or Rabbi Löw's visit to Görlitz in April of that year. Could Jacob have inherited the papers of the deceased Abraham? Is it possible that the young shoemaker looked on with a mixture of curiosity and disapproval as Dr. Balthasar Walter displayed the trinkets of his sensational journey to the East in his mother-in-law's bath house garden in Görlitz? Did Boehme acquire kabbalistic knowledge during or after the visit of the famous rabbi? One might imagine a spiritual challenge posed by the danger that an unborn child could die unbaptised, a crisis in which the free-minded father was overtaken by the terrors of the plague. One can theorize about Boehme's alleged participation in the conventicles of Pastor Moller. But these conjectures lack supporting evidence, and they also divert our attention from the broader context of Boehme's first writings. If his early readers responded enthusiastically to his fragment, they did not do so because of the imprint of its humble author. They did so because his writing addressed questions of general concern.

The Crisis of the Protestant "Weltanschauung"

What the author of *Aurora* tells us about his seminal moment of inspiration appears personal: it is summarized in the "scene" of the inquisitive young shoemaker who peers up at the stars and elements in search of answers to his questions pertaining to the deity. For the most part, however, the contents of *Aurora* are less personal. The *Memorial* of the brief moment of illumination has many themes: the inert lifelessness of elemental matter, the power of the sun and the power which, like gravity, holds the world together; the omnipresent life-giving spirit; the meaning of Christ's presence in the bread and wine of Communion, the relations of faith and knowledge, the validity of extrascriptural sources of truth, the reality of the free will; the issues of war and peace and of justice and tyranny; the hidden God, the hidden meaning of Scripture, and the hidden forces operating in nature, the design of macrocosm and microcosm; the utopian freedom of the angels, and the oppression and exploitation within human society. In order to interpret Boehme's vision it is necessary to discover a context which can encompass this array of themes—within one integral whole. How can we reconcile the images of the shoemaker whom we see struggling to feed his family, purchasing and selling properties, and aggressively taking part in the worldly affairs of his guild, and of the author of whom we know no personal history before 1600, and no life beyond his inspired authorship? If we imagine that only the latter existed, we will be jolted by the former. If we imagine the petty merchant and artisan as the true Jacob Boehme, we fail to account for the immense engagement and self-sacrifice of his alter ego. The first step toward a reconciliation of these two images lies in recognizing the larger context of Boehme's personal conflicts and perplexities.

Boehme arrived in Görlitz during a time when the local social tensions were overshadowed by the regional conflicts over doctrine. 1592, the year in which Boehme took up residence in this leading city of Upper Lusatia, was the year of restoration in Electoral Saxony; it was the year in which the orthodox clergy began implementing the harsh Saxon Articles of Visitation in an effort to enforce the Formula of Concord, a campaign which soon targeted the small neighboring territory as well. *Aurora* and the later writings react to these doctrinal conflicts.

The Formula of Concord codified the acceptable teachings. Salvation is obtained solely by faith and the word of God. The will is unfree in conversion. Understanding and reason are blind in spiritual questions. The body of Christ is present in the *Abendmahl*, just as the human and divine natures are personally united in Christ. The Saxon Articles of Visitation sharpened the orthodox attack on all independent positions. It is one thing to consider these documents as disinterested attempts to arrive at a satisfactory agreement on articles of faith. It is another thing to consider the consequences for an Upper Lusatia in which Philippists, Crypto-Calvinists, Schwenckfeldians, Catholics, and strict Lutherans managed to coexist. Impossible alternatives were pressed home by these Articles of Visitation. They disputed freedom in conversion but condemned the Calvinists for professing the logical corollary: that God both confers *and* withholds grace, saves *and* damns. They asserted the omnipresence and omnipotence of the divine will, while condemning the Calvinists and Crypto-Calvinists for professing that God is present in the world like the power of the "sun," which shines throughout the entire world "below." The Formula of Concord and the Articles of Visitation dogmatically spelled out binding articles of faith, but, at the same time, condemned those who maintained that reason and human understanding were capable of arriving at any truth concerning God, beyond the literal sense of Scripture. The Formula and the Articles made it possible to condemn Calvinists for predestinarianism, and Philippists for asserting the freedom of the will. In the spirit of Luther's own intemperate vituperations against his fellow reformer, the Formula of Concord classed the Schwenckfeldians with the Anabaptists and Antitrinitarians in a concluding catalog of errors.[11] Signatories, even if they agreed on doctrine, were obliged not merely to affirm their own beliefs but also to condemn other believers.

Not only Lutheran tenets but also a traditional vision of the world—shared by Luther—was implicated. Luther's major treatise and reply to Erasmus, *On the Bondage of the Will*, had argued that to admit the freedom of the will in conversion was to deny the gift of grace promised in the Gospels. Just as a stone falls by its nature, and can only be lifted back up again by an alien force, the fallen human creature can only be restored to grace by the omnipotent will of God. Whoever believes, Luther had contended, that this world is nothing but a battleground of Satan and Christ, whoever recognizes that mortal life amounts to an incessant warfare between the flesh and the spirit, needs no further proof that the human will is powerless to strive for the good or to stir itself toward its salvation, without the intervening hand of God. Salvation by faith and the word constituted a palpable unity with the impotence of the fallen will, with the dualism of Satan and Christ, and, by extension, with the doctrine of Christ's real presence in the *Abendmahl*. Even Luther's view of the cosmos was of a piece with his tenet of the unfree will: his insistence on divine omnipotence, on the Creation *ex nihilo*, and on the literal meaning of Holy Scripture were conducive to geocentrism. This is evident not only in the above-mentioned simile of the unfree stone, but also in his famous Scriptural refutation of heliocentrism, and in his remarks concerning the mastery of the divine Architect who could construct the vault of the heavens without employing visible pillars of support.[12] Nature, as well as Scripture, can be read literally.

Luther had justified his stand in the eucharistic controversy by means of his doctrine of divine ubiquity. Bitterly contested by the Calvinists, this doctrine enabled Luther to maintain the seemingly disparate scriptural assertions of Christ's presence at the right hand of God and in the bread and wine of Communion. Divine ubiquity meant that, just as the human and divine natures were united in Christ, so the elemental world contained a latent divine omnipresence. The bread and wine of Communion also had a dual nature, as elemental matter, beneath which the omnipresent divinity lay concealed. Luther's justifications of his doctrine of divine ubiquity were scholastic, owing much to Ockham. They stimulated further controversies among Lutheran divines and were far too complex for catechistic purposes.[13] The Formula of Concord put it quite simply: "the right hand of God is everywhere." It would be left to Boehme to develop fully the *mystical* implications of the bitterly contested doctrine of omnipresence.

One finds innumerable affirmations of the divine ubiquity in Boehme's writings.[14] These assertions occur in many variants. Though mystical, the terms do not suggest that their author has received any specific vision of the kind recorded by Hildegard of Bingen in *Scivias* ("I saw a great light, a celestial voice rang out..."). Boehme's ubiquitous divinity is seen and experienced by the inner spirit, not by the outer eye of the body (which perceives only the elements out of which it has been fashioned). True to the orthodox Lutheran doctrine, Boehme employed his mystical terms of divine ubiquity for the purpose of justifying the assertion that Christ is truly present in the eucharistic bread and wine. Relatively little attention has been expended on the fact that the mystic adhered to this doctrine—albeit in idiosyncratic formulations—throughout his life.[15] It is a preoccupation which disappoints both those who see him as a nondoctrinaire visionary and those who see him as a prescient philosopher. But preoccupied he was. His first three writings devote sections to justifying the Lutheran doctrine of the eucharistic *Abendmahl*, and many passages in his subsequent writings return to this doctrinal affirmation. One of his later treatises is entirely devoted to the sacraments.[16] Yet notwithstanding his insistent retention of a controversial orthodox Lutheran teaching, the author repeatedly condemned all quarrels over doctrine. How are we to interpret this contradiction?

That Boehme should have adhered to the doctrine of Christ's presence in the *Abendmahl* need not surprise us. The historical context of his mysticism was a Protestant territory lacking constitutional guarantees of freedom and faced with the encroaching influences of Lutheran, Calvinistic, and Catholic orthodoxies on all sides. Boehme's rationalizations of sacramental doctrine are couched in the conciliatory terminologies of his Spiritualism and esoteric mysticism; however, about his passionate sincerity there should be no uncertainty. The precedents of the Utraquist banner of the chalice, of the Calvinist symbol of the breaking of bread, or of the Lutheran popular uproar against the mandatory introduction of the Calvinistic sacramental practices—all confirm the immense authority of belief which was vested in the Eucharist as a means to salvation and as the rallying symbol for confessional, national, and popular aspirations.

The point of interest here is how the doctrines of divine ubiquity and of Christ's real presence could give rise to implications differing sharply from Luther's. Where Luther argued the omnipotence of the divine will, the servitude of the fallen human will, and the powerlessness of reason to grasp the truths of the spirit, Boehme *inverted* the relationship of divine omnipresence to human freedom and knowledge: *The divine spirit, manifesting itself in all beings, through its indwelling presence revitalizes the human will and illuminates the human understanding.* Thus, the human will is made free by the divine immanence; the graced human understanding is empowered to fathom the mysteries of the "unknown God." This voluntaristic twist is little more than a shift in perspective away from Luther, and it is a change which conforms to the differences of emphasis distinguishing Luther from Calvin.[17] However, for Boehme the shift had theological consequences which Luther almost certainly would have abhorred. The inversion revolutionized the relations of the Creator, the creation, and the human creature. The consequences eventually included Boehme's conception of evil as a developmental aspect of the divine nature.

Boehme's interpretation of the Lutheran doctrine of divine ubiquity not only provided the foundation for his voluntarism: together, these tenets would suggest to him that other doctrinal antagonisms could be resolved or transcended. The mysticism of the divine ubiquity could be adapted in order to disclose a path for circumventing the *Steinkirchen* in a kind of flanking movement of the "spirit," leading ultimately to a universal "Christendom" with open boundaries. Thus, in one characteristically defiant defense of Christ's presence in the *Abendmahl*, Boehme wrote that, like the sun, Christ shines "into all places and corners" of the world. In the same context, he rebukes the established churches for persecuting heretics and proceeds to envisage a universalistic "congregation of Christ."[18] Projections of this sort inform his writings from the first dawning of his *Aurora* to the reunion of Joseph with his brothers toward the end of the final volume of *Mysterium Magnum*. To the author and his approving readers, these prospects were nothing less than the last and most radiant hope for restoring the shattered peace of Christendom.

The Quest for the "Pansophic" Synthesis

The hope of a reconciled Christendom was nourished by the widespread movement toward a universal synthesis of beliefs and ideas—a synthesis invoked by the term *Pansophia*. The quest for this all-encompassing, "pansophic," wisdom presupposed the erstwhile perceived harmony of diverse notions which—from our distant vantage—appear to be divided between forward-looking theories and retrograde superstitions. *Pansophia* could entail philosophy as well as religion, esotericism, and even science. In Boehme's age, the longed-for concordance of knowledge and belief carried forward traditions of Renaissance Platonism and Hermetic magic, crossbreeding them with certain trends of the Reformation and of the new exact sciences.

The tendency toward synthesis has to take precedence over specific contents in the attempt to understand what *Pansophia* meant to Boehme. If not the magic, the synthesizing trend had been represented by Sebastian Franck, a Spiritualist reformer influenced by Humanism and mysticism, who had gathered teachings of heretics and ancient philosophers and recorded them alongside the doctrines of Luther and Erasmus.[19] Even the most advanced Renaissance science often considered its findings to be the resurrection of a secret wisdom held already by the ancient sages. (Just as Luther had restored the true Gospel, the sciences were now restoring the true, ancient philosophy.) The preface written by the Lutheran divine, Andreas Osiander, for Copernicus's *De revolutionibus* accorded the honor of prior discovery, fairly, to the Greeks. Hermetism and scholasticism, Aristotle, Plato, and Moses: all these sources of truth seemed to be falling into place within one pattern. Thus, for example, in 1610, a Leipzig professor and Paracelsian named Joachim Tanckius (a man whose style was not mystical) defended alchemistic medicine: he argued that the ancient *Magi* had been privy to the kind of knowledge which was being recovered by the new researches into nature. For Tanckius, this ancient tradition had encompassed Thomas Aquinas, Arnold of Villanova, and Albertus Magnus. It had also included Aristotle (whose pertinent writings had been lost), and, ultimately, Moses himself (whose alchemistic artistry was evinced by the fact that he knew how to burn a golden calf). Restoration of this ancient knowledge would lead to new advances in science and medicine.[20]

Around 1600, the search for synthesis was pursued above all by the loose convention of pansophic researchers at the court of Rudolph II in Prague. There, men of various disciplines, of differing confessions and nationalities, pursued complementary aims of construing the orders of the world. They did so by researching nature, consulting the wisdom of the past, and pondering the coherences of nature and Scripture. Their efforts encompassed religion, science, law, and the arts. Similar goals of synthesis had been pursued, more radically, by Bruno, who had sojourned briefly in Prague. The same studies still engaged men all over Europe: men like Robert Fludd, and perhaps even to some extent the early Galileo.[21] Characteristic of the pansophic universalist, the astronomer Kepler also engaged in astrology, addressed the eucharistic controversy, compared relevant passages of the Bible with the new astronomy, and modeled his idea of the solar system on the five perfect solid figures of Plato.

It is a commonplace of Boehme scholarship to pair him with his forerunner Paracelsus, as if they had been master and pupil. This distorts the relationship somewhat, since both of them were in reality part of a broader current, with more distant sources.

Boehme's writings contain evidence of the broader background of his speculations. *Aurora* refers to Platonic "figures" ("ideas" in a later gloss) and to the four elements (I 190/14.10; 396/26. 80). Within his extensive terminological inventory, there is a tension between the inert ("dead") element, and the universal vital spirit-medium, with its transcendent and perceptible manifestations. A brief juxtaposition with Pico della Mirandola can provide a measure of the Renaissance character and origins of Boehme's synthesis of scriptural and extrascriptural truths. The syncretism of the Florentine Humanist anticipated several of the shoemaker's themes: his mystical speculations on the Creation, his interpretation of the waters above and below the firmament, his interest in a divine, Hermetic magic (distinct from evil magic and false astrology), and his exultation of the human likeness of God from a clump of earth to a knowing being whose self-knowledge is a knowledge of God.[22] The Renaissance syncretism of Ficino and Pico also blended elements of Jewish Kabbalah with Christian currents of speculation. Certain of Boehme's most characteristic figures resemble kabbalistic prototypes.[23] In the wake of the Renaissance, Hermetism, Neoplatonism, and Kabbalism became so thoroughly mingled with the alchemistic, speculative, and mystical trends of thought sweeping Europe, that it is no longer easy to trace individual strands of influence.

Paracelsus and Weigel are, however, Boehme's more proximate predecessors. A contemporary of Luther, Paracelsus reinterpreted

Renaissance thought and disseminated it in the lands of Northern Europe. He interpreted and elaborated the Renaissance concepts of the macrocosm and the microcosm; and he recast the medieval trope of nature as the Book of the World. Paracelsus was particularly influential in directing alchemy toward the purposes of the healing arts and in admitting the traditional lore of the common folk as a source of knowledge worthy of the respect of medical doctors and philosophers of nature. A considerable stock of Paracelsian terms, concepts, and theories is found in Boehme's writings. Paracelsus's triad of principles (Sulphur, Mercury, and Salt) and his theory of the healing purposes of alchemy are of considerable significance at various junctures of Boehme's development.

In philosophical anthropology, the Paracelsian tradition was carried further by the heretical Lutheran pastor and mystic, Valentin Weigel. Like Schwenckfeld, Weigel was a doctrinal individualist of the Spiritualistic type. If Paracelsus directs our attention back toward the Renaissance, and toward its broad assault on medieval scholasticism, Weigel challenged the new scholasticism of the Lutheran orthodoxy. Weigel, like Schwenckfeld or Franck, tapped a tradition which extended, partly by way of the *Theologia Deutsch*, back to medieval German mysticism, and beyond it to Erigena, Pseudo-Dionysius, Augustine, and Origen. It is not certain when Boehme first encountered Weigel's work; however, *Aurora* already employs the Weigelian phrase: "How deep or broad is the *locus* of this world no human being knows."[24]

Like other Protestant and Catholic thinkers of his day and age, the shoemaker of Görlitz thus came to embrace the belief that ancient knowledge was resurfacing in order to reinforce and clarify the Christian articles of faith. Repeatedly, *Aurora* makes reference to certain ancient "wise heathens." These pre-Christian savants are said to have surpassed the Christians in the knowledge of nature; indeed, they even succeeded in coming before the very countenance of the hidden God in nature, though without recognizing Him behind its facade (I 324/22.29).

For Boehme, the "pansophic" synthesis addressed questions which were neither ancient nor academic. The Formula of Concord and the Saxon Articles of Visitation had sharpened the dualism of the Lutheran outlook, for which the bread and wine *either* embody the corporeal presence of Christ *or* are mere signs and things (in which Christ resides at most as an insubstantial power, like that of the sun which shines down but remains high up in heaven). The doctrinal either/or was the shibboleth of partisan divisiveness and bitter polarization. But what if the sun were not in an upper heaven, but rather at the very center of the created world? What if the solar or stellar forces were themselves both material and divine? And what if the dualism which knew no middle ground between matter and spirit (between the element or body, and the spirit, sign, meaning, or thought) rested on a false dichotomy, false because external nature and human nature were in either case triadically structured as aspects of the ubiquitous Triune God? All these questions of general concern were summoned up when the melancholy shoemaker pondered the unfathomable "*locus* of the world." What remains to be explained is why his own breakthrough occurred so precipitously and yet had such far-reaching consequences. How was it possible that the entire expanding and evolving agglomeration of his thought could continue to appear to him as the elaboration of one brief moment of integral insight?

Beyond the World of Dr. Faust

The author of *Aurora*, a man firmly convinced that the earth revolves around the sun, recollected his depressed state as that time, when he, like most people before him, had persisted in the error of imagining that "the true heavens," or abode of God, was many hundreds or thousands of miles above the earth. Only a few decades earlier, Michel de Montaigne's *Apology for Raymond Sebond* recorded a similar "scene" of bewilderment and forlornness:

> Man is the most blighted and frail of all creatures.... This creature knows and sees that he is lodged down here, among the mire and shit of the world, bound and nailed to the deadest, most stagnant part of the universe, in the lowest storey of the building, the farthest from the vault of heaven...[25]

Montaigne's defense of Sebond's Lullian mysticism foreshadows *Aurora*'s conviction that the study of the Book of Nature should complement what is learned from the Bible. It is quite apparent that many European thinkers in this period found themselves in a similar scene of puzzled inquiry. Around 1600, the North Italian peasant Menocchio was burned by the Inquisition for propagating the notion that God and the angels had arisen out of a cosmic "chaos," like worms in curdled milk.[26] The underlying question, whether the world was created *ex nihilo* or from some preexisting or coeternal material, could have far-ranging implications.

The interior monolog of *Aurora* hints that the question of the creation *ex nihilo* was debated in the shoemaker's vicinity. Hence the dialogical tone of *Aurora*'s discourse on this topic:

> You see in this world nothing but the depths, and therein the stars and the birth of the elements.... Dear fellow, what was in this place before the time of the world? If you say nothing, you are speaking unreasonably; you have to say that God was there, otherwise nothing would have come into being there. (I 271/19.42)

If the world had been created out of nothing, its substance would remain passive; the human creature would be entirely the product of a divine determination. In Boehme's thinking, the creation *ex nihilo* implies that the creature is beyond redemption, the human destiny of salvation or damnation having originated in the total causation of the absolute will. Conversely, to accept that the world is eternal, or has been fashioned out of some preexistent material, is to elevate nature to the level of the deity: the error of the wise heathens. The question of the creation from nothing or from something epitomized the doctrinal and political either/or at the highest level of speculation.[27]

Aurora's "scene" of the bewildered soul who stares up in wonder at the cosmic mysteries of nature was also the outlook of a celebrated and despised chapbook protagonist of Boehme's time: the Wittenberg theologian, Dr. Johann Faust. The shoemaker's recollected search for enlightenment incorporates similar motives of search, peril, crisis, and discovery. Like the fictional Faust, the cobbler pondered the heavens and earth and read the works of many "high masters." Unconsoled by learned tracts, he hazarded his soul with "heathenish thoughts," even assaulting "the gates of heaven and hell"—as if risking his life to force the hand of God. Boehme's search is a sequel to Faust's.

First published in 1587, the *Volksbuch* recounting the adventures of *Doktor Johann Faust* fictionalizes a state of mind which is very similar to the shoemaker's early melancholy. The focus of interest here is not whether Boehme read *Faust* or not. If we assume that he did not read it, then its similarities to the tone, theme, and language of *Aurora* only confirm that the preoccupations of the age were widespread enough to be identifiable in two works which arose independently of one another. However, it is perhaps no coincidence that both books utilize the dawn as an eschatological symbol. Boehme's title, *Morgenröthe im Aufgang*, corresponds in *Faust* to an unnatural aurora marking the barred gates of Eden. (In *Aurora*, Paradise is an eschatological "place," and not a geographical one; the imminent restitution of Paradise is heralded by the rising aurora.) Like the chapbook *Faust*, *Aurora* heaps contumely upon the legendary practitioners of evil sorcery, even accusing them of flirting with the devil. However, the work of

1612 is benevolent toward good esotericism, and perforce open-minded in matters of philosophical and theosophical inquiry. To be sure, *Johann Faust* also nourished the popular curiosity about astronomy, geography, magic, and classical learning. The graphic *Volksbuch* teased its readers with space flights, magic metamorphoses, and time-defying acts. Helen of Troy is sensationally fetched from the past and into Faust's bed. But in the famous finale of the tale, the Wittenberger is horribly punished for his illicit researches. His brains and eyes are splattered on his chamber walls, and his soul carried off to hell, brutally demonstrating that esoteric pursuits and improper inquiries lead to horrid damnation. The young cobbler entertaining his heathenish thoughts undoubtedly knew what it meant to fear for one's soul.

After bargaining away his prospects of salvation by striking his deal with the "evil spirit," the theologian of Wittenberg is overcome by melancholy (*Traurigkeit und Schwermut*). As if he did not have more grievous concerns to ponder, his mind turns to the structure of the cosmos. The evil mentor tutors Faust about the composition of the heavens. Like the young shoemaker, he learns of exact measurements of the heavenly bodies. Faust also learns that the world is divided into four spheres; and that these are composed of four elements. The sky is round and made of crystal. Its sphere would turn too fast and shatter if not for the detaining opposite motion of the planets. The lowest region of the air is inhabited by spirits and devils, which are responsible for the meteorological commotions of that region, and which also engender dreams, terrors, and apparitions. Faust acquires no awareness of any "hidden God" in nature: flying up to the outer limits of the world, he encounters no trace of the deity. The higher he rises, the darker it becomes: as if he were falling "into a black hole." Viewed close up, the planets and the stars rival the earth in size. From their dizzying height, the fragile mechanism of the celestial machinery is disquietingly evident. Through the eyes of Faust, the reader can see that the geocentric world is constructed like a gigantic machine which dwarfs the insignificant human being. (As Boehme recollected his own early melancholy perception of nature: "I considered the small little spark of man, of what account he might be against this great work of heaven and earth before God."—I 265/19.7)

In *Faust*, the great world-machine coincides with the metaphysical order. It provides the coordinates for what is up and what is down; it subordinates the lower to the higher, and cranks out the times of day and the seasons. Its hierarchical structure assigns the elements and creatures their spheres and properties. Hence, the created world is subject to the rule (*Herrschaft*) of its Creator. This same term for "regimen of properties" applies in the common usage of the time to political dominion and to the constitution of the elements. The power of the unseen deity in *Faust* is revealed in the retribution meted out to the protagonist for violating the rightful and natural order, and for questioning the mysterious facticity of the world. It would appear that the world is what it is for no other reason than that the inscrutable Architect has made it that way.

The chapbook *Faust* confronts its readers with consequences of the creation *ex nihilo*. A seductive lie of the evil mentor—judiciously introduced as a *false* answer to Faust's question—maintains that the world and man are uncreated and eternal. What the false mentor reveals to Faust is a caricature of Ptolemaic astronomy and Aristotelian physics. Faust's bargain is not honored by any new scientific knowledge, but only by the license to violate the old rightful hierarchies. His deal allows him to fly above the earth, to resurrect the past, and to transform objects. Even his carnal adventures are understood in reference to the symbolism of up and down: "Hell, the womb of woman, and the earth are insatiable," lectures the evil spirit. The theologian of Wittenberg is left to ponder the questions: "how God created the world, and about the first birth of man."[28] This same duo of questions will also confront the melancholy shoemaker.

The Breakthrough of the Spirit

For Boehme, "the spirit broke through," so that he "penetrated the innermost birth of the divinity," at the same time that he came to accept the truth of the Keplerian astronomy: "the earth turns and courses with the other planets as in a wheel around the sun" (I 376/25.61). The entire manuscript of *Aurora* is in some sense heliocentric, though its early chapters convey a symbolic and mythological heliocentrism.[29] An eloquent record of Boehme's struggle to acknowledge and incorporate the findings of the new mathematical and observational astronomy is given in two chapters where he writes candidly and in the first person of his struggle for knowledge. Chapter nineteen still ridicules the folly of the scholars who tried to survey the distances to the planets. But chapters twenty-two and twenty-five poignantly document a change of heart toward those skilled in the astronomers' art of *Cirkel-Messen* or "measuring with the compasses" (I 321/22.10). The implication that this applies to the science of the heavens is extended to what he calls the "formula of philosophy, astrology, and theology": that is, to all scholarly knowledge. "Their formula" is now acknowledged to have been his "master"—the first beginning of his own knowledge; "their philosophy" and his "philosophy" are said to have grown on the same tree and to have borne the same fruit (I 322/22.12–14). The context of this reconciliation with the practitioners of *Cirkel-Messen* is the discussion of the stars and planets. In the same chapter, he boasts of his theoretical knowledge of alchemy. He also praises the wisdom of the "wise heathens," criticizes Genesis for its improbable account of the Creation, and intimates that at the end of time humanity has become eager to uncover the root of the tree of knowledge. Chapter twenty-two writes of the "wheel of nature," apparently presupposing heliocentrism. This hint is definitively confirmed in chapter twenty-five (I 326/22. 41; *cf.* 376/25.61). All knowledge is due to the divinity of the knowing creature (I 322/22.12). Hence, what the common folk know is comparable to the knowledge of the learned. If he, the cobbler, has no right to ask questions "because the deity is a secret, which no one can research" (*die niemand erforschen kan*), then those who forbid his inquiry can have no basis to judge him (I 326/22.43). The reconfirmation of heliocentrism is immediately preceded by a defiant declaration of intellectual and spiritual autonomy: "thus, I intend to write correctly, according to my intuition, and to heed the authority of no one" (I 375/25.50).

The author of *Aurora* sees through the external structure of the world. He recognizes that the superficial reading of the eyes which perceive that the sun and the heavens are far above a fixed earth—is illusory. This suggests that the rigid and confining prisonhouse of the world is not its true and ultimate form. *Die Begreiflichkeit* is Boehme's term for the hard, impenetrable appearances of the things which are seen and touched. The distant enclosing vault of the heavens pertains to *die tote, äussere Begreiflichkeit*, to the dead, external palpability of this world. If the heavens have been opened up, the impenetrable surfaces of things can likewise be rendered transparent. The interior depths of the world—the reality discerned by the spirit—is quite different from the impenetrable surfaces of elemental things. The higher and deeper reality which even pervades the earth is a medium of ubiquitous spirit. Moreover, the inner depths are not an airless, lifeless realm, but rather a world accessible to *all* the senses, not merely to the sight and touch, which remain fixated upon the tangible. The true reality is not divided into discrete elemental things and spheres: it is a free-flowing interchange of vital forces. These spirit-forces are engaged in a perpetual rebirth and communication of properties (that is: a *communicatio idiomatum* more vivid than the one which describes Christ's presence in the Communion in the dry Latin of Lutheran doctrine). The divine light illuminates the spirit-world from within, like the central sun of the new astronomy.

Two seemingly contradictory aspects of the ubiquitous spirit world press themselves upon the author of *Aurora*: "God is a God of order" (I 148/12.20). Yet the true order prevails without any overt hierarchical subordinating of things. The reconciliation of order and freedom is expressed in a natural plenitude in which no quality is first and none last, no spirit is higher and none lower than the others, in which the entire divine being is wholly present in each sphere of an ongoing creation, hence in even the smallest circle of the created world:

> As if you were to draw a spatial, creatural circle, and were to have the entire divinity particularly (*Besondern*) within it; just as [the entire divinity] is born in a creature, so too, in the entire depth of the Father, at all points (*an allen Enden*) and in all things; and, in such a manner, God is an all-powerful, all-knowing, all-seeing, all-hearing, all-smelling, all-tasting, all-feeling God, who is everywhere.... (I 125–26/10.61–62)

The cobbler's seminal intuition was the intimation that a universal pattern reconciles order and hierarchy with multiplicity and spiritual freedom. This pattern was manifest in all objects of experience, as well as in the experiencing subject: (1) In the cosmos as a whole, the pattern was that of the sun-centered world, a cosmos held together by invisible forces, not by visible, mechanical vaults encasing an immobile central earth. (2) In all the objects of material nature, the universal pattern meant that the corporeal facticity of the things no longer had to be regarded as their predominant aspect. Hardness and impenetrability, these earthlike properties of objects, were reduced to the status of one quality alongside of six others, merged in the pansensual divine ubiquity—just as the once-central earth was relegated to its place as one among six in the invisible "planetary wheel." (3) The same universal pattern was apparent in the experiencing subject. For just as the elemental earth was not the center of the world, and just as the corporeality of objects was not their predominant property, so too, the "half-dead" corporeality of the fallen creature need not tyrannize a human life purposed for the recognizance and glorification of the eternal wonders. (4) This same spiritualization and reintegration of all discrete entities could provide a visionary model for the social, political, and doctrinal reintegration of the strife-torn world, and (5) for the secret coherences of time, space, and eternity. Philosophy and wisdom complemented the letter of Scripture and promised to resolve the conflicts engendered by the historical faith: doing so, not by means of new doctrines, but by means of a vision and philosophy which encompassed and reconciled all the conflicting doctrines.

Boehme's vision of his world in space is grounded in the doctrine of divine ubiquity, fleshed out and vivified by his intimations of a sun-centered cosmos, replete with visible and invisible spirit-forces. His vision of the world in time is rounded out by the chiliastic belief in a final age: an age coinciding with the restoration of an ancient knowledge which would clarify the letter of the Gospel and resolve all conflicts over its meaning. This rounded circularity of being—emblematized by mystical symbols and exemplified by the esoteric interrelatedness of all truths—realized the latent presence of eternity in time. It revealed the latent omnipresence of the hidden divinity within a fallen world.

What radically distinguishes this vision from those of contemporaneous science is the absence of mathematically conceived objective regularities. In other respects, even the rhapsodies of *Aurora* parallel the scientific theories of the age. The lingering popular idea expressed in *Faust*, of a geocentric world enclosed by vaults and threatened by the courses of comets which seemed to disrupt the celestial spheres, was discredited by Tycho Brahe in these terms:

> that the machine of Heaven is not a hard and impervious body full of various real spheres, as up to now has been believed by most people. It will be proved that it extends everywhere, most fluid and simple, and nowhere presents obstacles as was formerly held, the circuits of the Planets being wholly free and without the labor and whirling round of any real spheres at all...[30]

Liberated from the mechanical spheres, the celestial bodies were now guided through a fluid and continous space by spirit forces, by the planetary "souls" of Gilbert, or the *animae motrices* of Kepler. Boehme's "true heavens" are replete with transforming spirit-forces—familiar to him from an alchemistic experimentation based on Hermetic lore.

Kepler upheld the Copernican model of the world as an image of the Trinity—and as a reconfirmation of the ancient wisdom of the Sidonians, Chaldeans, Persians, and Platonists. He affirmed that, "most rightly is the sun held to be the heart of the world and the seat of reason and life, and the principal one among three members of the world."[31]

Like the scientists, Boehme attempted to extract the meaning of the new discoveries, albeit from a very different angle. His reflection upon the new findings was schooled by the emblematic and typological patterning of common knowledge in his time. Emblems presented the things of nature and of everyday life as the likenesses of eternal verities. The typology of Holy Scripture related the types of the Old Testament to the antitypes of the New Testament. Boehme's speculation combined the pictorialism of emblematic illustration with techniques borrowed from typological exegesis, thereby expanding the functions of both.[32] The figural types of Scripture are crafted into symbolic models of nature. Thus, John 4:24 confirms that the ubiquitous deity is spirit. Revelation 5:5–6 (the seven lamps, signifying the seven spirits of God) signifies that the universal pattern of divine forces is sevenfold. Ezekiel 1:16–24 (the vision of the divine creatures mounted on miraculously complex and mobile wheel bases) fascinated Boehme with its prototype of invisible, nonmechanical wheels mounted within wheels. A potential replacement for the visible machinery of the heavenly vaults, the mystical wheels from Ezekiel developed parallel to Boehme's "wheel of nature" and "wheel of essences."[33] The Spirit of God which hovers upon the dark countenance of the waters before the Creation has its antitype in the crystalline seas of the Apocalypse. The beginning of the world mirrors its ending in a pattern of perfect coherence.[34] The heliocentric world is arrayed around the likeness of Christ, as the light of the world, the power by virtue of which the life of nature is continually reborn in the dead element of the earth.

Everything in *Aurora*'s vision can be analyzed into its components and precedents. Nevertheless, the characterization of the "illumination" which Boehme memorialized in his first book would remain incomplete if one failed to acknowledge the ecstatic whole which is more than the sum of its parts. The rhapsodies of *Aurora* convey the triumph and joy alleviating Boehme's melancholy meditations upon the closed and remote vault of the heavens (I 266/19.11). The expressions of ecstasy recapitulate and transform the prerequisites of his earliest speculative thought: the revelation of the light, the omnipresence of spirit, the mythic-eucharistic "eating" of spirit by spirit, and the multiplicitous harmony of the spirits which represents the power of eternity in time and hence also the certainty that a restored Paradise will blossom in the fallen, strife-torn world. Radiating throughout the envisioned free-floating, yet stable, order of the cosmos, the emergent spirit-life eclipses the suffering and uncertainty of the mortal, earthbound existence.

> When the light ascends, one spirit sees the other; and when the sweet spring-water in the light penetrates all the other spirits, then one tastes the other; then all the spirits come alive, and the force of life penetrates everything; and in the same force, one smells the other, and through this surging and penetrating one feels the other, and everything is a cordial loving, a friendly seeing, sweet smelling, love-feeling, blissful kissing, eating, drinking of one another, and love-strolling. This is the blessed bride

who takes delight in her bridegroom, wherein is love, joy, and bliss; light and clarity; fragrant smell and an amiable and sweet taste. Oh and eternal! How can a celestial creature take the full measure of its joy! Oh love and bliss! You have no end. One sees no end to you; your depth is without measure; you are everywhere but in the grim devils that have corrupted you within themselves. (I 110–111/9.37–39)

These effusions are certainly mystical and lyrical. But the more they are considered in context, the less they appear to reflect an ineffable experience. Instead, the ecstasies of *Aurora* convey the author's spiritual and intellectual penetration of the surrounding barriers of darkness, fear, anger, doubt, and ignorance, symbolized by the heavens which were thought to be many thousands of miles away: "For the true heavens [*der rechte Himmel*] are everywhere, even where you stand and walk. If your spirit grasps the innermost birth of God and penetrates the sidereal and fleshly [birth], then it is already in heaven [*im Himmel*]" (I 268/19.24). With this, the dualisms of heaven and earth, of nature and the soul, have been breached. The world of the cobbler has been turned inside out and upside down.

3 The Twofold *Aurora*

The Work in Outline

Boehme's first and most famous work was at least twelve years in the making. The author mentions that there were a number of abortive attempts to "bear fruit" (I 267/19.16) before he was at last able to write out the 400 pages of *Morgenröthe im Aufgang* between January and June of 1612.[1] Miraculously enough, the paper he inscribed in 1612 survived numerous sales, transferrals, and disasters, and is now preserved in the Herzog August Library in Wolfenbüttel, West Germany.[2] This original is a fair copy from the author's hand, not his draft copy. The glosses and revisions inscribed in the margins of the autograph are apparently due to copying errors or to later editing. Passages of the profoundest pathos or keenest ecstasy are in the same steady hand that prevails throughout.

It seems probable that there were earlier draft copies or fragmentary sketches—the abortive starts undertaken before the author was illuminated again in 1610 (*pace* Franckenberg's report, X 11), or at least before he succeeded in writing out the long fragment at the end of the full twelve-year period (I 266/19.14; ep. 12.10). If we assume that *Aurora* incorporates transcriptions of previous drafts, this helps to account for the peculiarities of a compositional structure which contains non sequiturs and renewed beginnings.[3]

The author of *Aurora* insists on the planned structure of the whole. He counsels us to read him in order. His preface states that his first seven chapters are to discuss, "very simply and intelligibly," the being of God and the angels. There will be a step-by-step ascent "by means of likenesses" until in his eighth chapter the work will embark upon the "depths in the divine being," into which the reader will proceed ever further and ever deeper. He adds the promise that what is unclear in his first book will be explained in two sequels (I *Vorrede* 23/107–108).

Translated literally, the original title of *Aurora* means: "Morning Glow, Ascending"; it is followed by a long subtitle:

The Root or Mother
of PHILOSOPHY, ASTROLOGY and THEOLOGY
from the true Ground

Continuing, the subtitle promises a "Description of Nature," with discussions of the following points: (1) how all things were and came to be; (2) how good and evil are to be understood; (3) how things stand now and how the world will end; and (4) how Paradise and Hell are constituted, and how they are related to human beings.

Even this panoply of announced themes fails to prepare us for the confusions and intricacies of the contents. *Aurora* is the ruin of an unfinished edifice. Examining its floorplan, one might doubt that it could ever have been completed. Its center is the paradox of the entire divinity contained in even the smallest circumference of reality (I 152/12.42). This paradox satisfies Boehme's condition of divine ubiquity and allows him to reconcile human freedom with natural order. This may have been an impossibly difficult project. Certainly it was a premeditated one.

The complexities of *Aurora* urge a choice upon us: either to wend our way through every twist and turn, sacrificing the larger view, or to short-circuit *Aurora* by showing how this early work fits in with the subsequent writings. Neither path is appropriate for the present discussion. For the purposes of a biographical study, the very fact that certain terms and notions are later dropped or deemphasized only enhances their interest.

It is best to begin with interpretation, by summing up very briefly the underlying "center of gravity" in the 400-page essay. This may be what Gershom Scholem was alluding to when he suggested that there was an "Archimedean point," which, once Boehme had arrived at it, liberated his prodigious creative powers.[4] The author of *Aurora* has not yet arrived at this point; but since each trajectory of his essay moves in its direction, the content of his work will appear less disjointed if we begin with the implicit point of destination.

In tendency, if not by conscious intention, *Aurora* moves toward the synthesis of two notions of nature, each with its corresponding notion of God: two notions of the relationship of creation to Creator. These two concepts reproduce two interwoven strands within the intellectual and spiritual culture of Görlitz: that of the Humanist Scultetus, a man schooled in Melanchthonian Aristotelianism, a scholar whose observations, chronologies, and perpetual calendars reflected his mathematical and empirical outlook; and that of the Spiritualist Behem, whose mystical speculation displayed a Neoplatonic dualism and an inclination to view nature with reference to the soul. Though

Boehme was no scholar, his thinking indirectly reflected the tension between the Aristotelian and Platonic tendencies within the culture of his period. The first of the two notions of God and nature is oriented toward the experience of the senses in time, the second looks to the transcendent forms of being in eternity.

The first concept of nature is derived from the elements of earth, air, water, and fire. Aristotle's elements are identified by, and also transmuted by, the opposing pairs of properties: the hot, the cool, the dry, and the moist. Measurable time, with its absolute beginning in Genesis, is the scriptural correlative of this elemental nature for Boehme. The world was created out of nothing. Man was created out of clay. The materialized nothingness of the earthly elements, like the mortal flesh, is subject to change and corruption. Elements and flesh contrast with the imperishable spirit.

The second view of nature, then, has Platonic sources. As in Plato's *Timaeus*, nature is a living organism, a whole that is not reducible to lifeless elemental components. All of its parts are vitally connected, as are the limbs of a living body. In accordance with this conception of nature, one Soul, immanent in all of nature, is entirely present in each part of nature, just as the image of God is engraved in each human creature. Similarly, the one supreme Soul of Plotinus

> appears to be present in the bodies [of animate material creatures] by the fact that it shines into them: it makes them living beings not by merging into body but by giving forth, without any change in itself, images or likenesses of itself like one face caught in many mirrors.[5]

This second view accords with the Judeo-Christian tenet that man is created in the image of God. Just as man is an image of God, so also the created world of nature is in some manner an image of the eternal, divine and ideal, world.

Summarized schematically, these two notions of the relation of creation and Creator contrast as the God "beyond" (the Creator *ex nihilo*) contrasts with the God "within" (the immanent divine principle). The two notions contrast as the divisible, material nature contrasts with the indivisible divine world-spirit; as the lifeless elements contrast with the mysterious power of life; as a world created out of nothing contrasts with the Spirit of God that hovers upon and informs the primal waters; and, finally, as the human creature, shaped out of dirt, contrasts with the human replica of the divine being. If not for the controversies over predestination, over divine ubiquity, and over the eucharistic presence, these two views, both of which are conceived by Boehme in scriptural terms, would never have acquired philosophical dimensions in his thinking. Their foundation in the Bible would have granted them an unproblematic authority.

Although Boehme does not state philosophical preconditions *per se*, the above two perspectives are certainly in evidence in his first and subsequent writings. The synthesis attempted in *Aurora* and more nearly achieved in the second book aims at showing that *spirit is a vital substrate of elemental matter, latent in the element*. Since God creates nature not out of nothing but rather out of His own being, the indivisible divine life of the spirit is entirely present at every level, in every suborganism, in macrocosm and in microcosm, within every circle of the world. For the purpose of revealing that the divinity is present in all things, Boehme unveils the striking provisional conceptions of his first effort: the reification of *Qualität*, the hylozoism of the divine substance *Salitter*, the vision of the world of the *Quellgeister* (the seven source-spirits), and the multifaceted realm of the angels. These conceptions are later deemphasized, altered, or renamed; they are rendered more sophisticated, but less colorful. By contrast, the concepts of *Aurora* strive for a synthesis which the author would have us see, feel, and taste.

Nature as Quality

The first chapter of *Aurora* begins by defining *Qualität*: "Quality is the motility, the surging, or driving of a thing" (*Qualität ist die Beweglikeit, Quallen oder Treiben eines Dings*—I 24/1.3). Quality is the perceptible manifestation of the forces operating within things. Every created entity has its good and evil qualities. In all natural forces, in stars and elements, as well as in creatures, the good and evil qualities "are in one another like a single thing" (*in einander sind wie ein Ding*—I 24/1.2). The elemental and corporeal things of the world are tense conflations of the good and evil forces which are forever vying with one another and giving rise to good and evil effects in accordance with the engendered spirit of their combinations. Quality is thus both dynamic and reified. Its dynamic aspect is the divine force. Its reified aspect is to be subsumed as "spirit."

The same oppositions that defined the Aristotelian elements, the four simple properties of hot, cold, moist, and dry, are, in *Aurora*, composite qualities. Heat consists both of light and of the quality of *Grimmigkeit*, a fierce, destructive, incendiary quality which is present as well in coldness. Coldness has both the quality called *grimmig* and the soothing effect of coolness. Hot, cold, *grimmig*, gentle or soothing, dark, light, soft, and hard are joined by bitter, sweet, sour, and the dry or "salted" quality called *herb*. Initially, there appears to be no limit to the absolute number of mentionable qualities. What interests the author is their combining and multiplying powers and the good and evil influences that result. Even the good air that sustains all life can become inflamed, corrupt, and pestilential (I 29/1.23). Understood as quality, reality is dynamic and it is diverse. It is also dualistic, either good or evil (since even the opposites of hot and cold share the negative quality of *Grimmigkeit*). And finally, it is one (since everything is made up of qualities).

In the second chapter, the author continues to develop his theory of qualities. Simultaneously, he turns to the correspondences of macrocosm and microcosm, about which more will be said later. If we focus only on the thread of argument as it concerns the phenomenology of the qualities, these soon appear as the perceptible manifestations of forces flowing throughout the cosmos. Because of the qualities and their interchanges, the relations of microcosm and macrocosm are not merely imputed analogies:

> All of this, as recounted above [i.e., the permutations of the qualities described in chapter one], is called "quality" because everything in the depths above the earth, upon the earth, and within the earth interacts reciprocally like a single thing (*in einander qualificirt wie ein ding*), having various forces and effects, but only one matrix (*Mutter*), from which every thing originates and flows. And all creatures are made out of these qualities, and originate and live therein, as within their matrix. Thus, too, earth and stones take their origin therefrom, as does everything that grows out of the earth. All of this lives and flows from the force of these qualities. No reasonable human being can deny this. (I 30/2.1)

The good and evil qualities have a double source in the stars (I 30/2.2), which induce motion and growth in nature. Quality is thus a first conceptual endeavor to bridge the dualisms of heaven and earth and of good and evil. The same forces operating above in the celestial world also operate below, in stones, earth, and plants. The qualities are attributes of that aggregate of forces which is the very substance of all things. The force-aggregate is a vital medium which cannot be reduced to the affectations of lifeless matter. Even in the lifeless earth and stones, there is an afterglow of the divine substrate of forces.

Nature as Force

In *Aurora*, the divine substrate of forces is called *Salitter* and it exists in two variants: as a divine, pure *Salitter*, and as a corrupt, impure counterpart. What is in Paradise is made of the celestial *Salitter*. What is in the fallen world is made of the corrupt *Salitter*. The former is clear, bright, resplendent. The latter is dark, poisonous, and foul-smelling. The forces of the celestial *Salitter* give rise to celestial fruits, flowers, and vegetation. The corrupt forces of the earthly *Salitter* exert themselves, in vain, to do the same. And yet even the vitiated earthly *Salitter* can dimly attest to the powers of its divine counterpart, by bringing forth all sorts of useful and pleasant fruits and plants. These blossom in the likeness of a celestial world, even while bearing mortal corruption within them (I 54/4.16–17). The *Salitter* is complemented by what is called *Marcurius* (sic). If *Salitter* is the total potency of forces (I 53–55/4.9–21), its expression or discharging sound is *Marcurius*.

The divine substance *Salitter* is deemphasized in subsequent writings in favor of other concepts such as *Herbigkeit* or *Matrix*, and overshadowed by the assertion that God has made everything out of Himself. Nonetheless, the provisional characterization of this substance provides clues to the objects and intentions of Boehme's observations of nature. Influenced by science and by mainstream philosophy, we naturally assume that organic matter is synthesized out of inorganic components. For Boehme, the "dead" elemental matter is a mere residue of what was once the very stuff of life. The fact that this vital substrate is named after a particular substance tells us something about the raw material of his speculations.

The terminological inspiration for the dualistic substance of *Salitter*, which *Aurora* also calls *Salniter*, was a material which played an important role in the science and industry of Boehme's time. According to Grimms' Dictionary, *Salitter* is *Sal niter*. This once famous substance, otherwise known simply as "niter," indeed existed in two forms: refined and unrefined. The unrefined form of niter, saltpeter, was the nitrous earth found beneath stables and barns where it was synthesized through the agency of animal urine. The refined product was a pure liquor, capable of turning into pure, white, transparent crystals. Grimm specifies that in the late sixteenth century the word *Salitter* referred to the refined substance—said to be *klar, lauter und durchsichtig*: "clear, pure, and transparent." Refined "niter" (i.e., potassium nitrate), was much in demand as the essential ingredient of gunpowder. The German niter industry had long since worked out an industrial technique for artificially cultivating saltpeter in plantation beds. Professional *Salpetersieder* boiled and purified the crude niter to reclaim the gunpowder ingredient—known to Boehme as a "spirit of terror." What the divine *Salitter* has in common with refined niter from which it is otherwise so distinct is its concentration of force. Accordingly, the seemingly naive materialism of the *Salitter* in fact reflects the central thesis that the entire divine force is contained in even the smallest circle of nature.

Salitter was both mundanely familiar and esoteric: an object of common knowledge and an object of intense speculation. Around 1600, extraordinary claims were being propounded for niter by the wandering Scottish alchemist named Alexander Seton, whose influential work, *Novum Lumen Chymicum*, appeared under the name of his associate Sendivogius.[6] Seton's book propagated the theory that a "secret food of life" was contained both in the air and in the *sal niter* of the earth.[7] Helbach's *Olivetum* (1605) theorized on the fundamental distinction between *Salitter* and *Salpeter*. Other contributions to the niter discussion during this same period came from Blaise de Vigenère, Joseph du Chesne, and Oswald Croll.[8] Paracelsus may have inspired this new school of niter speculation by writing that fulgurous cloud formations contained the principles of Sulphur, Mercurius and (as an incongruent third, in place of the more general Salt) *Salpeter* or *Niter*. Paracelsus had written that the ingredients of gunpowder could be used to reproduce a flash of lightning, and that the latter in turn symbolized the Second Coming of Christ.[9] This school of speculation gave rise to the theory of a divine niter, paralleling the material niter at a higher level of being.

In *Aurora*, the celestial *Salitter* is a force of all forces, rather like the hydrogen that burns in our sun, and explodes in our bombs—but with the vast difference that it is also the substrate of pure life and awareness. In all probability, the author of *Aurora* saw the pure, transcendent *Salitter* as identical both with the divine spirit-waters in Genesis 1:6 and with the crystalline sea in the Book of Revelation. Washed round by the salnitrous seas of eternity, our fallen world corresponds to the stinking corrupt *Salitter* which has crude niter as its prototype. The nitrous earth was both foul and prodigiously fertile (rotting in the ground and aiding the resurrection of vegetative life). The refinement of impure saltpeter was a process which could aptly symbolize the very core of the Christian allegory of alchemy: the redemption of the soul. The two forms of niter were thus idealized by Boehme to represent the duality of the pure and the spoiled divine substance.

Aside from the symbolism, we can read Boehme's references to the *Salitter* as a clue to the kind of observations which provided him raw material for some of his earliest speculations. Most of the qualities mentioned in *Aurora* are functions of processes that could have resulted from transformations of niter. Niter could become earthen, liquid, fiery, gaseous, or crystalline: it could assume the state of any of the four elements, and of the *Quinta Essentia*. Mixed with vitriol in a retort, pure niter yielded *aqua fortis* (nitric acid), a biting, corrosive liquid that gave off red fumes. One part *aqua fortis* added to three parts hydrochloric resulted in *aqua regia*, used to dissolve gold. If, instead, ethanol or wine spirits was added to *aqua fortis*, a dulcified spirit of niter (ethyl nitrite) emerged, penetrating and volatile, it would smell like sweet apples—an association drawn by Boehme (I 86/8.22).

Qualities compatible with these transformations of niter are ascribed to the interactions in chapter eight. In this chapter devoted to explaining the angelic kingdoms, Boehme provided his first meditations on the sevenfold pattern of qualities, which was to acquire such central importance in his interpretations of nature. There are initially more than seven qualities. He names sweet, sour, bitter, trembling, burning, rising up, stabbing, penetrating, tempering, cooling, warming, drying, and soothing; there is a quality like a "rising source of laughter," and as an extreme degree of this quality one that is "like a tearing plague boil," as well as some related varieties of smell, shape, and color (I 85/8.15ff.). To an observer with the interests of the pensive young shoemaker, the alchemical transformations of niter must have seemed like a window into the concealed substrata of forces which transformed the elements, released energies, and engendered fire and light. Inert matter was teeming with hidden forces, eager to come to life.

In chapter eight, a dramatic ensemble of these forces begins to gather and rehearse its world-generating roles. The dry quality (*herb*) is introvertive, forever going into itself to produce what is cold and hard. Without the dry quality, there would be no cohesion, hence no determinate beings or objects. Yet when this quality goes too far, the harsh, cold, hard *Grimmigkeit* results. The feminine sweetness warms, soothes, or melts the dry hardness. The bitter quality is tremulous, penetrating, elevating, and triumphant; a great cause of joy, it is the quality that stirs spirit into life; but when stirred up too much, it, too, becomes dangerous, volatile, and even pestilential (I 88/8.28). Warmth, fire, water, light, and life make characteristic debuts. Heat is the core or heart from which the light that is ignited within the sweet quality issues forth.

The behavior of the qualities was dramatized by Hermetic thinking; the meaning of their interactions is the Holy Trinity. The *summa* of all forces is the Father. The warmth or energy within all things is the Son. The "flash" initially stands for the Holy Spirit (I 97/8.78–79). The fact that all things, even "stones, leaves, and grass," have a hidden fire within them suggests the omnipresence of Christ (I 98/8.82). The naive animism of these early observations provided the raw material for an incipient metaphysics. Inner spirit realms saturate the visible and transient world with invisible, nonindividual agencies.

The forces at work within the elements are at one with the astral influences which flow throughout the cosmos. Within the inner depths of the world, throughout the cosmic force field and flow, the sun is the focal source and central point of reference. It tempers the harsh forces in nature; it illuminates the obscure depths of space, and gives light to the stars out of which it is born. Even before chapter twenty-five of *Aurora* definitively confirms the new astronomy,[10] the sun already figures as the "heart" of all the radiating forces. The sun and heart is the likeness of the Son of God. In the cosmic pattern, the sun corresponds to the warmth and light generated in the chemical reactions in seemingly inert matter. The heliocentric world is therefore also a likeness of the Holy Trinity. The outer circle of the stars is the Father, centered upon the Son; the forces or qualities that pervade the cosmos coincide with the Holy Spirit. Though Boehme exercised caution so as to avoid turning his cosmos into a pantheistic world-individual, the cosmic model molded his understanding of human nature. The inexorable turning of the stellar circle led to his notion of an "eternal band" of necessity, to which life is bound by nature. The all-pervading spirit-forces were like the vital consensuality uniting the limbs and organs of the body, while the "heart"—as in our own dead metaphors—figured as the organ of a kind of knowledge which knows because of its own inner ground or reason. Thus the implications of his notion of a sun-centered world, constituted by invisible forces, extended from cosmology to theology and anthropology. If all of creation was held in a condition of harmonious free-play by ubiquitous, indwelling forces, these forces could hardly have been blind or indifferent.

Nature as Order and Spirit

In book after book, the discovered solar system provided an emblematic model for the interaction of the eternal forces at work in nature. The interaction of sun and earth suggested that the forces operating within the elements were identical with a preconscious will to life and awareness. Thus, in *The Threefold Life of Man*, the earth turns because it has two "fires," hot and cold, within it. The earth constantly rotates its dark side up toward the sun in an attempt to ignite a life of its own. The planetary longing for the sun stimulates germination and growth in the earthly matrix (III 198/11.1ff.). In *Six Theosophic Points*, the earth covets the sun, just as the external being hungers for the inner being (IV 46/6.9). The desire for life, consciousness, and self-knowledge is woven into the very fabric of the world.

Heliocentrism, as we can see, had its distinct advantages: it provided a natural symbol for the God within, it reconfirmed the ubiquitous presence of the triune deity, and opened the door to a new understanding of the relations of human microcosm and natural macrocosm. However, the advantages of accepting heliocentrism were accompanied by the disadvantages of abandoning geocentrism. Common assumptions concerning salvation, nature, and human life were indexed to the geocentric hierarchy of the earth, elements, planets, and the heavens. The behavior of the elements was explained by a theory of "aspirations"—by what Francis Bacon called "those original passions or desires of matter." The elemental "desires" made them seek their rightful place within the cosmic hierarchy, made the air rise up and made the stones sink down. The elements were in turn coordinated with the four temperaments or humors. If the manifest hierarchy of up and down was illusory, then all such relations ceased to be self-evident.

Boehme's common root of philosophy, astrology, and theology was designed to restore the one "true ground" to these several approaches to truth. This could be accomplished by envisioning the one single pattern present in all things great and small, by exposing the power of order present "in even the smallest circle of the world." The beginnings of this pattern are apparent in the "seven source-spirits" which are introduced in chapter eight—a pivotal chapter, we recall from the preface. The sevenfold pattern combines features of popular astrology with alchemistic lore; it intuits the common denominator of the natural, human, and divine worlds.

The order within the pattern is not firmly fixed: it varies slightly from presentation to presentation and from book to book. Its wealth of patterned motives tends to blur its contours. Its purpose is after all to reconcile freedom with order, and this is not easily done. The seven spirits or qualities perpetually give rise to one another: in this sense, the sequence of the qualities appears to be random. And yet the order in which the qualities are named is certainly not arbitrary for Boehme. We can only reconcile this contradiction by the recourse of an analogy: In a scientific or mathematical formula, the order of the terms is not arbitrary, even though the symbols of the formula can be reversed and inverted in various ways. Even though the term that appears first or last in the equation is not logically first or last, the order of the equation lends a distinct structure and direction to all the permutations derived from it. Similarly, the spirit-order of eternal nature is both stable and variable. The pattern which prevails in *Aurora* designates and orders the qualities or source-spirits as follows:

1. dry
2. sweet
3. bitter
4. hot
5. love
6. sound
7. *corpus*

The fourth quality is sometimes "sour" or "fire." The seventh is also referred to as "nature." At first glance, it may seem that this assortment of seven could only have appealed to the mind on the grounds of *credo quia absurdum.*

If the pattern of the seven spirits demonstrates that the forces at work in the macrocosm behave like those at work in the elements ("within the smallest circle of reality"), then the pattern resembles the hypothetical atom which schoolchildren were once taught to regard as a miniature of the solar system. But, unlike the terms of any scientific or mathematical formula, the qualities of the seven source-spirits cannot be reduced to quantities. The perpetual transformations of the spirits are called "births." This is logical, since a birth brings forth something that is fundamentally new, yet entirely made up of its antecedents. Moreover, the causal impulses which appear to enter into the interchanges of the spirit are subsumed by teleological purposes. Gradually, the trinitarian symbolism comes to the forefront. In general, the pattern serves to reveal the divine harmony and entelechy that prevail in nature and in human life, in all being and becoming.

Harmony in nature is called *die Temperatur*: the tempering of opposite extremes. The harmonious interchanges among the seven source-spirits provide a model for explaining how life and awareness come into being. In themselves, the first four *Quellgeister* are preanimate. Their reciprocal interactions only engender an animate spirit as their attractions and frictions ignite the *Schrack*, a "flash" or "fright," which arouses the "love of life" of the fifth *Quellgeist*. Love, in this sense, refers to various vital phenomena: to the reciprocal interaction of the spirits, to the sympathetic coordination of the limbs of the body, and to the coordination of the five senses which only in unison result in the consensuality of awareness (I 110/9.37). The limbs of the body and the spirits within the divine nature "love" one another, because they are in either case the several manifestations of one indivisible spirit. If the *Liebe* of the fifth spirit is manifest in this coordination of forces and senses within the cosmic flow of qualities, the sixth spirit, *Ton*, renders their waves into "sound"—*gleich einer lieblichen Musica*—

"like a delightful music" (I 130/11.10). *Corpus*, constituting the corporeality of things, is mentioned last, as spirit number seven. Last though not least, corporeality accounts for no more than the seventh component aspect of the flowing, bursting, harmonizing sea of divine nature. All the spirits are necessary for the whole.

In subsequent writings, the pattern of seven is altered and articulated more intricately. What is of interest here are its source materials, its designation as spirit, its heptamerous structure, and its strange selection of qualities. The seven source-spirits are not purely spontaneous in origin. *Aurora* offers more than one glimpse of its prototypes. Chapters twenty-five ("Of the Entire Body of the Birth of the Stars, that is, the Entire Astrology...") and twenty-six ("Of the Planet Saturn") discuss the stars, sun, and planets in terms of many of the same qualities and forces that make up the sevenfold pattern of source-spirits. The planetary forces of conventional or popular astrological lore provided one source of inspiration. Thus:

Saturn is the cold, sharp, astringent, dry regent which does not originate from the sun (I 385/26.1). Furthest removed from the sun, Saturn rules in a domain of death, and acts as a "dryer" of all forces. Its action creates stones and earth, as the least vital element (I 386/26.3). Saturn's quatitity is *dry* (*herb*).

Jupiter is a soother or softener (*Sänftiger*), and a source of the water of life (I 379/25.77). Jupiter is said to be an extension of the sun's flash of light. This may allude to the illumination of 1600. Jupiter was commonly associated with tin, of which pewter is an alloy. The vessel in which the melancholy shoemaker espied a "jovial gleam" was said to have been *zinnern*, pewter. Jupiter's quality is the *sweet*.

Mars bears a raging, storming, poisonous, and destructive force (I 372/25.34; 378/25.72). The quality of Mars is *bitter*.

Venus appears to be a feminine counterpart to Jupiter: "Venus, the most blessed planet, or igniter of life, has its origin or issuance from the rising of the sun" (I 387/26.15). Venus has as its quality *the love of life*.

Mercury. Curiously, this planet is not described under its own heading in chapter twenty-six. As a principle or substance, mercury (*Aurora* spells it *Marcurius*) complements *Salitter* in the divine substance. *Marcurius* is the agency of the perceptive and penetrating spirit and understanding. As previously mentioned, its quality, that of the sixth source-spirit, is *sound* (*Ton, Schall, Musica*).

Abstracting from scattered remarks in *Aurora*, one can add the following conventional qualities or associations: *Sol* is the regal source and center of light and life. *Luna*, as the celestial body nearest the earth, is held in low esteem by Boehme (I 300/21.4). As he later explains, Luna rules over the earthly waters and holds sway in the phlegmatic temperament (*cf.* IV *Trost-Schrift* 228/3.29). Earth, however, is not just the "dead" element of the same name; as a planet, it is also saturated with good and evil forces.

These more or less traditional astrological associations are the raw materials of Boehme's "system," not the final results. In *Aurora*, the attempt at constructing new models is at an early stage. Consequently, the underlying premises are all the more readily apparent. The tentative patterning collates the humoral passions with the elemental aspirations and planetary forces. Matter and the cosmos are thus informed by unconscious "passions" which rise to consciousness in human nature. In order to restore a sense of order to the free-floating world, Boehme envisioned this invisible and eternal order, within and beyond the visible transient world. This was his solution to the uncertainties of a new sun-centered world in which the relations of matter, mind, and cosmos were no longer self-evident.

The following juxtaposition summarizes the pattern of qualities, planets, and humoral-elemental associations, in line with the tendency of the unfinished fragment. The role of the moon is an extrapolation from the negative lunar qualifications in *Aurora* (*cf.* I 290/20.39; 300/21.4), and in the later works.

1.	*Dry*	Saturn	(*melancholy*, power of death)
2.	*Sweet*	Jupiter	(*sanguine*, gentle source of life)
3.	*Bitter*	Mars	(*choleric*, destructive source of life)
4.	*Water/Fire*	Moon/Sun	(night/day; evil/good; temptation to sin/triumphant virtue. [moon, later = *phlegmatic*, watery])
5.	*Love*	Venus	(love of life, spiritual rebirth)
6.	*Sound*	Mercury	(keen spirit, illumination, expression)
7.	*Corpus*	Earth	(totality of forces awaiting rebirth)

Boehme followed the alchemists of his time in counting his spirits seven. Ruland's *Lexicon Alchemiae* (published in 1612, based on earlier sources) named seven *spiritus chemiae* and subdivided them into four *principales* and three *secundarii compositi*. All were identified with colors and substances.[11] The shoemaker preserved their number and their subdivision of four and three. He parted ways with the alchemists by not identifying his spirits with substances. This departure from the alchemistic tradition enabled him to envision a metaphysical *mundus inversus* in which properties could be thought of as ontologically prior to tangible objects. Only the last of the seven *Quellgeister* rounds out the physical determinacy of things. *Corpus*, as the crux of weight and solidity, is, as we have seen, only one of the seven qualities in the eternal pattern.

In order to envisage the pattern as a dynamic whole, Boehme relied on the vision of Ezekiel, as mentioned in the previous chapter. The shoemaker integrated his spirit forces into the single figure of a complex set of wheels mounted within wheels, gradually adapting the figure from Ezekiel to new purposes (I 177/13.70ff.). At first glance, the construction seems wholly visionary; but as it evolves, the same language and imagery of wheels, orbs, and turning is employed to describe the turning of the earth in the "wheel of nature" (*cf.* I 300/21.5; 318/21.123; 321/22.8). Considered in the context of the entire book, the visionary model can best be interpreted as a prototype, abiding in the eternal nature, for the solar system. Hence Boehme's fascination with the hovering, free movements, and multiple and complex orbiting of the wheels. This also accounts for *Aurora*'s extension of the number of wheels, which are at first—true to Ezekiel—only four in number (I 40/3.10). The visionary model of wheels suspended within wheels is the mystic's reply to the competing cosmological models, with their unthinkable solar and planetary orbits. In later writings, however, the wheel becomes more abstract: it is said to generate *Essentien*, which are the impulses to vital particularity, responsible for the diversity of the world, and for the will to life.

Conceptually, the source-spirits mediate between the "clear divinity," or Eternal One, and the world of the elemental bodies. Since the world of the qualities is not a senseless chaos, a term is needed to capture the meaningful interrelatedness of everything. This term is *Geist*. "Spirit" is the agency of identity and discernibility in the world of diverse, interbreeding qualities. *Quell* means "source" or "well-spring." Owing to coincidence, *Quell* can be taken as the root syllable of *Qualität*. A *Quellgeist* is both the source, and the reified aspect of, a quality.

The Biblical prototype of the seven source-spirits is found in the Book of Revelation 4:5

> And out of the throne proceeded lightnings and thunderings and voices: and there were seven lamps of fire burning before the throne, which are the seven Spirits of God.

The seven spirits of the Apocalypse are an antitype of the seven days of Creation, and of the spirit that was upon the face of the dark waters in Genesis 1:2. ("God is a Spirit," reconfirms the Gospel of John, so frequently cited by Boehme.) The *Quellgeister* are the sources from which the qualities emanate. The fact that they are seven in number turns the "historical" Creation and the pivotal life of Christ into the natural pattern of a perpetual creation, corresponding to the astrological number and influences of the planets, centered on the "light of the world" (cf. I 389/ 26.25), and corresponding to the spirits at work within the seven metals or seven salts.

The seven divine spirits in the Apocalypse are thus linked to the temporal-eternal axis of the sevenfold pattern. However, before turning to this dimension, which leads to Boehme's angelology and eschatology, the colorful appearances of the source-spirits in *Aurora* are worth considering in greater detail. The seeemingly naive characteristics of spirit in *Aurora* anticipate the salient aspects of the metaphysical will in his later works.

Nature as Desire and Expression

The palpable aspects of *Aurora*'s source-spirits render them vivid and enhance the poetic beauty of the work—though at the expense of conceptual acumen. More than in his later work, the mystic is convinced that spirit, as a living presence, can be seen or sensed. The Holy Spirit itself is at work in the life-arousing quality (I 27/1.21). Spirit *qua* spirits can be extracted from grain by letting seeds ferment in water and igniting it to make the spirit become visible (I 95/8.69). One can even feel and taste the spirit and force at work within a root by placing it in one's mouth (I 314/21.97). The author of *Aurora* is still close to the peasant who tests the powers of his soil and the virtues of its fruits by tasting either.

When the sun's heat shines on the ground, everything in the soil—roots, worms, and even metal ores—surges and grows (I 91/8.43). *Aurora* describes the growth process of a stalk of grass. Ignited by the sun's warmth, the sweet quality (associated here with the sap) is pursued by the bitter quality (the cadmium layer), while the dry quality (outer layer, or bark) follows after. The knots or joints in the stem result from a tussle in which the sweet spirit escapes by leaping upward, leaving a tiny hole behind in the joint. In the end, the sweet quality can escape no further: it is caught and impregnated by the bitter and dry qualities. Seeds are formed incorporating all the qualities. The flowering and wilting of the plant comprise the course of the whole created world in the life of the part: "that is the end of nature in this world ... you will find this in [the account of] the creation of the world" (I 91–94/8.43–63).

The seven spirits perpetually give rise to one another within the parameters of their eternal sequence. In order to convey their nonhierarchical intermingling, *Aurora* makes use of erotic references, to lovers who wrestle, so that first one and then the other is on top. All seven spirits engage simultaneously in this blissful free-for-all. Their love-play takes place in the world of light. Its inverse, dark aspect is exposed in the description of the germination and growth of a root. As the dry, sweet, and bitter qualities struggle for domination, the dry and the bitter between them stifle and consume the sweet quality and raise a kind of changeling in its place (I 311–313/21.73–87). The sweet quality is crushed and transformed by the aggressive will of its more powerful and domineering neighbors.

In subsequent writings, natural processes no longer resemble the fairy tales of *Aurora*. Even *Aurora*'s source-spirits cannot readily be thought of as personal or individual creatures; eternal and ubiquitous, they are perpetually in the process of mixing and transforming themselves. They are closer to odorous spirits than to fixed, numinous presences. At some point in *Aurora*, all four primary source-spirits are identified with smells or tastes. This may strike us as utterly arcane, inasmuch as we think of smells and tastes as secondary, "subjective" properties, less substantial and less real than the primary qualities of weight and solidity. The divine communication of taste is in keeping with Psalm 34:9 ("O taste and see that the Lord is good"): this primacy of "taste" appealed to Luther as it had attracted Aquinas and many mystics.[12] Yet there is also a philosophical rationale to Boehme's odd scheme of things. The senses of smell and taste can convey presence and quality with considerable urgency. If the visual and tactile sensations reveal elemental bodies, the smells and tastes, by contrast, fathom the untouched and unseen. The messages received by the senses of taste and smell are rarely neutral or meaningless. We recall that to Boehme the "stench" of evil was not a dead metaphor. After *Aurora*, Boehme deemphasized the sensory immediacy of spirit, along with the *Salitter* and the animistic antics of the source-spirits. His *spirit* is not to be understood as something passively smelled or tasted. Spirit has a life of its own, compelling it toward self-revelation.

A further conceptual oddity is introduced in *Aurora* and maintained throughout Boehme's work: the so-called *Natursprache* or "language of nature." According to *Aurora*, this was the language spoken in the very beginning by Adam. It was the language in which the first man named the creatures led before him by God in accordance with their qualities and innate properties. Since the language of nature is the mother or root of all the languages of the world, it is more fundamental than Latin, German, or Hebrew. Touchingly, the author of *Aurora* reports that knowledge of this language is a "secret," conferred upon him by the grace of God (I 296/20.90–91).

In Görlitz, the pupils at the Humanistic *Gymnasium* spoke Latin even in street conversations with one another. In keeping with Humanistic usage, the scholars who dominated the culture of the city latinized their German surnames. (Scultetus had been baptized a prosaic "Schulz," Ludovicus was a Latinized "Ludwig.") Excluded from Humanistic circles as a man of rudimentary education, the shoemaker naturally enough regarded this dominance of the classical languages as an affront.

At one level, then, the *Natursprache* was his compensation. It allowed the autodidact to deconstruct German and Latin words in order to arrive at something even more fundamental. Usually, the words of the German Bible are translated into their meanings in the nature language; but the Latin *Ternarius Sanctus* is just as readily and specifically convertible into its natural meaning. Even when Boehme does not identify his construal of a word with the nature language, his interpretations are based on the same techniques. He discovers German words within Latin words (thus *Qualität* yields first *Quell*, and later *Qual*). He parses the number of syllables (*Mercurius* is composed of four subqualities; or *Ternarius Sanctus* is the three in seven forms). He discerns a second word embedded in the one to be construed (thus *Fall* is the root of *Teufel*, "devil"). His contrivances are diverse. It would seem that there is no cohesive method or thought behind his nature language. In practice, it serves to lend authority to his interpretations of the hidden meaning of words and sentences.

However, the single most important technique and dominant idea of the nature language involves attending to the issuance of "the spirit," that is, to the sound-producing actions of the organs of speech. This is not an unreflective makeshift; for it postulates the universal guiding force of spirit in nature. If the phonetic actions of the lips and tongue can hold the key to hidden meanings, this is because the same creative spirit that is at work in nature also brings forth the sounds. The spirit that is embodied in sound—but in far more than just sound—expresses itself in the articulations of the mouth and tongue, just as it has expressed itself in fashioning the objects of nature. The sound that is contained in the word *herb* (dry) (or the *mer-* of *mercurius*) both means and is the quality that it denotes. This is evident in his interpretation of the first syllable of *Er-de*, "earth" in the first sentence of the Bible. The first two qualities, dry and bitter, are operative in this syllable (I 255/18.71). The ignited anger of God is represented by the uvular resonance (*der zittert im hintern Gaumen*). The fearful tongue contracts and pulls back (*schmäuget sich im untern Gaumen*), thereby performing the spirit-reaction which is at work in the congelation of earth within the primal spirit-waters.

If not for the concurrent trend toward synthesis, the claims of the nature language might have rung hollow. These claims were implicitly reinforced by the Spiritualist precept that the mere letter of Scripture concealed the inner spirit, by the impact of a revived Kabbalah, and by the expectation that the Book of Nature was only beginning to disclose its secrets. Moreover, despite its makeshift applications, Boehme's nature language was theoretically consistent with his other ideas. Thus, the quality of *Herbigkeit* stems from the spirit-force of contraction. In water, this contraction is ice. In the trunk of a tree, it is the dry outer bark. In earth, it is dryness and cohesion. And in the tongue, the same universal spirit enters into, creates, and *is* the root sound of the word "herb."

The nature language postulates that not only words but also objects and processes originate in something like an utterance: "For it [the spirit] forms the name of the thing in the mouth, as the thing has come to be in creation; and from this we recognize that we are all children of God..." (III *Dreyfaches Leben* 109/ 6.3). The two salient corollaries of the nature language are the subordination of natural, causal processes to a mystical process of meaning, and the postulation of a universal brotherhood of all peoples.

Inasmuch as the ubiquitous divine spirit weaves its way through all creation toward revelation, the nature language can surpass its opportunistic applications and develop into a metaphysics of meaning, an "expressionistic" philosophy (to borrow a term applied by Isaiah Berlin to the thought of Herder[13]). The *Natursprache* is in the final analysis the formative power of the Word that would become flesh. The naive etymologies ultimately dovetail with the metaphysical and mystical expressionism of the "signatures of things" and with the theogony of the "speaking word" and the "spoken word" in *Mysterium Magnum*.

The Angelic World and the Mortal World

The world of the angels and the world of the mortals fit together like two initial fragments in the larger divine puzzle. The successive perspective of *Aurora*'s view of history has to be reconstructed from innumerable digressions. Time and eternity in his sense cannot be understood before considering why it is that God ever created anything at all, and how the creation was and is carried out. All these questions are answered in chapter twenty-three of *Aurora*:

> For the entire God stands in seven species, in a sevenfold form or birth, and if not for these births, there would be no God, nor

any life, nor angels, nor any creature at all. And these same births have no beginning, rather they have given birth to themselves from all eternity, and in this depth (*nach dieser Tieffe*), God Himself does not know what he is. For He knows no beginning, nor anything of His kind, nor any ending. (I 340/23.16–17).

Though inherently perfect, divinity would have no self-knowledge and no actualized being if it did not realize its potentialities. The eternal divine spirits bear out the inchoate intentions of eternity by bringing forth life, angels, and nature. The eternal spirit-forces mediate between the eternal God and His creation in time. Yet the spirits are obviously inadequate for actualizing the self-knowledge of God. Their hectic and nonindividualized being leaves them on the side of objective nature rather than on the side of the reflective subject. There is no hint that they possess powers of reflection or deliberation.

A new phase begins with the angels. As individualized creatures, they are the first subjects in successive time. Fashioned of the celestial *Salitter*, the angels are transparent and sexless embodiments of the divine "all-force," the totality of which is nothing less than the Divine Father. Since each angelic kingdom and each angelic creature is fashioned in the similitude of the whole God, the angels lead us from the divine totality, which is "greater than everything" (I 39/3.3; *cf.* John 10:29), toward the totality that is completely present in even the smallest circle of the world. The angels differ from God in their magnitude and origination (*cf.* I 83/8.1ff.).

Paradise is a realm of pure force and quality. Unencumbered by saturnine heaviness, the angels walk up and down in Paradise (I 159/12.81). Though each angel is created in the image of the entire God, the angels are finite and diverse. They dwell amidst the fruits and flowers of Paradise, which are as diverse as their earthly counterparts—but unspoiled by mortal corruptibility. Jubilantly, the angels bear witness to these eternal wonders.

It is clear that they have been created for the recognition and glorification of the wonders latent in the eternal deity. Within each angelic creature, the divine forces are incessantly exciting one another, harkening to the music of eternity, receiving impulses from without, and rising up to the head to sing forth the praises of the Son. In each angelic body, the seven spirits forge the five senses and coordinate the consensual and expressive faculties. Embodying pure force and pure sensory awareness, the angels are wholly alive, unlike the human "half-dead angel" that has fallen from grace. From the human vantage, the angels also represent the fulfillment of all betterment, be it of the soul in need of redemption, or of the world in need of improvement (I 60–67/5.6–39).

The angelic realm has a clearly utopian aspect. The angels live in harmony with one another and with their sovereign Lord. Each angel has a "natural right" (*Naturrecht*) to its own *Locus*, a right voluntarily respected by the Omnipotent Ruler. Only if an angel should oppose its Overlord and despoil its own *Locus*, is it disinherited and expelled by God: "worldly justice has its origin in heaven" (I 154/12.52–55). Moreover, the fact that an angel has a natural right to the *Locus* where it was born does not mean that it is bound to that place. The holy angels enjoy complete freedom of movement: between the territories of Paradise there is "no boundary" (I 158/12.77). No angelic prince would hinder the passage of foreign angels into its domain. To the contrary, the armies of Paradise are forever celebrating joyous reunions with triumphant music and dance (I 155/12.56–60). Moreover, just as the sun and the planets revolve in harmony, the King and Commander accepts the qualitative diversity of His subjects; and they, in turn, accept their own differences without begrudging any fellow angel its particular form and beauty. This should be a lesson to the greedy, proud, and violent of this world, admonishes Boehme—as if there were any danger of missing the point (I 148/15.19). The angelic kingdom is the Lusatian shoemaker's reply to the confused claims to dominion, the demands for confessional and political subordination, and to the avarice and enmity within his surroundings. Featured in the forefront only in *Aurora*, the angelic utopia is in reality topical. It addressed the overriding political issue during the very years when it was conceived. The relationship of God to His angelic subjects idealizes the Letter of Majesty which guaranteed religious freedom to the Lutherans of Bohemia. In the years 1609 to 1611, the political leaders of Upper Lusatia were engaged in efforts to secure their own Letter of Majesty from the emperor.[14] The angelic utopia faded with this passing hope.

In the eternal world, the succession of events first becomes manifest in the fall of Lucifer. The account of his fall extends intermittently from chapter twelve to chapter seventeen. In its narrative moments, it resembles a stirring chapbook epic of a princely vassal gone bad, and parallels Shakespeare's dramas of royal usurpation. Lucifer, the most beautiful angel, was seduced by his own vanity and pride. Disobeying his immediate overlord, Prince Michael, the satanic upstart attempted to usurp the place of God in order to rule alone in the entire kingdom. Dutifully, Lucifer's legions followed him into the rebellion. Defeated, his "light" was extinguished; his fiefdom became an abode of darkness and mourning. Its denizens, the corrupted source-spirits, remain locked into a quarantined realm, which, as it happens, is the very region in which our own world is located. However, before this world was created, Prince Michael conducted a victorious expedition which contained the forces of evil in the reified darkness of the created world. Prince Michael is one of Boehme's many idealizations of the good prince who creates order and remains obedient to God.

This idealization of the good ruler also reflects the concerns of Boehme's times. *Aurora* was conceived during the waning Rudolphine reign, a period rich in hopes and disappointments—both conditioned by the absence of a powerful central governing authority. The concepts of *Aurora* incubated during the fraternal quarrel between Rudolf and Matthias. The manuscript was written out largely during the interregnum after the death of Rudolf. Its cover was dated, and its composition probably discontinued, on a symbolic Pentecost, June 12. This was the month of Matthias's election to the office of Holy Roman Emperor—the event which confirmed that the "heat" of political antagonisms, alas, was to give birth to no new "light" in the "center"—as chapter eleven of *Aurora* had still expectantly foreseen (I 136/11.43). Near the very end of Boehme's fragment one finds a more darkly hued and cryptic intimation: "RA.RA.RP" (*Rudolph Austriae? ... Rechter Antichrist ... Römischer Papst?*) will be "thrown into the winepress outside the city," and with him "AM.RP." (*Antichrist Matthias? ...*) (I 401/26.120). We can only conjecture as to its meaning.

This prophetic shorthand was to inspire much speculation. In form, it is unlike anything else in *Aurora*. However, its importance should not be overestimated in a treatise which, more than all else, endeavors to convey the fluidity of a perpetually self-creating cosmos.

The Apocalypse in Time and Eternity

The end of time, which is announced as one of the titulary themes, is not taken up under any chapter heading. This is due in part to the fragmentary nature of *Aurora*, and probably in part to Boehme's ambiguous conception of the Apocalypse with reference to time and eternity. The ambiguous meaning of the Apocalypse is evident from the book's allusions. That the world must come to an end is clearly implicit in the proper understanding of its beginning. On the first day of Creation, God caused the dark, corrupt *Salitter* (which came into being through the inflammation of the divine anger) to contract and form the region where the external half-dead tangibility (*Begreiflichkeit*) of things was born (I 300/21.4). The darkness of the world is the prison in which Lucifer awaits the Judgment. God created the sun so that this world would not be entombed in darkness. To understand the sun is to recognize an imperfect likeness of the more perfect light which shone before Lucifer's fall (and which still shines within all things and creatures). The "light of nature," of wisdom and philosophy, and the "light of the world," Christ, are its twofold revelation.

Gradually, *Aurora* discloses that these are complementary truths. In the second chapter, all would-be philosophers are admonished to pray for the illumination of the Holy Spirit so that they will not mistake nature for the true God as did the wise heathens (I 31–32/2.11–13). Later in chapter nineteen, the words of Genesis are faulted for running counter to *Philosophia* (I 277/19.79). Thereupon, the image of the dawn's glow, together with that of the rainbow as a sign of the covenant, is presented as the symbol of awakening. This is the time when people become eager for the "root" or common mother of all knowledge: when God is resolved to reveal Himself completely, before the end of days (I 330/22.69).

Near the end of time, the light of nature and the light of revelation both shine upon the children of Adam. The nearness of the end is confirmed by the advent of a profounder knowledge; the historical faith is superseded by the awareness that what is in time is informed by an eternal pattern. To borrow an analogy from Boehme's own environment: the progress of the clockhands are forever completing the same stations and turns as they advance around the clockdial. In Boehme's period and region, clockfaces were elaborate works of art, often with several concentric circles of signs and ciphers.[15] Like the tangential intricacies of the clockface, the awareness of eternity surrounds the discrete moment with simultaneity and coincidence. The cycle of vegetation is said to complete the eschatological pattern in time. Just as the entire divine force is concentrated inside the smallest circle, the entire eschatological lifespan of the world is concentrated in each cycle of growth and death. Birth and rebirth are thus integral to the pattern of eternity.

Alchemy encouraged this kind of thinking by showing that the elements and organisms of the world were caught up in their small apocalypses. At the end of time, the world will be "sundered": the good and evil qualities in all things will be separated and reunited with their kind. This "separation" does not refer to the earth's being rent violently asunder (a notion which Boehme ridicules elsewhere—II 476/27.11). *Scheidung* is a complex metaphor derived from the alchemistic processes of refinement. Hermetic thought presents the elemental world as an eternal grim struggle of forces which crowd and menace one another in nature. Ruland's *Lexicon Alchemiae* defined the Paracelsian *Elementum* as subject to *mutationem, anxietatem atque necessitatem*, until the very *diem extremum consumtionis huius mundi*. To Paracelsus, the alchemist's art of transformation served to advance the status of matter along its path from *Materia Prima* toward *Materia Ultima*. The alchemist's separating fire rendered the impure pure. The alchemist thus performs the work of the Apocalypse in the here and now. "Separation" and clarification need not await the very end of the world.

But the perpetual clarification would not be real if not for the final one (any more than the microcosm can be intelligible if one fails to consider the macrocosm). Where the pure celestial *Salitter* once prevailed, the repurified crystalline sea of the Apocalypse must be restored. What lies between these two self-mirroring states of being grows organically, as a life which contains the seeds of its own death and destruction.

The preface of *Aurora* allegorizes this eschatology by means of a chronicle of the tree of revealed truth. Each stage of the allegory might be depicted in the form of an emblem. The main epochs of the tree stand for events of Scriptural history, the venal adulteration of truth by Rome, the renewal of Christianity in the Reformation, and, finally, the ensuing quarrels over the "root" of the tree of revelation. In the stage following the Reformation, the preface becomes self-referential. Before the tree of time is consumed in flames, its *root* (as in Isaiah 11:1) will give rise to one last branch in order to fulfill the tree's eternal longing to reveal itself. The battered and weathered tree of truth has been nurtured all along by the common root of theology, philosophy, and astrology. The present conflicts are caused by the widespread craving for the hidden root.

The "aurora" which ascends while the world is asleep heralds a celestial marriage rite: a motive of *Brautmystik* based on the parables of Matthew 22 and 25 and a common trope for the union of Christ with the church. Boehme's version of this motive is more complex and mysterious, and more conducive to hints of esoteric nature philosophy and folk prophecy. His contemporaries are the celebrants who have been summoned to the wedding. If Boehme's bridegroom is Christ, then his bride is associated with the new natural and philosophical wisdom which should restore the true church of all believers. The divine wedding is the last flowering in time, a final and complete triumph of truth. In the later writings, this sense of an imminent age of enlightenment fades. The celestial bride is superseded by the figure of the Virgin of Divine Wisdom who inspires the enlightened believers to struggle militantly and chivalrously for the cause of truth. The more joyous chiliastic imaginings in the earlier chapters of *Aurora* reflect the halcyon days of Prague, which, for all the turmoil, had offered some prospect of harmony and progress.

In order to see how Boehme's vision conveys the spirit of a particular time, it is instructive to compare his prophetic sense with that of a chiliastic poem by a later Lutheran Silesian poet—Andreas Gryphius, whose sonnet "The Final Judgment" expresses the outlook of a man whose lifetime (1616–1664) spanned the full duration of the Thirty Years' War:

> Arise dead! Up! The world cracks in final conflagration!
> The horde of stars fades! The moon's turned dark red,
> The sun has lost its glow! Up! whom grave and mud,
> Up! whom earth and seas and Hell held in detention!
> You who live: come on! The Lord who in disgrace
> Was judged appears; before Him fire and anguish race
> With Him stands Majesty, after Him come blaze and death ...[16]

The fact that Gryphius chose to portray a climactic moment of destruction says something about his attitude toward life and history. His eyes have seen enough. His other poems pile horror upon horror, when he writes of burning cities, hordes of insolent nations, thundering field guns, a stream of blood dammed up by corpses, but still flowing on, decade after decade. In an elegy for an infant niece, who perished as a city fell on the night of her birth, he represented her brief hour as the quintessence of life itself. The poetic absorption in immense destruction and irreconcilable division provides a hint as to why the two post-war poets influenced by Boehme, Silesius and Kuhlmann, went in such opposite directions. Where Boehme maintained his irenist ideal of a universal Christendom, Silesius could only seek this object in the Catholic past, and Kuhlmann in a future embodied in the excentric antipapal millenarianism of his "Kuhl-Kingdom."

In "The Final Judgment" of Gryphius, the fire of Armageddon arrives—true to the spirit of his times—as a sudden blow of avenging justice. Even the liberated souls scarcely know what has hit them. The salient fact is that some are on the winning side of the lightning offensive from on high. The bliss of the saved is weighed and measured solely against the woe of those who are irrevocably damned.

Boehme's apocalyptic vision differs by emphasizing Paradise over punishment and by insisting on the noetic resolution of the world's confusions prior to the final separating fire. Despite the shared premises, this difference of stress makes the chiliasm of the prewar illuminate into a very different affair. *Aurora* resounds with appeals to humanity to wake up from its sleep and adorn its lamps in preparation for the nocturnal wedding feast:

> The fiddler has already tightened his strings, the bridegroom is on his way: watch out that you don't have the infernal lameness in your feet when they're lining up on the dance floor; that you're not unfit for the angels' dance because you're not in angelic dress. Truly, the door will be locked behind you and you won't get in any more; instead you'll dance with the hellish wolves in a hellish fire: your scorn will disappear then, and remorse will gnaw at you. (I 62/5.18)

All who open their eyes and get prepared can evade the hellish wolves and join in the apocalyptic fun of being fully alive.

In the final greening of the world, the marriage of Scriptural truth with the philosophy of nature is consummated in an ecstasy like the bliss of the angels and the chaotic joy of the divine spirits in nature. After describing the realms of Paradise and the interactions of spirit, the pivotal chapter eight closes with more than a score of frenzied exhortations stretching over three pages and concluding with expressions of astonishment at what the spirit has now recognized:

> Oh you beautiful world, how heaven does accuse you! How you have darkened the elements! Oh, anger, when will you cease? Wake up! Wake up! And give birth, sad woman! Behold! Your bridegroom is on the way, and demands of you the fruit. Why are you asleep? Behold, he is knocking! Oh, blessed love and clear light, abide by us, for evening would draw near! Oh, truth, oh justice, and just judgment! Whence have you departed? The spirit is amazed as if it had never before seen the world. Oh! Why do I write the wickedness of the world, I who am compelled to do so, and the world thanks me like the devil? Oh! Amen. (I 103/8.108–109)

The spirit that is "amazed as if it had never before seen the world" resembles that of the reborn angelic Adam, whose first ancestor we will encounter in the next chapter.

Problems and Achievements of Aurora

In many thematic points, *Aurora* anticipates the subsequent writings; however, of equal interest here are the discontinuities between the first effort and those that follow. General problems are evident in the first book; these, together with the terms and concepts they generate, provide an insight into the speculative course of the writer. The problems concern the following nodal points in Boehme's speculation: (1) the balance of philosophical speculation and mystical contemplation; (2) the problem of evil; (3) Boehme's still rather undeveloped notion of human nature; (4) the difficulty of rationalizing the Lutheran sacraments; (5) the problem of expressing the imperceptible; and (6) the problematic relationship of the soul to the hidden deity.

What did the cobbler intend to convey with his literary visions? It is evident from *Aurora* that he was attempting to synthesize the structure of heliocentric nature with the esoterically conceived, vitalistic forces present in all things. This in turn revealed the Trinity in nature and the omnipresence of "the unknown God." Beyond this, other claims have been advanced for *Aurora*. It has been said that Boehme anticipated later philosophical developments. In judging these assertions, one would do well to consider that his thought was profoundly contemplative. Philosophy and science begin, as Plato tells us, with a sense of wonder; but they eliminate the wondrous by means of logical or causal explanation. The pious shoemaker probably did not set out with the intention of explaining things logically or causally. His methods instead aimed at maximizing the sense of wonder, by revealing that the same pattern was present in the solar system, in the interactions of the elements, in the inner life of the soul, and in the "inner word" of Scripture.

His world is magical, and not simply because he believes in supernatural events which defy the lawful order of nature. The "natural" events are miraculous in themselves. This is evident in chapter twenty, where he cites the astral-chemical influences of "sidereal spirit." His purpose is to provide a rationalization of Christ's consubstantial presence in the Eucharist. He accomplishes this not by showing how Christ gets into the bread and wine and coexists with the elemental matter, but rather by saturating all of reality with wondrous presences and births. The belief in natural magic in his writings also serves to extend the context of his Lutheran articles of faith to the point that other articles of faith can be accomodated alongside them.

And yet, even if Boehme did not begin with an intention of explaining things in what we would call a philosophical manner, his purposes nevertheless launched him upon an undertaking which could only be pursued by means of philosophical intuitions. He was forced by the very constraints of his materials to perform his labors of thought as a philosopher. The qualities were delimited by the number seven: speculative operations were needed in order to select and systematize the few qualities to be taken over into the core pattern of nature. The philosophical determinants of his solution are manifest in the relationships that connect the first quality, called *herb*, to those that follow. Since *herb* in modern German refers to a quality of wine which is called dry in English, *herb* is almost too easy to translate. Boehme's *herb* is both a taste and a feeling: an unripe or overripe taste and a rough texture to the touch. His *herb* can be a literal drying out and therefore a contraction or hardening (*Trocknung*). Stones as well as ice are congealed water or liquid. It seems that, aside from the weight and material solidity of things, they require a primal "dry" cohesiveness in order not to dissolve in the fluid medium of spirit. This primal condition of the object elicits various counterconditions, oppositions, frictions, and complementations. The drying contraction acts as a centripetal impulse which leads to a centrifugal one, as compression leads to volatility. Proceeding as if on the principle that each extreme calls forth an opposite, the coarse nature of the *herb* is complemented by a softness or gentleness, the *herb* taste by the sweet taste. A fiery state results from the frictions of the extreme qualities. The fiery is then cooled and harmonized by the watery quality, and so forth. Even the formless, lifeless, insensate elements are shown to be alive with the forces of attraction and oppostion. As these forces agglomerate and generate further tensions and oppositions, the ripening presence of the thing is rounded out. The qualities which presuppose smell, taste, and the tactile sense are supplemented by the visible (as presupposed in the flash or *Schrack*), and by the audible, which arrives with "sound." All of this has a sacral import, since the mediation of the sidereal force-qualities can rationalize the *communicatio idiomatum*. And yet it appears that the ensemble of qualities adds up to something like a phenomenology of experience. Instead of merely accepting the word of Scripture, interpreted to mean that Christ's body is in the host, the imagination is aroused to conceive of the existence of all things as a highly mysterious and meaning-laden state of affairs.

Boehme's modes of discourse often work at crossed purposes: this is true of the literal, historical mode and of the mode of speculative interpretation. Both are applied to the problem of evil. Evil, matter, and darkness appear in the two perspectives: as the consequences of personal deeds, and as circumstances in nature. At times, the two modes conflict so that the historical order of events is actually contradicted by the succession of the natural conditions. However, both modes of discourse retain their validity. Boehme's chief premise, that everything has arisen out of God, clashes with his project of accounting for evil. He explains the origin of evil in a nature which is the "body of God": First, there is the character study of Lucifer; this, in effect, traces the rise of evil to the evil motivations of the individual. A parallel explanation is referenced to the source-spirits in Lucifer which rose up too high.[17] Unfortunately, this second explanation merely transfers the motives of the person to the impersonal spirits in nature. As if to eliminate the circularity, additional speculative refinements are introduced: the interaction of the spirits in the wheel of creation squeezes out the sweet water of love—as if evil arose through a mechanical failure of nature (I 185/13.118ff.). The *Salitter* and the seven source-spirits serve as a kind of buffer between God and evil. They maintain the continuity of a creation that proceeds out of God—without transmitting any evil causation from Creator to creature and without relaying the responsibility for evil from Lucifer back to the good deity. A recognition of the makeshift status of these theories may have induced Boehme to eliminate the *Salitter* as a dualistic substance and to reduce the role of the *Quellgeister* as animistic agents capable of autonomous action. If, in *Aurora*, the angels serve as a buffer between Creator and creature, after 1618 the function of the angels and devils is recontextualized *within* the divine and human will. It is not the objectified spirit-forces in nature; it is rather the spirit *as subject* that holds the key to the problem of evil.

In *Aurora*, the pattern of the human subject is approached as the analog of the patterns of nature. Already, human nature is threefold: body, soul, and spirit.[18] Luther gave precedence to a dichotomy of "flesh" and "spirit." Boehme seems to sense that the heretical trichotomy of Gnosticism and Neoplatonism allows for free will and mediates between subject and object; and that the elusive third term of the trichotomy may also help to account for evil, and even assist in reconciling the doctrinal quarrels. For Paracelsus, the "sidereal spirit" implied intelligence (the stars were the teachers, *Lehrmeister*, of the spirit). In *Aurora*, this is only a secondary connotation of the sidereal "influences". Receiving influences from the stars, *siderischer Geist* behaves like a cosmically extended body. The context of sidereal spirit is not the analysis of intelligence *per se* but rather the universal power of the sacrament and the universal struggle between good and evil.

For the mortal human creature, the realm of sidereal spirit serves as a kind of defensive buffer territory surrounding the soul. The soul is portrayed as the inner being within the domain of the human creature. The soul is a power which may attempt to usurp the place of the heart. The inner struggles of the soul, spirit, and body are full of reversals, betrayals, crises, and critical reinforcements (I 237/16.95ff.). Because the sidereal spirit stands between the outermost birth of the flesh and the innermost birth of the soul, it is a no-man's-land through which eucharistic reinforcements are received. The mediating cosmic force fields of sidereal spirit not only relieve the soul; they also provide answers to the debate over Christ's real or nominal presence in the Eucharist. By virtue of the ubiquitous sidereal body of Christ, He is in both places: at the right hand of God, and in the bread and wine of Communion. This is presented as a stern rebuttal of the Calvinist position, but it looks suspiciously like a compromise notion for which orthodox Lutherans and orthodox Calvinists might have condemned the autodidact with equal justification (I 294/20. 73–76). He avoids committing himself either to the option of the mere "sign" and "thought" or to that of a physical presence. He does so by opting for the sidereal medium which mediates between the conscious inner soul and the external, insensate nature.

Another problem of *Aurora* has to do with the structure of its conceptual images. The world initially appears to Boehme as a kind of picture puzzle, as a code to be cracked: he is dealing with cipher-like images which mean something. Gradually, this kind of thinking proves inadequate. The weaknesses of his early, naively pictorial analysis of the world can be seen in chapter two of *Aurora*. There, he makes use of his definition of quality (stating that everything in the heavens and earth is reciprocally related since all flows from a single mother), by detailing the correspondences of macrocosm and microcosm: The hollows inside the body "mean" the chasm between earth and sky. Breath means air. Veins mean the orbits of the stars; entrails are stellar interventions. The heart is warmth or the fiery element; liver, the watery element; lungs, earth. The feet signify both closeness and distance; the hands, divine omnipotence. The whole body up to the neck means the starry vault, while the head signifies the heavens. But the heavens are also said to mean the heart of nature, referring to a certain finer matter which is composed of all the forces (i.e., the *Quinta Essentia*). The human figure is thus strangely dehumanized, in a manner analogous to the peculiar human portraits made up of allegorical details such as fruits and grains, painted by Arcimboldo for Emperor Rudolf II in Prague. In chapter three, Boehme's difficulties are compounded when he tries to interpret the Trinity by utilizing the same technique of allegorical correspondence. The approach breaks down because the divine side of the pictorial allegory contains three members that are contiguous with the totality of things.

The appropriate likeness of the Father is the round circle of the stars which has neither beginning nor end. The ensemble of stars represents the totality of divine forces. The stars also "mean" the angels. The sun represents the Son of God and, must therefore be born out of all the stars (I 44/3.22); but the sun is also the "heart or king of all stars" (I 31/2.9). Nature is the body of God. God, in all three persons, is all-pervasive, dwelling in *der rechte Himmel*, in the true ubiquitous heavens (I 268/19.24). This has troublesome implications. If the Son is the heart in nature *and* in the Father, nature coincides with God. Since pantheism runs counter to Boehme's intentions, he amends his solar allegory with stern admonitions against heliolatry (I 373/25.41).

The scheme of the correspondences is eventually saved by sacrificing pictorial literalism. Beginning in 1618, a theory of "principles" will enable Boehme to evade the limits of his pictorial relationships: by tripling one and the same totality of things to obtain three interpenetrating—and yet distinct—spheres of being, united in the Godhead.

To the extent that *Aurora* already surmounts the limits of pictorialism, it does so by developing a visionary language. The correspondences which dissolve objects also restructure the representation of reality. The coherence of *Heiliger Geist, Quellgeist* and *Qualität* creates a metaphysical and nonspatial equivalent of heliocentrism. God is Spirit, and the divine center is ubiquitous. The notion of the sun stirring up the spirit-forces in nature is subsumed by the ubiquitous self-emanating power of spirit. If Boehme begins with a literal and pictorial thinking, his language succeeds in envisioning an all-encompassing ocean of animating processes and interactions, a world which can be expressed but not depicted. In this language of ubiquity, verbs overshadow objects and the intransitive supercedes the transitive relation. Reciprocal influences are captured by characteristic verbs: *inqualiren mit* and *sich inficiren mit*. His *inqualiren* (which found its way into Hegel's *Logic*[19]) suggests a perpetual self-impregnation of the indwelling spirits. *Aufsteigen* and *aufgehen* are used in the sense of the alchemistic *sublimare, sublimatio*.[20] Eventually, spatial relationships are contorted into graphically inconceivable spiritual equivalents, as when the prepositions, "*in* sich *aus* gehen," are combined in order to express a movement of spirit which unfolds outward by going into itself. In *Aurora*, a verb of frequency and importance is *wallen*. This is what *Geist* does: "to waft or flow in waves." *Wallen* contains the same root as *Welle* (a "wave" or a "flow"), and it is associated in *Aurora* as well with the term *Wille* ("will"). These verbal refinements assist in elevating the secondary qualities of taste, smell, color, and motion to a primacy equal to that of the weight, hardness, and impenetrability of earthly objects.

The net effect of his usage is the integration of all facets of experience in a nonhierarchical vision of the world: a vision in which spatial, moral, and metaphysical precepts are related in a new and more complex manner. Angels are explained by the same design that accounts for metals or for wild flowers. The angelic and natural orders reveal that variety can flourish in harmony.

This vision of ubiquitous plenitude is both a strength and a weakness of the fragment. Compared with the later writings, its ecstatic presentation fails by not providing an adequate interpretation of the deity as subject. The great *Memorial* is both unfinished and inconclusive. The half-pantheistic notion of God as the sum of all forces blurs the distinction between good and evil. The soul has no special access to a passively ubiquitous God. *Aurora* has postulated an "innermost birth" but has not explained it. There are seven divine spirits, but there is no singular subject of which their universal *Wallen* can be predicated. *Aurora* thus fails to find its way into the interior, the subject's side of the objectified spirit-forces of nature.

The last chapters contain waymarks of the future direction of Boehme's thought: a shift from nature to subjective spirit. The birth of the stars is linked to human birth. The fall of man is previewed. The author ponders over the function of the brain, and lashes out at the *Medicos*, who are said to dissect living human bodies in a misguided search for the principle of life (I 391/26.41ff.). In his final pages, the intrepid thinker is still attempting to penetrate the closed firmament and still cogitating over the seven planets in search of what he calls *das Cirkel des Lebens*, the mysterious "circle of life."

4 The Three Worlds

Between 1613 and 1618

The 400-page *Aurora*-fragment was written down and dated during the first half of the year 1612. A year later, on July 26, 1613, the author was castigated first by the city magistrates of Görlitz and two days later by the contentious Pastor Richter. According to Boehme's defensive presentation of the affair, the personal *Memorial* was entrusted to someone who acted without the knowledge or permission of the author in copying and circulating it (ep. 12.12). Scholars have theorized that Carl von Ender was the culprit.[1] According to Boehme, it was the borrower who seized the initiative in circulating the manuscript, eventually in multiple copies. This suggests that the *Aurora* scandal was a private matter that got out of hand.

The affair poses many questions. Is it possible that during the composition of such a dialogically argumentative work, its gregarious author would have said nothing about his writing to those who influenced his thinking? Could he have been unaware for so many months that *Aurora* was being copied and circulated? What about the readers, copyists, and circulators? To transcribe a 400-page manuscript might have required as much as a month of painstaking sessions. This is what it would have come to for Johann Rothe, a lawyer who copied another of Boehme's manuscripts in 1622 for waiting readers—at a rate of three *Bogen* (sheets) per day (ep. 23.4), with a *Bogen* being equal to about five pages in the edition of 1730. A reader who read for personal edification, who saw no permanent or general importance in the treatise, would have perused it, perhaps made some notes, and then either returned it or passed it on to others. Yet multiple transcriptions eventually came into existence and circulated widely in Lusatia and Silesia. By the standards of the period, *Aurora* set forth no miraculous claims.[2] Its prophetic message was subtle, if not vague, its philosophy difficult, not to say abstruse.

If it was heretical, why were its readers and copyists not persecuted? Why was there apparently no attempt to trace and destroy the circulating copies? How odd that Ender, assuming it was Ender, who brought disaster upon the shoemaker, became his most important patron after 1618. Were there no hard feelings? What are we to make of the fact that, barely a year after the incident of 1613, Richter himself wrote a fawning dedication to Carl von Ender, at whose estate members of the pastor's family took refuge during the plague scare of 1614?[3] Why was Richter, himself a Philippist, intent upon supressing *Aurora* and punishing its author?

As in the plight of Pastor Franz Rotbart a century earlier, many factors played a role. Some issues were local and personal, others more general. The shoemaker undoubtedly knew his friends, enemies, and neutrals. Those who resented newcomers and non-conformists were not well disposed toward him. Neither, we may surmise, were his old guild rivals, the tanners. Richter also knew his friends, enemies, and neutrals. The latter category included some who were important enough to be wooed. Ender was in this category. Ender was rich and well educated. He was a scion of one of the aristocratic families that had been hounded as Schwenckfeldians in the 1560s. His father, Michael von Ender, was a member of the Convivium Musicum, to which Pastor Richter also belonged. Carl von Ender's good will was thus worth obtaining—but not if this meant sacrificing the dignity of one's own pastoral office.

Richter's status in Görlitz was more insecure than it would seem. Like Boehme, he was of humble origin, the son of a blacksmith. The patronage of an important council member in Görlitz had been decisive for his career. Richter's classical education and literary skills were impressive, but he held no degree from his studies at the University of Frankfurt an der Oder. As a Philippist, Richter was as vulnerable as Martin Moller had been. Richter's conservatism was that of a man who had worked his way up, only to find his hard-won authority weakened and destabilized from every side. The doctrines that Richter opposed were those authored by the so-called "autodidacts," like the despised Schwenckfeld.[4] Richter fought to preserve the prerogatives of his official authority, dignity, and academic credentials—prerogatives which had indeed been challenged by the shoemaker.

The miscreant cobbler had violated a hidebound maxim of his station on at least two occasions in the years before his formal reprimand, once as a guild member by challenging the traditional prerogatives of the rival tanners, and again in 1612 by selling his shop to enter the profitable yarn trade with the active support of his wife. "Shoemaker, stick to your last!"—must have been the first reaction of many in Görlitz. The fact that his writings were filled with insolence toward those trained in the canon of the written word probably offended the parvenu pastor of Görlitz more than their content. The political implications of *Aurora* could be interpreted in two ways: either as a potentially dangerous attack on authority in a city imperiled by revolt from below and impeachment from above; or as a circuitous appeal for toleration and confessional harmony in a region badly in need of them. The second interpretation of the scribblings of a simple cobbler was too farfetched for the year 1613.

Soon afterwards, the same scribblings must have begun to look like farsighted visions. No sooner had the cobbler been silenced, than the Rosicrucian writings came onto the scene. In the town of Kassel in Brunswick, the first of these cryptic books appeared in the year 1614, announcing in its title the program of a "General Reformation of the Entire Wide World." The slogan had been taken, along with an extensive excerpt, from a recent work by the Italian Trajano Boccalini. In 1615, other Rosicrucian tracts were printed in various cities. In 1616, *The Chemical Wedding* came out. At about this same time, writings attributed to Weigel and Paracelsus began making the rounds in Boehme's region. In a similar vein, Johann Arndt's books *Vom wahren Christentum* were reinforcing the mystical speculative trend among Lutherans.

The first Rosicrucian writings created enough of a stir that even Descartes harbored hopes of meeting up with members of the secret fraternity during his stay in Frankfurt am Main in 1619, and was suspected of Rosicrucian affiliations when he returned to Paris.[5] Neither the inquisitive Descartes, nor the others who more earnestly declared their intention of joining the Brotherhood of the Rosy Cross met with any recorded response to their inquiries. But even if it was only a phantom, the Rosicrucian Brotherhood furnished the scattered circles of dissenters and seekers with powerful slogans, symbols, appealing myths of organization, and a fabled tradition. Here was a confirmation of the link between Hermetic tradition and the Lutheran Reformation. The covert order of Christian Rosenkreutz was stepping out of the shadows, a Protestant response to the feared and hated Society of Jesus. The Rosicrucian myth orchestrated alchemistic and apocalyptic symbols, heralding a final victory over the Papacy.[6]

Boehme did not share the clandestine zeal of the Rosicrucian Brotherhood. But two of its slogans are echoed in his writings: the "age of the rose" (which he transformed into the age of the rose-lily, and then just of the lily—II 202/15.26; 316/19.66), and the "new reformation."

Those in the vicinity who read, exchanged news, reflected on the state of the world, and watched for the signs of the times must have noticed before long that the shoemaker who lived between the inner and outer Neisse Gates of Görlitz appeared to have anticipated this mysterious movement which was only now beginning to emerge from its concealment. Now, the very fact that Boehme was only an uneducated cobbler and tradesman must have accentuated his aura of prodigy and sharpened the curiosity of all seekers.

At the same time, Boehme was travelling in pursuit of his commercial livelihood. This brought him into contact with the network of tradesmen who had additional contacts and sources of information. Whether he and his associates talked about business or about religion, they could scarcely have ignored the political events in Prague. In the summer of 1617, the ailing Emperor Matthias nominated a successor to the throne of Bohemia: his adopted son Ferdinand of Styria, known as the champion of the Counter-Reformation. Ferdinand had already suppressed and exiled the Protestants of his native Styria. In 1617, the estates of Bohemia, Moravia, Silesia, and Lusatia were convened in a general diet. Despite their reservations, the estates confirmed the nomination of Ferdinand. The era of relative tolerance was at an end. Protestant freedoms throughout the region were jeopardized.

In Görlitz, popular sentiments were divided between the rosy optimism of some and the anger, rebellion, and anxiety of others. In 1617, Dornavius, the rector of the city's *Gymnasium*, held and published a celebrated oration, *Felicitas seculi*—in praise of the superb good fortune of the inaugurated century. He heralded all manner of scientific, scholarly, technological, and industrial progress: the invention of the telescope, resultant astronomical sightings, the discovery of logarithms, the improvements of surveying, bold navigational explorations, the development and practical uses of pumps, the new refinements of agriculture, the exportation of local textile products to lands as far away as Africa, the invention of the pocket watch, and the creation of ingenious automatic machines for the collection of Rudolf II in Prague.[7]

However, there were also social and political rumblings inside Görlitz in 1617. The craft guilds—still excluded from participation in city government—were distributing rebellious proclamations against the city council. Emmerich, the new mayor, recorded in Latin in his official diary the words of one of these denunciations: *Propter Tyrranidem libidines et Idiolatriam periit primus mundus. Quid fiet Gorlicio?*[8] In an aside of this period, Boehme refers to a certain writing of prophetic admonition (*die Schrift der Weissagung*). He warns that a "deluge of fire" (*Sündfluth des Feurs*) awaits those who scorn "the spirit of knowledge" (*Geist der Erkenntniß*), like the Flood that destroyed "the first world" (II 78/8.16). Boehme's admonition echoes the popular prophetic warning from the streets of Görlitz but redirects it toward his own chiliasm of spiritual enlightenment.

By 1618, the city council was sufficiently concerned about the situation to dispatch observers to Prague.[9] The widespread mood of crisis reverberates in the book begun at the very end of 1617 (a disputed date which we must accept on the best available evidence from Boehme's own hand).[10] The new project bears the dire forebodings of the period, even while trying to swim against the current of the time. The preface of the new book admonishes that "horrid wolves are among us" (II 4/6). In chapter twenty-four, a bestiary conceit is expanded into a nightmarish parable:

> Truly, I tell you, and it is no joke; as I was at Jericho my dear companion opened my eyes that I might see, and behold! a great generation and horde of nations of men were mingled and a part of them were like animals and a part like human beings, and a struggle was among them.... (II 420/24.10)

Boehme explains his rationale for resuming his writing by elucidating this lurid vision of "Jericho": the human and animal men are both trapped in the devil's garden where they are being fattened for the slaughter. Those who flee are hunted down like wild game. The animal humans are the hunting dogs. Love of his fellows has compelled the author to resume writing; this is why he is ignoring the voices that tell him to leave well enough alone and let the paid pastors have their say, since the way of the world cannot be changed. The world has fallen under the sway of the fratricidal church of Cain (II 347/20.116). The crowned whore of Babylon rides an apocalyptic horse; the drink she offers is God's wrath. The nations are becoming drunk from it. They are turning into murderers, thieves, liars, scoffers, traitors, and the like—each thinking his path correct (II 350/20.128).

There are also those who "play with secrets," writing one thing and professing something else to please the mighty. Rejecting the example of these unspecified opportunists, the long-silenced author declares that one should write and speak "freely, from the abyss of the heart, without disguise" (II 271/18.1). Public intentions thus played an important role in the decision to write *The Three Principles of Divine Being*.

Boehme's public purposes were bound up with the central themes of his mystical speculation. On January 18, 1618, just after beginning the new book, the author characterized his project in a letter to his patron, Carl von Ender:

> Thus in body, as well as in spirit, he [man] has become a child of this created world, which now rules, drives, and leads him, and

feeds him and quenches his thirst; he has received unto himself its destructibility and suffering [*Peinlichkeit*] and acquired an animal body which must rot in its mother [i.e., nature]: For he should not have its monstrous form. The stars of the great world should not rule over him. Rather, he has his own star within him, which is infused [*inqualiret*] with the holy heaven of the second principle of divine being, that is, with the rise and birth of the divine nature. (ep. 1.8)

Since the mortal world is lodged between two eternal realms, its perspective is peculiarly condensed: the reign of material nature, of hunger, fear, darkness, and hostile elements, blends with the political reign of power, anger, violence, venality, hypocrisy, and war. Those under the sway of the *Geist Maioris Mundi*, the spirit of the animal and elemental realm, include the evil tyrants and venal clergymen, the hated "Belly-Servants of Antichrist." The "monstrous" human form must be liberated both from its state of thralldom to nature and from all the satanic-apocalyptic encirclements of the times.

The Three Principles of Divine Being

The title and subtitles of the second book again promise a whole universe of topics. The Latin and German titles, *De Tribus Principiis*, and *Beschreibung der Drey Principien Göttliches Wesens*, are followed by three long subtitles, promising discussions: (1) of "the eternal birth, without origin, of the Holy Trinity (*Dreyfaltigkeit*) of God" and how through and of it arose the angels and the heavens, stars, and elements, "together with all creatural being"; (2) of "man, out of what, and to which end, he has been created," and about the fall from Paradise into the wrathful grimness of mortal being, and how the mortal creature has been helped; and (3) of the meaning of God's wrath, that is, of sin, death, devil, and Hell," as well as an explanation of how the aforementioned once stood in eternal calm and great joy; and of how everything originated, what it is now driving towards [*wie es sich ietzo treibet*], and how it will once again come to be.

Even compared with *Aurora*, the second book is an uncommonly difficult volume. The naive exuberance has vanished. The reader is confronted with a many-layered complex of relationships and references, a kind of symbolic-esoteric palimpsest. Terms are multiplied beyond any conceivable requirement of thought or contemplation, points of discussion repeated with constant shifts of emphasis and meaning. Yet, surprisingly, the author boasted that in the second work he developed not only a deeper and more fundamental knowledge but also *einen besseren Stylum* (ep. 12.13). His modern critics have not accepted the claim of a better style.

Our goal is to understand what the new style conveys. This was an age of riddles and conundrums, of curiosity cabinets and mazelike gardens, byzantine conspiracies and intricate theoretical constructs. This same *Zeitgeist* is manifested by two books published even as Boehme resumed writing, Robert Fludd's *Utriusque Cosmi Historia* and Michael Maier's *Atalanta fugiens*: two men who wrote for the cognoscenti, and to whom the Rosicrucian tracts spoke the language of the initiate. Around 1618, the passion for the intricate was attaining its zenith. The symbolic texture of *The Three Principles* is truly that of a palimpsest. The central symbolic patterns of the "principles" are superimposed over the whole hierarchy of speculative objects. That the principles are three in number alludes to the ubiquitous Triune God, and to the trichotomy of soul, spirit, and body, and finally to the alchemistic triad of *Sulphur, Mercurius,* and *Sal*, which again refers back to the Triune God and the trichotomous human nature.[11] The three principles, which are in fact three "worlds," remain dominant in almost all of Boehme's writings from this juncture on. The fact that the chemical triad is discussed near the beginning of *The Three Principles* should not be taken as an indication that what follows is *derived* from alchemistic reflections on nature. The difficult development begins with the question of God's origin. As in *Aurora*, the terminology projects from what is lowliest (the alchemical statement of the principles), to what is most sublime (the "clear divinity"). If the new book greets its readers with a conceptual conundrum, this is done, not to put them off, but to lead them on, by enticing them into the quest for the simple core beneath the maze of symbolic terms of an alchemistic nature:

> Accordingly, even if I were to speak and write purely of heaven and only about the clear divinity, it would mean nothing to the reader who lacks knowledge and gifts. However, I intend to write thus both in the divine and in the creaturely manner, in order to make the reader covetous to contemplate the exalted things (*den hohen Dingen nachzusinnen*); and should he find that he is not able to do this, that he may in his desire seek and knock and ask God for the Holy Spirit, so that the door to the second principle may be opened to him... (II 15/2.5)

The "clear divinity" is the divine light and Eternal One. As opposed to the corresponding "divine manner," the "creaturely manner" of writing refers to the creation and employs the whole array of alchemistic terms. Accordingly, these are intended to facilitate understanding and stimulate interest.

The Three Principles of Divine Being attacks the intractable problems of *Aurora*: the problem of evil, the rationalization of the sacraments, the problem of conceiving the ubiquitous God as subject, and the difficulty of expressing what cannot be seen or depicted. The language and themes are not intelligible if they are read in isolation of their doctrinal and exegetic context.

This begins with the title itself, of which the last word, *Wesen*, is often erroneously translated as "Essence." *Wesen* is distinct from the alchemistic spirit-essences, for which Boehme possessed other terms. Luther, we recall, used *wesentlich*, an adverb derived from *Wesen*, to characterize Christ's real presence in the *Abendmahl*. Christ is truly and really, or truly and consubstantially, present in the bread and wine: "Darum wird im Sacrament unter dem Brod und Wein sein Leib und Blut *wahrhaftig und wesentlich* dargereicht und empfangen." Luther's meaning is that Christ's words at the Last Supper, "This is my body," are to be taken literally. How the sacramental miracle can be true is no one's business to inquire. (All the same, Luther's strident defense of his doctrine opened the way for the kind of scholastic controversies that were so noxious to Boehme.[12]) *The Three Principles* staunchly defends the Evangelical sacraments. It defends Christ's ubiquity and real presence, and, in so doing, it employs the terms *Wesen* and *wesentlich*.[13] However, *Wesen* is also all substance and all living being. *Wesen* is Boehme's ontological designation for the reality of a world which is made real by the indwelling presence of a God who is nothing less than "the Being of all Beings," *das Wesen aller Wesen*.

It has been argued that each of Boehme's many terms has a precise meaning within a philosophical "system." The true context of his terminology is not a philosophical system in the usual sense, but rather the sacramental and absolute mystery of presence and transcendence. There are notably many expressions for "being in": *im Wesen, im Centro,* and *im Ternario Sancto. Im Centro* and *Centrum Naturae* convey the indwelling presence of the total divine being in each circumference of reality. *Ternarius Sanctus,* according to one theory, designates the last three, the holy qualities of the seven. However, the dwelling-like aspect of the usage, *in Ternario Sancto,* is also reminiscent of Luther's discussion of the Tabernacle. Though Luther elsewhere rejected the trichotomous anthropology, he made use of it in discussing the symbolism of the Ark of the Covenant, designating its three compartments as *atrium* (symbolizing for Luther the body), *sanctum* (the soul), and *sanctum sanctorum* (the concealed dwelling of

God and spirit).[14] If *Ternarius Sanctus* indeed alludes to Luther's exegesis, the term serves to salvage the reformer's suppressed mysticism, reclaiming its validation of the Gnostic trichotomy and assimilating Luther's *sanctum sanctorum* to Trismegistos, the legendary "thrice great" founder of Hermetism. The *Tinctur* or mysterious energy which sublimates and tranforms things is also characterized as if it were a dwelling, even though this does not jibe with the implicit imagery of the word.

Boehme's terminology of immanence and transcendence envelops all being, all becoming, in a veil of mystery. *Aurora*, we recall, conceived of sensible objects as composite qualitative presences, of which corporeality was only a foreground aspect, beneath which illocal forces communed. By the same token, the whole of nature can be conceived as the presence of the unknown eternal deity in time and space. If that which cloaks itself in presence in the here and now comes from outside, or if it comes out of some other thing, then what is present everywhere arises out of nowhere and nothing, which is to say from another mode of being. This is the structure underlying Boehme's peculiar and paradoxical doctrine of the "principles." The term *Princip* is consistently defined as a "birth."[15] *Wesen* as substance or being encloses the indwelling presence of spirit: *ein Princip* is the realm into which spirit is reborn. Hence, if *Wesen* is the absolute form of the eucharistic immanence, *ein Princip* is the correlative of Boehme's concept of "rebirth": a theosophical notion which dissolves baptism into a field of further allusions to contrition, conversion, and grace. The three interpenetrating principles, as *worlds*, are an absolute form of the union of divine and human natures in Christ. Hence, just as all being has its center in the indwelling divine spirit, all becoming strives for spiritual birth and rebirth in eternity.

These complementary projections of the sacramental mysteries shape even the syntax of *The Three Principles*: the turgid, dense phrasing of the "better style" contains innumerable appositives introduced by "as"; it contains long concatenations of seemingly redundant genitive and dative constructions which split up the objects of speculation between passive media and indwelling forces, reinforcing a thesis which is asserted in the book: that all things are concealed within and born out of all other things. Tedious and difficult as the new style now seems, it conveys the mood and sentiments of a certain moment: a balance of despair and hope based on the perception that long-contained forces are about to erupt. A work composed five years later by the tragic last bishop of the Moravian Church, Jan Amos Comenius, *The Labyrinth of the World, and the Paradise of the Heart*, thematized the concealment of things in a mood of bitter disillusionment (as in the riddle of the bright Rosicrucian boxes, which are labeled as containing exalted mysteries but prove empty when opened). The two men were affected by the same events in the same region. Boehme, by far the luckier of the two, remained serenely confident that the Paradise of the Heart could be disclosed *inside* the Labyrinth of the World. He urges his readers to take heart accordingly:

> For he [the reader] shall here see as in a mirror in the mother of the womb all things. For each thing lies within the other; and the more he seeks, the more he shall find; and he need not propel his spirit beyond this world, he will find everything in [it], and in himself... (II 73/8.1)

The very syntax of nature is wrapped up and interwoven into its own being. Each element, hermetically contained in the others, is struggling to be born. The symbolic cross-references render the evocation of divine nature all but impenetrable. A kind of terminological thicket which the reader cannot traverse without becoming mired and enmeshed envelops the first chapters.

Viewed from our distance, this nature resembles the multiple conflicting allegiances and alliances which crisscrossed Middle Europe on the eve of the Thirty Years' War. Confronted with this situation, the author of *The Three Principles of Divine Being* is firmly resolved to defend his Lutheran tenets. Pursuing these, as if by the light of an "inner star," Boehme labors to interpret them in order to regain the path toward peace and reconciliation.

The Riddle of Being

As Boehme says elsewhere, the "great mystery" is the human creature. Human existence and being-in-the-world are therefore presented to us as a convoluted knot of riddles which must be unravelled altogether. Chapter four addresses a battery of questions to the reader concerning human existence and the being of the world. Raise up your thought and mind—he advises the reader—and ride on the "wagon of the soul." Consider yourself and all creatures. Ask how the "birth" of your life could have come to pass, and how that light of your life (*deines Lebens Licht*) was born that enables you to travel, without the light of the sun by the sheer force of "imagination," into a great expanse which the eyes of your body could not penetrate. Ask how it happens that you are more reasonable than all the animals. Consider the elements, their origin, and how fire could be born in water; and how the light of your body is born in water. Reflecting on these things, you will arrive at God and the eternal birth (II 33–34/4.23).

He continues with further questions intended to demonstrate that everything before our eyes must have a concealed, "higher root." How does it happen that the starry firmament persists in its stable order and does not shatter, float up, or sink, given that there is no up and no down? (Here he introduces two of the three principles into his speculative questioning.) This same permanence indicates, "in the first principle," that the "eternal birth without beginning" is an indissoluble, "eternal band." In "the second principle," one recognizes the "separation"; and one discerns that the third and most external principle, the created world with its stars and elements, has arisen out of the first one. Why? Because, in the elemental realm, there is always a cause to explain why something comes into being, yet one finds here no *first* causes. In the visible, external realm, one finds only destructibility (*die Zerbrechlichkeit*). One discovers the origins of this realm only as it comes to an end (II 34/4.24).

The next set of questions moves to the inner being of what is: In all things there is a wonderful force, life, growth, and rising up, a beauty and gentle inner activity. Examining a plant or a woody growth, you discover the four qualities: dry, bitter, fire, and water. If you separate these four, and then put them back together, the object remains dead. You can't restore its life or its pleasant smell. Even if you could return its color and make it grow once again, you could not restore its smell and taste (II 34–35/4.25–26). (So it seems that the origin of these two forms of sensory experience, smell and taste, has to lie in another principle.)

This brings us to the phenomenon of human life. You are made of elements, just like all animals and plants. Yet they are capable only of nourishing themselves and multiplying. Moreover, in themselves the stars are mute, without knowledge or feeling. Only the motions of this astral ensemble stir up a surging in the "water," a rising (i.e., a seeing, feeling, hearing, and tasting) in the *Tinctur*, the vital powers of the blood. If you inquire about the source of this tincture, in which the noble life rises up out of the dry and the bitter, out of fire and water, no other source can be discerned but the "light." But how do we explain the light which shines forth from a dark body? And what about the light that shines in the night, that guides your senses and understanding, that enables you to "see" (i.e., to know what you are doing) even with closed eyes? You may wish to maintain that it is the *senses* that animate the mind (*Gemüthe*), but where do the senses and the mind come from, and why is it not the same with the animals (II

35/4.27–28)? (Boehme thus introduces the *locus classicus* of mysticism, the seeing with closed eyes, but in a context reflecting the insight of a peasant who knows that cows are not capable of orienting themselves when blindfolded—as if he had compared this animal blindness with the human faculty that can project its inner sense into the external darkness.)

Look at your body, look at the stars, the elements, at all creatures, plants, and metals, and you won't find the "key," he goes on. What is the "first root" (*die Erste Wurzel*) from which such visible and sensible things emerge? You can find the answer in John 3:5, "Jesus answered, Verily, verily, I say unto thee, except a man be born of water and of the Spirit, he cannot enter the kingdom of God."

This citation of John appears as an abrupt about-face from philosophical wonderment to Scriptural authority. Does Boehme mean to suggest that whoever is baptized and reborn will receive the answers to the philosophical questions previously outlined? This is not what he means. Instead, he is suggesting that John 3:5 and the other verses, especially of the fourth gospel, hold the "key" to an imaginative vision which will provide answers where "reason" fails. As he proceeds, the clue from the Gospels is incorporated into a philosophical rejection of the *Creatio ex nihilo*.

You think, then, that God alone is behind all these mysteries, and that He is a spirit who has created all things out of nothing. Fine and good: God is a spirit, and before our eyes He is indeed like a nothingness (*wie ein Nichts*). We would have no knowledge of Him at all if we did not recognize Him through the Creation; and nothing would have arisen from eternity were He not (II 36/4.30–31). But what do you suppose there was before the time of the world? Whence arose the earth and stones, stars and elements? What was the root of these things? What do you find in these things but dry, bitter, and fire, together like a single thing? This complex whole was only a spirit, and in these three forms you will not find God. Beyond these three forms of the transcendent, eternal nature, there is the *pure Gottheit*, mentioned already in *Aurora*. In its homogeneity, the "pure divinity" is like a nothingness. The pure divinity is a light that is immaterial or incomprehensible (*unbegreiflich*) and nonsensible or insensate (*unempfindlich*), but also omnipotent (*auch Allmächtig und Allkräftig*) (II 36/4.31–32).

Immediately, Boehme then climbs back down the ladder of divine being in order to pose a further question; and this leads to an audacious turn of thought: If God is only good, where does evil come from? What is the origin of God's anger, of the devil, and of the fires of hell? If, before the time of the world, there was only God, there must have been a will within his spirit to create the source of anger—"or so reason judges." If the devil was once a holy angel, what moved him to become angry and evil?—This is Boehme's most agonizing problem; and, though he never solves it satisfactorily, it leads him to formulate ever bolder conceptions. If God had made the devil and the human soul out of some extraneous material, then no sin could be attributed to either (II 36–37/4.33–37). The logic here is unmistakable: material objects that are merely fashioned are unfree. Animals that have no ability to penetrate to the root of things are also unfree. But Boehme goes beyond these implications of freedom to affirm that the root of evil extends into the divine nature itself. One reason for taking this additional step is that the author is unwilling to accept that God could have initiated evil through an intentional, "historical" act, out of a "will" which is one faculty among others in the divine mind. If He had done this, then evil in the world would be a "work" of the Almighty Creator. Had God chosen and predetermined what is evil in the world, He would be the predestinarian deity rejected by the mystic. Evil arises as an eternal moment of the theogony; it arises, so to speak, as a necessary phase and aspect within the eternal self-realization of God, a process reflected also in the created natural and human world in time. The original sin of the human creature and the evil present in nature have a protoform in the eternal nature.

The philosophical questions of chapter four guide the speculations of *The Three Principles*. Here, again, Boehme is trying to formulate an understanding of a creation which is neither *ex nihilo* nor *ex materia*, but rather *ex Deo* (and therefore both out of *nothing else* and out of a *divine material*). The Creation *ex Deo* is the pattern of his theogony and of all birth and transformation in the world. The inner "being of all beings" is the self-creating deity. This must also account for the order of the physical and psychic aspects of the world, most especially for the birth of life out of matter. In a word, all being—of God, Creation, nature, matter, and the human mind and character—is configured alike, only at different levels of being in time and eternity. The terms employed in the discussion are both sacramental and speculative: the light, the dry, the bitter, fire, and water are all used in a double context. For example, the dry, as a contracting force, creates *Wesen*. *Wesen* houses an opposite spirit, the bitter, which attempts to escape and give birth to itself in order to obtain release from the womb of the dry *Wesen*.

The pure divinity is the divine light in John 1:5, identical with the Word which was "in the beginning." The prolog of John is praised by Boehme above Genesis; it is the key to the underlying vision of *The Three Principles of Divine Being*. The light shines in the darkness without being "comprehended" by the darkness. This metaphor for

Christ's temporal presence in a world which does not accept Him is interpreted by Boehme as a mythic occurrence in the eternal nature (II 78/8.17–18). Sunlight can shine into things without being touched by them; it can affect them without being affected by them, without mixing with their materiality. In accordance with the properties of the materials, the light can have various effects: passing through things, dwelling passively within them, energizing or transforming them, or even engendering life, as in the soil. Similarly, the light of the soul shines in the body, but it is not one with the flesh. All of the above speculative questions and Biblical motives are encoded in the Hermetic puzzle presented in the first two chapters. In *Aurora*, the second quality, between the dry and the bitter, was the sweet. In chapter one of *The Three Principles*, the first three qualities are cast negatively. The dry contracting force, *herb*, engenders, as its counterforce, the stabbing and abortively fleeing quality of the bitter. The opposition of the two generates a turning in place, called "the wheel of essences" (*das Rad der Essentien*). A figure of terror and abortive flight, it represents the inner unconscious driving force in nature. The friction and opposition between the constricting dryness and the fleeing bitterness engender fire and a flash of light. The dry resistance of the *Prima Materia* of *Herbigkeit* is subdued and transformed into a passive materiality by the *Schrack* as a bolt of light. The liberation from the tension results in the fourth quality, the "water-spirit" (II 12/1.11–12). Water exists in two forms. Before the *Schrack*, the quality of the water spirit is sulphurous and foul. The *Schrack* turns it into a sweet spirit of love.

The three alchemistic principles are superimposed upon the sevenfold pattern: Sulphur is broken down into *Sul* ("soul") and *Phur* (the *Prima Materia* of the soul). Mercurius is *Prima Materia* as well. As such, it contains four components, identified by the four syllables which designate the four subordinate urges of the dry contraction (*Mer*), the bitter stabbing pain (*Cu*), the turning wheel of essences that generates particularity (*Ri*), and the release and liberation which breaks the trapped turning and results in the "cross birth" (*Us*). *Sal* is their "son." *Sal* is the root of materialization (*die Begreiflichkeit*) (II 13/1.13).

The interactions of the first four spirits codify the Creation *ex Deo*. Borrowing from Kabbalistic theosophy, Boehme thus succeeds in combining his two initial premises from *Aurora*: that of the elemental nature (thought to have been created *ex nihilo*), and that of a world created in the image of God. The self-cause of his First Mover Unmoved is generated *internally*, by the primal contraction of a desire for the eternal light. The first four qualities represent the eternal driving forces within the mutable elements, earth, air, fire, and water. The first three qualities also represent the driven, preconscious, or prevital forces which bring forth life. They are the first principle. The two forms of water, bifurcated by the *Schrack*, are the waters separated at the beginning of the world. This world, including even its hard stones and earth, is a congelation of the water-spirit, which is thus the matrix of the third principle (II 55/5.30). The second principle begins with the flash and the sweet water.

The three interpenetrating principles are analogous to: (1) matter; (2) light; and (3) the transformation of matter by light, yielding a suspended whole. Not all permutations are reversible. The second principle, the goal of the soul, is a sublimation of the first principle, the realm of blind insensate urges. What is in the first principle is transmuted into the second principle by being sublimated to a higher level; however, a willful regression must have dire consequences for the soul. Evil arises out of the eternal nature of God; but, in God, this evil nature is eternally overcome and sublimated, so that it cannot be said that there is evil or darkness in God. If evil is prefigured in the eternal nature of the Father, so is the mercy and salvation of the Son. The motive of the "cross-birth" elevates the Passion of the Son into the Father's eternal agony to give birth to his Heart.

The pattern of qualities is intended to reveal the coherence of eternal forces as they inform both the elements and the inner life of the human creature. The first five qualities refer to the four elements plus the *Quinta Essentia*. The original desires of the elements pertain also to the corresponding "complexions" or humors. Boehme constantly ascribes psychic affectations to the qualities. In his treatise of 1620 on the four "complexions" (*Trost-Schrift von 4. Complexionen*, IV 222, 227–230), the pertinent psychic affectations overlap with and expand upon the ones introduced in the first chapters of *The Three Principles*.

The new pattern of qualities can be summarized and compiled. Simplifications are unavoidable since the interactions are characterized as simultaneous or overlapping occurrences of a single, many-sided process displaying different features when one focuses on one or another of its facets. Of the elemental associations, that of air with the bitter is the least self-evident. (However, Boehme draws it explicitly—II 66/7.13.) Most of the elemental associations for the first four spirits are found in chapter one.

Column A. shows the simple force ascribed to each of the qualities. Column B. represents the cumulative force that arises from all the preceding qualities. Column C. shows the resultant spirit-quality as it informs the respective element. Column D. indicates the element (which can come into being only insofar as the indwelling spirit has materialized). And Column E. shows the corresponding humor, as it is delineated in the later treatise on "the four complexions." A vertical row on the left, omitted for lack of space, should be labeled: (1) dry, (2) bitter, (3) fire, (4) water, (5) love-spirit, and so on. (Since the enhancement of spirit-forces progresses both down and across our compiled table, a Column F. might present the human, and a Column G. the angelic, typologies, progressing downward from evil to good.)

A. Simple Force	B. Complex Force	C. Spirit	D. Element	E. Humor
1. attraction or contraction,	1+2= *rubbing, opposition* . . .	"hardness" [=cohesion]	EARTH= Melancholy (as sadness)
2. agitation, pang, fleeing,	1+2+3= *revolving* . . .	"sulphur-spirit" [=volatility]	AIR/ Melancholy (as fear)
3. movement (as liveliness),	1+2+3+4= *flash flares up* . . .	"dark fire" [=heat]	FIRE= Choleric ("rising up")
4. release and passivity,	bolt [*Schrack*] . . . *purification*	"water-spirit" [=fluidity]	WATER=Phlegmatic ("materiality")
5. softening and melioration	*brightening light*	"sweet water" [=cooling]	QUINTA- /Sanguine ESSENTIA[16] ("joy")

6. The sixth spirit, as *sound* or music, can be interpreted as a complex of the foregoing movements and spirits (II 18/2.12).

7. The *multiplication* of the "circles of life" combines all the spirits and disseminates them as offspring (II 41/4.55).

This compilation is not a fixed system. Again, it is a symbolic construct, collating several sets of varying allusions. Aside from the elemental aspirations and the conventional elemental-humoral associations, the variable palimpsest synthesizes overt references to an escalating chain reaction of mechanical forces, adding subliminal allusions to sexual intercourse (fire and water are male and female respectively), and to a breaking storm (the third column alludes to the accumulation and agitation of clouds, the thunderclap, and precipitation). The concatenating complex forces of the second column overlap because of their reciprocal actions and reactions, and therefore cannot be neatly assigned to the qualities. The birth of the light has at least three stages: (3) heat or dark fire; (4) the fearful bolt or *Schrack*; and (5) the tempering and brightening of the light, which transmutes the crude spirit into a love-spirit. The chain of forces describes (from an "inside" point of view!) the purifying transformation of matter, the emergence and birth of life, and the purification of the soul. Implicitly, the chain also accounts for the stability of the world by delineating the constancy of the eternal nature. For example, the wheel-like spinning of the first two qualities, the dry and the bitter, helps explain the stability of a cosmos which does not rise up (like air) or sink down (like earth and stones). The rotation sets the pattern of the wheel of nature, which becomes embodied in the planetary wheel as a generator of life. The seventh form, here multiplication, refers us to the reproduction, out of one, of many vital centers, each of which continues and varies the generating qualities. The stability of the world in space is necessary for the generative continuity of life in time. (Comets and stellar irregularities, we recall, could induce monstrous births.) The subjective significance of the pattern undoubtedly lies in the contemplation of the divine order and meaning of all things, seen and unseen.

The overall paradigm (if it can be called that) draws upon meteorological, astrological, alchemical, mechanical, and psychic prototypes. It soon becomes apparent that all these references are subordinated to the overriding theosophical and metaphysical context. The seven qualities are a figure of the Trinity and of the three principles as the *dark-world* (later: "fire-world"), the *light-world*, and *this world* (which is formed in the middle, where the first and second principles overlap):

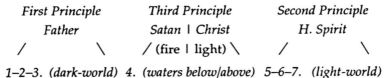

Christ is the light of the world, the central focus of time, and the personal union of the divine and human natures. As the formula of eternity works itself out in time, it moves toward an age illuminated by the Holy Spirit, in which the full significance of Christ appears in the light in nature—the leitmotiv of *Aurora*. In eternity, the self-transcending divinity does not evolve, any more than, to employ our own analogy, a mathematical equation evolves from left to right on the printed page. The equation is true and unchanging—though its truth and meaning would remain hidden if no one were to work through it. Eschatological time is prefigured in the eternal nature. The Creation, the Fall, the Virgin Birth, the Passion of Christ, the Resurrection: all these "historical" moments have counterparts in the eternal nature.

How can we know all of this? We know because the light of the soul has an a priori knowledge of God. As a free being, the reborn soul recreates itself. To recognize this self-creating self is to know God. Self-knowledge, that is, recognition of "the hidden man," the soul, is a knowledge of the hidden God.

Self-knowledge also involves a recognition of the evil that lies at the root of human nature, and in external nature (which, ultimately, is not external). Without the evil or venom which makes creatures struggle blindly with one another, to live, to aggrandize their mortal existences, and to reproduce their kind, nothing would exist except the eternal calm of the pure divinity. Therefore, *Aurora*'s vision of a violent, evil, fallen nature is revisited within the human and divine nature. Boehme states that "in the root and substance of the eternal birth of the soul" (II 29/4.7), in its "eternal band," one finds the most terrifying, antagonistic torment: a conflict within itself (*eine Feindung in sich selber*), and an opposition to God, equal to that of the devils which are excluded from the divine light. In accordance with this turn of thought, the root syllable *qual*, associated in *Aurora* with *Quell*, *Qualität*, and *Quellgeist*, is recovered in the German word for "torment." The struggle in nature is thereby equated with the tormenting conflicts in the root of the soul. It appears that quality as particularity is rooted in the torment of separation from the the eternal oneness of the transcendent God. This same fierce torment is experienced in the soul, in the very spirit of life imparted by God. As radical as this sounds, Boehme's thinking is consonant with the homiletic assertions of Luther, for whom the soul was a blind will to live, a will so immersed in the mortal flesh that it valued its transient existence more than eternal life itself. This problematic divine and human will becomes the overriding theme of the second book.

The World as Will and Reflection

The eternal God creates Himself and everything in the world out of the "nothingness" of a hypostatized free will. *The Three Principles of Divine Being* presents a succession of corollaries of the self-creating eternal divine nature. The consequences of the eternal self-generation of the divinity extend down the chain of being, thus: (1) We know already from *Aurora* that the angels were created out of God; they are finite but perfect miniatures of the Divine Being. (2) Man was not created out of a mere clump of earth, but rather out of a finer material, a *Limbus* or *Quinta Essentia*, which came into existence during an apotheosized cosmogony (II 102/10.2; 104/10.10). (3) God did not create the first woman out of a mere rib extracted from Adam, but rather out of all the vital "essences" of Adam (II 152/13.18). (4) Even the animals are not simply formed out of clay; for they have a spirit in them that is not reducible to mere earth and water (II 83/8. 37). (5) Plants have a life in them that cannot be resynthesized from the materials into which they decompose. (6) Finally, even lifeless elements are penetrated by the force of the Word which revitalizes vegetation. Hence, when the elements separated off from one another at the beginning of the world, each element was left teeming with invisible "elemental spirits" of its own kind. This shows that the "circle of life" is everywhere, complete in each creature and latent in each element (II 72/7.37).

The birth of this world begins with the origination of the created heavens: matter and space have been rendered dark by the fall of Satan. (Here, too, is the usual ambiguity between the historical perspective required by evil and the internal account of the same events as aspects of the divine nature.) The concealed birth of the elemental world is recognized both in nature and in the hidden man of the soul. In nature it is plain to see that the elements are contained in one another and give rise to one another. "Desire"—though not necessarily a conscious desire—is attributed to the separated strata of the elements. Having been together as one before the creation of the world, the fiery stellar heavens lust for the watery matrix or spirit which filled the world space before it separated further and formed up into elemental realms. Hence, the "limbus" out of which man is made also lusts for the "aquastric" being of the woman, and vice versa. Tormented by separation from the primal unity, all things male and female lust after their opposites in accordance with the eternal pattern of nature (II 84/8.40). Their instinctive drive is "a great secret" which holds clues to the eternal mysteries. Like chapter nineteen of *Aurora*, which it resembles, chapter seven of *The Three Principles* offers a rare glimpse of Boehme's thinking in progress. Before chapter seven, the term *Wille* has been used mainly in the everyday sense: in order to designate one faculty among others within a divine or human constitution of faculties. Beginning in chapter seven, the apotheosized will acquires a central importance which it retains in this and nearly all subsequent major treatises. Like chapter nineteen of *Aurora*, chapter seven of *The Three Principles* instructs the reader on the modalities of the mystical inquiry. The key passage in *Aurora* had recollected the "scene" in which the troubled young shoemaker peered up at the elements in search of the hidden God. Here, the reader is told to undertake a similar mystical search—with unmystically opened eyes and mind—by observing the elements in space:

> If now you open the eyes of your mind, you shall see how fire is in water, and becomes visible in lightning.... You shall see, too, how all about there goes out a great power of air, and the one is in the other. In addition, you shall see how the water is born in the storm. (II 53/5.20)

This mixing and transformation in the elemental world provides evidence against the doctrine that the world was created out of nothing. What is, is perpetually created out of something else. Moreover, at this point, a new perspective leading to the same insight opens up: "For the origin can be recognized in the human being as well as in the depths of the world . . ." (II 53/5.19). Where *Aurora* equated microcosm and macrocosm, *The Three Principles* carries the logic of correspondence one step further by seeking the common *origin* of consciousness and cosmos. Correspondence is thus no longer the static collage of *Aurora*, in which each organ of the creature was equated to some part of the cosmos: the correspondences of microcosm and macrocosm are now focused in their shared patterns of birth and development. If (Boehme appears to reason) the human and elemental worlds are both likenesses of the eternal world, then they must also be likenesses of one another, that is, their developments must be complementary, like two sides of the same process. In considering the birth of the cosmos in this perspective, chapter seven of *The Three Principles of Divine Being* accomplishes a spectacular feat of mystical speculation.

We know in advance that the "setting" is the darkened and spoiled region which surrounds the locus of this world—as the seas surround an emergent atoll. (The created heavens "float" in the "eternal matrix" between Paradise and Hell.—II 64/7.8) In this margin of eternity, the world-to-be is preceded by a matrix or womb (*Matrix* or *Mutter der Gebärerin*) of the heavens and the earth. The incorporeal dry quality of *Herbigkeit* is the matrix and cause of all that is (*Matrix und Ursache aller Dinge*). It is "like a nothingness": a mere hunger or longing, without life or awareness. Aroused by the reflecting light of the pure divinity, it becomes a desirous will, a longing for the light. Possessing no object for its aroused desire, the primal dryness contracts into itself; and the contraction creates the internal bitter pang of longing. This in turn arouses fear, frustration, and terror at the impossibility of satisfaction or calm. Refusing to surrender to death and darkness, this "will or pang of desire" (*der Wille oder der Stachel der Lust oder d :s Begehrens*) rubs inside the *Herbigkeit*, slanting or tilting its desire and will toward the concealed light of the deity, until the startling firebolt of fear (*Feur-Schrack* or *ein schielend Blitz*) fulfills the dry spirit which becomes as if dead, turning "sweet and material, into water" (II 65/7.11–12). The released bitter quality becomes the air. The covetous fearfulness is the fire. The contraction (which is also identified with Lucifer's fall) creates the earth and stones. The created elemental hierarchy of the world is then complete (II 66/7.13). The separated elements are embodiments of the opposing forces that crave for, and clash with, one another. Because the materialized force cannot hold the light from beyond, another light has to be given: that of the sun shining within the creation (*Geschöpfe*), so that it is revealed (II 80/8.23). Further impulses spin off the planets. This sets the pattern for all generation within this world. Even the basest sexual desire is a longing for something higher, a longing for the eternal light and a flight from death and darkness. The primal darkness, impregnated with the divine light, gives birth to the sun (II 79/8.19). The veracity of the sexual allusions lends solemnity to Boehme's findings. But to assume that all of this sprang spontaneously from his subconscious mind would be to fall for the sly tricks of the writer who would have us believe that by turning his gaze inward he has recollected the birth of the solar system.

The philosophical, epistemological corollaries of the vision emerge more clearly in later writings: the unity of the inner and outer worlds accounts for the ability of the subject to know the world. The subject can perceive its objects only because the subject's "light" (the sense of sight) contains within itself a "chaos" of the natural light of the sun and stars (VII 8/2.5). The mind's eye apparently recognizes the external world because the latter is, in a manner of speaking, a distant family kin.

Until now, Boehme's speculative progression has been guided by an enormously complex scheme of correspondences. From now on, however, the philosopher can simplify all the correspondences of forces and concepts. The elemental attractions and oppositions of the seven source-spirits can be discussed as manifestations of the will. The insensate *element* is the contracted aspect of the divine will (II 239/17.8). Matter, like the flesh, is therefore a garment "put on," or congealed, by the fallen will and a medium in which the eternal wisdom of God is mirrored. *Spirit*, as a conscious life, is the ascending, sublimated aspect of the root torment (*Qual*) of the will (II 79/8.21). Eventually, the same pattern is applied to the Holy Trinity, making it possible to envisage the Triunity of God as three aspects of the divine will. Where *Aurora* refracted the human figure beyond recognition into the correspondences of microcosm and macrocosm, the second book recaptures the human figure in its volitional development. The three "principles" are in fact rendered specific by transferring the cosmogony of will to the human organism, with its desires, its emergent consciousness, and resultant growth:

I. The darkness in you, which longs for the light, is the first principle.
II. The force of light in you, by means of which you see in your mind without eyes, is the second principle.

> III. And the longing force, which issues in the mind and attracts to itself and fills itself, from which the material body grows, is the third principle. (II 69/7.26)

The limbs and organs of the body are formed by the inner desire which struggles against darkness (*cf.* II 171/14.14). The human microcosm therefore recapitulates the birth of the macrocosm. We understand Genesis because of our own human genesis.

The will is at root an impulse to emerge from darkness. Its first compulsion is now called a "fearing toward the light" (*sich ängstigen nach dem Lichte*). The polarity of darkness and light is therefore the inner orientation of will. This provides new coordinates to replace the annulled symbolic directions of the pre-Copernican cosmos: "There is no Below and Above, only the rebirth from darkness into gentleness is called Above" (II 190/ 14.78). The sun, in the third principle, is still the analog of the spirit in the divine eternal nature; but now Boehme traces the force of growth in nature from the "first will" (II 81/8.29), as the desire to rise out of darkness into light. The heliocentrism of *Aurora* has been supplanted by a metaphysics of will.

In order to discover the intended significance of the new voluntarism it is necessary to look beyond the intricacies of symbol and correspondence. The hypostatized will substantiates the union of the inner "hidden man" with the "hidden God"; in so doing, it attempts to reconcile the contradictions of theology and theodicy. The rationalization of evil in God's world and the rationalization of human freedom in regaining grace are two sides of the same problem. The hypostatized will is both free and oriented. God is called God by virtue of a divine, free transcendence of the "darkness," that is, of the will as blind, angry force. Trapped in its own darkness, this will is the evil being that vainly covets the forms of Paradise. Although it has arisen out of God, the unredeemed divine nature is not to be called God.

The Androgynous Adam

Similarly, human salvation is obtained through a rebirth of the free will, paralleling within time the eternal divine birth out of darkness. The angry, evil, ignorant human creature is not the first, the true, or the ultimate human form: in order to show this, *The Three Principles of Divine Being* takes the surprising step of recasting the heretical myth of the first Adam.[17] This step is surprising because the myth amends the "historical faith" by adding on a new *Historia* with little foundation in the Bible. The clear purpose of this amendation is the reinterpretation of the Genesis account of the fall, a revision intended to establish that knowledge rather than ignorance stands at the beginning and end of the drama of human salvation. The myth also suggests that the same drama may be reenacted in the life of each individual, and that its reenactment is exemplary for the very time in which Boehme is writing. The character of the first Adam demonstrates that the goal of salvation is not achieved by blind obedience to a capricious God. It is foolish, writes Boehme, to think that God could have ruined such a fine creature as Adam by allowing him to take a bite from a forbidden apple: God has forgiven far graver sins than that (II 108–109/10.23).

The background modifies the eschatological framework of *Aurora* in order to bring it in line with the context of *The Three Principles*. Rooted in the volitional *Prima Materia* of God, the soul is exiled from its true *Vaterland*, thrust into the created world of the third principle. Intermingling the dark world of matter and the light world of the spirit, the created world was born after the fall of Lucifer and his angelic legions. Their place in the divine order was left desolate by the celestial uprising. To heal the desolation, God has created the third principle, fashioning it as a likeness of the spiritual Paradise of the second principle.

After praising the Fourth Gospel above all other books of the Bible (II 78/8.17ff.), Boehme recounts the Creation as a conflation of Genesis and John, of the *Fiat* and *das Wort*, the light of the sun and the light of awareness (II 81/8.29). Animal life is brought into being. Since every animal is born from one single being, there is a powerful hunger in beasts, one for the other; their drive to procreate exemplifies this (II 84/8.40). Within the will, there is a sexual longing for unity and completeness, so that all the unreasoning creatures are blindly given over to their procreative urge. The reflective aspect of the will, the intangible tincture toward which things grow and mature, is present in the blossoming forms and colors of nature. The driven life of nature, fired by the instincts of procreation and hunger, is what Boehme calls the "spirit of the great world," or *Spiritus Mundi*. What this spirit blindly covets in vain is the heavenly Paradise of calm perfection and beauty. The blind procreative drive of nature can never attain "the paradisiacal child of love" (II 86/8.44).

In chapter ten, this paradisiacal child is revealed in the first Adam. Adam before his fall resembled the angels of *Aurora*: he was made, not of earthly materials, but of a celestial *Limbus* or *Quinta Essentia*, that is, of the divine forces which had no mortality in them; his bones were not hard and calcified; and he had no animal reproductive organs and no foul intestines. He was androgynous, neither man nor woman (hence, not hermaphroditic). This fine Adam could have given birth to an angelic host without tearing open his body. When God led all the creatures before him, he named them in words of the nature language. This Adam experienced reality more completely than his corrupted successor:

> ... his seeing was day and night with wide open eyes without lashes [or lids: *Wippern*]; there was no sleep within him, and no night in his mind. The divine force was in his eyes, and he was whole and complete.... He was neither man nor woman, just as we will be neither after our resurrection." (II 107/10.18)

The total awareness of the first Adam is symbolized by his wide open eyes without lids (a Kabbalistic motive[18] later applied very aptly by Heinrich von Kleist to perspective in Friedrich's famous painting of the Monk at the Seashore). The first man has a heightened power of seeing because the Divine Virgin is within his being. But pristine Adam has to be tested in the treacherous terrain in which Satan's spirits are banished. To this end, Adam is to be tempted for forty days (the same challenge of temptation which Christ later withstands in the desert—II 132/12.9). The mystical attributes of darkness and light are the poles between which Adam's soul struggles and falls. In Boehme's account of the temptation, the three principles, as his soul, "the mind of the great world" (*das Gemüthe maioris Mundi*), and the Virgin, are supposed to contend within Adam for forty days and nights. The crisis and denouement arrive, in the discursive pseudo-narrative, when an unseemly lust for the Virgin is aroused in Adam. Fearing that her brightness will be darkened by his desire, the Virgin shuns Adam. As a result he can only become mortal. Exhausted by the struggle of the three principles within him, Adam the "youth" falls asleep. While he is asleep, the Noble Virgin vanishes into the second principle. Henceforth, her presence in this world is mirrored in the highest and brightest tincture, in which the human mind originates (II 149–50/13.9). In place of the Virgin, Adam is assigned earthly Eve, who is described as fickle and weak (II 152/13.20). It is the fate of man to drag this disappointing female counterpart with him through life. (Assuming that this is to be taken literally, it is a dim and uncharitable view of woman and marriage, but still a view which refuses to blame the ills of man and the world on woman—as in a conventional interpretation of Eve's role in the fall from grace.[19]) Adam is responsible for the fall. However, the male and female readers are also warned against smugly imagining that they would have held up better than he. To convey the struggle of the three principles in Adam, the author shrewdly calls upon his readers to imagine an attractive young man and woman, brought together and given all liberties, but commanded not to allow lust to enter their hearts. Only wretched reason, Boehme concludes, deceives itself that it could withstand temptation (II 139/12.38). After Adam fails the first test of temptation, it is a foregone conclusion that the human pair will also fall. Their expulsion from Paradise is therefore an anticlimactic episode in act one of the human drama of failure and redemption.

How are we to interpret this strange account, which is discursive rather than narrative, and interwoven with nearly every motive the writer can muster? An interpretation that captured the imagination of Boehme's Pietistic epigons reckoned that the tale summoned believers to maintain strict celibacy by contrasting celestial love and bliss with earthly lust and lasciviousness. (This was the interpretation of the Rappite sect that founded its communal-celibate New Harmony on the slippery banks of the Wabash River.) At first glance, this seems quite plausible. It is as if a subterranean vein of sexual preoccupations and repressions were coming to the surface here. Carnal desire, even the sheer imagining of the flesh, taints the entire relationship of man to the world. And yet, this interpretation ignores the fact that Boehme deliberately inflated his sexual motives. It also ignores the entire palimpsest of references superimposed upon the account of the youth and his desire for the Virgin. A one-sided sexual interpretation leaves no bridge to the topical, social, and political significance which Boehme attached to his work. He can hardly have meant that the current ills of his time stemmed solely from the fact that men are unable to control their carnal lust for women. A narrow sexual interpretation also ignores the tone of the tale, which hardly reads as if it were written to excoriate the carnal lewdness of man. It seems that, for Boehme, sexuality was surrounded by powerful proscriptions and strictures. But they were not puritanical in spirit. Unlike the brutishness of hunger, sexual desire always has an ideal aspect. (For example, no matter how lascivious the parents, their reproductive act begins with the celestial *Tinctur*—II 295/18.93). The great *Mysterium Conjunctionis* of Jung stimulated his speculative imagination more than his loathing.

Several contexts of allusion should be distinguished in the characterization of the first Adam: (1) the context of scriptural exegesis; (2) the dual context of Boehme's anthropology and metaphysics of will; (3) the context of the active and contemplative purposes of human life; and (4) the social and historical context which was surely in the minds of contemporaneous readers. Each of these contexts refers us to an "in the beginning": (1) of the Creation; (2) of the human birth; (3)

of the reborn human; and (4) of the reformed world. The common terminological denominator for each is the insistent characterization of Adam as having all three principles within him.

1. The exegetic context refers us to the foregoing account of the Creation, which distinguished between (a) the Fiat of Genesis; (b) the Word, hence also the light, of John; and (c) the power by which life in this world moves and grows. At the beginning of chapter ten, Boehme solemnly announces that the purpose is to see behind the "veil of Moses," in order to recognize the real truth of Genesis. The Creation should be approached in these three senses: in terms of the "historical" account of the beginning, in terms of the Spiritualistic and mystical rebirth of the divine light in the world, and in terms of an external nature which perpetually grows, dies, and is reborn as a likeness of the two eternal worlds. Since *The Three Principles* gives emphasis to the Gospel of John, the light of knowledge comes first in human history. Hence, Adam's state of total awareness.

2. However, we know about the Creation because of the fact that it is exemplified *within* the human spirit, Boehme asserts (II 111/10.34). It must be possible to recover the drama of the primordial three principles within every individual human life. All three principles were in Adam; he was the model human being, hence the "hidden man" who awaits redemption. If not for the fall, we would still be like him, creatures with an absolute awareness. The connection between Adam's androgyny and his total seeing can be interpreted with reference to remarks found in *The Three Principles* and elsewhere. Since the first and second principles constantly operate upon and within human nature, the mind (*Gemüthe*) can be represented as a "pair of scales." As one side falls, the other rises up. What links one scale with the other is the senses. As spirit, they are the bridge between the inner and the outer; they balance the two sides (*die Sinnen sind der Angel*, II 358/21.23). This implies that the blind will, with its inner compulsion and torment, can outweigh and darken the senses—or that the reflection of the spirit world can tip the perception of the senses back to the translucent vision of the perfect eternal forces. In another passage, Boehme argued that the potential mental faculties of the newborn child are derived from three forms of will, prefigured in the sexual impulses and "mingling" (*Vermischung*) of the parents. Their mingling sows the darkness, through the animal craving of the parents, and sows the "*centrum* der Liebe," through the affectionate love of mixing that is inevitably also present in copulation (II 203/15.30). The fall of the child of Paradise can therefore be understood as the prototype of the fall from the childlike state in which the male and female sides which were once as one still coexist in harmony. Accordingly, the three

principles represent the congenital human nature and destiny.

3. The principles continue to tyrannize and attract every individual soul throughout its life. Therefore, they also describe the circumstances of rebirth. The first principle stands for the compulsive, willful, base instincts. The animal reproductive organs (*viehische Glieder*) are characterized as repulsive in the account of the first Adam. They are rejected along with the other organs which suffer in the animal condition of human beings: the foul intestines (which must be filled and relieved), and the hard bones (which ache from gout because of gluttony). The "spirit of the great world" is generalized to signify greed, gluttony, and the hedonism of "eating, drinking, gambling, and dancing" (II 131/12.5) and power and wealth (II 133/12.13). Had Adam remained loyal to the Virgin, he would have eaten *vom Verbo Domini*—lived by the Word of God. Instead of seeking his own honor and satisfaction, he would have savored the Incarnate Word as it existed even before Moses recorded the Creation in the Book of Genesis—as the celestial qualities in the Book of Nature. The angelic Adam was not only androgynous; he was also enjoined to abstain from eating the earthly fruit. We are told that he was even allowed to eat it in his mouth—but not in his body (II 107/10.19). Assuredly, this is not meant to signify that he chewed it and then spit it out without swallowing it. He was to savor its paradisiacal qualities without turning it into the material of his own self-aggrandizement, thereby despoiling it. Had he done so, he would have been able to take delight in the Virgin without desiring to enter and possess her.

Along with his mission of androgynously begetting a new angelic host to replenish Lucifer's desolate realm with life, this Adam named the living creatures that were led before him in words of the "nature language": his mission was not simply to resurrect life, but also to glorify Creation. The presence of all three principles in Adam can thus also be interpreted to signify: the inner willful power of desire, the power to reflect and know, and the power to mediate beween inner and outer worlds—either by reflecting and expressing what is, or by "imagining into" things and becoming infected with their worldly spirit of greed, vanity, and power. Adam was intended to rule over all things: his ideal figure is thus also a model for the rulers of this world, and a warning to the free burgher or peasant who has become the master within his own small domain.

4. The parable of the first Adam describes the historical "new man" of an age of awareness which combined the values of burgher and noble, of Renaissance and Reformation. Like the first Adam, the Reformation was to have replenished the world with redeemed souls without tearing open the body of Christendom. The Noble Virgin

embodies the wisdom and knowledge prized by the Renaissance and by the Reformation. The reborn world which should have come into being would have incorporated the virtues of faith and wisdom. But instead, the false Christians have fallen to worshipping the golden calf of a "Belly-God." Boehme's tale pillories the avarice and arrogance of his fellow Protestants. The standing of Adam within the hierarchy of eternity is important. Adam was created by God to be an *immortal* angel, but the Noble Virgin is an *eternal* being. Hence, in desiring to possess and wed his being to that of the Virgin, the exuberant young Adam aspires to a *mesalliance* with a being who is, "after all, one degree higher in birth than he" (II 144/12.54). Responding to other hints of social class, Koyré compared Lucifer with Adam: the former fell out of *superbe*, the latter out of *bassesse*.[20] As the true feudal aristocrat, Prince Lucifer tried to conquer the highest throne. Adam is more the naive burgher than the rogue: he would pull the exalted down to his own level, coupling himself into bliss. Confounding passion with possession, he repeatedly utters his desire to own the Virgin: "to have as property" (*zum Eigenthum haben*) (II 141/12.43–46). Lucifer acted decisively. The ingenuous Adam instead falls because of moral indecisiveness. Boehme writes that Adam "hypocritically flirts" (*heuchelt*) with all three principles (II 126/11.35).

The abstinence praised by Boehme is chivalric rather than monastic; it is guided by an attraction to the ideal rather than by a revulsion for the flesh. Like Schwenckfeld, the shoemaker often employs metaphors of chivalry in order to evoke the heroism demanded for the struggle to defeat evil and attain the good. In *Forty Questions on the Soul*, Boehme provides a cogent gloss on the social context of the Adamic Paradise and Fall. In a passage anticipating Weber's thesis of the Protestant Ethic, this advice is offered to the new free man of the Protestant age:

> You are in the world: you have chosen an honest profession without falseness, so stick to it, work, toil, acquire what your needs demand. Seek wonders both in the elements and in the earth.... Seek in the earth for silver and gold. Craft artful products from them. Build and plant. It is all to the glory of God (*zu GOttes Wunderthat*). But heed this ABC: You should not allow your spirit to go into these things, and to fill itself with them, and to make a Mammon out of them, and to put itself into them, as into darkness. Otherwise [your spirit] will be God's fool and the devil's ape... and your noble image will be transformed, in accordance with your imagination, in accordance with your will which is in greed.... (III *40 Fragen* 86–87/12.22)

Adam "imagines into" the things of this world and succumbs to the *Gemüthe maioris Mundi*, forfeiting the celestial qualities of his pristine vision. The Noble Virgin parts from him and the first man sinks into the sleep of all mankind (II 147–48/13.2ff.).

Grave perils and tribulations will beset Adam and his human consort beyond the gates of Paradise. They face the thorns and goads of a bitter exile. But even the tragic loss of Paradise must have some necessary meaning in the divine purpose of self-revelation. The indomitable youth, before whom the wild beasts shrank in terror, who lived without sleep, knowing nothing of darkness, and naming all the creatures brought before him by God, obviously lacked *self*-knowledge. We can only interpret his fall with reference to what has now become a perpetual leitmotiv: *Know thyself*. This explains the tragedy and higher purpose of Adam's fall. Unlike him, we should be aware that self-knowledge is necessary for salvation. Self-knowledge, acquired through Adamic guilt and infused into a firm resolve, should reform the will and lead the reborn soul back to its lost Fatherland.

The Noble Virgin of Divine Wisdom

The salient embodiment of the second principle, of the world as reflection and ideal, is the Noble Virgin of Divine Wisdom, a figure based on the allegory of Wisdom in Proverbs, a book which was excluded from the clear canon by Luther, and was still ranked as apocryphal by the Lutheran divine Chemnitz in 1603.[21]

Beginning in *The Three Principles of Divine Being*, the Noble Virgin of Divine Wisdom assumes a spectacular profile in Boehme's writings. The Noble Virgin is the serene and reflective aspect of the Deity. As her title makes abundantly clear, she is not a "Mrs. God." Nor is she equivalent to Christ, though the Virgin is in Christ and the divine nature. By insisting on the role of the Virgin in the divine nature, Boehme made himself vulnerable to charges of heresy. These charges were forthcoming—from some orthodox pastors during Boehme's lifetime, and from illustrious churchmen like Carlov and Hinckelmann after his death—and not easy to refute.[22] Still, it can hardly have been his *intention* to break with received Lutheran doctrines. *The Three Principles of Divine Being* is in other regards his most orthodox work. Only the firm conviction that Lutheran teachings were complementary to the extrascriptural sources of wisdom and truth can account for Boehme's odd hybridization of orthodoxy and heterodoxy.

The emblem and embodiment of the metaphysical principle of knowledge, reflection, and self-transformation through reflection only later acquires the proper name "Sophia." One misses the intention of this figure if one sees her only as a "person" (though she is a person in the sense of the persons of the Trinity). The Noble Virgin is the same as the "eye of eternity" in which the wonders of God await revelation, or as the self-mirroring mirror which sees into itself, thereby creating *Wesen*. She is inherent in organic processes as the "noble tincture."

The theosophist, the devotee of divine wisdom, has learned his ABCs *in der Jungfrauen Rosen*, "in the rose of the Virgin" (II 287/18.63). Very soon, this mariological "rose" is replaced by the "lily." In the same context, the consistent Lutheran writes that supplication to Mary and the saints is idolatry, comparable to worshipping the golden calf. The scriptural antecedent of the Virgin appears in Proverbs:

> The LORD possessed me in the beginning of his way, before his works of old. I was set up from everlasting, from the beginning, or ever the earth was. When there were no depths, I was brought forth; when there were no fountains abounding with water.... Then I was by him, as one brought up with him; and I was daily his delight, rejoicing always before him; Rejoicing in the habitable part of his earth; and my delights were with the sons of men. (Proverbs 8: 22–24, 30–31)

If God the Father is increasingly identified with a fiery anger, redeemed through the Son, Boehme's Virgin of Divine Wisdom is a coeternal, female principle, standing for calm, cool reflection: According to Proverbs, she was there, "When [God] prepared the heavens... when he set a compass upon the face of the earth..." (8: 27). Since "her delights were with the sons of men," she is an inner common bond of the divine and the human. The Virgin vouchsafes the eschatology of a knowledge that is at the beginning and at the end of human history. Her placid wisdom counterbalances the fiery deity of battles and punishments.

The Virgin is a passive power at work in nature. Ruland's *Lexicon Alchemiae* of 1612 defined the "work of Sophia" in the same sense as Boehme: *Labor Sophiae, id est, paradisus, alter mundus*. The Virgin also subsumes the role of the unworthy moon goddess Luna, as the patroness of growth. The mystic held Luna in contempt, but he apparently recognized her good counterpart in the mysterious woman on the moon who is pregnant with the sun and is chased by the dragon in the Book of Revelation (II 132/12.11). The most important symbolization of the virginal wisdom in the sphere of nature, growth, and transformation is the emblematic concept of the celestial *Tinctur*. The identity of the Virgin and the *Tinctur* is established in a long and enigmatic digression in chapter thirteen. Numerous circumlocutions are provided for the tincture. The tincture transforms iron and copper into pure gold; it transforms little into much (II 155/13.26). It is also called the friend or companion of God (*GOttes Freundin*). The tincture represents the rebirth of fire as light and as serene joy, *liebliche Wonne* (II 153/13.23). In vegetation, the tincture symbolizes the contrastive aspects of the sweet smelling blossom and the dryness and bitterness of the root. As the Virgin, the tincture "makes nothing," yet lends the essences their power to grow. The tincture is "the most secret and the most revealed of all things" (II 154/13.24). Moreover: "Its [or *her*] way is as subtle as the thoughts of human beings; and the thoughts also arise from it [or: *from her way*]" (II 155/13.26[23]). Boehme's long discourse on the tincture formulates a riddle rather than a definition: the purpose is the invocation of the divine mystery. Yet the metaphors of his disquisition make it clear that at all levels of nature—in the transformation of stones and metals, in the growth of plant life, as well as in the "birth" of thought, consciousness, and self-knowledge in the human soul—the same principle is in evidence: the principle of the "light" which, as the "clear divinity," precedes even the "first will." The tincture is the reflective gleam of metals, the paradisiacal flowering in nature, the inner light of human awareness; the tincture represents the transparent sea of the Apocalypse, the pure waters of eternity, the spirit waters in which the soul has to be washed clean for eternal life. Just as the Virgin does and makes nothing, the mysterious tincture is like a nothingness. This of course refers back to the central problem of the Creation *ex nihilo*, which Boehme cannot let stand in the mythic form of a personal Creator who fashioned the world out of nothing for some inscrutable reason—rather, "through the great longing of the darkness for the light and the power of God, this world was born out of darkness, when the holy power of God mirrored itself in the darkness" (II 177/14.33). Creation itself and everything in it grows toward the divine self-knowledge which was intended from the beginning. The divine attractive power induces all things to grow toward the realization of eternity.

It is axiomatic that in the eternal divine nature one hidden pattern must underly all opposites. Boehme's method of arousing the reader's imagination with riddles and enigmas is responsible for our unconfirmed but irresistible supposition that the Virgin, the tincture, the "eye," and the "mirror of eternity" are inverse aspects of the terrifying "wheel of essences." The wheel, as a generator of particular qualities, and as an instrument of self-torment, contrasts with the serene figure who presides over birth and higher awareness. The movement of the wheel is a centrifugal flight from one into many. The movement of the mirror or of the eye of eternity is a reflective absorption into being. Whereas the wheel blindly spins out diversity, the Virgin oversees birth, assuring that what comes into being reflects the tranquil figures of eternity. The spinning circularity of the "eternal band" contrasts with the bent of the mirror or eye of eternity, which involves a magical self-absorption, a centripetal, concentrating antipode to the centrifugal flight into particularity—hence a leaning from the many, back toward the One.

The wheel of essences and the Celestial Virgin hold the balance of diversity and unity. Out of particularity and likeness, they fashion the individuality and identity of things, including that of the human individual. In the maternal womb, the stars, sun, and elements struggle to shape all that the embryo possesses in common with the animals. But the stars and elements are not responsible for the qualities by virtue of which the infant is born in the image of God. The higher awareness associated with language and the ability to recognize all three principles is present in the immaterial tincture of the Virgin (II 182–183/14. 54–57). Only in human nature, in the two related moments of birth and rebirth, can the will regain the intimation and certainty of Paradise. In *The Three Principles of Divine Being*, Boehme's own awakening is superimposed on the birth of an infant. We recall that the illumination of 1600 occurred in the spring or summer, not long after the birth of the mystic's first child in January. Twenty years later, birth has become generalized to convey all the processes of theogony, cosmogony, physical birth, baptism, contrition, and spiritual rebirth. This is evident in the discussion of a pregnancy and birth in chapter fifteen.

At first, the will of the prenatal embryo is pure, neither dark nor light. Then it begins to covet the light. Since there is no light to draw upon, the desiring will of the embryonic soul draws into itself the spirit of the stars and elements, darkening itself and becoming fearful. This, in turn, engenders the will to give birth to the light. Finally, a glance, like a flash, breaks through the "wheel of essences" and the dry hardness of death. A thought shatters the darkness and breaks the wheel that is bound to its place. This "flash" (*Schrack*) attempts to find a voice. Still inarticulate, the flash returns to the heart, where it ignites the love-will, and then into the head where it arouses a will to attain the celestial realm and to defeat the forces of darkness (II 207/15.43ff.). Birth actualizes the potential freedom of the embryonic soul. The newborn will is ironically thrust into free selfhood: "Therefore it no longer remains in darkness, but rather must be free" (*Darum bleibet er nicht mehr in Finsterniß, sondern muß frey seyn* ... II 208/15.45).

The birth of the infant soul approximates in each stage of its agony and joy the eternal birth of the divine nature, the embryonic emergence of this world, and, finally, the main stages in the author's own spiritual rebirth. The earliest state of the embryo is beyond darkness and light—beyond good and evil. This is the harmonious childhood evoked by the author's metaphors of innocence. The embryo's longing for the light represents the youth's spiritual fears and longings. The absorption of the dark world of the elements and the stars is the early melancholy meditation on the cosmos. The first "glance" or "flash" is the illumination of 1600. For the shoemaker, this flash was followed by an inarticulate sense of joy, and then by the finding of his voice, and finally by his new seeing.

Everything in nature, including its lowest forms, is part of the same process, in which the Virgin functions as an attracting force. The essences in nature forever strive to possess the Virgin, just as the cosmic darkness hankers after the light (II 173/14.22). Until the end of time, the essences of particularity will go on striving to attain her, tormenting themselves with the vanity of their desire. Yet even their torment fulfills a higher purpose. For without it, no good creature would come into being, and the world would be a grim and hellish place (II 177/14.34).

By the same token, the present strife and conflict are motivated by the longing for light. Error arises because of the bad faith of those who view God as the remote World Maker, as the supreme instance from whom their own power (*Gewalt*) arises. This belief not only runs counter to "reason," it legitimates false claims of worldly authority. (Here, Boehme even uses the anti-Calvinist formulas from the Visitation Articles: ... *also wäre GOtt ... gleich der Sonnen, welche hoch über uns schwebet, und die Kraft und das Licht zu uns scheust ... und überall wircket* II 68/7.19.) This is directed against rulers who bolster their tyranny and war powers by sanctimonious deferences to the King of Heaven and Earth, and perhaps specifically against the Calvinist candidate for the Bohemian crown: "the realm of the Antichrist is born of these thoughts" (II 68/7.19). At least until the second book is finished in October of the year 1619, the author appears to remain hostile to all parties in the escalating conflict.

In the course of *The Three Principles of Divine Being*, the hellish strife and eternal longing in nature become overlaid with intimations of an increasing hysteria. We read that great wars and insurrections are being launched in the name of faith. At the instigation of the pastors and scholars who claim to be the mouthpieces of God, the common folk are being incited to persecute all those who hold a different opinion (II 466/26.13–14). Christendom is turning into Babylon. Those who still bear the human countenance pine for "the Age of the Lily." In accordance with Boehme's significant condensation of his time perspectives, his present situation is compared to that of the first humans who have just been expelled from Paradise and already find themselves ensnared in the thorns and brambles of the most bitter exile.

Boehme adapts the hunting metaphor used in war propaganda of the Thirty Years' War in order to evoke the dire circumstances of the human soul. The soul is a hunted animal that has been driven by the Satanic huntsman's "beater" (*der Treiber*) into a "bath" of thorns and thistles: "Behold, poor soul in your bath of thorns, where is your home? Are you at home in this world?" (II 366/21. 63) Confused in its search for the Kingdom of Christ, oppressed by earthly tyrannies, and hounded by the devil's beater, the soul is a wild animal, trapped in a thicket of brambles. The Noble Virgin draws the hunted animal out of its thicket and exacts from it a pledge to assist its brothers and sisters in a like manner. Its thorn wounds are to be the mark of a new knighthood, pledging it to spread truth: "your mouth shall not be closed, you shall enter my laws and speak the truth" (II 367/21.67).

In the last lines of *The Three Principles of Divine Being*, Boehme takes a stand consistent with this devotion to Sophia. He warns both against rebellion by force and against sacrificing one's true opinion, both against calculating on the stronger side, and against submitting in spirit to a conquering power:

> The Lily is not won in war and strife, but rather in a friendly and humble love-spirit, with reasonableness (*mit guter Vernunft*). This [spirit] will break up and expel the devil's smoke, and [it] will turn green for a time. Therefore, let no one think, that that one (*der*) will win when the conflict starts, and it will be fine. And the one who is lying on the ground must not think: I've been judged to be in the wrong and should stand on the other view and help hunt this pack. No, this is not the way, and is only into Babylon. (II 482/27.34)

5 The Fire-World

Philosophus Teutonicus

Ghosts were inflaming the hearts of Middle Europe, inciting the living to resume the heroic projects of centuries past: the Hussite insurrection, the Protestant upsurge, the Imperial containment and reversal. The war that would not acquire its final name from its causes or combatant states promised at its outset a decisive epoch in the life of the world.

During the gradual but inexorable escalation of hostilities, Boehme observed from a vantage like that of few other intellectuals of his time. The former cobbler who now earned his living by small-scale commercial undertakings moved in and out of the storm centers. John Donne's journey to Germany in 1619 was safe and superficial by comparison (though, as chaplain to Viscount Doncaster, Donne preached a sermon before Elector Friedrich V of the Palatinate in Heidelberg). Another contemporary who followed the events from close at hand was René Descartes. While Boehme was visiting Prague and reporting on events there to his friends, Descartes was encamped with a Catholic army in Ulm, where he is said to have experienced his own signally important illumination (vowing in gratitude a pilgrimage to the shrine of the Virgin of Loreto).

Golo Mann's *Wallenstein* conveys the tone, momentum, and emotions of the public acts and pronouncements in Bohemia. On May 22, 1618, the "furious" Count Thurn led his fellow conspirators into the council chamber of Hradschin Castle in Prague. They were determined to challenge a forged imperial response to Protestant grievances concerning violations of the Letter of Majesty. Resolved to force a break with Ferdinand, they had agreed in advance to show no mercy to the Habsburg governors: "talking themselves into new and better fulminations ... because what they proposed to do was impossible to perform without fulmination"—the conspirators pronounced death sentences on the executors of Imperial authority and threw them, along with a hapless clerk, out the castle window. The victims of the new Defenestration of Prague landed largely unscathed, much luckier than the peoples that bore the consequences for the next three decades. Ferdinand and those loyal to the Empire were just as brutally resolved, though their retaliation came more slowly—but then remained in effect much longer Next, the Protestant cities of Bohemia were pressed to follow suit with Prague. Count Thurn threatened the reluctant people of Budweis with an assault that would not spare "the child in its mother's womb." In the following year, first Moravia and then Silesia and Lusatia were coaxed and compelled to undertake the *salto mortale* of confederation with Bohemia.[1]

The Lusatian nobles generally favored confederation. The cities at first hesitated and then assented. In return, the Lusatians were granted the guarantee of religious freedom they had sought in vain ten years earlier. In May 1619, fear of a pro-Imperial military intervention by the Elector Prince of Saxony led the Görlitz *Stadtrat* to station contingents of guards at each of the city gates.[2] On July 31, 1619, their allegiance to the Bohemian Confederation was formalized.[3]

The confederated territories chose the youthful Calvinist, Elector Friedrich V of the Palatinate, the man from Heidelberg, as their new sovereign. With this, the possession of the Styrian, Ferdinand's prior claim to the throne, was forcibly overturned in favor of the young leader of the Protestant Union, the son-in-law of King James of England. From England, munitions rolled through Görlitz to reinforce Friedrich's position in Prague.[4] Ferdinand, the ousted regent, the champion of the Counter-Reformation, was elected to succeed Matthias to the office of Holy Roman Emperor. No prophetic gifts were needed in order to foresee that the conflict was threatening to become a universal conflagration of "Babylon." The conflict that would be fought mainly in Germany was entering its second year; already it involved armed forces of several nations, with mercenaries from many countries.

On October 31, 1619, Friedrich (dubbed the "Winter King" by his detractors who expected a short reign) held his ceremonial entrance in Prague. The rearguard of the parading contingents was a detachment in Hussite regalia. The stately arrival of the procession at the Hradschin was witnessed by a visiting merchant, the erstwhile shoemaker of Görlitz. In his letter of November 14, 1619, to Christian Bernhard of Sagan, Boehme solemnly reported that the new king had received from the estates all the ceremonial dignities accorded to kings of old. Boehme's remark is far removed from the excited reactions of many Protestants who vested such great hopes in the man from Heidelberg. But it acknowledges the legitimacy of the elected monarch. The same epistle formulates other expectations: that the *Siebenbürger* (the Hungarian-Transylvanian Gabriel Bethlen) would soon join forces with the "Turk" in order to carry out a victorious sweep through Germany to the Rhine, smashing the moribund Holy Roman Empire. In the same letter, Boehme advises his friend not to expect that the events in Prague herald the imminent advent of the "true German Emperor": before that, a great war, involving an immense devastation of cities, castles, and powerful lands, would take place (ep. 4.38–41).

No treatise and no section of any treatise is specifically devoted to the events of the war. Political and historical events are dominated by spiritual imperatives and eschatological perspectives in Boehme's writings. His reactions to events are contained in his impassioned, but often contradictory, asides and invectives. But even these merit consideration, if only because they scratch through another of the layers of cliché and generalization which make it difficult to bring the mystic and his times into clearer focus. Boehme's increased output as a writer at the beginning of the Thirty Years' War raises questions about his status as a *Philosophus Teutonicus* and about the prophetic role that has been claimed for him. During the war, Boehme accepted this pseudonym from his supporters. Several of his letters are signed "Teutonicus." This together with his prophetic reputation helped shape his legend in later times.

In the Age of German Romanticism, the national status of Jacob Boehme was an elective affinity, untroubled by its own contradictions. Hegel could emphatically praise him as the founder of German philosophy and just as emphatically berate him as a "barbarian" among true philosophers. Schelling was accused of stealing ideas from Boehme. The accuser was Arthur Schopenhauer whose own *magnum opus* immediately elicited the same jaundiced allegation from a Lusatian critic named Rätze.[5] In a charming, though silly, gesture of adulation, the German patriot, Romantic writer, and Prussian officer Baron de la Motte Fouqué, riding with his comrades-at-arms to fight Napoleon at Lützen, stopped off at the *Landeskrone* outside Görlitz in order to carve reverent graffiti on what he and his companions took to be the cave site where the young Boehme had discovered his treasure.[6]

Later German nationalistic veneration harbored oddly mixed feelings about the *Philosophus Teutonicus*. The Protestant Peip honored him in 1860 as *der deutsche Philosoph*, but at the same time disputed his national credentials. Peip wrote that, whereas Luther had "cleansed" what he had received from German mysticism, Boehme had not. In Peip's judgment, Boehme therefore merited only the qualified and lesser predicate of *teutonisch-deutsch*.[7] Referring back to the aspersions cast by Peip, Elert concluded in 1913 that it should suffice to compare Boehme with "the Jew Spinoza" to answer the question whether the

Teutonicus was truly *deutsch*.[8] Peuckert's biography of 1924 ridiculed the "scurrying little shoemaker" as a coward who should have had the courage to volunteer for frontline duty in "the German War." This characterization was left unaltered in the biography by Peuckert, which is included in volume ten of the postwar facsimile edition edited by Peuckert.[9]

A certain *je ne sais pas quoi* made it hard to rejoice whole-heartedly in *Teutonicus*. What could it have been? Hankamer's biography of Boehme (1924) hinted at the contamination of his mysticism with something un-Germanic: "What was German had to degenerate into what was Eastern in order to bring forth new essence from a new mixture of blood and juice" (*Das Deutsche mußte ins Östliche entarten, um aus neuer Blut- und Saftmischung neues Wesen zu bringen.*).[10] The nationalistic caricature of *Teutonicus* was not challenged directly after 1945. Even its National-Socialistic overtones did not disappear altogether from the public discussion of Boehme. Thus, in 1976, Herbert Cysarz could still declare him "a vanguard fighter for 'Aryan-Germanic' Christianity" (*ein Vorkämpfer der Reinigung und Reinhaltung des "arisch-germanischen" Christentums*).[11] While still in power, the guardians of the "Aryan-Germanic" culture had vacillated between venerating *Teutonicus*—and ordering his rediscovered original writings seized and held by the Gestapo. The autographs only survived the war by quirkish chance.[12]

As scholars, Peuckert and Cysarz were not reluctant in acknowledging that Boehme was influenced by Jewish mysticism. Something else in his writings compelled Peuckert to allege his cowardice (mawkishly claiming at the same time that the heart of "this simple peasant" veritably swooned for all things German), and induced Cysarz to canonize him so absurdly in terms of Alfred Rosenberg's *Myth of the Twentieth Century*. These contradictions very probably stem from the fact that Boehme's pertinent utterances concerning the partisan causes of his day, and specifically concerning the cause of the German nation, were quite negative and even outright antinationalistic. Hence arose the tendency either to deprecate his credentials as a German, or to pretend that he was somehow an early predecessor (*Vorkämpfer*) of an as yet unborn *true* national spirit.

Reactions to War and Nationalism

The real partisan spirit of the early Thirty Years' War is evinced by the propaganda songs of the time. In the nineteenth century, these texts were collected and edited as "folksongs." Many of them originally appeared on broadsheets, accompanied by striking graphic illustrations, with intricate political allegories.[13] By comparing their public portrayals of the war with Boehme's half-clandestine discourse, it is possible to place his views into a contemporaneous spectrum of opinion.

The songs were rarely neutral. They made use of demonifying portrayals of the opposing "Antichrist" and voiced predictions that the final victory was drawing near. These printed presentations of the war assigned a major role to the clergymen. Thus, opponents of the Bohemian Confederation made much of the actions of Friedrich's Calvinist court pastor, Abraham Scultetus. The party of Protestant rebellion blamed the war on Cardinal Khlesl of Vienna, as the conniving author of the forged response to the Bohemian petition. The prevailing ideology found on either side claimed to know that men of false faith were pulling the strings and misleading the simple folk on the enemy side. In Protestant songs, the enemy was not the Catholic *per se*; in Catholic songs, not the Protestant *per se*. The real villains were the ominous powers at work in the background. Depending on one's allegiance, this could mean cruel Spaniards, subversive Jesuits, Roman Pope, Satan, and Antichrist; or it could mean Calvinist rebels, vicious Turk, the apostate Transylvanian, and, as always, Satan and Antichrist. Rosicrucians made a debut as subversive phantoms. The *Pragischer Hofe-Koch* (printed in the winter of 1620) envisaged them emerging out of concealment after the precipitous flight of the Winter King. The nobles of the "noncombative red rose" were ridiculed for practicing the art of conjuring gold—by plundering the coffers of the papists.[14] Soon the monetary inflation of the early 1620s suggested another enemy for the litany: "Isn't it a sin and calumny/ That Jews mint in Germany."[15]

The patriotism of the time was, for obvious reasons, a plastic sentiment. A Protestant song rhymed *Germania* with *Concordia*. German songs celebrating the Confederation rhymed *Vaterland* with *Böhmerland*, and *spanisch* with *tyrannisch*. German nationalism could be affixed to the Empire or hooked up to the issue of religious freedom. It could be extended to include the old Czech reformers Hus and Žiška, or focused in some territorial entity such as Saxony or Bavaria.

The so-called *Volkslieder* also clamored with awesome prophecies. Virtually every statement about the future was couched in the voice of an oracular authority. The Book of Revelation was only one prototype among many. "Sibylla" was also a popular mouthpiece of oracular forecasts. The prophetic composers may have remembered her from the Catholic hymn: *Dies irae, dies illa . . . Teste David cum Sibylla*. Implausibly enough, Sibylla now found herself seconded by the shades of Hus, Wyclif, and the anti-Hussite preacher, Saint John

Capistrano—in a Protestant prophecy sung for the benefit of Friedrich, the new German king of Protestant Bohemia.¹⁶ A "most ancient prophecy" (*uhralte weissagung*), which came out in 1620, had long ago foretold the coming victory over the pernicious Jesuits, much to the glory of the praiseworthy *Teutsche Nation, unsers vielgeliebten Vatterlands*.¹⁷ Not just by chance, the new victorious king would also be named Friedrich, thus recalling the chiliastic legend of the great Hohenstaufen Emperor and foe of Rome, Friedrich Barbarossa. When, soon thereafter, the new Friedrich was put to flight and his rebellion suppressed, the Protestant broadsheets entered the breach with further prophecies, laying out the schedule of his comeback year by year. Some of the song composers may have gotten unnerved by so many omens. "Five Tidings" (*Fünfferley Zeitungen*, anno 1621) expressed generalized *angst* at the rising spiral of destruction: ominous astral configurations appear above the entire Holy Roman Empire.¹⁸ Although these prophecies now strike us as transparent concoctions, at the time even the sober-minded Comenius journeyed to Friedrich's Dutch exile court in order to deliver the hopeful prophecies of a certain Christian Kotter who had been among Boehme's acquaintances. Suffice it to say that the prophecies did not predict victories for the enemy.

When one compares Boehme's utterances to those of the propagandistic texts, it is apparent that he spoke the same language but sang a different tune. Beginning in *Three Principles of Divine Being*, he developed positions that used the same images, altering and generalizing their meaning. His world was also polarized: between the anger of God and the mercy of Christ, between the church of Cain and the persecuted church of Abel. All those who justify war and oppression, who denounce others as heretics (a favorite theme) are in *Babel*. The war is *ein Bruder-Mord*, a fraternal conflict of Christendom, conducted by the same tyrants who oppress, exploit, and corrupt the people. There is a sense of confusion in his formulations; but even in this, they differ from the war propaganda of the time.

Boehme's stance was not pacifistic. The concluding words of *The Three Principles* caution against involvement in the conflict. However, *The Threefold Life of Man* is ready to countenance the need for military self-defense: "For whose house is on fire should put it out; [God] after all allowed Israel to defend itself." He immediately adds: "Whoever starts and causes a war is an official (*Amtmann*) of the devil" (III 249–50/12.40). To be sure, the papacy is called the "devil in Rome" and made responsible for the falling away of the "Turks" from Christendom (III 242/12.18). (Perhaps this aided in rationalizing the "Turkish"-Transylvanian support for the Bohemian Confederation.) The name of

Germany is invoked. Protestant Germany is compared to the Prodigal Son, the pope and the emperor to the scornful older son: "Listen, you Roman Pope and you Roman Emperor, why do you rage at us poor lost sons in Germany who want to return unto our first, true Father?" (III 307/16.17). This was certainly an understandable diatribe in the light of Ferdinand's Counter-Reformation. Though Boehme was consistently opposed to papal authority, he did not greet the war as an opportunity for an offensive against the enemy in Rome.

On the whole, his militant statements are outweighed by his calls for peace and toleration, by his rejections of the partisan spirit, and by his opposition to tyranny. The author now eschews the authority of dogma, whether based on the opinions of the pope, or on those of a Luther, a Calvin, or a Schwenckfeld (III 130/7.8). Where the war propaganda blamed Cardinal Khlesl or Chaplain Scultetus, Boehme indicted the clergy in the most general terms. In referring to *Teutschland*, he invokes *die Christenheit* and the universal congregation of those who have retained or are open to the true faith. Only this universal congregation now has the right to administer the sacraments, since the faithful in Germany have dwindled from a thousand to ten. To be sure, the sacraments thus administered are not just "signs," they are *Wesen*; and those who deny this are still the Antichrist (III 263/13.27–28). However, the true congregation includes God-seeking people of all continents. Even the American Indians—still undeserving "barbarian peoples" in 1600—now lead "a more godly life," in greater simplicity, than "Antichrist" in Europe (III 228/11.92). By now, Boehme's Lutheranism implies virtually no adherence to the organized confession. The allegiance to the Calvinist-led Confederation has isolated the Lusatian Lutherans even further from their orthodox neighbors in Electoral Saxony. Without ceasing to be fervently held articles of faith, the Lutheran doctrines take on the role of religious-political precepts, formulated in a manner that can justify the religious autonomy of Lusatia within a posited universal body of Christ. Christendom extends even beyond Christianity and includes all those who seek the truth. The self-contradictions in his exhortations are glaring, but this does not obsure their intention:

> Whoever wants to slay the Antichrist, is the beast on which the Antichrist rides; he only becomes more powerful through quarreling... (III 228/11.94)

> People think in Germany that they have now left the Antichrist behind them with their struggle; but this is not yet so. For those who curse others as the Antichrist... are themselves branches

> growing from the tree of the Antichrist and are the bears and wolves of the Antichrist... (III 245–46/12.28)

If Boehme had gone no further than these desperate fulminations, his mission as a *Vorkämpfer* might have been conveniently tailored to the anticlerical campaign of National Socialism. However, he pressed his point further, proclaiming the universal kinship, the flesh-and-blood kinship of all peoples, including most definitely the non-German ones, the "Jews, Turks, and heathens." (Despite his strain of Christian anti-Semitism, Boehme firmly asserted the spiritual equality of Christians and Jews, a stance considerably more fraternal than that of the older Luther.) "So, look, you dear peoples of the world, you are all of one flesh. That you have separated yourselves is the work of the devil in the Antichrist" (III 241/12.16). Perhaps this too could also have been overlooked in a mere *Vorkämpfer* of the Aryan culture, but the *Philosophus Teutonicus* finally pressed his universalism to an extreme that was surely unpalatable. His utterances appear to anticipate the nucleus of a future nationalism, the notion that Germany is fundamentally distinct from other nations, and to condemn this coming nationalism as a new "Antichrist," destined for sure destruction. Boehme's reply to the sect leaders, Stiefel and Meth, had this to say about their view of a special salvation (which the mystic interpreted as implying a German elect status):

> Dear brothers! Just look, it is not far from the birth of a new Antichrist. Germany surely will have it with its certainty that one can live securely beneath Christ's purple cloak, and [that we] titillate ourselves with his sufferings... And this is a sure picture of human security: that we praise ourselves as children of Christ, moreover holy, and that we claim to be distinct from other peoples. Thus, with this image, God lets us know that we stand before Him with mouth adorned. But the spirit is a false man. (V *Anti-Stiefelius* 272/283)

Not Germany, and not the warring Christian states, but rather a redefined, envisioned, universal *Christenheit* of all peoples, including the non-Christian ones, is the polity to which Teutonicus held an undivided allegiance. One need not recast Boehme as an antifascist prophet, in order to recognize that his words, no matter how they were intended, were highly objectionable to the guardians of Aryan culture.

The German nation which once claimed to lead Christendom toward its evangelical rebirth now deserves to have its light taken from it and passed on to other peoples, according to an indictment in

Boehme's *Mysterium Magnum*:

> Thus, in this world, Christ is to wander only as a light from one people to another, as a witness over all peoples: And to you, Germany (you, who for such a long time walked with a heathen heart beneath the mantle of Christ, who boasted of your childhood [i.e., restored Evangelical faith], but lived only in the anger of the flesh), it is now being shown, just as [it was shown] to the peoples from whom you were born, with the name of Christ, that your Judgment is at hand.

This indictment rolls as inexorably to its conclusion as the Day of Reckoning itself:

> For the Judgment-Angel in the sound of the trumpet cries out to the other children of Abraham in Christ to go out from Sodom... where one brother scorns and reviles another for the sake of the knowledge of Christ... the city of Jerusalem and Babylon, in which you have strutted for so long, shall now be cast down, Amen. (VIII *Mysterium Magnum* 465/ 45.12ff.)

Peip and Peuckert may well have had such passages in mind when they faulted Boehme for his less than satisfactory Germanitude; however, their allusions remained oblique. Peuckert's grotesque depiction of him as a shirker of his soldierly duty at the front confounds the sentiments of 1918 with a conflict three centuries earlier. (*Wäre er stark und kühn gewesen, dann wäre er wohl ins Feld gezogen und hätte sich einen Feind genommen, der sichtbarer war als Luzifer.*—X 125) What obviously galled Peuckert was that Boehme viewed the world in a perspective in which "nation" played hardly any role. Boehme is thus ridiculed as a "Silesian prophet of doom" (*einer der schlesischen Gram-Propheten*, X 126), as well as an unpatriotic coward.

Certainly, these scholarly episodes are only marginalia of German cultural history—and scarcely worth mentioning in view of the real horrors of history. The nationalistic and National Socialistic distortions of Boehme's image may be no greater than those of many other German authors who have been reevaluated by the scholarship of the postwar decades. What distinguishes the case of Boehme is the difficulty of his writings: his work is far less likely to be taken up by the kind of reader who approaches a novel or play with no preconceived notion of its message. As a result, his reception continues to be filtered through a secondary literature which perpetuates unchallenged myths of the past.

Historical Prophecies Attributed to Boehme

Boehme's status as a folk prophet is part of the myth of the German national character that clouds his reception. Before turning to the meaning of his prophetic role as he conceived it, it is therefore necessary to consider the substance of certain claims that have been advanced by German scholars in publications appearing after 1945.

In arguing for their Germanic folk-seer, Grunsky and Peuckert made much of a letter of February 1623 (ep. 41). The letter itself is down-to-earth, but a "P.S." is appended to it. Without any transition, this postscript relates a series of visionary images: The destruction of Babylon is approaching. The storm clouds are gathering above all locations. Hope is in vain, since the tree is soon to be destroyed, as has been recognized in the "wonders." "The indwelling fire harms its fatherland" (*Das einheimische Feur schadet seinem Vaterland*). Truth and justice have almost been finished off, and so on. Many of the allusions are apparent to us as Boehme's emblematic shorthand. A "tower of Babel" that appears to be propped up will be blown over by the next wind. Just before midnight a light will proceed from the sensory properties that are natural to all beings; the sun gives life to some things and death to others. So far, this mostly recapitulates Boehme's theme that Babylon is destroying itself. Of course, this too is "prophetic"—but what political commentary was not prophetic in that day?

But there are also images which seem to have arisen from a prophetic dream or vision: the "Oriental beast" receives a human heart and countenance and uses its claws to tear *Babel* asunder. An eagle has hatched lion cubs in its nest in the hope that they will grow up to feed it with their catch. Now they are tearing out the eagle's feathers and biting off its claws. Fighting with one another, the young lions destroy the eagle's nest. Their anger will soon ignite and burn up the nest. The imagery is borrowed from the night visions of Daniel.[19] Of course, this would not preclude Boehme's having dreamed or envisioned such things.

In fact, the prophetic images were the political clichés of the day. *Das Orientalische Tier*, who receives a human heart and face, is either the Turk or the *Siebenbürger* (the Transylvanian prince, Gabriel Bethlen).[20] Bethlen was a Christian vassal of the Turks. He was commonly, if erroneously, thought to possess the will and military capacity to finish off the moribund Empire. Boehme mentioned him and his prospects of wrecking the Holy Roman Empire in his letter of November 1619. *The Threefold Life of Man* augured that when finally the Christians were converted to love, "the Turk" would also be transformed and given eyes to see the truth: "for thus his wild heart will acquire a countenance with eyes" (III 228/11.94).

The eagle, the lion cubs, and the burning nest were not part of Boehme's standard repertoire of images and references. This enabled Peuckert to suggest that they were symbols welling up out of the "subterranean" depths of Boehme's German folk-psyche.[21] Their source is more likely to have been banal. In the propagandistic folk songs of the period, the eagle is invariably the Habsburg emperor.[22] The lions are either those rulers who have the lion as their heraldic emblem, or, through a process of generalization, all the warlike princes and territorial rulers, as in a song of the year 1621: "The lions are heard roaring/ everywhere in Germany" (*Die Löwen hört man brüllen/ In Deutschland überall*).[23] These symbols were the commonplaces of numerous songs about Emperor Ferdinand and the Winter King. In "Secret Hint concerning the Supposed King" (*Gehaime Andeutung über den vermainten König*), the lion is the unlucky Friedrich. He plucks plumes from the noble eagle in order to feather a nest for his cubs and foreign mate. However, the lion is soon laid low by a menagerie of biting and stinging beasts, representing various leaders of the Imperial side.[24]

If Boehme's postscript is read as a down-to-earth political commentary, it conveys an estimation of the general situation, to wit: Emperor Ferdinand has nurtured warring subalterns, hoping to profit from their aggressive potential. His young lions will turn upon him and destroy the Empire. This reading captures the gist of Boehme's political views. It also presents a sober and reasonable, though not necessarily prescient, assessment of the prospects in 1623. The Emperor, like the eagle, hovered high in nominal power above his earth-bound lions. But the eagle was powerless *on the ground* (in point of actual power), therefore (so it must have seemed) at the mercy of his own rapacious predators.

Given the universal prevalence of bestiary symbols in the rhetoric of the day, and given also the fact that Boehme's *Post Scriptum* did not identify its contents as part of a prophetic dream, the reader of the letter could have had no way of knowing that this was a prophetic vision welling up *ex profundis* from the German "soil" or folk-psyche (rather than a political assessment couched in conventional terminology). Indeed, the reader surely did not know this; for the recipient of the letter was none other than the same Abraham Franckenberg who so eagerly seized upon all providential hints in Boehme's life. Since Franckenberg did view Boehme as a prophet, it is surprising that he failed to comment upon this—purportedly miraculous—prophecy in the otherwise so credulous account on his *Teutscher Wunder-Mann*.

Another prophetic utterance bolstered Boehme's German folk credentials for Peuckert and Grunsky. In 1622, he wrote a letter to Dr. Christian Steinberg, alias Thirnes (ep. 28), a correspondent in the North German city of Lübeck. Lübeck, near the Danish border, harbored Rosicrucians and was open to mystical influences from Holland. Boehme was replying to inquiries concerning the interpretation of certain words in *Aurora*. These words included the figure of the "Midnight Crown." The Görlitzer averred that there could be two possible interpretations of this figure: as the crown of life (the spirit of Christ), or as a figure in the "external realm or empire" (*des äusserlichen Reiches*), revealing which nations would win out in the military struggle. This is written in response to an inquiry, not in order to trumpet forth some great prophetic vision. Yet Grunsky hailed the reference as a true prophecy of the victory of the Swedish King Gustavus Adolphus. Peuckert was moved by profound reverence for Boehme's Nordic soul: "this is after all folk-faith and folk-religion" (X 127). Again, a modern pattern, vindicating a later ideology, is superimposed upon Boehme's own theories.

Now it was well known in 1622 that the Scandinavians—not only Gustavus Adolphus but also King Christian IV of Denmark—were partisan to the German Protestant cause. One of the wittier pro-Habsburg propaganda songs even suggested that the ousted Winter King should be crowned King of Lapland, since the winters lasted longer there.[25] The claim that Boehme's folk instincts made him envision a Nordic salvation is so lacking in substance that the more significant question is why Grunsky and Peuckert had such a compulsion to cast him in the role of the Germanic folk-seer. They did so, I believe, in order to insinuate that the modern German *völkisch* ideology of National Socialism, with its chiliastic and racist myths, was deeply rooted in the past character and culture of the German people (not just concocted by an assortment of right-wing intellectuals and foisted on the people, to its ruin, by a self-appointed elite, eagerly abetted by many professors). Thus the desired rationalization: *As educated men, we professors stood above these folk superstitions—though we nobly stood by our German folk (therefore: stood by the party that embodied its deepest aspirations) throughout all its struggles and tribulations.*

The Prophet of the Will

Logically speaking, there is no reason why prophecy and the German national character have to be linked in the discussion of Boehme at all. The Germans certainly did not corner the supply of illuminations, prophecies, and apocalypses in the seventeenth century. Christopher Hill has shown that the English people of that century were "a nation of prophets." These included more than a few English "Behmenists" from all stations of society, from commoners to high aristocrats. One of these noble Behmenists, Lord Pembroke, inadvertently provided an instructive and humorous demonstration of the touchstone of prophetic truth. According to an account, Pembroke "took his master's teachings too literally," and therefore came early one morning in April 1665, to the bedside of King Charles II, and

> kneeling told his Majesty that he had a great message to deliver to him, and that was, the end of the world would be this year, and therefore desired his Majesty to prepare for it. "Well," says the king, "if it be so, yet notwithstanding I will give you seven years' purchase for your manor of Wilton" at which he replied "No, an please your Majesty, it shall die with me" and so went away, making his Majesty and the whole court merry with this fancy.[26]

If the anecdote is correct, Charles II shrewdly perceived that the first test of a prophecy lies in the consequences which the prophet and his followers are ready to draw from it.

Boehme's own understanding of prophecy also emphasizes the consequences that are drawn, rather than the certainty of coming events. To be sure, he believed that foreknowledge is, or should be, possible. However, with minor exceptions, he did not attempt to base his reputation on the precise foreknowledge of particular events. Moreover, he forfeited the trump card of all millenarians by disclaiming any knowledge of when the world would end. Thus his reply to the chiliastic theorist, Paul Kaym (*Von den letzten Zeiten*), who had prophesized that the destruction of Babylon would occur in the 1630s:

> ...I have no knowledge of the 1000-year Sabbath; nor do I know how to establish it sufficiently with Scripture; for one always finds something contrary; one can interpret the Scripture as one will....

There is no way of knowing what units of time are intended by "day" or "year," Boehme had written to Bernhard in 1619 concerning the "true German Emperor": "before God a thousand years is like a day" (ep. 4.42). And further below, to Kaym:

> ...and thus, too, the revelation of the 1000-year Sabbath makes little difference for the world. Because we do not have sufficient

grounds of it, it properly rests in the Omnipotence of God; for the sabbath of the new rebirth is enough for us.... (V 417/part 1. 67, 69)

The choice of words is noteworthy: "makes little difference for the world" (*ist der Welt an der Offenbarung ... nicht viel gelegen*). Instead of discussing prophecy as a function of German national character or of the Christian tradition, it is more instructive to inquire about the pragmatic sense of prophecy in his specific historical context. Prophets abounded; he was only one among many. The question is how Boehme's prophetic utterances were to be understood in the context of his region and period. What effect were his prophecies intended to have on the behavior of his fellows?

There were *action-oriented* prophecies, like those of the propaganda broadsheets, or that of Christian Kotter. This kind of prophecy aimed at inspiring men to fight for the final victory by sanctioning it and making it seem inevitable. And there was also a *quietistic* prophecy: that of the sect of Ezekiel Meth, whose followers sold their property in expectation of the approaching "Zion." To these chiliasts, Boehme replied that they might as well stay at home, since wherever they took refuge, they would still be the same, until their Zion came about within (ep. 12.47–48). Boehme's own propheticism calls neither for the action of the war propagandists, nor for the quietism of the adherents of Zion, but rather for something that stands on its own ground between action and quietism: responsibility. He recognized two eventualities: the great "conflagration of Babylon" and "the Age of the Lily." These two perspectives combine and shift, often reflecting the sentiment of the moment. Both will surely come to pass, yet neither is bound to a known timeframe. Prophetic certainties are not those of the "outer man," but those of the soul and the will. This he had stated already in *Aurora* (I 267/19.17–19). In chapter thirteen of *The Threefold Life of Man*, the prophetic gift of inner certainty is explained in greater depth, in a context which brings together Boehme's central motives: the issues of real presence and divine ubiquity and the corollary notion of an all-inclusive organic growth which leads Christendom toward its final true revelation. The tree of the world is growing toward its measured end; the divine will is working its way toward its own final greening and "crown." *The Threefold Life* combines the tree from *Aurora* with the metaphysical will from *The Three Principles* in explaining the meaning of prophecy. History unfolds as the growth and division within the One Will: it "grows" from unity to conflict and then back to unity. Like the tree, the One Will raises up its inner contrarities higher and higher until the limits of its innate growth possibilities are attained. The crown corresponds to the chiliastic thousand. The innate growth *within* the will recognizes *in itself* the end, and then resolves either to attain or "break" this immanent limit of its own growth. At this stage: "the prophet is born, and he is his own prophet, and he augurs concerning the errors in the will" (III 265/13.31). The prophet denounces greed, arrogance, and strife. The prophet understands the causes of aggression: "For what has room is not easily crowded; but what is bound in and blocked always desires to surpass its goal, and it thinks that its neighbor's dwelling is its own too, and it always desires to break the ring or band" (III 267/13.32). "What is bound in and blocked" describes the condition of the will which has not yet been reborn into the light: the condition of the bitter spirit which attempts to break out of its dry confinement. What is bound in and blocked also echoes Boehme's hatred for the aggressive self-aggrandizement of the tyrant rulers. To covet a "neighbor's dwelling" anticipates the impending invasion from neighboring Saxony. As another passage of *The Threefold Life* concludes: "thus God lets come what men themselves have awakened, as war, hunger, and pestilence; now, it is not God who does this, but man himself; he makes war . . ." (III 211/11.51). One can safely conclude that the true prophet has the wide open eyes of the first Adam, and the self-knowledge and responsibility of the restored Adam. By penetrating to the eternal patterns hidden within the present confusions, the prophet foresees the way of the world. But this involves no startling foreglimpses in the manner of Nostradamus, and no deep political futurology. It is a matter of visionary common sense.

The message of prophecy is pragmatic, not doctrinal. The learned church authorities who claim to have a superior knowledge of Scripture are in reality murderers and wolves, responsible for war and bloodshed (III 94–95/5.75–76). The historical faith with its doctrinal "opinions" is not decisive, but rather "good will" and "good actions," *Wolwollen* and *Wolthun* (III 112/6.20). Instead of listening to these false shepherds, each individual should turn inward and assess the truth (III 138/7.38–39). The path to God—the path of return to the lost Fatherland of Paradise—is the inner way. This way leads into the inner universe of the soul. The author is aware that not everyone can follow him into its most rarified regions, nor is this necessary (III 193/10.48). For in the final analysis: "the true faith is the true will" (*Der rechte Glaube ist der rechte Wille*) (III 274/14.6).

As a prophet, Boehme is not a voice crying out specifically to the German nation. *The Threefold Life of Man* concludes with an exhortation to all peoples. The whole world is now strangely present and implicated in the course of events:

> Oh you worthy Christendom, behold yourself! Oh Europe, Asia, and Africa, open your eyes and just look at yourself, just seek yourself! Let every human being seek himself, or it will not turn out well: a grave bow has been drawn back; seize the arm of the archer, and turn around, and find yourself, or you will be shot off and will never return. Do not let yourselves be rocked like infants, walk on your own feet: The time has come! Your sleep is at an end! The angel has sounded the trumpet, delay not! Consider what the Revelation of Jesus Christ has spoken, that those who cling to the Whore of Babylon shall go as well into the mire that burns with fire and brimstone.... (III 340/18.14)

Although salvation and damnation are individual destinies, this prophecy is directed to the world and all its peoples. The Whore of Babylon refers not only to Rome, but by now almost equally to all of Christianity insofar as it relies on external forms of authority. The peoples are to wake up and stand on their own feet before it is too late. "The time has come" does not signify that the world will end tomorrow. It means that what is decided (or not decided) now will determine what lies far ahead, both in the eternal life of each individual and in the future existence of all humanity.

The Threefold Life of Man

Boehme began work on *The Threefold Life of Man* before the end of the year 1619 (ep. 5.9). The work was still in progress in June 1620 (ep. 7.10). By September 1620, it was completed and copied (ep. 9.13). However, by August 1621, he listed not only his first three works but also *Forty Questions on the Soul*, *The Human Genesis of Christ* (*Die Menschwerdung Jesu Christi*); two other major works were finished or in progress, in addition to a number of smaller tracts, many of which were not copied before he sent them to his friends (ep. 12.68–70, 74). The year 1620 therefore marks a turning point in his productive activity: the year during which his momentum rapidly increased. *The Threefold Life of Man*, *Forty Questions on the Soul*, and *The Human Genesis of Christ* all bear the date 1620. What one might call Boehme's middle period is around this year: in the interval after it had become certain that Lusatia would sever its connection with the House of Habsburg, but before the short-lived Confederation had vanished into oblivion.

The periodization and analysis of Boehme's works now has to come to grips with a rate of production considerably more rapid than what has gone before. No longer do ideas and symbols evolve gradually as products of many years of trial and labor. In the works of the middle period, concepts tend to become formulistic and emblematic; what is original often flashes only briefly in the torrent of words. If up to this point the purposes of an intellectual biography were best served by a relatively detailed analysis of his works, the perspective will now be widened and at the same time fragmented.

Analogous to the concentric circles of the Baroque clockface, the thematic evolution from work to work is surrounded by contextual circles. In *Aurora* and *The Three Principles*, there was the continual progression from the angelic kingdoms and the rebellion of Lucifer to the creation of this world, the existence and fall of the first Adam, and then on toward the postlapsarian world. Now it becomes apparent that this linear progression is encompassed by a revolving passage from the outer to the inner, from an external nature and cosmic creation, to human life, its origin, its struggle in nature, its inner bond with God through the soul, and then eventually to a world of signs and utterances which synthesizes the previous outer and inner phases. Beyond this circle, there are reminders of the three main conflicting interpretations of the Eucharist: as body, as spirit, and as sign; and there are equivalents of the trinitarian Father, Son, and Holy Spirit. At last, encompassing all the other circles, there is the mysterious pattern of the seven forms. Never wholly translatable into the figures of the other circles, this rotating and changing dial seems inexhaustible in its allusions, radiating outward to probe the unknown, even while giving expression to a central code of authorial meaning and life experience.

The works of the middle period form a group in that the content of each is concerned with the human subject: as an unredeemed human existence in nature, as the soul that stems from God, and as the God who is reborn as a human. Though there is much thematic overlap in all Boehme's writings, the three middle works suggest by their titles and openings the three levels to which humanity has attained. If we focus on this progression, a continuous thread of development will come to the fore. It is a slender thread, which winds through countless turns of thought, but one which clearly links the main works of this middle period to those written earlier and later. *Aurora* already asserted the freedom of the will. *The Three Principles* expanded the assertion into a voluntaristic metaphysics. The ultimate major works again will propound theories of nature and Scripture, interpreting them as expressions of the divine free will. In the entire sequence, there is a thematic movement from nature as "the body of God," to human life, the soul, and Christ, and then to the natural and historical utterances of the Word (which are called the "signature," the "speaking Word," and "spoken Word").

The middle three treatises fit into the overall pattern by developing the notion of freedom with prime reference to the human subject. Influenced by the instability of the world around him, Boehme pursued this cardinal theme by formulating more and more daring evocations of freedom: as a human, divine, and even material-natural condition of being. Freedom is latent in the vital substance of objects, and it is experienced in the terrible transience of life.

The Threefold Life of Man makes increasing use of Gnostic symbols and images to depict earthly alienation. The Christian is a pilgrim wandering in search of the lost Paradise of his true Fatherland. We are not at home in the external world, the author declares at the outset. There is another life within us that longs for the eternal. The soul is therefore like a prisoner condemned to death. Renouncing all hope of a commuted sentence, the imprisoned soul begins to consider the source of all life, in search of an inner avenue of escape.

Phenomenal existence is evoked by images of attrition and starvation. Existence is a self-consuming fire that burns itself out. Since life is fueled by the body, and the body by food, all earthly life faces death by starvation. The blossoming fields of wildflowers, which symbolized the diversity of life in *Aurora*, now symbolize the certainty of doom, that of a field when its water supply has vanished (III 3/1.3). The seven qualities or spirits of nature will reappear as evil "archons" (Gnostic planetary rulers). They tyrannize human life and open up the way to the soul for the devil, the "executioner" (III 280/14.21). The "wheel of nature" has become a "fire-wheel" (III 282–83/14.27). The entire life of the elements, all of nature, is a seething mass, *ein Sud*, ignited by the stars (III 4/1.7) No object is permanent in this fire-world of flux, self-immolation, and exhaustion. The "wheel of nature" winds inward toward the central light of a deity beyond depiction (III 171/9.58). The powers of the stars hold sway over human birth and development, generating character types which are represented as wrathful (*grimmig*) animals, as "tyrant lions, bears, wolves, and the like." The stellar powers govern through the princes of this world, causing "war, murder, and all misfortune" (III 208/11.39–40). The dark-world, the driven world of the essences, is the principle in accordance with which God is called a jealous, angry God, and a consuming fire (III 30/2.58). This implies that the divine wrath consumes the godless and visits an inexorable chain of suffering upon whole generations to come. The implication takes on greater resonance from Boehme's now repeated allusions to crowd scenes in which Christian hypocrites stir up the people to burn heretics, shouting: "Here is Christ! . . . There are the heretics! On with the fire!" (See: III 138/7.38; 159/9.1; 224/11.84; 227/11.90.) One passage (III

242/12.18) specifically recollects a Catholic time in which the simple folk was incited to hysterical hatred. This recollection sufficiently troubles Boehme that he attempts to exculpate the folk participants by noting that their simple faith had been misused by the instigators. These scenes are not what was happening around him in 1620; they are projected fears of past persecutions, known to him by oral tradition. His answer to persecution is a religion in which each soul goes into itself in order to assess the truth (III 138/7.39). "Priests" should be nothing more than the elders of the congregation, not its masters, but rather its servants (III 254/13.5). This blow is aimed as much against the Lutheran pastorate as against papal authority.

The human creature is not a fixed, shaped thing of flesh; the soul is not predestined for salvation or damnation. Human life manifests itself as desire and will, as the ineluctable, tormenting freedom which cannot escape from nature (III 61–62/ 4.5–8). This is the sense of the "fire-will," the "fire of life," "the fire-wheel," and "flaming world" (*die feurende Welt*).

This world is a self-consuming freedom in which no thing is eternal and none wholly dead: even stones "give weights" and have the noble "tincture" that enables them to be refined and rendered luminescent (III 65/4.21). Everything consists of bundled energy, released into the calm entropy of the light-world, or remaining as an eternal residue from the divine process. This vision of nature leads to some correspondingly radical definitions of the Word and Deity: God is the Word, and the Word is "its own self-eternal Maker" (*sein eigener selbstewiger Macher*), as a self-speaking Word (III 12/1.42). "For we cannot say that God has a maker; thus too the will has no maker; for it makes itself from eternity to eternity, and . . . is not a making but an eternal birth . . ." (III 19/2.7). The eternally self-spoken Word and the self-made God coincide with "the divinity within us."—"God appears to us in the will" (III 29/2.51).

Within the eternal pattern of nature, the fire of life is generated by the latent impulse to escape from the darkness of dead materiality: this indicates that the third and fourth qualities reveal how "feeling" is aroused in dead corporeality. Life is fire; but fire can also burn without the flame of light. Life proper is the light. The life of the soul can endure only in the light of eternity. The idea of the origination of life is thus evolving conceptually. In *Aurora*, the source-spirits were animate but lacking in self-awareness. Gradually, the sevenfold pattern is articulated more finely to convey the emergence of life and consciousness in the "dead" element, in accordance with the qualitative stages of trapped containment, of breaking out, of ensuing terror and dark fire, followed by the psychic light and the light of eternity. Later still, the emergence of a life and consciousness which develops toward wisdom is codified in the "table of seven qualities" (ep. 47), as: (1) Desire; (2) *Szientz* (i.e., movement, life, feeling, and "cause of enmity"); (3) Fear, senses, fire-root of heat; (4) Fire, seeing, separation; followed by (5) Love; (6) Sound; and (7) *Wesen* or Wisdom (*wesendliche Weisheit*). The emergence of the sevenfold pattern in all its ramifications also coincides with a prophetic revelation of the meaning of history, as Pältz' discussion of the "seven ages" has shown.[27]

The Threefold Life of Man concludes with a reference to the theme of individual responsibility, linking it to the motive of spiritual hunger, and encompassing both the theme and the motive in a eucharistic figure: each soul should assess its own quality and weed and replant itself before it is too late. The harvester will come and tie the weeds into bundles, and cast them into the fire. Only the good fruits will be placed upon the table of the Lord. Salvation means becoming palatable to God, just as faith itself is an eating of God's being. In conclusion, Boehme pronounces that his book is faithfully served up by its author for the delectation of all hungry spirits: "whoever is hungry should eat, whoever is thirsty should drink . . ." (III 344/18.23).

Forty Questions on the Soul

The first three books are similar in structure: each of the three incorporates and, at the same time, reworks motives from the creation and destruction of the world. *Aurora* recounts the first three days of Creation. *The Three Principles* recounts the creation of Adam and Eve and their expulsion from Paradise. In *The Threefold Life of Man*, again Biblical motives, allusions to the Apocalypse, strongly influence the development. However, *Forty Questions on the Soul* frees itself from this structuring influence of succession. Instead, it is the multiple of four in the title that ties the fourth book to the pattern of the seven qualities. All temptation and transformation comes in multiples of four. The decisive transformation occurs between the fourth and fifth of the seven qualities.

The prompting of Dr. Balthasar Walter led to Boehme's *Forty Questions on the Soul*. Walter, we recall, was older, widely travelled, and a friend of the late Scultetus. Walter carried on extensive talks with Boehme as a guest in his house; however, the stern *Medicus* was not altogether compatible with his more easy-going host, according to Franckenberg. Boehme may have felt constrained to provide a virtuoso performance in his replies to the questions posed by such a man.

In certain respects, *Forty Questions* appears to be intent upon outdoing the culture of elite Humanism in Görlitz. This ambition of the shoemaker was evident in the nature language and in *Aurora's* critique of mathematical "astrology." The numerological and graphic modes of presentation of *Forty Questions* can be viewed in the same light. *The Threefold Life* employed the simpler, triadic emblem of fire, light, and air, the candlestick, flame, and smoke. However, *Forty Questions* develops ten "forms" of fire in order to account for the origin of the soul. Walter, the man who had researched the secrets of Kabbalah in the Near East, may have influenced both the questions and the answers. The sefirot or ten emanations of the Kabbalah may be the prototype for the ten forms of the soul.

Ten is also of eschatological significance as a divisible of the millenial thousand. The number ten consists of a one and a null. The mystical being of the deity (now for the first time called the *Ungrund*, the "unground") is everything and nothing, unity and nullity (III 11/1.15). The author is openly conjuring with his symbols. The O is the empty mirror or eye of eternity. Its mystical cell of Divine Being is then polarized: the V (for *Ungrund*) is set opposite the A (for *Anfang* or *Alpha*). Numerous other elements are then added in order to work out the design of the "Philosophical Globe" or "Miracle-Eye of Eternity."

The design of astronomical world-models, of *solaria* and *planisphaeria*, was an activity of the Humanistic mathematicians and scientists of the time, including Mayor Scultetus.[28] Boehme knew that the wise *Magi und Mathematici* had constructed a planetary "sphere." He considered that they had not gone far enough in interpreting its subtle symbolism (III 190/10.41). He therefore diagrammed his own design of the solar system in *The Threefold Life*. This first attempt integrated only a few of his concepts and symbols. He therefore carried the enterprise of interpreting the spheres of Divine Being to a higher degree of intricacy in *Forty Questions on the Soul*. The "Philosophical Globe, or Wonder-Eye of Eternity," can be seen as a most elaborate response to the celestial globes and cosmological models of the scientists. "The Philosophical Globe" is intended to demonstrate that the created world is circumscribed by the mystical mirroring spheres of the intersecting darkness and light. Boehme's "Globe" stands in a tradition of mystical circle-symbolism that goes back to Cusanus and, ultimately, to Parmenides.[29]

In *Forty Questions on the Soul*, Boehme gravitates toward the Neoplatonic pole of his thought. The first and longest of his replies is to the question: "Where, from the beginning of the world, does the soul originate?" The reply advises the readers that they should know by way of reason (*aus der Vernunft*) that all things have their origin in eternity (III 8/1.3ff.). "All things are in God," he cites Paul (*Acts* 17.28), "in Him we live and move and are of His kind" (*In GOtt sind alle Dinge, in Ihme leben und weben wir, und sind seines Geschlechtes.*). Paul had begun his sermon to the Athenians by observing that they had erected an altar "To the Unknown God." Paul had proposed to reveal the true God as the fulfillment of this "unknown deity." Preaching to the Athenians to convert, he converted the legendary Dionysius the Areopagite—the Pseudo-Dionysius whose writings established the Christian Neoplatonic tradition. As if returning to this nexus, Boehme's fourth book rotates its focus from the objective realms of nature and external experience to the eternity of forms within the soul.

This gradual shift in perspective is essential to the understanding of a famous term introduced in *Forty Questions*, the term *Ungrund* (which I will refer to in German, since "unground" is not a felicitous translation). The unusual term, *Ungrund*, was once considered to be an equivalent of the Gnostic "abyss"—with which there are indeed some shared connotations. Koyré has convincingly disputed this interpretation, providing instead the following definition: "*L'Ungrund* . . . est l'Absolu absolument indéterminé, l'Absolu libre de toute détermination."[30] This seems applicable, too, though only if Boehme is interpreted from the vantage of German Idealism. Considering the matter from Boehme's own point of view—as suggested by his own terminology—Koyré's *l'Absolu indéterminé* implies an unwonted degree of abstraction. It is noteworthy that Boehme's *Ungrund* often behaves as a subject: it "seeks," it "longs," it "sees," and "finds." Before the divine *Ungrund*, there is nothing, no source of determination. However, prior to the textual occurrence of Boehme's noun *Ungrund*, there is his adjective: *ungründlich*. This word of frequent use in his mature writings means "unfathomable" or "incomprehensible." It is close to the modern German word *unergründlich*.

To say that something is unfathomable or inconceivable is to designate it as an *objective* unknown. The subject dwindles to an impotent eye peering after its unattainable object. That which is said to be *ungründlich* is placed in the same region of speculation as Kant's neumenon or his antinomies of pure reason (all absolute unknowables being equivalent to one another). The chain of becoming, the causal chain in time, can be thought of neither as infinite nor as finite. But, unlike the philosopher, the mystic cannot accept silence where reason fails; the "ground without a ground" therefore has to be named and drawn into the circle of discourse. Thus the *Ungrund* arises as the substantive form of the adverb *ungründlich*.

But of course this is no mere change of phrase. The substantive not only designates the unknowable. It retrieves the unknowable from the realm of the unknown and assimilates it to the experience of the devout seeker. In the substitution of the noun *Ungrund* for the adjective *ungründlich*, a shift comes about, as between the two similar utterances: "About the final ground of God one cannot be certain." And: "The final ground of God is Uncertainty." In the first instance, the seeking subject is cut off from the unknown object of its contemplation. In the second instance, the subject has recognized its inner longing for the deity as akin to the Divine Unknown. In the first instance, any believer, preoccupied, as Boehme was, with the divine will, must remain in the grip of doubts and trepidations about his standing with God. In the second instance, the uncertainty and tormented freedom of the self has been recognized in its relationship to the ultimate ground of divinity. The unknown divine object is reflected in the self-knowledge of the subject. The *Ungrund* is the uncertainty which precedes the divine will's arousing itself to self-awareness (though in the deity this "happens" in eternity). The truth-seeking believer stands closer to the divine indefiniteness of the *Ungrund* than to the false personal God who is thought to have predestined chosen individuals for grace. This paradoxical sense of the *Ungrund* is clearly formulated in *The Human Genesis of Christ*, the book which follows *Forty Questions*:

> God is in Himself the *Ungrund*, as the first world, about which no creature knows anything, for it [the creature] stands with its body and spirit in the ground alone: Even God would therefore not be manifest [*offenbar*] to Himself in the *Ungrund*; but His wisdom has from eternity become His ground (*Grund*), for which the eternal will of the *Ungrund* has lusted, from which the divine imagination has arisen.... (IV *Menschwerdung Jesu Christi* 127/II.3.5)

Here, the mystic uses antithesis to explain the *Ungrund*: (a) God is the world beyond this world, about which no finite being can know; but (b) God would not know Himself if not for His longing for the wisdom of the "ground." Hence, (c) just as the divine desire and longing for the mirror of wisdom engenders this world in a magic act of self-impregnating imagination (as the passage goes on to explain), the believer, too, approaches the unknowable deity through the transforming process of longing and imaginative faith. The soul likewise impregnates itself by reflection, thus transforming itself into the mirror of the hidden God.

The Human Genesis of Christ

The fifth book bears the title *Von der Menschwerdung Jesu Christi*: "the human becoming of Christ." Given that the birth of Jesus, like all birth and becoming, recapitulates the one archetypal genesis at the root of all becoming, the title is best translated as: "The Human Genesis of Christ." Though this title leads us to expect an approach to the Jesus of the Gospels, the expectation is not fulfilled. *The Three Principles of Divine Being* was more literal and "historical" in its treatment of its articles of faith.

The exposition of *The Human Genesis of Christ* begins with a condemnation of all quarrels over the person of Christ. The true object of the Christian faith is not to account for the distant event. Instead, one should attempt to recreate in oneself the process in which Christ was born as a human, the *Menschwerdung Jesu Christi* (IV 2–3/I.1.3). The prerequisites of this process are generated from two sides. On the one side, the deity must be brought into the purview of the human understanding. On the other side, the human creature must be elevated above the level of an elemental clump of earth: for God would hardly have become human for the sake of a mere clump of dirt.

The Virgin of Divine Wisdom accomplishes these purposes as a *tertium comparationis*: God, Christ, the first Adam, and we who are to restore ourselves to the pristine Adamic Paradise *all* reflect the Divine Virgin. In God, the Noble Virgin is a passive mirror and ideal form of the divine nature, a principle or world hovering before the eternal deity, representing the eternal *Magia* of what is and is not. In a philosophical sense, she stands for an immaculate conception, a Platonistic virgin birth. What is created comes into being as a reflection of the figures in her eternal wisdom. She is the mirroring of darkness as light, the bringing to light of what is latent in the Father. Since she embodies the magic process by which the principle of darkness is reflected as light, her role is a more striking one in Boehme's writings than that of the historical Christ.

The historical life of Christ in this world was a brief but paramount episode in the drama of Creation, Fall, and Rebirth (which are now declared to be the three points of the Christian religion). These three points are eternal motives, expressed in every phase of the unfolding being of the deity. On the clock-face of eternity, these three moments completely overshadow the historical continuum of time. The same drama of sin and redemption is always entirely present. Boehme's term "imagination" is the key to this eternalization of the "historical" religion.

The term imagination is used throughout Boehme's writings in an unusual sense based on, but going far beyond, the customary one. In *The Human Genesis of Christ*, imagination is specified as the transforming activity of faith. Salvation for Boehme occurs by faith and the word of God, but since the word of Scripture is not historical, the creative activity of imagination acquires a decisive importance in constituting the act of faith.

> For the word "faith" is not historical, it is rather a taking from God's being (*Wesen*), an eating of God's being (*Wesen*), [it is an] introducing of God's being (*Wesen*) by means of the imagination into one's soul-fire, in order to calm its hunger with it ... [the soul] must eat of God's bread, in order to become a child. (IV 88/I.11.8)

Faith thus remains symbolically eucharistic. But it is also an imitation of God: "Now it is up to our going into ourselves [*unserm Selbst-Eingehen*], that we may follow after the way which He has made [or gone]. We may introduce our imagination and entire will into Him, which is called faith [*welcher Glaube heisset*]..." (IV 154/2.6.11).

Imagination as the transforming power of faith draws various strands of thought together. We have already observed that the Creation consists of a divine process of concentrated desire and reflection; and that theogony is this same creation in eternity. Imagination, as unbridled desire, is responsible for the fall of the first Adam. The reflective imagination is also instrumental in spiritual rebirth. The three eternal moments—the Creation, Fall, and Regeneration of the soul—are therefore all capable of being represented as the magic transformations effected by the imagination. *Magia* can be construed as the root of *imagination*. *Magia* (magic), as opposed to evil *Zauber* (sorcery), is a sacred generation of something out of the nothingness of the will. In nature, there are parallels to this: Sunlight "spontaneously" generates life in the lifeless soil. Matter is transformed by fire into a light "free" of matter (V 93/1.12.6), or into the tinctured metallic ground that admits and reflects the light. The believer partakes of the divine being by recognizing in God and in the soul the eternal self-creating will of the fire which transforms itself into the light (V 88/1.11.7–8). The wondrous forms and figures of the Divine Wisdom are imagined into *Wesen*.

This conception of the imagination as magical has roots in the medical theories of Paracelsus, which have been analyzed and summarized by Pagel. For Paracelsus, the power and importance of imagination derived from the occult faculty of the human microcosm. The imagination possessed a sunlike power that could work its will upon the surroundings of man. By virtue of its magnetlike force of attraction, the power of imagination drew the outside world into itself and "impressed" its acquired force upon outside objects and persons.[31]

The German verb for "to imagine," *sich einbilden*, interprets the Latin *imaginatio*. *Einbilden* hints at the divine act of creating man in the image (*Bildnis*) of God. Hence, the cluster of words linked to "imagination" ties in with a whole field of concepts: the entire world with everything in it is an expression of the divine magic; a form or idea (*Bildnis*) was the prototype of things; and man is created in the image (*Bildnis*) of God. The concept of imagination reinforces the thought that the whole is entirely reflected in each part. The faith of imagination thus reacts against the historical faith, the latter being the creed of an authoritarian, unregenerate Christianity.

The first of the three parts of *The Human Genesis of Christ* closes with a creed or confession for the reborn. One can gauge the evolution in Boehme's understanding of Christianity by juxtaposing this new ten-point confession with an eight-point catechism in *The Three Principles of Divine Being*. Anticipating the title of *Die Menschwerdung Jesu Christi*, the earlier summation bore the heading "The Gates of the Human-becoming (*Menschwerdung*) of Jesus Christ, the Son of God" (II 267/17.121). The earlier eight "strong articles of faith" offered a rather conventional, historical, enumeration of the objects of gospel faith: (1) the Immaculate Conception; (2) the human death and interment of Christ; (3) Christ's descent into hell to defeat Satan; (4) His atonement of human sins; (5) His resurrection on the third day; (6) His return on the Day of Judgment; and so on in a straight-forward catechism devoid of alchemistic or Hermetic terminology.

By contrast, the new ten points register a striking change of emphasis, if not substance, in Boehme's Christology. This is evident in his alchemistic language, his allusions to the false authority of the official church, and his angry condemnation of violence and oppression. Above all, it is evident in his stress on human freedom and responsibility which overshadow the historical Gospel events in his statement of what "we" confess:

> I. That the new reborn man, who is hidden in the old one like gold in stone, has a divine tincture and has divine flesh and blood in him; and that the spirit of this flesh is not an alien spirit, but rather its own, born from its own essences.
> II. We confess and say that the Word, which became man in the Virgin Mary, is the first ground of the rising tincture in the sulphur; and we confess that Christ's spirit which fills all of heaven, everywhere dwells in this tincture.

III. We confess that the divine flesh is Christ's flesh in which the Holy Trinity dwells undivided.
IV. We confess that it is possible that the same flesh and blood in the time of the old Adam can again be corrupted through imagination, as happened in the case of Adam.
V. We say that the divinity loses nothing through corruption and is not touched by any evil; for what the love of God loses falls to the wrath of God: what falls out of the light is caught by the fire; and God's spirit remains uncorrupted in itself.
VI. We say that in all men there is the possibility of new birth, otherwise God would be divided up and in one place not as in another; and we herewith confess that man is drawn by fire and light: where he turns with the scales, there he falls, yet he may in this time still swing the balance back high; and that the Holy Clear Divinity wants no evil. It wants no devil, never wanted one, much less man in the hell of God's anger. Rather: since there is no light without fire, we can see in ourselves how the devil by virtue of imagination becomes enthralled by the wrath-fire; just as all men who are damned don't want to accept counsel, but rather themselves fulfill the greedy fire-torment (*Feuer-Qual*); they let themselves be drawn in, yet could stand firm.
VII. We say that the true temple in which the Holy Spirit preaches is in the new birth: that everything is dead, deaf, bent, blind, and lame which is not, or teaches not, from God's Spirit; that the Holy Spirit does not enter into the sound uttered by the mouth of the godless, that no one who is godless can be the shepherd of Christ....
VIII. We confess and say that all teachers who pass themselves off as Christ's vassals and church-servants, and do so for the sake of gluttony and honor, yet are not reborn, are the Antichrist and the woman on the dragon in the Book of Revelations (17:3–4).
IX. We say that all unjust tyranny and violent measures, with which the wretched are oppressed, exploited, crushed and tormented, and because of which they can also be drawn to luxury and injustice, are the vile, abominable beast upon which the Antichrist rides.
X. We recognize and say that the time is near and that the dawn is breaking in which the beast with the whore shall pass into the
abyss, Amen, Halleluiah,
Amen.

In summary, Christ and the Trinity inform all things (II, VI). Moreover, because the ubiquitous balance of anger and love, fire and light, bifurcates every human soul, each, in principle, can yet be reborn. Without spiritual rebirth, no sermon or ministry possesses the authority of the Holy Spirit. Hence, all the tyrants and Pharisees, all warring princes and toadying clergymen, stand stripped of their authority—and soon to be hurled by their own anger into the fiery abyss.

The Fall of Bautzen

The ten-point confession ending with its damnation of "the beast with the whore" was written not long before August 1620—when the brief summer of the Bohemian Confederation was already on the wane. In June 1620, Ferdinand entrusted Elector Prince Johann Georg of Saxony with the task of subjugating Lusatia, granting him the territory itself as a forfeit for the military expenses incurred during the invasion. In September, an army of 12,000 threatened Bautzen. Although the city would have been willing to surrender, the negotiations were unsuccessful. What followed was a monthlong siege, during which some 4,000 cannonades were fired into this sister city of Görlitz. During the siege, 1136 houses and 5 churches were reportedly destroyed. Only about 200 houses and buildings remained standing.[32] A propaganda song of the time portrayed the siege as a sporting event. The Elector Prince was cast in the role of the huntsman who poured lead and pitch into the thicket and merrily gave chase to the game, which gave up and "rendered unto Caesar his own" (*Gaben dem Kaiser das Sein*).[33]

One of Boehme's letters records how those in Görlitz became aware of these events. People had seen smoke rising beyond the horizon from the direction of Bautzen, but they had had no idea of the course of events. Only after the city had fallen on October 5th was Boehme able to piece together an account from the reports of withdrawing soldiers. His summary of the events is addressed to Balthasar Walter. The letter presents a balanced, though not dispassionate, narration of the behavior of the besieging Saxon forces of Elector Johann Georg, the defenders inside the city, and their Silesian allies (who remained encamped at Görlitz and failed to relieve the beleagured city).[34]

The Saxons first bombarded Bautzen from a distance for three weeks. This terrorized the inhabitants and induced some to throw out messages, either pleas for mercy or collaborationist advice to the attackers. The elector then moved his placements closer and stormed the city, incurring heavy losses. When the defenders saw they were in danger of losing the districts beyond the city walls (*die forstette*), they burned what they could not defend and withdrew into the fortified perimeter, still hoping that their appeals to the Silesian relief force of the Margrave von Jägerndorf would be answered. If only 1,000 men had been sent, Boehme sadly reports, the fine city could have been saved. The Saxons then bombarded Bautzen with burning pitch, setting most of the houses ablaze. During the bombardment, the defending soldiers plundered property that had been stored inside the city from outlying estates. During the continuing bombardments, many inhabitants, especially womenfolk, were burned or asphyxiated by smoke when they fled onto open squares or into cellars in an attempt to escape the spreading conflagration.

After repeated negotiations and renewed assaults, the defenders, who had "chivalrously" (*Ritterlich*) stuck to their guns, at length came to realize that no relief was on the way. They then allowed the opponent to enter the city. Further negotiations followed. These ended when the elector permitted the defenders to withdraw with their weapons on the condition that they not fight again for two months. He thereupon attempted to win them over to his side with a promise of two months' pay. When they refused, they were allowed to depart for Silesia, "with flags flying and with all their wagons and plunder" (*mit fligenden fahnen/ mit allen wagen und raub*), leaving behind the devastated city. The survivors in Bautzen were required to swear loyalty to Johann Georg and to forfeit additional property as tribute to the conqueror. The city was then occupied by Imperial forces. These forces in turn summoned the nobles into Bautzen to swear loyalty to the emperor.

The tone and attitude of the letter correspond to Boehme's general attitudes, expressed in his writings and letters. He is horrified at the reported sufferings of the citizenry of Bautzen (*solche Nott . . . das es schrecklich und Iemmerlich zu Melden ist*). But his account is not characterized by one-sided pathos. The plundering defenders are not idealized, but their staunch defense and refusal to change sides is in their favor. By the same token, Johann Georg's respect for their loyalty is to his credit. The point of view of the letter is that of a Lusatian (*unsers landes lauslitz*) and of a subject of the King of Bohemia (*unserm könige*). The writer devoutly hopes that the arrogance of the Saxon Elector will soon meet its proper due (*ver hoffen dem Curfürsten werde Balde sein hoch mut geleget werden*). The letter pays close attention to details having to do with the betrayal of conscience. Its author is against changing sides and swearing allegiance under duress. As usual, however, he reserves his most acerbic epithets for the type of the clerical "belly-servants of Antichrist." His conclusions are gloomy: Those who try to save their material fortunes will either hasten their own downfall or lose their souls. One broom—one force of self-righteous wrath—will sweep up after the other. *Babel mit dem Thir und der huren stehet im Bra[nde].*[35] Babylon, with the beast of violence and the whore of betrayal, is in flames.

6 The Mirror of Darkness

"Babel brennet in der gantzen Welt"

1620—a year of fateful consequences for all of Middle Europe during the next three centuries—came to a close with Görlitz occupied by the troops of the Confederation. After procrastinating while Bautzen fell, the ineffectual Margrave of Jägerndorf skirmished with the invading army before returning to Görlitz in November to set up his winter quarters. A resolute Calvinist, he violated the *de jure* autonomy of Lutheran Görlitz by mandating church services in his own confession. His troops behaved badly so that a gallows and pillory had to be set up in the Lower Market Square for punishing the reprobates. The people of Görlitz had no choice but to feed and house an army, with all its attendant camp followers, while assisting in the construction of battlements around their city.

A letter written to Christian Bernhard in November 1620, (ep. 67) reports on continuing skirmishes between the forces loyal to the Confederation and those loyal to the emperor. The country is said to be more than half "ruined and plundered," and very nearly at an end (*unser Land wird bald fertig seyn*). Eight days earlier, Boehme had undertaken a perilous journey into Bohemian territory, where Wallenstein was on the march. The Görlitzer took note of the terrible devastation of Northern Bohemia. His letter records personal impressions and hearsay of the war without claiming to know the further consequences of events. The same letter comments that news has just arrived in Görlitz of a great battle fought before the gates of Prague. The reference is obviously to the Battle of White Mountain, fought on November 11, 1620. Prague was captured and the Winter King put to flight. To Boehme, this most decisive of battles could as well have been an inconclusive preliminary encounter of armies.

By the end of the year 1620, the Bohemian Confederation had joined the airy phantoms of Middle Europe. On December 23, the Winter King fled the Silesian city of Breslau, to Brandenburg. The Silesian potentates initiated separate secret negotiations with the Saxon

Elector. After the new year had begun, the Upper Lusatian estates secured the permission of their exiled king to negotiate a peace settlement with the elector.[1] In February 1621, the forces of Jägerndorf withdrew to Silesia. In the following month, the Saxon army occupied Görlitz.

In June 1621, the forty condemned leaders of the defeated Bohemian Confederation were executed in front of the Prague City Hall in a grisly theater of retribution. The Jesuits returned to Bohemia in order to institute the Catholic Counter-Reformation. Against the wishes of his Saxon ally, Emperor Ferdinand soon began forcibly catholicizing his reconquered kingdom. Aside from the destruction of Bautzen and the plundering of their territory, the Lusatians were luckier than their exconfederates in either Bohemia or Silesia. Having been conquered by the Elector of Saxony, they were at least delivered from the Jesuits.

This bit of luck notwithstanding, they still faced extreme hardships. What was harvested by the peasants was seized by the *Landsknechte*. The shortages caused by the foraging armies in the countryside and two military occupations of Lusatia worsened the widespread inflation. There were bread riots in Görlitz. In the countryside, bands of discharged or deserting mercenaries terrorized the roads, attacking travellers around the city. The League of Six Cities returned to the pattern of the Hussite Wars, hiring a mercenary force of sixty men to maintain order.[2]

For the time being, the theater of war shifted to the west and north of Germany. However, the whole region appeared to be on the brink of renewed warfare, continuing so until Boehme's death in November 1624. His letters of the period convey the impression of a perpetual chaos and danger on all sides. In November 1622, he wrote that "the Antichrist in Babylon now holds power in Christendom" (ep. 31.2). He had good reason to speak of "killing the Antichrist in ourselves" (ep. 31.4). For, he, too, pinned hopes on the "beast" of violence. The Transylvanian "Turk," Boehme's Oriental Beast (ep. 41), still threatened to sweep from Hungary through Germany, "tearing asunder the Tower of Babel with his claws"—or crushing the Holy Roman Empire under hoof. "Cossacks," who were probably Polish cavalrymen, are said to be galloping through the region. Boehme made mention of their *Teufeley* or devilish rampaging (ep. 34.23). Expecting them to complete their march in Lusatia, he reckoned that it was high time to go out from *Babel*. The war and turmoil were slated to intensify (ep. 36.3). By 1623, the mercenary armies were again maneuvering in Moravia and Silesia. In June 1624, the prospect of peace was still remote. Six months before his death, he wrote from

Dresden that, "We behold the time when Babylon burns in the entire world, and woe is upon all streets..." (ep.64.7). However, this is only one side of his letters during the 1620s.

Not long after the fall of Bautzen, Boehme's state of mind manifested a surprising turn. As the winter passed into spring and then summer, a dreamy optimism began to assert itself alongside the gloom of his letters. On June 8, 1621, he wrote to Bernhard that a "golden age" would blossom from the flames of *Babel*. Not long ago he had spurned those who spoke of the new golden age. Now his new sanguinity transformed inner aspirations and pitfalls into signposts on the path to a dawning era:

> Seek, says Christ, and ye shall find. The noble pearl reveals itself only in those who will now seek. For it is a pleasing time. Both to Heaven and Hell, the doors now stand open with their desire. It is a time to seek oneself. Let no one think this a joke or he'll fall prey to the grim wrath of God, and will be seized up in the grim jaws (*im Rachen des Grimmes ergriffen*). (ep.13)

These notes of optimism also continued during the 1620s, as he wrote of "the destruction of Babylon," the "Age of the Lily," the "New Reformation," and the "New Man." How are we to account for this rising spirit in the face of worsening conditions? What can he have meant: "It is a time to seek oneself"?

The most deferential answer is that the mystic had entrusted his life to God and was now graced with increasing serenity. But Boehme had long since entrusted his life to the will of God, and only a year earlier he had depicted existence as a seething hell. The most damaging answer that the findings of scholarship can suggest is that Boehme was doing tolerably well in the worst of times. He had learned to combine his mercantile activities with what interested him most. The letters written during the fighting in Lusatia contain references to various transactions, sales of tin and gloves, and a scheme for selling wine supplied by the customs official Bernhard to the Silesian officers and camp followers in Görlitz.[3] Boehme and his family probably suffered less from the shortages and rising prices than others in Görlitz. His supporters among the landed gentry supplied him with grain and vegetables during winter months. Beginning in 1621, the earlier mercantile journeys were replaced by visits to his contacts and supporters among the Protestant dissenters. He repeatedly undertook journeys to Silesia and paid visits to his acquaintances in Sagan, Zittau, and the area around Görlitz. His spiritual discussions may well have been accompanied by business dealings. The Protestant mystic was fond of quoting Christ's parable of the faithful servants who lend out the master's talents for interest. Though his references were to spiritual talents, he was not above applying the same standards to his material ones. The "Theosophical Letters" contain numerous references to provisions and sacks of grain. A certain M. Weigel, who refuses to return three grain sacks, is said to have been seduced by the spirit of the "Babylonian Virgin" (ep. 33.6). For years already, Katharina Boehme had been engaged in the yarn trade. By 1621, their sons were old enough to bring in income.

Yet enterprising as the family Boehme may have been, the kind of living they eked out while its head spent his time composing his long treatises could hardly have been much better than a passable hand-to-mouth existence. If he had wanted to earn more money, he would have done better to return to the workbench in order to cash in on the demand for military footwear. The roads travelled by the spiritual "pilgrim" in his last years were perilous enough. He could have led a safer existence if he had stuck to his shoemaker's last, inside the fortified walls of his city. Having authored more than a thousand pages by 1620, he could have rested on his laurels. In some instances, his books were copied with his knowledge for money. If his main object had been "royalties" of this sort, or just increased influence, the sheer size of the books he penned was counterproductive.

The motives of Teutonicus are accessible only through his writings. The activities of his last years are documented not only in several major works, but also in a variety of occasional writings: in the "Theosophic Letters," in tracts on the issues of grace, baptism, and Communion (*On the Election of Grace* and *The Testaments of Christ*), in his polemics against such doctrinal rivals as Stiefel, Meth, Kaym, and Tilke, as well as in numerous shorter works concerned with contemplative themes or with the spiritual practices of the worshipper.

In order to reconcile the apparent contradiction between his profitmaking and his self-sacrifice for his sublime cause, it is necessary to revise the image of Boehme's role and calling. The cobbler-mystic was the greatest propagandist of his own myth. It was he who never wearied of repeating that his writings had been inspired by a God-given gift, his inspirations pouring down from heaven like thundershowers, and that, as far as his own humble person was concerned, he had never sought anything but refuge in the loving heart of Jesus. These are stock phrases.

The same formulistic imprint of rationalization also frames his often-cited account of his illumination of 1600 in the letter written in 1621 to Caspar Lindner (ep. 12.7ff.). In the letter to Lindner, the author detailed a suspiciously long, and even more suspiciously worded, inventory of what he had "seen and recognized." The advocates of the spontaneity theory cite this letter as proof that Boehme experienced visions in the most literal fashion. The "seen and recognized" things include concepts that occur in his writing as it evolved after *Aurora*. His assurances that he was a mere instrument of a higher power with no desire for followers may have had an important legal significance. Such assurances deflected the charge that his goal was to found a new sect in his own name, or was pretending to theological qualifications. In point of legal defense, the author could indeed state with some justification that he had written for himself and his friends. But one is misled if one reads these sworn affidavits as psychological descriptions of the creative process of an "illuminist" or even as creditable disclaimers of a systematic dissemination of his doctrinal views.

As early as October 1619, he had written to Carl von Ender: "Since, however, I recognize in force and light that it is a pure gift of God, who thus also gives me a driving will so that I have to write what I see and recognize, I want to obey God more than man, in order that my episcopal office (*mein Bisthum*) shall not be taken from me again and given to another, which I would regret eternally" (ep. 2.8). This reference to his *Bisthum* need not be taken as a sign of inflated self-importance. This is apparently meant in the sense of an informal spiritual authority. (*The Threefold Life*, written at this time, states that "bishops" are worth as much to the world as a "fifth wheel is to the wagon."—III 278/14.14) Yet a note of authorial vanity is clearly blended into his passionate sincerity when he disengenuously pledges to redouble his efforts in order to prevent his God-given covenant from being taken from him and handed on to another, which *he*, the passive and reluctant instrument, would eternally regret.

During the 1620s, the hidden man behind the expanding galaxy of symbols increasingly becomes cloaked in his self-defined calling. Two important nonmystical aspects of this calling have to be distinguished: (1) that of the doctrinal polemicist eager for influence; and (2) that of the author who writes and behaves as if engaged in a kind of literary endeavor.

Doctrinal Polemics

In spring 1621, the Protestant intellectuals in Silesia and Lusatia began to meet, discuss, write, and defend their views in the wake of the collapse. Not all of these newly emergent voices were amicably disposed toward the self-appointed spiritual leader from Görlitz. The Silesian noble Balthasar Tilke wrote against *Aurora*. Boehme replied to

Tilke, telling him that his criticism was a willful distortion, motivated by Calvinistic sentiments. Two virulent "apologias" to Tilke were complemented later by a milder anti-Calvinist tract, *On the Election of Grace (Von der Gnaden Wahl)*.

Boehme actively promoted his own polemical writings in his letters to his contacts. In early summer 1621, the mystic was bested in a dispute that took place at a meeting of Protestant circles in the Silesian region of Striegau. Pitted against an academically trained opponent and forced to defend his earliest manuscript, the autodidact stood at a clear disadvantage. The opponent, Dr. Staritius, insulted Boehme by throwing the word *Flacianer* into the debate (ep. 15.7). The epithet implies that Staritius and his supporters dismissed their Lusatian rival as the adherent of the most conservative of Lutheran doctrines.

Vis-à-vis other sectarians of the time, the theosophist from Görlitz did exert a conservative influence. This is evident in his relations with the followers of Stiefel and Meth, who turned to him for support around Easter 1621. It is also evident in his response to Tilke and to the customs official Paul Kaym who, in 1620, had sent him his own tractate on the Day of Judgment. Stiefel and Meth were proponents of a Weigelian mysticism. Worse than this: in Boehme's view, they were antinomians who justified their libertine conduct on the grounds that the sanctified flesh could sin no more. Against Stiefel and Meth, Boehme fired off the three-principled response of the *Anti-Stiefelius* of 1621 and 1622. In reproving them, the doctrinal polemicist laid aside the nonrestrictive guise of the contemplative mystic.

The debates with Staritius and Tilke likewise demonstrated that Boehme was no less opinionated than his opponents. On one day alone, July 3, 1621, he wrote no less than five letters polemicizing against Tilke and Staritius (ep. 15–19). The epistolary flurry served: (a) to justify *Aurora*; (b) to challenge the value of all public disputes; (c) to cast doubt on the utility of "logic" in deciding doctrinal questions; and (d) to praise the author's own writing on the "election of grace" as the definitive answer to all the debated points. This is the same voice that repeatedly reassured readers (most recently in the first "apology" to Tilke) that the "author" had written his books only for himself, had never wished to receive burdensome divine talents, nor sought anything but refuge in the loving heart of Jesus. A mere child learning his theosophical ABCs, the author was only persuaded by the coaxing of his wise friends to write down the inspirations which he spontaneously received from God. Like official seals of affidavit, these unvarying assurances are stamped into treatise after treatise, letter after letter.

However, more was at stake than a zealously defended reputation or a cautiously maintained defensive posture. If Boehme's self-effacing characterizations are contradicted by his self-promoting actions, his doctrinal positions were nevertheless longstanding and impassioned ones. He remained true to himself in his opposition to Lutheran literalistic Biblicism and in his rejection of Calvinist predestinarianism. If his humility is couched in stock formulas, his views on salvation are not. It would surely be an error to look for ulterior motives behind his expressions of faith in the divine and human nature of Christ. And any interpretation which construes his Christology as a mere pretext for nonreligious motives cannot penetrate to the core of his thought and symbolism.

But the prospect is just as dim for any interpretation that ignores the fact that Boehme's objects of faith were quite bound up with his personal, social, and historical experience, so that one can only approach what he meant by attempting to reconstruct this broader, evolving experience. The disputes with Staritius and Tilke occurred at a time when the region was constantly on the brink of continued warfare. The supranational Confederation had vanished. The propagandistic claims that the nation of Hus and Žiška would regain its fighting prowess were no longer tenable. The English king had failed to intervene on behalf of his German son-in-law. Spanish troops and Polish Cossacks were threatening German Protestant territories. German Protestants who were determined to carry on the fight—which in Boehme's view could only make matters worse—must have been attracted at just this juncture to a revived German nationalism: either to Luther's stirring German nationalism of the early Reformation era, or to the military rigors of the Calvinist Second Reformation.

Tilke, Kaym, Stiefel, and Meth adhered to different doctrinal positions; but in replying to all of them Boehme criticized the same latent spirit of militance and nationalism. "Zion" would come about when people stopped warring and laying waste to their own land, Boehme wrote in response to Kaym's chiliasm (V *Von den letzten Zeiten*, I 406/23). All peoples are equally favored in the eyes of God, he wrote in the first apology to Tilke, in defense of *Aurora*. Foreign and non-Christian peoples born "in the light of nature and the spirit" may all be graced with salvation, even without "the name of Christ" (V 65–66/404–09).

Boehme's rejection of intolerance was in part aimed against the consequences of nationalistic militance. The second apology to Tilke concludes with a declaration against its spirit. Like the antinomian voluntarism of Meth and Stiefel and the prophetic speculations of Kaym, Tilke's doctrinal views offended Boehme by intimating the notion of an elected grace of the *nation* favored by God. The touchstone of harmony among peoples is recognition that God bestows equal favor on all, Christian and non-Christian peoples alike. The alternative will be a life-and-death struggle in which nation consumes nation:

> Can you not assess (*prüfen*) what will soon follow upon this? Unless, being equal in life and will, they are also accounted as equal before God, and if one only fights and seeks nothing but quarrels, it will result in such a mixing up in conflict, that one people will swallow up the other. For God withdraws His hand from the peoples ... thus, anger has seized its sword of desire, and powerfully compels the minds of men to the end that one people will ruin and consume the other: What our fathers have dished up with their scorn and contempt, their children will finish eating with swords and blows. (V 161–162/316–317)

With this, the critique of nationalism (elsewhere merely implicit in his spiritual stance) becomes explicit and acquires prophetic contours. A confessionally conditioned worldview is at issue. The first treatise against Tilke argues that the most dangerous of warmongers are those who engage in prophecies of the Second Coming: these are the same ones who condemn others as heretics, who "make laws out of Christian freedom" and "seduce the elect" (V 20–23/108–25). Boehme portrayed in Tilke the type of the paranoid Calvinist mind that forbids all open questions about salvation, yet secretly falls prey to obsessive doubts concerning the elect status of others (V 75/470). Whether this was justified against the man Tilke is hard to judge and need not concern us here. Of interest is the type which Boehme perceived and opposed.

If antinationalism is not a central theme of Boehme's works, it is certainly very characteristic of the productive core of his thought and feeling. This core cannot be exhaustively captured in distinct propositions. Like the associative flow of a reverie, it acts as a strong undercurrent in his thinking, giving rise to various tenets by linking similar qualities and positing related oppositions. In nature, the mystic reacts against the stubborn facticity of things, embodied in their discrete and determinate forms, their hardness and tangibility. These qualities contrast with the flowing sidereal force fields which transform all qualities and effect the sacramental miracle. In the sphere of life, this coincides with his rejection of predestinarianism; in the sphere of organized devotion, with his hostility to the "stone-church" or "church of walls," which excludes others[4]; and in the sphere of war and peace, with his opposition to a national elect status.

The principle of ubiquity implies that God does not reside separated off from the world in a heaven above. Those who see God as the summit of a hierarchy only serve the "Antichrist" by making themselves into the executors of God, investing themselves with divine powers in the world below (II 68/7.19). The belief in the "historical faith" entails the principle of hierarchy and succession, fundamental to the relations among rulers and ruled. The earthly authority of laws and restrictions parallels the literal-mindedness of bibliolatry. The state, in its then common model, presupposed both the ruler who stood above its internal hierarchies and the aliens or enemies who stood threateningly outside its inner domain of order. Just as a temporal ruler is legitimated by his relation to the founder in the remote past, the historical dogma of Scripture is referenced to the events that took place in "history."

Yet these sentiments cannot give rise to a clear political program. Boehme does not deny the reality of elemental objects, nor exclude the literal truth of the Gospels, nor eschew the need for a strong ruler who guards against anarchy and suppresses violence. The extremes are transformed, not abolished. The base ore is turned into gold by the power of the celestial tincture. The benighted heathen becomes a Christian, if not in name, at least in principle, by seeking God. In the end, even the unjust prince can be reborn spiritually, and therefore also politically, in order to rule with clemency and justice.

The Litterateur

The illuminist theory of Boehme's writings also ignores his numerous self-characterizations as a writer, his allusions to the variety of styles and to their appropriateness for the times (ep. 12.24), and his frequent references to the planning of projects. Whether one focuses on these references or on his assurances of his divine inspiration is determined in the final analysis by the beliefs of the interpreter; and if (logically) the two approaches need not be mutually exclusive, the choice between the two has certainly been operative in the kinds of interpretations which resulted. My argument here is that we can see more clearly the processes of Boehme's writing and of his readers' reading if we allow that his work emerged as an ongoing synthesis of initial inspiration and new external experience. Moreover, the notion that he wrote in thundershowers of passive intuition has led commentators to ignore the fact that his writings appear to be carved out of a material of inspiration and fitted together like blocks fulfilling a masterplan. The preface of *Aurora* promises a second and third book to supplement the understanding of the first one. The fourth book states at the outset that no one can understand this *Tractat* without having read "the third part of our writings" (III 8/1.2)—the third *part*! Looking back in 1622, Boehme calls *Aurora* "the first part of my writings." To the author, the whole of his illumination is a recognition and reading of "my own book, that I myself am"—of which *Aurora* was only "the first part." (ep. 34.9–10). The author's recommendations for the reading of his works indicate that he viewed the sequence as significant for the understanding of the whole. If scholars have largely ignored the question of the meaning of this sequence, if they have failed to inquire why Boehme was compelled to compose so many thick tomes, their failure was conditioned by the postulates of a *Zentralblick* or *mystische Schau*—the terms employed to uphold the claim that his works were written out as a kind of involuntary dictation.

His references to his writings leave little doubt about the order and priority. Disregarding the numerous shorter and occasional or doctrinal writings, seven lengthy treatises trace the evolution of his thought. These treatises average well over 300 pages per work in the edition of 1730: *Aurora* (403 pages), *The Three Principles of Divine Being* (482 pages), *The Threefold Life of Man* (344 pages) *Forty Questions on the Soul* (178 pages), *The Human Genesis of Christ* (221 pages), *Signatura Rerum* (244 pages), and *Mysterium Magnum* (896 pages). Of these only *Forty Questions on the Soul* derived from an external stimulus (the urging of Walter). These major works convey a progressive interpretation and refinement of Boehme's "illumination." Each of them confronts us with an expanding survey of his visionary imagination. Just as the first three works were said to be part of a larger plan, these seven writings also appear to outline a grand design.

The polemical writings on doctrine may be excluded from the masterplan since they were spun off by the debates which occurred after 1620. *The Election of Grace* and *The Testaments of Christ* (on the sacraments), the two long replies to Tilke, and the shorter ones to Kaym and to Stiefel and Meth, are important expressions of his views—but they do not alter or add to the overall configuration of his thinking in any significant way. The shorter pamphletlike works were also occasional in nature. He sent many of them off without even retaining a master copy for himself. The "little book on melancholy" mentioned to Lindner is of interest because it systematizes his understanding of the four "complexions"—but it adds nothing new to the developing system.

There is also the brief but significant *Six Theosophical Points* (82 pages), a work which the author regarded as exceptional in nature—and about which more will be said subsequently in this chapter. Finally, there are the late, eclectic works which will be discussed in the next chapter.

Boehme wrote seven extensive works in order to expound his ideas consecutively: seven books which he cited and defended as the body of his inspiration. Considered side by side, the seven appear to stand in a *rough* relation to the sevenfold pattern of divine qualities. The last work, *Mysterium Magnum*, resumes many themes of the first, and generally recapitulates everything that has gone before it. *Signatura Rerum* utilizes the major concept corresponding to the sixth spirit, "sound": The "signature" is introduced as an interpretation of the relationship of sound to understanding, and although the signature is in fact extended far beyond the audible, the concept is nevertheless epitomized by hearing and understanding.

The works written rapidly between the end of 1619 and the end of 1620 introduce concepts which interpret the third, fourth, and fifth qualities. The third quality, fire, gives rise to an, as yet, unredeemed life: the fiery life in nature of *The Three-fold Life of Man*. Out of this firelife, the light-flame shines forth, the light of the soul in its freedom: the stated subject of the fourth book, *Forty Questions on the Soul*. Christ, whose path the believer follows, is associated with the transition from fourth to fifth—from the forty days of temptation, to the pure and transcendent *Quinta Essentia* of the reborn soul[5]: the fifth book is *The Human Genesis of Christ*. The transition from fourth to fifth also epitomizes the rebirth and purification following the first human birth in nature. Respectively, the first, third, fourth, and fifth books have as their themes: (1) nature, viewed through its own qualities; (3) human life within nature; (4) the supernatural origin of the soul; and (5) the soul-redeeming human genesis of Christ. In Boehme's letter to Lindner, *Six Theosophic Points* is called "the sixth book or part" of these writings (ep. 12.71). However, this sixth book in order of emergence has an exceptional status with respect to the thematic order of seven.

Likewise, the second book, *The Three Principles of Divine Being*, does not fit readily into the pattern. In *Aurora*, the second quality was the sweet; however, in the sevenfold pattern after 1618 the second quality is the bitter: a mere precondition for life and redemption. The second book seems to miss a beat. In fact, it marks a shift in the master plan, resulting from the unforeseen way of the world. *Aurora*, we recall, knew nothing of the coming cataclysms, foreseeing instead the imminent advent of a restored Paradise. This Paradise was to have coincided with the return of an Adamic knowledge and wholeness, anticipated in *Aurora* and slated for elaboration in the second and third books (announced already in the preface of the first, optimistic one). But in 1618, the final realm of harmony and enlightenment was dislocated in time. The new *Bitter-Stachel* ("bitter-pang"), the thorns and brambles of a most bitter exile, lengthened and rerouted the journey to the final destination of the soul in the Fatherland of peace, enlightenment, and harmony. Henceforth, the angelic world, with its dawn glow and invitation to the heavenly nuptials, would lose its naive radiance. The path to the angelic reunion would lead through an unexpected vale of dark fire.

Though Boehme did not say so explicitly, he provided some indications that the tendency embodied in the sequence of his major works followed the tendency of his seven qualities: a tendency toward ever higher degrees of "life." In February 1624, he was persuaded by Siegmund von Schweinich and Abraham von Franckenberg to write out tables explaining the system of his principles. In his "table in seven spaces," summarizing the seven qualities, the seventh property is called: "the eternal Substantial Wisdom of God, as the *Mysterium Magnum*." The sixth property is identified with "understanding, as sound" (which is the introductory and guiding motive of *Signatura Rerum*). The fifth property is "the true spirit." The fourth is now "life itself," while the first three are "only properties for [or toward] life" (*nur Eigenschaften zum Leben*). Of the first three, the "third form of nature" is "fear" and "a cause of the fiery life." The second is "the ground of contrariety," in which hardness and movement are pitted against one another. Only the first quality of "magnetic desire" fails to match the overall tendency of the series of works. The "magnetic desire" is like the world-making contraction which was first introduced in the second book. The four elements are associated with the first four qualities. The seven properties progress from darkness toward light, from death toward life eternal, and from the first principle toward the second principle, while the third, the mixed world, stands in between. The "flash" (*Blitz*) separates the dark world from the light world. The fact that the flash occurs *after* the midpoint provides a clue concerning the location of *Six Theosophic Points* in Boehme's view of his oeuvre. (See: IX *Tabulae principiorum* 65–69/ 52–55, 46–49, 37, 33–36) The scheme of correspondence between the seven qualities and the seven major works is never perfect, indeed could not have been so, since it was developed by a writer who remained open to external influences while working out his initial inspiration.

The humble and prophetic God-taught shoemaker subordinated himself to the divine will—as a writer. The inspired author apparently sensed that the spirit within him had more to reveal before the completion of his cycle in *Mysterium Magnum*. More than once, he intimated that if only he were stronger, the spirit might reveal far more to him, including a prophetic knowledge in the strictest sense. This hope reinforced his unrelenting drive, as well as his caution about going public before the sequence was completed. But, as it came to completion, the writer showed no restraints against allowing his works to be printed. Despite his erstwhile pledge to silence, he was eager to see them circulate.

Like the associates of Scultetus, the circles around Boehme also possessed the prerequisites of a philosophical and literary discussion society. The fact that a number of the theosophical letters can stand as tractates in their own right tells us something about the role of this devoted readership in eliciting and conditioning his compositional efforts.

His expanding flock of adherents consisted of landowners and of professionals (lawyers and doctors). There were three customs officials: Paul Kaym, Caspar Lindner, and Boehme's most devoted friend, Christian Bernhard. In social composition as well, these circles were like those of the *Convivium Musicum*—except for the fact that here clergymen played only a very minor role. It is also conspicuous that there were no female recipients of the theosophic letters that have come down to us. This is rather surprising since women figured prominently in medieval mysticism and would do the same in the eighteenth-century Pietistic movement which owed much to Boehme's circles. Perhaps his letters were not addressed to women because fewer women were allowed to become literate in his time: a principal activity of the circle lay in reading the works of the master. In any event, all the evidence indicates that the man who called for devotion to the Noble Virgin of Divine Wisdom directed his message to a male following. Katharina Boehme was an energetic businesswoman, but if she actively participated in her husband's other involvements, no word of it has come down to us either in her husband's letters or in the brief report of Franckenberg—who merely testified to the harmony of their marriage.

The structure and composition of the writings are further evidence of their literary nature. Stylistic devices play an important role. Repeatedly, we have encountered the stylistic riddle: in the preface and the title of *Aurora*, in the opening chapters of *The Three Principles of Divine Being*, in the definition of the *Tinctur*. All of *Mysterium Magnum* is a typological decoding of Genesis in terms of the philosopher's own systems, with the Gospel of John superimposed upon the first account of the Creation.

The riddles are often rhetorical. The cognoscenti no doubt knew the real identity of the *Lapis Philosophorum* even before *The Threefold Life* gave the "secret" away: "the same stone is Christ" (III 136/7.30).

The art of Boehme's discourse lies in its ploys for turning the familiar into a mystery. The answer is always near at hand, like the cornerstone for Solomon's Temple, said to be banal, and yet most precious. The hydrolith or *Wasserstein der Weisen* is a base stone, found everywhere. Nonetheless, it has been sought by all the savants throughout the ages. The human being is the book of all secrets, the "great *arcanum*," Boehme writes to a new reader (ep. 20.3). Since the beginning of the world, philosophers have puzzled over the meaning of the "two realms" (2 *Reiche*). Now this ancient mystery is about to be solved (III *40 Questions* 17/1.41). God is "the most secret and the most revealed" of all things (III *40 Questions* 19/1.51).

Given the importance of Boehme's rhetorical mystifications, it is fair to conclude that the efforts to discover a full-blown philosophical system in his writing are misguided. By the same token, those who accuse him of ambiguity and inconsistency miss the point. To look for the integral system of his thought and then to fault him for his multiplication of terms and for the ambiguities of his thought is somewhat like compiling the motives found in the paintings of a Dürer or de Chirico, and then taking the painters to task for redundancies and inconsistencies. Many of his writings are only superficially structured as treatises. They are more like great series of thematic cycles and epicycles, dominated by briefer expositions, each of which treats its topic by bringing the literary equivalents of emblematic symbols to bear upon it. Each part contains, or attempts to contain, the whole. The thematic-symbolic circle with its impromptu cluster of images is therefore the integral unit of Boehme's writing. There are circles within circles in the revolving pattern. Literary techniques are responsible for the plastic effects of his language: qualities are hypostatized, and actions ascribed to the hypostatizations. Antithesis and oxymoron are utilized to convey the dynamic and movement of what is at rest in eternity. The riddle and the contradiction are carried over into his language and symbolism. The resultant indirect presentation overcomes the pictorialism of doctrines. The world has turned away from Christ and preoccupied itself with the "pictures and questions," out of which conflicts have arisen (ep. 39.8–9). Boehme's solution is to replace pictorial literalism with an expressive evocation of the objects of faith.

All things are manifestations of the single divine mystery. Boehme's terminology reflects this by creating numerous partial synonyms. It is not conceptual differentiation that necessitates a range of designations such as *Lapis philosophorum, die Tinctur, das Öl* ("elixir"), and *das Universal*. The first is vested with Biblical and legendary associations as something to be sought. *Die Tinctur* and *das Öl* are readily applicable in discussions of "natural objects," while *das Universal* bears the connotations of ubiquity and of that which is prior and opposed to *das Particular* (roughly equivalent to *Essentia*). Material creation occurs in processes involving "concentration": *Coagulation, Compaction,* or *Impression.* These processes engender the evil of *Selbheit* and *Ichheit.* Their self-centering force is the inverse of the self-knowledge which liberates from selfhood. Yet the same force of concentration also marks the beginning of all higher awareness.[6] Efforts have been made to compile the prolix terminology. The first was Boehme's own *Clavis, oder Erklärung der vornehmsten Puncten und Wörter* (IX). Registers were composed by his excellent early editor, Johann Georg Gichtel. They are included in volume eleven of the facsimile edition. On the assumption that all his terminology has a distinct role to play in an overall "system," Grunsky, followed by the even more serviceable work of Solms, analyzed and grouped Boehme's concepts.[7] However, valuable as their compilations may be, their compiled systems can no better summarize the meanings of Boehme's individual usages, than could the aforementioned hypothetical register of a painter's symbols impart the meaning of his images as they appear in the individual canvasses. In Boehme's prodigiously repetitious writings, nearly every context is distinct. Ambiguity is necessary in order to sustain the forcefulness of his evolving enigmas.

The cryptic beginning of *Forty Questions on the Soul* is far more engaging when read as a conventionalized puzzle rather than as a reported vision or philosophical exposition. In answer to the question, whence the soul has arisen, Boehme writes that the *Ungrund* looks into itself and finds itself: the *A* (for Alpha) is below and the *V* (for *Ungrund*) is above; and the *O* (for Omega) is an eye or mirror as yet without *Wesen* (III 11/1.16). To the modern secular reader, this and the ensuing presentation, which extends over sixty pages, may well resemble a series of abstract expressionistic themes, executed with words. His contemporaneous readers were no doubt sufficiently schooled in the code of types, antitypes, symbols, and allusions to grasp the philosophical and doctrinal message. Christ, as the Alpha and Omega, is coeternal with the *Ungrund* or Father, who finds Himself in the Son. The Alpha and Omega are the coordinates of eternity and time, infusing the beginning and ending of all things into their being in the world, with the omnipresence of the Son. Another question, "How the soul is nourished from the Word?" is a riddle keyed to Christ's real presence in the Eucharist. The reply is that the sacraments are not spirit without body, and that the external world is a likeness of the inner divine world (III 90/13.5–6).

Since the divine world is also a likeness of the inner human world, Boehme's trinitarian mysticism must evoke the life of the soul. In *The Threefold Life of Man*, the generative power of the Father is compared to the human mind (*Gemüthe*), which is also a single desiring will that generates countless wills or impulses within itself (III 72/4.64–65). In *Forty Questions*, a Baroque Trinity is fashioned from the three aspects of will:

> Thus... there is in God an Eternal Will, which He Himself is, [a Will] to give birth to His Son or Heart; and the same Will makes the impulse or issuance out of the Will of the Heart, which is a Spirit; so that eternity stands in three eternal figures, which are called persons, as we have explained quite clearly in the third book.... (III 9/1.5)

This voluntaristic Trinity contorts the spatial references, "*in... ist... aus*," to convey the torment of an eternally self-creating will. Analogous to a medieval plague crucifix (in which the normally linear figure of the cross curls upward, as if in pain and entreaty), the expressive artistry of this Trinity of Will twists triunity out of identity and difference. Like the "knotty Trinity" in Donne's *Divine Meditations*, Boehme's "three eternal figures" conjoin the human with the divine. For the reader who is able to empathize with what is expressed by the verbal figure, something like a phenomenology of the inner life as freedom may be evoked: Being, as willing, is a dialectic of the focusing power of resolve, of the conceived focus of resolve, and of the expression of the resolve which is born from this same self-concentration.

If one reads *Forty Questions on the Soul* as an attempted systematic exposé of philosophical, theological, and psychological themes, the work appears as a chaotic failure. One is left with the impression that its author and his readers were escaping into a kind of vague "inner emigration" to ignore and suppress the world around them. But one can also consider the book as a series of discrete thematic expositions. These illuminations focus the social, psychological, and historical experiences of the author and his readers. His contemporaries could scarcely have failed to notice the topical references. Confronted with the question, what the soul does, and whether it looks forward to the Day of Judgment, after departing this life, readers must have been reminded first of personal reflections and doubts concerning their own justification. Their ardent curiosity aroused, they encountered a succession of conceits: The son of a family sets off for foreign parts in pursuit of a craft and honor. All the while, he is eager to return to the bosom of his family, bringing with him the art and knowledge acquired while a journeyman. Thus too, the soul longs for the Final Day when, returning to its true Fatherland, the apprenticeship of its knowledge gained will have been completed. Further emblematic images are brought to bear. A condemned soul is led to the scaffold; and some "highly damned souls" who flaunt the mentality of the *Landsknechte* storm God's fortress, forfeiting their eternal life in the process (III 114–18/22.2, 17, 21). The journey into the beyond is thus also a panorama of the hopes, vagaries, and perils of the here and now.

In *The Human Genesis of Christ*, "reason" inquires why God allows so much oppression and exploitation in this world—why everyone oppresses everyone else, so that even he who has much only lusts after more wealth. The answer holds that there is an agency of class conflict in the *Centrum Naturae*, an *acquisitive* will to create where there is nothing. One force, *Herbigkeit*, greedily appropriates unto itself, while the second force, the bitter, becomes the oppressed "worker" of the first: "he is the worker, which means the one who is lower..." (IV 170/II.8. 9ff.). Their dialectical conflict pits the acquisitive and exploitive spirit against the angry and rebellious spirit. The servant "storms the house of the master." The incensed master is then driven on to greater and greater excesses. Going round and round with each other, their "wheel" of greed and class hatred generates a spiraling enmity, resulting in conflicts, wars, destruction of countries and cities, and so on. The mystical symbol of the wheel spinning with force and counterforce is thus adapted in order to express the notion that history is generated by class conflict, and conflict in turn by the tyrannical power of nature. The answer to the question posed by reason is neither irrational nor incognizant of the harsh realities and material determinants of historical events. More often than not, Boehme's diatribes against what he calls "reason" are directed against the content of certain deliberations, not against rationality itself.

Boehme's overall designs leave us with the question which was with us from the very beginning: how could a self-educated shoemaker have been inspired to conceive such a grandiose project? The aura of pansophic Prague, with its grand cosmographic undertakings in the arts and the sciences, was undoubtedly one source of stimulation. But a more time-honored well-spring may have stemmed from the popular sources of his Spiritualism: from a *Volksfrömmigkeit* which antedated the Reformation. Late medieval "folk piety" had luxuriated in cults of the saints and the Holy Family, in all manner of fanciful *sacramentalia*, spun around the seven sacraments, the seven deadly sins—around the sevenfoldness of all things good and evil. As Huizinga has shown, such devices had served as popularly accessible creative expressions of faith. One might call them "proto-Protestant," in the *limited* sense that they were instituted from below, and were frequently discouraged by the church authorities and mainstream theologians.

The habits of medieval folk piety can hardly have vanished into thin air at the first light of a Reformation with which they shared their popular orientation. One finds the same patterns of thought transformed and spiritualized in populistic reformers of the first hour: in Thomas Müntzer who, in touch with chiliastic peasants, wrote of the seven stages of the baptism of the spirit—based on the references to water in the first six chapters of John; or in the peasant and preacher Georg Haug, who construed the sevenfold gift of the spirit in Isaiah as seven successive stages of the ascending spirit on its path to perfection.[8]

We recall that in Upper Lusatia the implementation of the Protestant reforms occurred haltingly, with setbacks, and without the monitoring supervision of a local church consistory. Under these circumstances, the old habits of devotion from the culture of "works righteousness" could persist long enough to be spiritualized by the new Protestant culture of individual faith and the Book—long enough even to be reintegrated with the renewed speculation on nature. In Boehme's mysticism, the cult of the Virgin Mary is superseded by the more intellectual devotion to Sophia. The expectations of Purgatory are replaced by the vision of the cleansing fire-world in eternal nature and historical time. The topological pilgrimage undertaken by the penitent is overshadowed by the internal odyssey and metamorphosis of the self-tranforming spirit. The stubborn pattern of the seven sacraments is echoed by Boehme's dynamic seven phases of the ubiquitous spirit-life.

The claim has been made (most recently by David Walsh[9]) that Boehme's mysticism is an important link between medieval and Renaissance thought, on the one hand, and the modern philosophies of German Idealism and Existentialism, on the other. This claim appears more creditable when one puts aside the postulate of the visionary *Zentralblick* in order to place Boehme's work in its own setting. His work stands at the confluence of two transitions: (1) the reabsorption of philosophical speculation and folk "enthusiasm" into a Lutheran religiosity which for a time suppressed their impulses; and (2) the shift of German aspirations from the medieval Empire to the smaller territorial dominion—moreover: to an inner domain, ruled by a divided and tormented Will. Because of these transitional aspects in Boehme's oeuvre, it appears as a kind of missing link between premodern philosophical currents and the modern philosophies of German Idealism and Existentialism. However, it should be borne in mind that these resonances arise because of the associative and nonrigorous methods of Boehme's thought—not out of a systematic integration of ideas.

The modern reader who is unfamiliar with esoteric lore and

unappreciative of emblematic and typological modes of presentation is likely to find Boehme's treatises virtually unreadable. The vast matrix of allusions has long since disintegrated. Its components, which once reflected debates in science, politics, and theology, have survived only as objects of a faddish obscurantism. In his time, the arcane and obscure terms and queries were shared with artists and scientific researchers. This applies not only to the sun, stars, and planets, to the power of the magnet and to the design of the cosmos, but also to numerous minor details which now appear to be exclusively mystical: to his discussion of the rainbow or to his distinction between elemental fire and nonelemental light.[10] If our science and mathematics is someday discredited by more advanced theories, so that our own knowledge likewise falls into oblivion, readers in some future century will regard the allusions of a Thomas Mann or a Hermann Broch as hardly less bizarre and mystical than the references of the Baroque author Boehme.

Six Theosophic Points

By August 1621, the increasingly prolific Boehme was able to mention two important additions to the growing list of his writings: *Six Theosophic Points* and *Signatura Rerum*. The first work is dated 1620. Its tone echoes his mood of anarchic serenity during the period of collapse and before the normalization of the new order. In *Six Theosophic Points*, the law of freedom has become the sovereign rule of life. The transformation of darkness into light is the only law ruling over human nature:

> Otherwise man has no law—except for not becoming inflamed in the quality of the dark world, and acting in accordance with this quality—otherwise he is free in everything. Whatever he does in gentleness and love—he is free in this. It is his own being; and no one's name or opinion has any bearing on it. (VI 70/9.22)

This is radical evangelical freedom, with a visionary tone which echoes the historical "zero hour" and new beginning.

A new tone of gnostic secrecy is also evident in the preface of *Six Theosophic Points*: "We have written this work not for the unreasonable animals which have an exterior human form, yet are evil and wild animals in the [internal] image and in spirit... but rather for the human image that blossoms from the animal form into a human image that belongs in God's realm..." (VI 1). The "human image," in reference to Boehme's readership, means the "children of the secret," the hidden congregation that knows its own identity and waits for the propitious moment to step into the open. The human beings differ from the fierce beasts by virtue of a blossoming inner *Bildniß* or image: the flower of a transforming imagination through which the human creature recreates itself in the likeness of God.

The letter to Lindner likewise stresses the secret aspect of *Six Theosophic Points* (ep. 12.71). The sixth book is the deepest of all. It is a "secret" which has been "childishly brought to light," and it is a key to alpha and omega. Despite the esoteric tone, the further themes summarized for Lindner are familiar: "how the three principles give birth to themselves in one another and get along with one another, so that in eternity there is no conflict, and each rests within itself; from what conflict and disunity arise; from what good and evil arise: entirely derived from the *Ungrund*, from nothing into something, as into the *Grund* of nature" (ep. 12.71).

What is the "secret, childishly brought to light," in *Six Theosophic Points*? One possibility is that the theosophist had decisively shifted his thinking to a religion of introspection, a philosophical religion generalized beyond Christianity. In *Six Theosophic Points*, the historical Christ is almost completely absent. The light world is balanced, almost motionlessly, against the dark-world. During the early 1620s, Boehme began to write about religion in more and more simplified terms: "Our entire religion is only a children's path, so that we can leave all our knowing, wanting, running, and disputing behind, and resolve how to enter upon the path that leads back to our lost Fatherland... to our mother, who gave birth to us in the beginning" (ep. 46.53). Although Boehme retained his belief in eternal life as punishment or reward, he understood it in terms of the transcendent dimensions of this life. He was aware of the connection between the punishments of God's "anger" and the punitive, vengeful reactions of the warring authorities in the world around him, and aware that the belief in a life after this life reassured the fierce "beasts" that they could rage with impunity. His rejection of the principle of "God's anger" led him to conceive a Spiritualistic autonomy of internal rewards or punishments. Everyone bears heaven and hell within: whichever of the two is ignited within, the same one burns in the soul (IV 72/9.34).

Here again we are confronted with the problem of Boehme's understanding of Christ. The reader becomes increasingly aware of the obvious paradoxes in the concepts of Christ. Orthodox in his insistence on the miracle of Christ's human birth, Boehme ardently held forth against Weigel and Schwenckfeld for denying that Mary had been wholly human, thereby impugning the dual natures of Christ as man and God.[11] He pontificated that the human Jesus had been constituted by divine and human *Essentien*. But alongside this Christological orthodoxy, we encounter his persistent deemphasis of the historical person of the Savior. In *Aurora*, there are few specific references to Christ. Although the second book devotes more attention to the historical Christ, many of the subsequent treatises, including *The Human Genesis of Christ*, contain surprisingly few references to the life, deeds, and death of the Savior here below. On the one hand, the author repeatedly proclaims that he has never sought anything other than refuge in the heart of Jesus. On the other hand, he makes use of a phrase which exudes contempt for the pious contemplators of the Gospel Jesus: "titillating oneself with the sufferings of Christ" (*sich mit Christi Leiden kitzeln*). This is what the false Christians are said to engage in when they presume that they have been saved because Jesus died for their sins. As we have seen, *The Human Genesis of Christ* allows the Virgin of Divine Wisdom to overshadow the historical person of the Savior. She embodies the magic process by which the principle of darkness is transformed into light. The flash of terror or *Schrack* separates the world into two realms, the realm of light and joy and the realm of death and darkness (IV 172/2.8.12). The same images of the dark-world and the light-world are prominent in *Six Theosophic Points*. The division between the artistic writings and the polemical tracts can be illustrated by comparing *Six Theosophic Points* with the treatise *On the Election of Grace*. The latter was promoted by Boehme as the conclusive word on predestination. Although the book summarizes mystical themes beginning with *Aurora*, the reader is left with no doubts that the overriding purpose is to address a doctrinal question. Indeed, the subordination to the doctrinal issue is instructive because this correlates Boehme's esoteric symbolism with the issue of widespread interest. The book begins with the question of election and ends with a lengthy exegesis of scriptural passages pertaining to providence and predestination. Everything in this book of 224 pages argues its announced thesis. By contrast, *Six Theosophic Points* must be approached through the codified pattern of Boehme's symbolism.

With reference to the sevenfold pattern of Boehme's works, the brief and compact *Six Theosophic Points* equates to the flash that bifurcates the seven. The transforming *Schrack* is the shock of human self-recognition. It is an acknowledgment of the tragic ground of life. As reflection, the *Schrack* stands for the Wisdom of Sophia. As a transforming process, it symbolizes redemption through Christ. In the codified pattern of Boehme's mysticism, Christ therefore retains an unspoken, sublimated centrality.

The apparent shift away from Christ is thus a matter of perspective. *Six Theosophic Points* contains only brief allusions to the Passion and Resurrection; however, these establish that the pattern of the two worlds is constituted by life eternally resurrected from death (IV 15/73). The fact that Christ is scarcely mentioned by name cannot be taken as an indication of a shift of emphasis. In *Aurora*, Christ was rarely mentioned, but His name was, in a manner of speaking, written in the stars. In *Six Theosophic Points*, the role of the Redeemer is engraved in the structure of Boehme's imagery. As usual, sacramental doctrine is not neglected. The book reservedly addresses the issue of infant baptism, rationalizing it even in the process of justifying it (*cf.* IV 59–62/4–22).

In terminology and structure, *Six Theosophic Points* is more austere and more cryptic than any other work. The array of terms has been simplified. Here too, the underlying rhetorical conceit is that of a sophisticated riddle. The reader is forced to draw the balance between the two worlds by coming to terms with the enigma of life. Life is the central category of *Six Theosophic Points*. "And man need not research any further, for he is himself the being of all beings..." (IV 70/9.21). "Thus man is in person... the great mystery in the three worlds..." (IV 55/7.30). Human life unfolds between the charged polarities of anger and wisdom, just as the soul develops between the poles of desirous self-will and reflection.

The exposition itself is dualistic, as if two very distinct thematic developments were occurring simultaneously: a development as will and as reflection. This is evident in the first exposition of *Six Theosophic Points*. The first sentence encapsulates much of Boehme's earlier thought: "We see and find that each life is essential; and, furthermore, that it stands within the will, for the will is the driving (*Treiben*) of the essences." (IV 4/1.1) *Aurora* began by defining quality as the driving or driven aspect of things. The term *Essentia* correlates with *Qualität*. In *Six Theosophic Points*, life is animated by its drive toward particularity; this driving of the essences is the living force itself. Life is the "son" of the essences; the will is their "father" (IV 4/1.6). The peculiarly visionary aspects of the exposition combine rarified abstraction with vivid expressiveness, to paint a vital experience conceived *sub specie aeternitatis*.

There is a hidden fire in the will, Boehme writes. The will is intent upon awakening and igniting this fire (IV 4/1.2); for the will which has not yet awakened the fiery essences is without capacity, mute, lifeless, without feeling, without awareness or immanent presence (*Wesenheit innen*). Prior to the emergence of life, the will exists in a preconscious, prevital state. Yet the preconscious will contains within it the ground of the conscious life. The will as *Ungrund* is like a nothingness (IV 4/1.7); yet its nothingness prefigures the vital aspects of consciousness and particularity. The prefiguration of the *Ungrund* is captured in its mirroring aspect which can be conceived as a disembodied power of imagination that looks into itself and forms everything out of nothing in accordance with its innate, ideal forms. The mirror that contains everything as nothing gives rise to potentiality as a prefigurative seeing of that which is not yet. The inturned mirror or "eye of eternity" creates a ground within itself, a will in the dual sense of a determined resolve and a determinate entity (IV 5/1.12). The dark fire-world arises out of the *Centrum Naturae* in the *Ungrund* of the Father, which lies beyond the terror of the birth of life, in the region which cannot be researched further (IV 23/2.33). The second world is the light-world which exists in freedom. The light proceeds from the dark fire-world but is not touched by its fire; accordingly, it is the intermediate or central world: *die Mittel-Welt* (IV 23/2.34). The third world is the external one, where human beings dwell in their external bodies (IV 23/2.37). The three worlds are not located and separated from one another by boundaries. They are the three moments in a process of self-revelation of the divine will, a process by which the volitional *Nihil* makes itself into something (IV 45/6.7).

Because the three worlds are inextricably bound together, there is no redemption without terror and tragedy. Not only is grim death a root of life, there would be no joy if not for woe (IV 15/1.69). The First Will is the Father, the Second Will is the Son: their relationship is not without tragedy. Life only emerges out of death for the purpose of revelation. The external principle of nature is caught up in a perpetual war and strife. What the light of the sun builds is shattered by the cold and consumed by the fires of corruption (IV 27/2.51). The life of nature and the warfare which rages in the human domain are one. Even the forms of nature accuse each other of evil and engage in mutual destruction (IV 66/9.2). The dark-world is like the tyranny of this world: the more evil and vicious a creature, the greater is its power (IV 69/9.15).

Yet the dark-world is *necessary* for the divine revelation. It is necessary, not as a contrast, but as a ground or source; for life is a symbiosis of darkness and light:

> For all life is steeped in poison (*stehet in Gift*), and the light alone withstands the poison, and yet is also a cause that the poison lives and does not languish. Therefore, we can recognize that the life of darkness is but a languished poison, like a dying torment

(*Qual*). And yet there is no dying there; for the light-world steps toward the mirror of darkness, from which the darkness stands eternally in terror (*im Schracke*). (IV 67/9.9–10)

This convolution of mirroring surfaces and mirrored depths can be interpreted in the following manner: The "mirror of darkness" *is* the light-world, the serenely redeemed world. The darkness in this world is quickened by and drawn toward the light; but the darkness also stands in eternal terror of light, recoiling from it as an opposite. The light in this world steps toward "the mirror of darkness," thereby recognizing its own shadowy being, discovering that its existence is blindness, terror, anger, and death. Through self-knowledge, the light is mortified and awakened to an eternal world which is free of darkness. The light thus both redeems and torments. The unredeemable powers of darkness covet the good in vain. The light prevents the poison of life from becoming wholly vitiated.

It is significant that Boehme cited much the same idea as is expressed in the above passage when recounting the sense of *Six Theosophic Points* in his first *Apology to Tilke* (V 52/322). This indicates that the above passage is close to the thematic center of Boehme's most cryptically fascinating book. Its symbolism of darkness and light, epitomizing the *Schrack* of Christ and Sophia, unites Boehme's doctrinal interests with the hopes and anxieties of his cultural and existential experience. At the center of his cycle of works stands the mystery of good and evil. There is no resurrection without tragedy. The light-world and the dark-world are two sides of the same coin. They are two eternal dimensions of the one perishable world: "What gives joy in the light, gives mourning in the darkness" (IV 67/9.12).

The "poison" of life is the encompassing world of nature, a nature that includes the societal reign of terror. Just as this world came into being through a darkening or thickening of the primal matrix, mortal life arises spontaneously out of "dead" matter. Frogs, vermin, and maggots arise directly from the matrix of life. By the same token, the body's death is not the absolute cessation of existence. Death is a withdrawal of light and a submersion in the dark-world, not nonexistence but another kind of existence:

> Superficial reasoning imagines when it sees with the external eye: this is good; beyond this, there can be no seeing.... when the external mirror shatters, what should [the soul] see with?... Therefore it often happens that when the poor, imprisoned soul perceives the inner root, and thinks about what will happen when the external mirror shatters,... it is horrified, and the body

is plunged into fear and doubt. For it can see no place where its eternal peace might exist. Instead, it discovers in itself nothing but unrest and darkness, and [it discovers that it] has the external mirror only on loan. (IV 52/7.14–16)

Inner agitation and death are contiguous with the dark-world. To a remarkable degree, the "mystical light" is still conceived by invoking the common "darkness" which the light surmounts and sublimates. Darkness is necessary for the process of revelation. The sources of quality and consciousness lie in the dark-world:

> For Hell has in darkness the greatest constellation of the grave force; in them [i.e., in the forces of hell which are death, enmity, sadness, sin, and the "hellish worms"], all is audible as a great resounding. What rings in the light, knocks in the darkness.... The bell receives a blow, as a [mute] knock; and from the hard knock, the sound issues forth. (IV 29/3.7)

It appears as if this world originated in evil:

> For this world stands on the ground of the dark-world; the dark-world gives this world essence, will, and property; and if the good had not also been enclosed in it, there would be no other action or will in this world than that which is in the dark-world. (IV 69/9.17)

But the triunity of distinct, interpenetrating principles enables Boehme to skirt these Manichean implications and avoid identifying the world of the Divine Father with a hellish state of things: "Although the fire of God is the root, it does not belong to the realm of God" (IV 44/5.18). This would be an ineffective sort of special pleading if not for the notion of God's adcrescence toward the light of an indwelling Heart and Son. Evil is the type of the good that has been stunted and perverted in its growth.

Because of this underlying developmental notion, Boehme's mystical speculation seems to anticipate psychoanalysis. The dark-world and the light-world can be compared to the *id* and the *ego*. These and other parallels have attracted scholarly comparisons with Freudian psychoanalysis.[12] The similarities are discernible in all of Boehme's works, but are particularly obvious where the religious context recedes behind the central categories of life and awareness.

Boehme was led by his own premises to draw the conclusions which resemble those of psychoanalysis. In his mystical concept of the deity, the prototype of the family and its inner relations predominates over other prototypes (such as that of the King of Heaven). If eternity is construed in the manner of time, then we are the distant offspring of a first Father. Since time loses its sequential meaning in eternity, the divine family relations are wholly immanent in each moment, place, and person. Morever, since nothing arises out of nothing, consciousness rises out of its own dark ground. Although what grows out of this dark ground is not causally determined by the darkness, the light-world is a positive mirror image, a sublimation, of the forces operating in darkness. (The term itself stems from the symbolic processes of alchemy.) Consequently, Boehme's mysticism universalizes these "family" relations. It stresses the preconscious origins of conscious life and the growth or development toward a latent or inherent end. Growth and likeness, will and reflection, are metaphysical polarities of human existence. Self-knowledge is the criterion that divides the two societal worlds of redeemed and unredeemed souls.

Six Theosophic Points evokes a sharp division between the "children of light" and the "children of this world." Though the latter are compelled to persecute the former, both will continue to exist side by side (IV 32/3.20). This theme of persecution connects the gnostic dualism of Boehme's secretive work to the situation of the author whose role in the world was as uncertain as the conditions of his times.

The Politics of Piety

Six Theosophic Points is the work of a man who sees himself as misunderstood, isolated, and vulnerable despite his scattered adherents. He is threatened by "God's anger," by punishment for his views, and by the equally grave peril of plunging into the "maw" of wrath to be swallowed up within the "beast" of raging violence. In *The Three Principles of Divine Being*, Boehme wrote of the metamorphosizing power of anger:

> Take as an example man, when he is incensed, [consider] how his spirit contracts, so that he trembles bitterly, and if there is not soon a resisting and extinguishing, the fire of anger is ignited within him, so that he burns in wrath: [so that] there arises soon thereafter in his spirit and mind a substance or a whole being to take revenge. (II 11/1.9)

Franckenberg was at pains to portray his friend as a gentle and lovable soul. However, two anecdotes of the biographer seem to corroborate the wrathful side of Boehme's personality. On one occasion, apparently after he had already become famous, the author received an unannounced visit from a small man of curious appearance who came bearing a strange request. The visitor had heard that Boehme possessed a "personal spirit," *ein Familiar-Geist*—a sort of genie. The small man of curious appearance wanted to buy it or rent its services. The author made several attempts to persuade the visitor of his error, advising him that he should pray to the Holy Spirit for illumination. But the man was not to be dissuaded, and instead began to conjure with magic formulas. At length, writes Franckenberg, "J. B." lost his temper and seized the visitor by the hand. Tempted to curse the man's "perverted soul," he commanded him to desist from his "simony and devilry." Thoroughly terrifying his uninvited guest, Boehme ordered him to be gone at once (X 16–17). Even if witchcraft persecutions did not occur in Görlitz, the terrors and unshakable superstitions which led to them were clearly not unknown. And as to the gentle mystic, the threshhold between mildness and transforming anger was narrow indeed.

The second anecdote illustrates what must have been the general vulnerability of a cobbler who professed an unheard of calling and associated with men of a higher station. Boehme was invited to the estate of David von Schweinich, a sympathizing noble. A village boy was supposed to meet the visitor and lead him up to the manor house. However, as Franckenberg recounts, Schweinich's doctor and brother-in-law (who happened to be present with his own wife and children) despised the renowned former shoemaker. The doctor therefore paid the village boy to push the arriving visitor into a mud puddle. The boy was so conscientious in fulfilling his contract that the weary wayfarer fell, cut his head on a stone, and began to bleed profusely. Remorseful, the boy ran and confessed his deed; and the guest was brought to the manor house. Soaked and bloody, he was bandaged and given a change of clothing. Having recovered sufficiently, Boehme went into the manorial room in order to greet his host and his host's family, including the brother-in-law and his family. Offering everyone his hand, the shoemaker also extended greetings to the Schweinich children who were lined up for his inspection. Coming to one of the Schweinich daughters, he paused and declared her to be the most pious of all who were present in the room. Laying his hand upon her head, Boehme pronounced a special blessing upon her (a blessing which, as we have seen, recalled the providential benediction he had received in his own youth).

This seemingly harmless gesture, coupled doubtlessly with a striking air of humble authority, so enraged the hostile brother-in-law that he began to taunt Boehme as a prophet, daring him to prophesize something for the assembled company. At first, "the good Boehme" protested vigorously that he neither had, nor professed to have, any sort of prophetic gifts. But the malicious relative was not appeased, not by the disavowals of the humble visitor, and not even by the entreaties of the lord of the manor. At length, "the good Boehme" lost his temper and told the whole gathering what "a godless, noxious, and frivolous life" the bullying nobleman had led. The upstart burgher held forth about his tormentor's life, about "how things had gone so far, and how they would continue to go, which"—as Franckenberg insinuates, ambiguously—"all truly came to pass" (X 18–19). Only the active physical intervention of Schweinich saved his expatiating guest from a violent retaliatory assault. The unlucky visitor was packed off for the sake of his own safety to spend the night at the village parsonage. The following morning, he was cautiously transported back to Görlitz.

One can safely assume that in his dealings with the gentry Boehme contended with animosities which were not just personal or religious in nature. The defeat of the Confederation caused new conflicts of interest between Silesians and Lusatians and between the cities and those nobles who had most vigorously supported the Confederation, and were now forced by Saxony at the behest of the emperor to pay a higher price for their disloyalty.[13] As early as June 1621, in a letter to his good friend Christian Bernhard, Boehme had been able to state the claim that his writings were known "to nearly all of Silesia, as well as to many places in Saxony and Meissen" (ep. 60). If this was an exaggeration, it nevertheless suggests the momentum and excitement of his success. Around the same time, he initiated his close association with the von Schweinich brothers, Hans Sigismund and David, of Silesia. A year later, we find the shoemaker already on familiar terms with the important East Lusatian nobleman, Rudolf von Gersdorf. One letter suggests that Boehme was coordinating the dissemination of his doctrinal propaganda with his noble patrons (ep. 32). In preaching conciliation, he was prophesizing against the continued armed pursuit of the cause of the Confederation: a partisan stand most disagreeable to those who were unable to countenance defeat.

7 The Will to Revelation

Waiting Out the Storm

We have arrived at the author in his last years, the figure whom Franckenberg knew well, describing him as a man prematurely aged, yet vital and charismatic in his mid-40s. Since no portrait of Boehme was drawn from life, this verbal description is the most authentic representation of his appearance that we have:

> His ... external bodily form was wizened (*versunken*), and of a simple appearance (*von schlechtem Ansehen*), small of stature, with a low forehead, high temples, slightly bent nose, gray and almost sky-blue sparkling eyes, moreover like windows in Salomon's temple, short thin beard, small voice, yet graceful of speech (*holdseliger Rede*), mannerly in his gestures (*züchtig in Gebärden*), modest in his words, humble in his demeanor, patient in suffering, gentle of heart. (X 20–21)

We know from Franckenberg's previously cited anecdotes with what powers of self-mastery the humility, gentleness, and equanimity were maintained. Boehme's type is that of the stoic sage rather than that of the miracle-working saint.

The biographer was not yet twenty when he met the Lusatian mystic during the dispute with Tilke and Staritius. Boehme's letter to Franckenberg of February 1623, recalls the watershed Silesian dispute and marks the beginning of the closer association of the two men. The postscript of the letter discussed in chapter five concluded with the advice:

> Whoever remains thus in his own will, like a child in its mother's womb, and lets himself be led and guided by his indwelling ground (*seinen inwendigen Grund*), from which the human being has sprouted, is the noblest and richest man on earth. (ep. 41.*P.S.*13)

Moreover: the sword and the six winds which rule the earth will pass by and give way to the seventh wind; a new fire will be revealed, a great light will shine forth. A font of grace will flow with pure waters to refresh the wretched (ep. 41.14–15).

These are the words of the acknowledged prophet, the man convinced that the forces of the Antichrist will exhaust themselves or destroy one another, and that the "storm" is the necessary prelude to the final calm which will ensue. The prophet of coming times tells his followers what they already know or want to believe. The prophet rejects the "logic" which posits necessary opposites and oppositions in the sphere of faith. All contrarities will be resolved prior to the end of time (ep. 41.8–9).

Translated into political terms, this meant that if one remained calm the storm would eventually pass and the antagonistic differences of doctrine would no longer be seen as reasons for quarrels and wars. There was common sense and farsightedness in this view. But from the vantage of the biographer who survived his friend by three decades, the hopes aroused by such prophecies were not slated for fulfillment.

In the same month, February 1623, the Lusatian prophet wrote to another Silesian noble and medical doctor—Gottfried Freudenhammer von Freudenheim. Deliverance is possible, Boehme speculates, but if mankind remains godless, a hard rain and hail will drown many thousands of souls. One broom will sweep up after another in Babylon, though no one can say just when. And, furthermore, it is no less certain that a lily will blossom from noon toward midnight, and that a light will shine for all peoples (ep. 42.39–49). The strategy is one of principled hope tempered by caution, not of principled quietism or of prophetic certainty. To intervene in Babel's conflagration, he advises Freudenhammer, would only shore up the flames: better to wait out the storm.

The former shoemaker of Görlitz acted as the spiritual counsellor of his followers. He did not condemn the rival teachings of Weigel or Schwenckfeld (though he disagreed with their alleged denial of Christ's humanity). Instead, he believed that, "the present time is in need of another doctor" (ep. 12.52, 54, 59).

A Silesian noble, von Schellendorf, inquires concerning his deceased wife's grave effigy: tears have appeared in the stony eyes. He would know the agency of this wondrous happening. Disavowing any certain knowledge in such matters, the man of Görlitz replies that, though the effigy is lifeless, still all things are permeated by the sidereal spirit and by the three alchemistic principles; therefore these could have been the medium of transmission between the grief and concern in the soul of the deceased woman and the stony eyes of her grave effigy (ep. 22). (Enthralled, Franckenberg attached a notation to the letter, that Boehme only later learned of the woes of Schellendorf's poor spouse who had lost two sons in the Turkish wars.)

Through contacts of this sort the initially small circle of sympathizers widened further. In May 1623, Boehme wrote to his chief patron, Ender: the book on the sacraments (*Von Christi Testamenta*) is finished. He conveys to Ender the greetings of the nobleman, Fürstenau, who has recently undergone a dramatic spiritual transformation (and now intends to employ his village pastor for copying Boehme's writings!). Schweinich, the man with the obstreperous brother-in-law, has also undergone a spiritual transformation witnessed by Boehme (ep. 44). A letter of the same period tells of this religious experience: Schweinich had realized that before God he was as nothing, like excrement. For hours during his experience, Schweinich had humbled himself with his unworthiness, repeating the words: *GOtt, Koth!* ("God/dirt!") (ep. 45.4). But there was also a pragmatic consequence of this conversion: Schweinich recognized that all *Zank*, all quarreling and fighting, is unworthy. In the same passage of his letter, Boehme reports that his writings are now sought after by high "potentates," even by certain "scholars" with whom he now enjoys much *Conversation* (ep. 45.7–8). In his letter of May 1623, to Ender, Boehme discusses plans to publish part of his treatise on the sacraments: a shortened version is to be edited for those who are "simple"—while those whose understanding is higher should read the full handwritten version (ep. 44). The treatise on the sacraments ends by characterizing the Lutheran and Calvinist doctrines of the Eucharist, condemning both for their literalism and appealing to put an end to all quarrels over doctrine, and an end to all religious warfare (VI *Von Christi Testamenta* 111–115/ 5.7–16). Another letter of the year 1623 writes: *Es ist kein wahrer Verstand in keiner Partey*: "no party is truly reasonable" (ep. 46.48).

Signatura Rerum

Signatura Rerum, the most famous and characteristic title after *Aurora*, is mentioned in the letter of August 1621, to Caspar Lindner (ep. 12.73). A letter to von Schellendorf of New Year's Day 1622, cites the authority of *dem Buche "de Signatura Rerum"* (ep. 22.16). A letter to Christian Bernhard of November 1622, calls the book an "excellent, high work of forty-one [quarto] sheets," mentioning its length for the first time. At this point, the work is already being copied and circulated (ep. 32.3).

Despite the fame of its title, *Signatura Rerum* is said to be the least accessible to modern readers of all Boehme's writings. This is due less to the innovations of the book. For the most part, it recapitulates and reworks the mix of alchemy, astrology, and Christology present from the very beginning in his writing. *Signatura Rerum* polishes and systematizes the time-honored alchemical allegorization of the spiritual. The innovations are relative to the pattern of Boehme's oeuvre, which moves from regarding Creation, to analyzing the subjective freedom of Creator and creature, to depicting the world as expression: that is, as the meaningful "utterance" of the eternal Word, revealed both in Genesis and in the Book of Nature. Boehme's pattern of speculation thus comes full circle. The incarnate utterance is deciphered in the created world of nature. The motives of the first book are resumed in the last two.

Signatura Rerum must be read in reference to the persistent pattern of themes in his writings. Of the seven qualities, the "signature" corresponds to number six: the mercurial spirit of "sound" and "music." The sixth spirit stands for the penetrating insight of the Holy Spirit, for the moment of exaltation which follows rebirth, and for the source of a receptive understanding which not only registers the sounds spoken by others, but intuits their meaning as well. The signature represents the hope that a new community will arise as the basis of a stable order. The concept of the signature enabled Boehme to postulate a principle of understanding which should restore the rent fabric of society. The signature is the key to the spirit of Scripture, and it is the proof that all human beings are rooted in the same divine One: "Therein we recognize that all human quality comes from One, that they [all] have only a single root and mother, otherwise a human being could not understand another in the sound [*im Hall*]" (I 4/1.3). The signature, like the nature language, proves the universal kinship of all humankind.

Signatura Rerum attempts to restore a sense of order to the human world by uncovering the concealed design of the divine and natural worlds. The clear premise of this attempt is the belief that a kind of knowledge which is more fundamental and inclusive than all the doctrinal positions can reconcile and harmonize the superficial oppositions which rend the body of Christendom. In his *Harmonies of the World*, Kepler expressed a remarkably similar faith in his invocation to "the Father of Intellects," summoning all who are enlightened to respect "the sanctity of life":

> that we should keep at a distance all the discords of enmity, all contentions, rivalries, anger, quarrels, dissensions, sects, envy,

provocations, and irritations arising through mocking speech and the other works of the flesh.... Holy Father, keep us safe in the concord of our love for one another, that we may be one, just as Thou art one with Thy Son, Our Lord, and with the Holy Ghost, and just as through the sweetest bonds of harmonies Thou hast made all Thy works one; and that from the bringing of Thy people into concord the body of Thy Church may be built up in the Earth, as Thou didst erect the heavens themselves out of harmonies.[1]

The rediscovered harmonies of nature are a model for restoring harmony to the strife-torn world. This hopeful vision is shared by the author of *Signatura Rerum*, when he describes the cosmic likeness of the world as signature:

For God did not give birth to the Creation in order to become more complete, but rather for the purpose of His Self-Revelation, to his great joy and glory. The Creation is the same playing out of itself (*dasselbe Spiel aus sich selber*), as a model or instrument of the Eternal Spirit upon which He plays, and is exactly like a great harmony, a multitudinous play of lutes, which are all directed into one harmony.... just as an organ of many voices is driven by one single wind, so that each voice, indeed, each pipe gives its tone, and yet the same wind is in all the voices, which resounds in each voice, after the instrument is fashioned. (VI 231/16.2–3)

The harmonies of the celestial orbits and the harmony of voices in the pipe organ—like the diverse colors and virtues of the flowers of the field, which do not envy and begrudge one another their singular beauties—represent the plenitude and plurality of a divine will, of which this world is the manifest expression: the world as expression reconciles unity and diversity, order and freedom. The symbol of the harmony of voices is more dynamic and mysterious than the static image of the flowering meadow, or of the colorful spectrum of the rainbow. The harmonization through expression recalls the angelic glorifications of the Son in the angelic kingdoms of *Aurora*.

Evil emerges when one voice, one spirit, attempts to rise too high and thus departs from the "temperance" (*Temperatur*) of the clocklike divine plan of self-revelation. The allusions to the "clockwork" (*Uhrwerk*) of the Creation should not be confused with the later metaphor of Deism. The extraordinary clocks of Boehme's own time were devices which coordinated several hands, dials, and mechanical figures. Boehme may have viewed the clockwork more as a symbol of harmonious simultaneity—not as a model of a mechanically predetermined linear progression.[2]

The "expressionistic" element was implicit in his thought from the very beginning. The signature of things is the common denominator of nature and meaning. *Meaning* is both relation and process, a timeless signification and an utterance in time. The process by which the latent intention comes to be embodied in an external expression, that is, in a thing, creature, or word, can be represented both as free and directed, both as voluntary and as bound to its own distinct end. The willed act and process of meaning and uttering something (as opposed to the pure mechanics of producing a sound or sign) is noncausal, and at the same time nonarbitrary. Meaning as relation and process therefore reconciles freedom with necessity and unites the one with the many. One word as a willed "sense" can be expressed in countless spoken or printed words, all the while remaining, as meaning, one and indivisible in each of the exemplars and utterances.

The *Signatura* is defined as the unfolding of the concealed inner being of a thing in its external manifestation. What lies concealed within all things is the omnipresent will, with its blind drive and its refraction of the wonders of eternity into time. Since the will and the essences of all things unfold and reveal themselves in the external forms of things and creatures, all the morphological concepts hitherto introduced by Boehme are summed up by the mystical signature of things. The morphology of plants and the phonology of language, the typology of beasts, and that of human character—these all fall within the category of the signature. All are external manifestions of the omnipresent inner "will to revelation" (VI 7/1.15).

This being the case, one is no longer confronted with a blind and senseless chaos of conflicting forces, incapable of understanding or reconciliation. We know from the theory of the "nature language" that the spirit in nature articulates sounds, just as it shapes the things in creation. As a parallel to this, the inner will in its quest for the light shapes human beings as individual organs of "sound" which are capable of resonating like tuning forks in sympathetic communication with one another. All organic beings, plants, animals, or human individuals, are like lutes fashioned by the will. Each organism has its own "natural spirit," engendered in its birth. And yet the good or bad nature of the created being or thing can be altered by the sympathetic powers of circumstance. An herb can be transplanted from a bad soil to a good soil. An animal which is by nature evil can be tamed. The human creature, which is unique in freely expressing its inner character in words, actions, and habits, is capable of resonating to a sympathetic chord when its human "instrument" is struck by an "artful master" (VI 4–7/1.6–16). The transforming blow does not contravene the divine will that crafted the instrument. The artful blow only liberates the latent potentiality of the instrument. The theory of the signature therefore militates against predestinarianism and at the same time lays the groundwork for the hope and belief that the appeals for peace and reconciliation may find an ever wider resonance.

The signature is the key to Holy Scripture and the codex of all discourse on divine matters:

> Everything which is spoken, written, or taught about God without knowledge of the signature is mute and senseless (*ohne Verstand*), for it only comes from the historical delusion, from another mouth, in which the spirit without knowledge is mute. But if the spirit opens up the signature to him, he understands the mouth of the other, and, further, how the spirit has revealed itself with the voice out of the essence, through the principle, in the sound. (VI 3–4/1.1–2)

Thus, where *Aurora* fell short in its project of reconciling order with freedom, the signature symbolically envisaged a resolution of this perennial problem.

The sources of Boehme's signature go back to the medieval trope of the Book of the World. This trope gained wide currency in the applications of Paracelsus. Paracelsus had written that the healing "virtues" of plants could be identified by examining their forms and colors. The salient model for the Paracelsian theory of the signature was the work of the artisan. The work of the divine Craftsman could be seen in His products, just as the craft of the tailor is visible in the coat sewn by him.[3] In the intellectual circles of Rudolphine Prague, the significance of the signature was expanded further by men like Oswald Croll and Jakob Typotius in an environment of scientific observation and artistic experimentation.[4]

According to Curtius, the trope of the *Liber Mundi* underwent a revolutionary transformation in the seventeenth century through Galileo's stipulation that the Book of the World is written in the language of mathematics.[5] Without a doubt, this change from the Paracelsian artisanal marks on things to their mathematical relationships heralds the subsequent triumph of modern thought. But "revolutions" very often result in secondary movements which appear highly important at the time, but then lose out and pass into oblivion. Boehme's understanding of the signature of things represents just such an offshoot in the evolution of the term, a branch, however, which taps the very root of this complex notion. The signatures in Boehme's "Book" are neither artisanal marks nor mathematical relations; instead, they resemble the inspired works of a creative artist. To be sure, the "artful master" who knows and manipulates the signs of the world is modeled on the alchemistic "adept." But like the poetic genius of later provenance, Boehme's *Artist* possesses a keen empathetic knowledge of the inner being of things and people. The artist of *Signatura Rerum* anticipates the imaginative power of the Romantic poet or thinker.

The signature of things is embodied in the individual word, sound, organism, or object, as well as in the world in its entirety. The signature is the externalized "mirror" of the one inner will that moves or animates all things. We have already seen that the Divine Wisdom effects a magic "birth" in eternity, and that it induces the introspective self-transformation of the reflective believer. In *Signatura Rerum*, the outer world in its totality is said to be the mirror of the Divine inner world: "the inner [world] holds the outer before itself as a mirror in which it beholds itself in the property of giving birth to all forms; the external is its signature" (VI 97/9.3). This implies that one need not search for the meaning of the world in some occult, fatalistic design, hidden behind the manifest processes of nature and history and hence wholly distinct from experienced nature and history. Understood in its absolute depth, *the world means just what it is*. The Divine Word and Will articulates itself in the world, in order to reveal itself and to know itself. The divine process of self-articulation informs the all-encompassing world-process, as an awakening of the Will of the *Ungrund*, and as its expression in the emanations of the divine spirit. The world is the progression from the inchoate desire for self-knowledge, articulating itself in Creation, to the end that the Eternal Being becomes self-transparent through its works of self-revelation.

In the signature, time is assimilated to eternity, as the inner being recognizes itself in the external manifestation, and as the full significance of the *Ungrund*, as all and nothingness, is balanced in a final equation of purpose and fulfillment. The "true spirit of the high power of eternity" (VI 5/1.6) touches the human instrument and elicits from it a chord. The godlike artist and physician who prescribes the cure of "nothingness" employs his remedy to bring the will into a state of harmonious equilibrium or "equality":

> And it is to be understood how the physician [i.e., the cure] stands in the equality of each single thing, for in equality stands the fulfillment of the will, as its highest joy. For each single thing desires a will of its kind; and it is made sick by the opposing will (*mit dem Wiederwillen wird es gekräncket*). But when it receives a will of its own kind, it takes delight in the equality, and sub-

merges itself therein into the state of calm; and out of animosity arises joy. (VI 9/2.3)

The state of calm in which the will, reaching equilibrium, sinks and becomes will-less, is identical in the Divine Being with the "calm nothingness" of the "clear divinity." In the practices of faith, this state is called *Abstinenz*, a term defined already in *Aurora* as "calm" (*Ruhe*). The healing medicine of abstinence, as administered by the alchemistic physician, regulates what *Signatura Rerum* designates as the "magical process," or the "process of Christ." This process is capable of producing what is called the "magical child."

As a *Magus*, or adept theorist of white magic, and as an alchemistic physician, the "artist" prescribes the cure of nothingness both for the individual soul and for the world. This odd prescription implies many things. What it does not imply is a nihilistic rejection of life and the world. The artist as world-healing physician recognizes the purifying powers of fire and therefore retains his faith that a better world may emerge from the flames of destruction. The artist as adept prescribes the ethical and spiritual corollaries of the alchemistic science of nature. Boehme's inner circle of readers included enough adepts or dabblers who could appreciate his allusions. (In addition to the Paracelsian doctors, several of the nobles, among them Fürstenau, practiced the alchemistic "art.") Boehme's own approach to alchemy stressed its spiritual allegory. He was influenced by *Der Wasserstein der Weisen* of Ambrosius Sibmacher.[6] The hydrolith, or ignoble castaway stone, is a magical foundation stone of wisdom, capable of transforming base metals into gold and of healing mortal ailments. *Signatura Rerum* states that the true philosopher's stone is the Eternal Word (VI 63/7.26). What counts most in the symbol is the paradox of the stone: It can be used to transform gold from base metals—but only if the device is employed by the artist who does not covet earthly treasures. By the same token, rebirth through Christ transmutes and prepares the soul for eternal life, but only if the soul seeks the good without coveting the reward. Those who console themselves with the treasure are sure to lose it. Babylon titillates itself with the stone, but holds in its hand nothing but a coarse piece of masonry, *einen groben Mauerstein* (VI 63 7/27). The true artist knows that transformation requires the fiery annihilation of the selfish will. Annihilation purifies the base substance of the mortal creature and prepares it for eternity. These are the reflections of the Stoic sage for whom the highest *desideratum* of this world is to be free of base desires. "Nothingness" is thus the remedy recommended by *Signatura Rerum*: "What has been found again desires [to return] into the will of the calm nothingness (*des stillen*

Nichts), so that it may therein have peace and calm; and Nothing is its medication" (VI 13/2.19). "Nothingness is the highest good" (*Das Nichts ist das höchste Gut*—VI 111/9.59). Here again it will become evident that Boehme is not recommending a monastic denial of life of the sort that might find expression in asceticism and celibacy.

The Magical Process

Boehme, as we have seen, does not rely on scientific laws or on causal necessity. All processes of becoming have to be viewed as manifestations of a single underlying divine process. If the inner structure of "elemental" matter resembles the workings of the mind, this is not because mind has evolved from matter, but rather because both mind and matter are rooted in the one divine process. In elemental nature, the divine process brings about qualitative distinctions in metals. In plants or animals, the process effects growth and maturation. In the human creature, the universal process regenerates life, engenders the awareness of freedom, and imbues the creature with the capacity for knowledge.

No reductionism is permitted by the concept of the universal divine process. What is elemental rises to the organic and what is organic is in turn sublimated in the human, not by causal and quantitative changes escalating into qualitative ones: the one divine process unfolds all the wonders of time and eternity by a *magic* which is also the exercise of the Divine Wisdom. *Magia* is therefore the power by which something arises from nothing, by which distinctions emerge from indifference, and also by which differences return to the state of "equality," or harmony with the one will, and thereupon sink into the blissful calm of the nothingness. Magic is intrinsic to the freedom and self-transcendence of the will. All life is fundamentally magical.

The "magical process" in *Signatura Rerum* is the conjoining of opposites and the birth of new things from their conjunction. The process takes place at three levels: in the world of stars and elements, in the sphere of human life and birth, and in the eternal birth, life, and suffering of Christ. The prospective *Magus* is instructed concerning the three aspects of the magical process. The magical process includes both the *Process Christi* (the process, or trial, of Christ), and the "actual process of the figuration of the magical child" (VI 72/7.59–60).

The figuration of the magical child is also the creation of a real child. The process has both a natural aspect (in that the interaction of qualities first produces a "vegetable life" before the emergence of the soul), and a supernatural aspect, since the "magical soul" is the "modelling" of eternity within the mortal being (VI 72/7.61).

Although the Noble Virgin is not personified in *Signatura Rerum*, she is nonetheless present in the magical process.

In the production of the "magical child," a real virgin is assigned to a bridegroom by the *Magus*. The virgin first tempts the suitor by projecting all her love into him. This period of temptation preceeding the nuptials represents the forty days of Christ's temptation in the desert. Here, the guiding *Magus* must pay special attention to the process, seeing to it that the temptation is neither too strong nor too weak. Either extreme could have an adverse effect on the suspended mixture. The procedure is said to be entirely in vain unless the "angels" appear at the end of the symbolic period of temptation. But once they appear, the process has been successfully initiated:

> As soon as [the *Magus*] sees the figure of the angels, he should lead Christ out of the desert, and let the bridegroom have his own food again, and get rid of the devil, so that he doesn't bother [the bridegroom] any longer. Then Christ will reveal wonders and signs, astonishing and pleasing to the artist. From then on, he has nothing to do. The bride is in her bridegroom; they are already wedded. He can only make their bed. They will warm it for themselves. The bridegroom heartens the bride, and the bride the bridegroom. This is their food and their diversion, until they conceive a child.... (VI 75/7.71–72)

The process is modelled on a "chemical wedding." But it is also a prescription for a real betrothal and wedding guided by the wise adept in the art of life. The trial banishing of the bridegroom expands on the common practice of posting church bans, or of imposing a prudent waiting period before consummating the marriage. Here, the state of equality or nothingness or *Temperatur* is the balanced harmony of the couple. *Abstinenz* and *Temperatur* pertain to the wise conduct of life, which must be guided by the harmonies of the great and small worlds. Far from counselling complete renunciation, the adept artist of *Signatura Rerum* is closer to the wise Magus of Shakespeare's *Tempest* who advises Ferdinand not to break Miranda's virgin-knot ere the "sanctimonious ceremonies" are ministered, lest, "No sweet aspersion shall the heavens let fall, to make this contract grow."

Mysterium Magnum

Mysterium Magnum rounds out and completes the cycle of great treatises. Like the seventh spirit-quality, this longest of all his books ties together in nearly 900 pages virtually everything that precedes it. In this sense, *Mysterium Magnum* encompasses the full *Corpus* of Boehme's works. Analogous to the ultimate spirit, the sabbatical work recapitulates the themes and resolves the tensions of the first work. Both *Signatura Rerum* and *Mysterium Magnum* reinterpret *Aurora*.

Though the original manuscript of *Aurora* was confiscated on orders of the city council and held at the *Rathaus*, its offshoot copies continued to circulate. Boehme's reputation continued to derive from the suppressed manuscript, even after he had revised his thinking in many subsequent writings. This surely meant a vindication for the silenced cobbler, but it also became a source of embarassment for an author who considered his first "Memorial" to be an obscure work, in need of interpretation. In the dispute with Tilke and Staritius, *Aurora* still provided the standard of his views.

As early as 1619, the author and his noble patron hoped to recover the original manuscript or a reliable circulating copy of *Aurora*. Ender wanted to have it printed, but Boehme was probably more interested in reviewing its contents in order to justify or revise its problematic formulations (ep. 4.45). Sometime in the year 1620, a copy was obtained from the Silesian nobleman Abraham von Sommerfeld. Examining it, the author pronounced it reliable (ep. 10.35). His letters of the 1620s bespeak his efforts to come to terms with the inspiration recorded in *Aurora* (epp. 18, 28). In July 1621, he wrote to Sigmund von Schweinichen that his first book had been the vehicle of a true, though "childish," recognition which was in need of further explanation and better clarification (ep. 18.13). *Signatura Rerum* already reflects a renewed attention to *Aurora*.[7]

Boehme's hints and allusions suggest that the author, at the zenith of his productive activity, is still engaged in studying and interpreting the first manifestation of his inspiration. This augmented the unity of his work. The letter to Lindner recounts the initial attempts to record the illumination and states that in struggling to write he had retained only as a "chaos containing everything" (*ein Chaos, da alles inne lieget*—ep. 12.9). In *Signatura Rerum*—in association with the "sal-nitrous *Schrack*"—the term "chaos" is given a special signification, based on a Paracelsian usage; a *chaos* is:

> a view of great wonders, in as much as all colors, force, and virtues are contained in this one chaos or wonder-eye, which chaos is God Himself, as the being of all beings who reveals Himself in the particular with the eye of eternity. (VI 28/3.40)

This provides a further indication that the author conceived his own agonies of self-expression as the divine will to revelation. (Why should we be surprised that the reverse side of Boehme's humility was his identification of his authorial labor with the divine birth and self-recognition?) *Mysterium Magnum* carries the reevaluation of the first work one step further. Where *Aurora* impugned the authority of the *Scribent Moses* and rejected the "historical faith," *Mysterium Magnum* written for the purpose of an "Explanation of the First Book of Moses," vindicates Genesis as an account of the Creation and first steps in the pilgrimage of humankind; it does so by rendering both the Creation and the "history" into terms that are present and eternal.

It is not clear when Boehme first began writing *Mysterium Magnum*. A letter written to Carl von Ender on February 14, 1622, mentioned a *"Materia über Genesin,"* which promised to be pleasing and useful to certain people (ep. 23.6). This and some similar references suggest that there may have been a draft version of *Mysterium Magnum* (without the final title) in circulation soon after the completion of *Signatura Rerum* (*cf*. ep. 71.5, 73.1). Grunsky places the composition of the first half of *Mysterium Magnum* in the fall and winter of 1622 and of the second half in the spring and summer of 1623.[8]

Mysterium Magnum combines the Genesis version of the Creation with the *logos* version from the Prolog of the Fourth Gospel. The two "beginnings" are merged in his usage, *Verbum Fiat* (the *Verbum* being the Word of the Gospel of John, while *Fiat* is the "Let there be" of Genesis). The title also symbolizes the typological concordance of the Old and New Testaments, as well as the correspondences of nature philosophy and Scripture. *Mysterium Magnum* contains "Moses" and "Messiah." The first few chapters are dominated by the Word. The Word is conceived both as a power of creation and as that which is created: as the "speaking Word" and the "spoken Word." The word *mysterium* is the Latinized Greek word for "sacrament." The evocation of the sacramental mystery of the world is here complemented by the interpretation of Moses' account of the creation of the world and of the beginning of its history.

Mysterium was a concept of the influential Paracelsian or pseudo-Paracelsian *Philosophia ad Athenienses*—which had once led to a controversy in Görlitz. Pagel has summarized the concept of the *Mysterium* as formulated in the *Philosophia*:

> It first introduces the concept of the "Mysterium." By this is meant any "Matrix" or "Mother" in which an object is generated. Thus milk is a "mysterium" of cheese and butter, cheese a "mysterium" of maggots and worms.... They all in turn descend from the "Mysterium Magnum" which is the "one mother of all things" and of all elements and "a grandmother of all stars, trees and crea-

tures of the flesh." It is the "materia of all things," incomprehensible, without properties, form, color, or elemental nature.[9]

The North Italian peasant Menocchio was thinking in terms of a *Mysterium* when he claimed that God and the angels had been generated from a "chaos," like worms from curdled milk. In chapter seven of *Mysterium Magnum*, Boehme characterizes the seven "forms of nature" as a *Mysterium*, thereby defining the term in the sense of the *Philosophia ad Athenienses*:

> But this is to be well noted: that each property is also essential. In the realm of heaven, the same being (or essence) is mixed up together like One Being, and is a *Mysterium* from which the celestial plants sprout from the property of each force. In the same manner, the earth is a *Mysterium* of all trees and herbs, of grass and worms; and the four elements are a *Mysterium* of all living things, and the stars a *Mysterium* of all actuality in living and growing things. (VII 35/7.23)

For Boehme, the *Mysterium Magnum* is the radical of everything that is, the primal condition of all creation. *Signatura Rerum* and *Mysterium Magnum* contain references to the "salnitrous *Schrack*." As a divine substance, the *Mysterium* is the *Salitter* under a new name: a divine protoforce laden with all the qualities and potentialities in the world. The first conceivable form of the *Mysterium Magnum* is the vaporous exhalation of the eternal Word (VII 9/2.6). The *Mysterium* is pure hypostatized expression: the Word as a self-generating, world-generating power. The usage follows the lead of the *Philosophia ad Athenienses* in positing the implicit presence of all the objects of the world in the great *Mysterium*. The primal reified expression, informed with its latent meaning, is the utterance of the eternal Word which means the world to be, and into being.

Mysterium Magnum is a deliberately self-referential work. It not only summarizes Boehme's concepts and symbols; it sums up his life, times, hopes, and ideals as well. An important point of transition leading into the realm of historical reference is found in chapters twelve and thirteen, where the harmony of the sun-centered world symbolizes the stable, proper order of the political world. In chapter twelve, which treats "of the six day-works of the Creation," the "regime of the planetary wheel" is grouped around a *puncto solis*, or "Royal place of hierarchy." The erstwhile "prince of hierarchy" has been thrust into darkness, because he has "risen up" for the sake of occupying the "center of eternal nature." Hence, God has created in the same spot "another prince, but without divine understanding, to be the ruler of essence, that is, the sun" (VII 74–75/12.4). The solar system thus reflects the ideal situation for a Lusatia which is gradually being reintegrated into the political orbit of Dresden rather than of Prague. Satan is the deposed rule of force. This is not the vanquished Winter King, toward whom Boehme retained an attitude of reserved respect. (Even a letter written in Dresden during his last year still wistfully recalled *Friderici, unsers gewesenen Königs,* "our former king."—ep. 63.4.) The "prince of hierarchy" is the tyrant Satan who acted through his worldly instruments. The solar system which replaces his reign is an emblem of political freedom and order. In chapter thirteen, more symbolic detail is added; as a result, the cosmos appears as a reconstituted League of Six Planets. Each of the four elements has its guiding star within it. In the analogy of the political and cosmic systems, this may well symbolize the four estates of peasants, burghers, clergymen, and nobles. (We have already seen that the elemental forces can coincide with social forces.) The four together give birth to the *Amtmann* of God in this world, who resembles an elected *Landvogt*. In nature, he is the "soul of the external world"—a "nature god" and a positive variant of the *Spiritus Mundi*. The ruler in the world of nature is supported by *sechs Räthe*: "six counsellors," who represent the "six planets," and thus recall the Six Cities (VII 87/13.16). On the third day of Creation, vegetation sprouts: and this means that "the violent one" (*der Gewaltige*) has lost his power over the earth and must remain imprisoned in the darkness between time and eternity, to await his Judgment (VII 81/12.35). Without presenting an explicit program, the solar utopia gives voice to new hopes.

The balance of eternity and time has been restored. The enclosing firmament distinguishes between the dual aspects of the "speaking Word" and the "spoken Word." The world beyond the firmament is the eternal world. Its power acts through the forces that operate in time. The outermost world is therefore also the innermost being of things (VII 78–79/12.19–27). Time and the cosmos are looped into the eternity which is within.

The "inner" world beyond the firmament is the Word and the light; the "outer" world of brute force is the power of darkness and evil; the order of the cosmos around the central sun and the rejuvenation of life represent the pervasive power of the Word in this world. These three realms also refer, respectively, to the "inner Word" of Scripture, the "letter" of Scripture, and the inspiration which penetrates through the letter to the spirit. The three can be interpreted as symbolizing: (1) the eternal faith, inspired by the Fourth Gospel; (2) the historical faith, which is concerned with Genesis or with the synoptic Gospels; and (3) the Spiritualistic inspiration that discovers the *logos* concealed within Genesis, thereby reconciling eternity with history. In terms of chiliastic typology, the Age of the Father prefigures that of the Son; and the Age of the Son prefigures that of the Holy Spirit. The final age returns to the first root of the hidden God, to the *Mysterium Magnum*.

The dawning Age of the Spirit is clearly outlined in the explication of Enoch at the end of chapter thirty. Boehme echoes Gnostic and Kabbalistic accounts of Enoch's living ascent into heaven, as an ecstatically transported visionary's journey[10]: "His ecstasy was not death and not a laying aside of nature and creature; rather, he entered the *mysterium* between the spiritual and external world, as into Paradise..." (VII 274/30.48). Out of Enoch's "line" came the "spirit of prophecy" which was slated to prevail at the end of time. Hence, the "voice" of the miraculous Enochian tree of time was destined to recover what had been lost to the earlier ages:

> For what is lost shall be rediscovered in the spirits of the letters, and the spirits of the letters [shall be rediscovered] in the formed Word of the Creation; and in the Creation, the Being of all Beings shall be discovered and recognized; and in the Being of all Beings, the eternal sense [*Verstand*] of the Holy Trinity, and then all conflicts over the knowledge of God, of His Being and His Will, shall come to an end. For the branches shall recognize that they stand within the tree, and shall no longer say that they are trees unto themselves. Rather, they shall all take delight in their [common] stem, and shall see that they are altogether nothing more than the branches and twigs of one tree, and that they all derive strength and life from the one single trunk. (VIII 275/30.52)

Enoch prefigures Boehme's own spiritual and intellectual growth, which assuredly also proceeded from letter to spirit, from spirit to nature, from nature to the recognition of the oneness of all being, and from this recognition to the fervid hope that all conflicts might soon be resolved, that all "branches"—all peoples and faiths—might soon recognize that they grew out of the same "root" and toward a common destiny or "crown." The realization of this growth toward unity is one with the paradisiacal ecstacy of the old and new Enoch.

Joseph and His Brothers

Mysterium Magnum progresses toward the vision of this unity. The work elaborates a mystically expanded religion, intended, in the first place, to secure the philosophical basis for his own articles of faith, but also to stake out a common ground broad enough to encompass various other religious beliefs or practices, including some non-Christian ones.

The murder of Abel by Cain, as always, typifies the schism between the two "churches" of Abel and of Cain. Cain's desire was for power over the earth. He typifies the church of worldly lust, power, honor, and of the eternal god Mammon. Abel is the church of all who are persecuted and scorned in the world (VII 202–203/ 26.24–25). The next chapter treats the offerings of Cain and Abel. The burnt offerings of the two brothers are construed as a justification for *Räuchern*. This may refer to the burning of incense, the sort of extrascriptural church custom despised by Protestant purists. Lutheran practices, we recall, only very gradually replaced Catholic rites in the converted churches of Upper Lusatia, where a Catholic minority remained. Boehme never dropped the Catholic term for "Trinity," *Dreifaltigkeit*, in favor of the more abstractly tempered Lutheran *Dreieinigkeit*. The burnt offerings of the brothers are compared with the alchemist's transforming fire, the *Magisch Feuer* (VII 215/27.8). Already in *The Three Principles*, the divine and natural qualities of fire were used in order to provide a rationalization for the Catholic doctrine of Purgatory—though with vehement rejections of the Catholic claim of a mediating role of the Church (II 297/18.104). In *The Threefold Life*, the symbolism of the soul-fire was cited in order to rationalize Jewish dietary law (III 147/8.11). The mystical religion tends toward a concordance of all beliefs. This concordance reaches its apogee near the end of *Mysterium Magnum*.

The commentary on the tale of Dinah's seduction and the revenge of her brothers (Genesis 34) contains sweeping condemnations of intolerance. "Dinah" is the type of a religion that reduces faith to laws, ceremonies, and opinions, while whoring around with fleshly lust. However, Dinah also represents "the first, true, virginal Christian ground"—which is still worthy of matrimony. The brothers of Dinah are all those who cry out that the true church has been violated. These same criers are also the representatives of the titulary Christendom which denounces others as "heretics" and violates the true faith by resorting to murder and the sword. "This Dinah is now nothing but the church of stone...." (VIII 659–660/62.13–17) When the sons of Jacob deceitfully convert the Hivites in order to murder them, this treachery is likened to the far-ranging conversions of heathen peoples. The use of force in proselytizing heathens is condemned in words evoking the evils of missionary colonialism:

> Thus, the same thing [as in Jesus' denunciation of the proselytizing Pharisees, in Matthew 23:15] can be said of the Christian Levites, who persuade the peoples to be baptized and to call themselves Christians; and, when that is accomplished, they thrust the sword of murder in their hearts, so that [the heathen peoples] learn to curse and damn with words other peoples who are not of their name and opinion; and they give cause that one brother should persecute, curse, and damn the other.... (VII 664/62.36)

According to the author of *Mysterium Magnum*, the non-Christian peoples will soon see that the false, titulary Christians are only interested in murder, tyranny, and persecution. Because of Christian hypocrisy, certain nations, notably the Oriental ones, have already fallen away from Christianity to become Muslims (VIII 666/62.40).

Non-Christians are represented by the trio of "Jews, Turks (i.e., Muslims), and heathens." The latter category refers both to the ancient "wise heathens" and to the newly discovered "barbarian peoples." Heathens, whether ancient or barbarian, can be excused for their unbelief because they have not heard of Christianity. "Turks" are excused by having heard and seen too much of it. However, the Jews would seem to have reacted arrogantly to the premier opportunity to embrace the new faith; and this casts them as the type of all subsequent "scribes and Pharisees." This mainstay of Christian anti-Semitism is not alien to Boehme. But at the same time, it runs counter to his insistence on toleration and rejection of the exclusionary Christian confessions. Beginning in *Aurora*, he employs his natural-philosophical extension of Christianity in order to include Jews, Turks, and heathens in the purview of the true faith. Characteristically, *Aurora*'s firmest statement of this sort follows upon the author's justification of his own authorship (I 326/22.43; 328/22.52ff.). Though his defense of toleration reflects his native dislike for persecution, it was of course also a matter of self-defense.

Mysterium Magnum redefines the notion of grace and salvation in order to extend it to non-Christians. Boehme even formulates a rationale for unbelief. There is a good reason why not all Jews were brought over to Christ. God gave them the law, which is the same as the law of nature; their continued adherence to the law of nature signifies that, in the end, "the law" should dwell in the same house with Christ (*so muste die Figur des Gesetzes bey etlichen Abrahams Kindern, als bey etlichen Juden bleiben, anzudeuten, daß das Gesetze Christi Hausgenoße sey.* VIII 534/51.25). The idea of conferring an honorary "grace" on nonbelievers may now seem like backhanded largesse. But since the judgment that others were condemned to eternal perdition provided a pretext for hating and persecuting them in this world, such special pleading had its clear pragmatic import. Moreover, the use of typology as a justification for toleration anticipated the same kind of rationale in England and America after 1648.[11]

However, it must be said that there are real vacillations in Boehme's toleration. Tolerance and the rejection of intolerance are not one and the same: the rejection can always find more to reject in others. Moreover, the same typological thinking that provides grounds for toleration can turn Jews into the type of those who are enslaved to "laws" and "ceremonies," and "heathens" into the type of all devotees of wicked superstition. In the *Mysterium Pansophicum*, dated May 1620, the characterizations of heathenish superstition and Jewish "greed" are a case in point.[12] However, Boehme was fairly consistent in opposing the intolerance and self-righteousness of organized Christianity. At his best, he was resourceful in formulating esoteric and typological justifications for the acceptance of "Jews, Turks, and heathens." This is evident in his exegesis of the story of Joseph and his brothers.

The story of Joseph no doubt appealed to Boehme for many reasons. Betrayal, exile, and discord are surmounted by faith and reconciliation. In addition to its symbolic figures, including its type of the Lord's Supper, the account of Joseph and his brothers is rich in realistic details—of jealousy, temptation, hard times, shortages, purchases of grain, and negotiations with the powerful. Although these details are treated figurally, they also constitute a universalized portrayal of Boehme's own life and times. Joseph is the "dreamer and enthusiast" whose unusual gifts, symbolized in his coat of many colors (*der bunte Rock*), inflame the jealousy of the less favored (VIII 693/64.45). This is the author himself, and all who are graced with an inner life open to the divine world. Joseph's ability to interpret dreams is equated with the rediscovered art of *Magia Naturalis*. This art was known to the ancient Egyptians before it degenerated into a sorcery which was rightly rejected by the early Christians as idolatry and consigned to oblivion for a time. Natural Magic, exemplified by the wisdom of Joseph, must now be resurrected in order to "research the ground of nature" (VIII 744–745/68.3–8). For Boehme, as for John Dee (who was associated for a time with the pansophic milieu of Rudolphine Prague), the belief in natural magic offers a rationale for toleration by implying that the full truth of religion has yet to emerge.[13] Hence, in Boehme's *Six Mystical Points*, "Magic is the best theology" (IV 95/5.23).

In addition to Joseph's inward Spiritualism and his Natural Magic, his uprightness as the steward of Potiphar and minister of Pharaoh characterizes him as the type of the reborn prince and ruler who knows that he is only temporarily exercising an office for a higher Ruler during a sojourn in a strange land. The contrast to the prince's ideal servitude to God is the cruelty of *Leibeigenheit* (VIII 836/74.34–38)—the serfdom that was a resurgent phenomenon of the Thirty Years' War.

Certain details appear particularly biographical. This applies to the forced travels and purchases of grain. It applies to the fear and amazement of the brothers when they open their sacks to discover not only the grain but also the money paid to Joseph for it. Similarly, confides the author, a person is often so amazed to find himself the recipient of "temporal nourishment" (*zeitliche Nahrung*), that he suspects that it has come to him as an evil temptation (VIII 766/69.38). Benefitting from donations of his aristocratic patrons, Boehme must have wondered if he was betraying his integrity by taking their gifts.

The most important interpretation is that of the common meal: unaware of the true identity of their host, the brothers break bread with their vanquished, now triumphant brother. The meal of Joseph with his brothers attempts a symbolic resolution of the problem of toleration. The separate meal of the Egyptians is the type of all those who reject Christ's real presence in the Communion bread (it is said to be an abomination to Jews, Turks, and heathens, as well as to a "titulary Christianity" which proceeds from the false dichotomy of body and spirit). At the same time, Boehme interprets the sacramental presence itself as a warning against all who claim that, because "Jews, Turks, and unknowing heathens" do not accept the *Abendmahl*, they should be condemned: an error of blind "reason" (VIII 785–786/70.68–71). The typological explication of the supper of Joseph and his brothers acknowledges that all, including the "Turks, Jews, and foreign peoples" whose desires and prayers go out to the one God, "speak with the same mouth." Although the sacramental miracle is not revealed to the unbelievers, in spirit they are nonetheless in Christ (VIII 786/70.71, 74). Jews, Turks, and heathens can, it seems, attain to a state of grace without knowing it. They are closer to achieving grace than the Christians in name only (VIII 788/70.83–85). Unaware of their true kinship, therefore in terror for their lives, and entrapped by their guilt, Joseph's brothers share their common meal with the unrecognized brother whom they have betrayed and sold into bondage.

"Holy Kabbalah" and the Chaste Goddess "Idea"

In Boehme's later years, Kabbalistic, Neoplatonic, and Gnostic allusions move into the foreground. Where, beforehand, these traditions were blended in his work, now individual strands are singled out and taken up explicitly. Without adding much to the conceptual system of his thought, the eclectic writings of this period give rise to symbolic usages of enduring appeal.

His *Betrachtung Göttlicher Offenbarung*, or "Consideration of Divine Revelation" (*Questiones Theosophicae*), employs Kabbalistic and Neoplatonic terms. Outside of nature and creature, God is an infinity. Unity, as the Good, emanates from itself to pervade the unity of *Wollen oder Wallen*: a pun based on the gerund "wanting," this depicts desire as an undulation of divine energy. In the "ground of the soul," God is immanent as an eternal "Idea." The term Idea here subsumes the sapiential-angelic light-world of the "second principle."

Boehme's discussion of the *Tetragrammaton* looks back to the tradition of Christian Kabbalah associated with Pico della Mirandola and Johannes Reuchlin.[14] The same tract also produces one of his most memorable coinages: the divine life prevails in the two "Central Wills," in the eternal *Jah* and *Nein*, the Yes and No of God's love and anger (IX Questiones 27/9.4). The free life of the Divine Being steers itself "yes-wards" and "no-wards" in all things. The "Yes" is "the One ... pure force and life ... the truth of God or God Himself," the "No" is the contrary force, or counterthrust (*Gegenwurf*) of the "Yes," without which He could not be revealed (IX Questiones 6–7/3.2, 8/3.10).

Franckenberg recollected that, upon hearing the word "Idea," Boehme remarked that it evoked for him, "an especially beautiful and chaste goddess" (X 16). Presumably, the biographer's recollection coincided with a vivid memory of his late friend: as a figure, surrounded by a devoted circle who supplied his fertile imagination with notions to be "tested in the sensual manner in the understanding" (*sensualischer Art im Verstande probiren*), as Boehme once explained his manner of reflecting upon propositions without recourse to exclusionary logic (ep. 41.8). The tyrant logic with its either/or was replaced by the eternally free *Ja* and *Nein* of the divine life. At root, Boehme's method lay in his creation of a symbolism, with which religious teachings could be taken up and contemplated without imposing a strict dichotomy of propositional truth and falsehood.[15]

The Path to Christ

After Boehme's death, his friends collected and published an anthology of his shorter writings under the title, *Der Weg zu Christo* (*The Path to Christ*). A smaller version of *The Path to Christ* had been published already during the author's lifetime, in Görlitz at the very end of the year 1623, but it probably contained only two of the nine short pieces that made up the posthumous work: *On Penitence* and *The True Spiritual Calm* (ep. 50.6). Siegmund von Schweinich paid for the printing and distributed the copies. The pieces composed in various years,[16] comprising the posthumous edition of *Der Weg zu Christo*, provide a measure of the range of Boehme's devotional writings, as well as of the impression of his teachings which his supporters later wished to propagate.

The posthumous *The Path to Christ* offers advice to the believer ranging from spiritual exercises for the practice of faith (the booklets on penitence and prayer) to detailed psychological advice for troubled souls (the treatise on the four complexions). For the more advanced readers, there are works on introspective contemplation which show the influence of older German mysticism. A central place in the collection is occupied by the explication of the all-important doctrine of spiritual rebirth. This 34-page exposition is both concise and sufficiently broad in scope to touch on most aspects of Boehme's speculative thought. Rebirth is linked to the cosmogony, to the story of Adam, and even to the birth of water from fire as lightning, all figures of the eternal rebirth. The triune human nature and the androgyny of the first Adam are patiently explained, as is the mirrored dualism of the darkness and light. The treatise concludes with simple restatements of Boehme's program of faith: the sacraments and the church are meaningless without spiritual rebirth. For the sanctified Christian, the church is everywhere in the world and it is within the soul. On the whole, the Christian religion is concerned with self-knowledge, that is: what we are, whence we come, how we have proceeded from unity into division and strife, and what is our destination (IV *Von der neuen Wiedergeburt* 109–142).

The initial tracts of penitence and prayer can be understood as applications of the faith of imagination. Imagination provides a practical technique for effecting the inner transformation by way of remorse and determination. The penitent passes through the "process of Christ," enacting the siege of Satan's *Raubschloß* and undertaking the perilous pilgrim's journey to salvation. The soul dallies with Noble Sophia in a chivalrous *frauendienst* full of sublime eroticism (*Penitence* 1). Here (as in the collection's concluding *Coversation of an Illuminated with an Unilluminated Soul*), Boehme proved that, had he desired to do so, he could have composed clear-cut narrations and dialogues to contend with the writings of those more learned than he. Nevertheless, these polished little productions are not nearly as original, nor as vital, as those other tracts which challenge the reader and verge on turgidness.

The practical examples of private prayers for the daily worshipper provide a rare insight into what must have been the inner life of the mystic. Day by day, almost hour by hour, the devout soul transforms daily life through prayer into the odyssey of the first human beings. There is perhaps a certain unintended whimsy or inspired childishness in this. The prayers to be said upon rising from bed on Monday morning recall the naked innocence of Adam and Eve. Setting off to work on Monday morning recalls the expulsion from Paradise. Preparing oneself to retire at night evokes the angelic garments which the soul should soon don for eternal Paradise (IV *Vom Heiligen Gebet* 60–62/44–45, 71–72/49).

Boehme created something like a manual for spiritual counselling in his treatise on the four complexions (*Trost-Schrift von vier Complexionen*). Presumably the diagnoses rely on the experiences of the author. The treatise outlines four character types, corresponding to the four elements and humors. Constructive advice is offered to those who find themselves either perpetually or occasionally beset by such symptoms. Each of the four types, melancholic, choleric, sanguine and phlegmatic, displays the affectations associated with the interactions of the first four spirit-forces within the divine cosmogony. The most impressive of the four types is the one associated with the dark, earthen complexion of melancholy. The melancholy soul dwells in fear and darkness and is the most vulnerable of all to Satanic raiding parties at night. The melancholy soul is advised against reading treatises on the special election of grace (*Trost-Schrift* 244/92). The soul has to declare its freedom and then launch its counterattack against the bastion of the oldest enemy.

Several other tracts in the collection offer a more abstract and refined form of mysticism. The tracts on the "supersensible life" (*Vom übersinnlichen Leben*, or *De Vita Mentale*) and on the "divine contemplation" (*Von Göttlicher Beschaulichkeit*, or *Theoscopia*) make interesting use of the concepts of nothingness and oneness. Mind or consciousness is conceptualized as unity and opposition. The second tract explicitly conceives God as the One Will. Wanting or willing itself, it creates its counterpart or object. The human mind therefore exemplifies the Divinity. In order to attain self-knowledge, it issues forth from itself. Through sensual awareness, it establishes both a counterpart to itself (*ein Gegenwurf des Gemüths*) and a center of the Ego (*ein Centrum der Ichheit*). Seen from another angle, the principle of contrariness (*Contrarium*) refracts the One Will (*Einiger Wille*) into the innumerable sensible centers which are necessary for revealing the wonders and virtues of the Divine Wisdom (IV *Von Göttlicher Beschaulichkeit* 169–170/18–20). Boehme's dialectic of subject and object and his metaphysical notion of the imagination are in a tradition extending from Weigel to the *Wissenschaftslehre* of a later Lusatian countryman, Johann Gottlieb Fichte.

Von wahrer Gelassenheit (*De Aequanimitate*) is dated 1622. Its title is the untranslatable classical concept of German speculative mysticism. *Gelassenheit* is inherited from the masters, Eckhart and Tauler, and from the *Theologia Deutsch*. *Gelassenheit* was also a term employed in common with Müntzer, Karlstadt, and Weigel. *Gelassen* has roots in the verbs for *leaving* and *relinquishing*. It conveys abandonment, calm, and selfless serenity.[17] The attainment of *Gelassenheit* requires abandonment of one's own will. For Boehme, this perspective is advantageous because it blurs the distinctions between all the doctrines formulated by the imprisoning "selfhood as reason" (*Gelassenheit* 8/26).

In addition to the tracts in *The Path to Christ*, the previously mentioned work on the "Testaments of Christ" presents Boehme's programmatic message to the adherents of the Christian confessions. As early as May 1623, he wrote to Ender of his intention to simplify and publish the part on baptism (ep. 44). His interpretation of the sacraments is both Lutheran and magical. The context of magic is intended to alleviate the antagonistic nature of all disputes over doctrine. Reason is presented as the "pictorialism of the understanding" (*Bildlichkeit des Verstandes*). (VI *Christi Testamenta* 52/14) All "natural knowledge" is tormented by the question whether a thing "is or is not" (*Dann alles natürliche Wissen ... lauffet in Wahn, ob ein Ding sey, oder nicht?*). Here, reason and logic are the source of all hostile disputes, most especially of the quarrels over the question whether Christ is present in the host or seated in heaven at the right hand of God (VI *Christi Testamenta* 56/36). Here again, Christ is present in the Eucharist, just as the sun's invigorating power is present in vegetation. In a plant, the solar rays of light and warmth engender a *spiritus* and awaken the pleasant qualities that labor to bear fruit (VI *Christi Testamenta* 89/4). Despite his central concern with spiritual rebirth, Boehme still justifies the practice of infant baptism—but with an argument that has less to do with the sinful nature of the infant than with the active good will of the parents. He wholeheartedly embraces the magic process *per se*. Through the magic process, the elemental water is transformed into a spirit-water, just as the elements are to be transformed when the world in the end passes back into an invisible state (VI *Christi Testamenta* 45–46/44–50).

The sacramental miracle thus remained a keystone in Boehme's cosmic architecture. Though in his later works there are some hints of attempted compromise formulations of the disputed articles of faith, the sacraments remained a magic-ritualistic access to the hidden, divine world. And in the end, the divine magic and mystery could be counted on to reconcile the opposing views.

8 Boehme's Last Year

The New Reformation

All dynamic ages may view themselves as conclusive ages: as decisive for the final state of a world poised between perdition and deliverance. The Baroque Age in which Jacob Boehme finished his life was, by this measure, agonizingly dynamic. A climactic stage action, its outcome seemed on the verge of working out the final design of all things. Donne's elegy, *An Anatomy of the World*, evoked and mocked this sense of resolution, linking it to watershed advances in the exact sciences. Unlike Boehme's vision of things, the sciences here appear to ensnare the once-free heavens in a web of mathematical-astronomical coordinates:

> And in these constellations then arise
> New stars, and old do vanish from our eyes:
> As though heaven suffered earthquakes, peace and war,
> When new towers rise, and old demolished are.
> They have impaled within a zodiac
> The free-born sun, and keep twelve signs awake
> To watch his steps...

Through science and graced imagination, wars and explorations, spectacular moral and spiritual visions, and even through common deeds and sufferings, the true "anatomy of the world" was being laid bare. If we allow for this heightened luminescence of experience, we may better understand the larger-than-life meanings which accrued to events that now appear obscure, if not absurd.

Boehme's final and most eventful year was ushered in by the publication of the short version of *The Path to Christ*. The year 1624 was marked by two dramatic events: a new clash with Pastor Richter, prompted by the printed book, and a journey to Dresden, where the shoemaker-mystic met with some of the most influential men of Electoral Saxony. These events resulted from a calculated decision to step out of the shadows and reach out for a wider influence. In May 1624, in a letter to Bernhard, Boehme mentioned having sent several manuscripts to Balthasar Walter for the book fair at Leipzig. They included, in addition to the single printed book, the works on grace, on baptism, all or part of *Mysterium Magnum*, and the *Clavis* or "key" to his system (ep. 57). Boehme was looking for further contacts and distributors: he was evidently aiming to influence the entire German-reading public. By journeying to Dresden, he hoped to secure powerful sponsors for his response to the religious conflicts of the age. Both the printed collection and the journey to Dresden challenged and antagonized Richter.

Influential men in Silesia and Lusatia stood behind him in his public campaign which bore the slogan of a "new reformation." What this slogan meant is nowhere spelled out programmatically. The political expectations of his reformation must be extracted from the moral, social, and religious ideals of his writings—projected as a dawning universal age: an age of toleration, in which the quarrels over the sacraments are no longer causes for war and persecution, an age in which no one is accused of heresy, in which doctrines are not imposed from above by learned experts, an age of spiritual enlightenment and self-awareness, of justice and brotherhood, of open confessional boundaries and free opinions, their latitude measured by that of Boehme's own writings, as well as by the views of the liberal-minded Lusatian scholars and nobles. In a word, the new reformation would reconcile freedom with order, with the new order—provided of course that the Elector Prince of Saxony was sufficiently reborn to favor it.

Three months after the publication of the short version of *The Path to Christ*, all of Boehme's chickens came home to roost. He received what was understood to be an official invitation to visit the court of Electoral Saxony in Dresden. At about this same time, Richter launched a concerted attack on the influence and person of the now famous shoemaker.

There are traces of a gnawing anxiety in the letters which register Richter's printed denunciation and charges. In a letter of March 5, 1624, the threatened author writes of a cross-shaped mark (*Mahlzeichen*) ingrained on his forehead; he writes that it would deflect the "poison rays" of Satan caused by Richter's denunciatory pamphlet (ep. 50.3). This curious stigma reminds one of Franckenberg's description of Boehme as already old in his late forties. Perhaps this "wizened" man (who gave credence to phrenological theories) peered into a dim mirror and noted that the wrinkles of his forehead formed the sign of the cross above his "sparkling, almost sky-blue eyes."

There were good reasons for his anxiety. Richter had attacked his writings and character in violent terms. The *Pasquill* went beyond insult in its portrayal of the shoemaker as a drunken scoundrel who drank expensive foreign wines and brandies and made fun of the Bible. Richter denounced his opponent as the "shoemaker Antichrist," as a purveyor of the poisonous Arian heresy that had caused the Near East to turn away from Christianity. The accusation played on popular fears of Turks and heresies, of magic and sorcery, all of Near Eastern origin. Brandishing his classical education, Richter denounced Boehme as an "Oedipus"—an interesting charge that did not escape the notice of an early Freudian analyst of Boehme's writings.[1]

Richter's charges were not without their theoretical underpinnings. In the previous century, the Basel professor Erastus had denounced Paracelsus as a restorer of Gnostic apostasy, as a fomenter of the "pestilence of Arian and Mohammedan heresy," as a disciple of Satan, a friend of the lowlife, and an inspirer of witchcraft.[2] More recently, the Wittenberg professor Hunnius, author of the strict Saxon Visitation Articles, had published devastating charges against representatives of a tendency which, in his opinion, originated with Paracelsus and included Weigel, Schwenckfeld, Osiander, Meth, and the Rosicrucians. The date of Hunnius's *Principia Theologiae fanaticae*, 1619, indicates that it was composed just before Boehme broke his silence, hence his absence from the index. Hunnius denounced Paracelsus's influence as "poison to the soul." He denounced the Paracelsian trichotomy of body, soul, and spirit; denounced the Paracelsians for rejecting the learned academy in favor of the "light of nature"; denounced Paracelsus for leading men to "desert Scripture."[3] All of this could have been applied also to Boehme, whose circulating writings provided ample material to substantiate such charges.

Already in 1623, Valentin Grießman in Thuringia had come out against Boehme. In 1624, Peter Widmann in Leipzig published a warning against the *Path to Christ*.[4] When Gregor Richter began casting about looking for allies, he found a useful one in Pastor Frisius of Liegnitz, who wrote to the city council of Görlitz that the shoemaker was disturbing the religious peace in Silesia. In his home parish, Richter began to use the pulpit to inflame an impressionable congregation. What the pastor recorded in his diary must have been voiced in his public sermons or his private slanderings, since it made the rounds to the slandered shoemaker: the "Shoemaker Antichrist" reduces God to brimstone and quicksilver.[5] Blasphemy, it must be remembered, was the most serious of accusations. Since Luther's own time, this charge had been hypocritically employed by Protestants for persecuting heretics while pretending to respect their freedom of conscience.[6]

It is an error to assume that, because Boehme succeeded in

dying a natural death, he was not at risk in the spring of 1624. If, through some shift in the political winds, through some unguarded utterance, or through the zealous manipulations of the pastors, matters had taken an unexpected turn in Görlitz or Dresden, neither his powerful friends nor his good intentions would have been a sure deliverance. After all, Schweinich, on his own estate, had just managed to save his guest from his own kinsman.

Görlitz and Dresden

When the Görlitz *Stadtrat* received the formal complaint from Pastor Frisius of Liegnitz, it was obliged to act. *The Path to Christ* had been printed in Görlitz without the permission of the clergy or the council, and both claimed the right of censorship. Moreover, the city council was obligated to safeguard against violations of the Augsburg Confession. While the patriotic councillors of Görlitz had to resent Richter's bringing a complaint before them by way of a Silesian colleague, they were unsure of their jurisdiction under the Saxon occupying power; and they knew that Boehme had been invited to Johann Georg's capital. The *Rat* met, summoned, and questioned the shoemaker. It examined his writings and deliberated upon the charges brought against him. In the interest of keeping the peace, the city councillors were obliged to resolve the matter one way or the other. They could either exercise their supervisory powers by taking Richter in hand, or they could uphold the complaint of Frisius and punish Boehme for violating his sworn rule of silence. Instead, they declined to act on the accusations of heresy, and suggested to Boehme that he take leave of Görlitz for the time being. The shoemaker hailed this as a victory, but prepared to leave. The pastor continued to incite the congregation against him.

Before leaving town, Boehme composed and circulated an eloquent defense against Richter's pamphlet, "The Defense Speech against Gregor Richter" (*Schutz-Rede wieder Gregorium Richter*); and he attached a short written statement addressed to the city council. Before the conflict could result in further altercations, he was gone from Görlitz.[7]

On May 8th or 9th, Boehme journeyed to Dresden. En route to his destination, he stopped in the League City of Zittau and met with several of his supporters, including the wealthy and worldly wise von Fürstenau (ep. 61.13), from whom he no doubt received advice, instructions, and perhaps messages to be relayed to the court in Dresden.[8] In Dresden, the court alchemist Benedikt Hinckelmann saw to the needs of the guest. Boehme was received by the politically influential nobleman Joachim von Loß, by the court chaplain Dr. Hoë, famous as a resolute anti-Calvinist, by the Lutheran superintendent, Ägidus Strauch, who may have tested the beliefs of the visitor, and by various other officials or officers of Johann Georg, but never by the Elector himself.

In view of his humble station and the furor against him in his home city, the friendly reception is astonishing. From all sides, Boehme heard repeated assurances that his works were read and loved. The climax of the visit occurred in Pentecostal week, on Whitsunday afternoon: it was evidently to be a day of the Holy Spirit's descent as a dove, a day of speaking in tongues and of understanding among the peoples. Eight high officials of the court interviewed Boehme in his quarters. The meeting went well. They promised him their support and led him to believe that the Elector himself might take interest in his books (ep. 63.2). On the following Thursday, the shoemaker was driven in a carriage to the imposing Renaissance palace of the aristocrat, Privy Councillor von Loß, in Pillnitz. Here, too, the meeting proceeded pleasantly; the Lusatian was again reassured of the benevolent intentions of his interlocutors.

The details of Boehme's stay in Dresden are too inconclusive to reveal anything certain about the true motives of his hosts. The question whether his beliefs received and passed the test of an official colloquy has led to insupportable claims and counter claims.[9] Since the content of the discussions and the motives of the Saxon court are probably irretrievable, we can only consider the range of the *possible* reasons for the exceptional invitation extended to a shoemaker accused of heresy.

(1) One can view the invitation to Dresden in the light of Boehme's doctrinal and political "conservatism." His doctrinal polemics had been directed against the new sects and against the Calvinists. The Silesian Calvinists loyal to Jägerndorf were a threat to the fragile, transitory peace of 1624; and they stood in the way of an expansion of Saxon influence into Silesia. The Lusatian and Silesian interests represented by Boehme were not of this party. By sending him as their emissary, they reassured the Saxons of their willingness to accept the new status quo, and at the same time staked out a claim to the traditional independence of their territories. The Saxon court officials had some reason to regard Boehme as a potentially useful subject.

(2) It is also possible to interpret the official invitation and the sojourn in Dresden as an unpolitical matter for all concerned parties. One can interpret the talks in Dresden in the light of Boehme's own ambitions, as well as in the light of the private spiritual interests of his

hosts. His honor had been besmirched, his spiritual reputation challenged. The kindnesses of the Saxon officials conferred an unprecedented vindication. His letters from Dresden revel in what amounted to a triumph over Richter. For their part, Loß, the court alchemist Hinckelmann, the court chaplain Hoë, and the other officers of the court may have been truly fascinated by his writings. Boehme wrote that they all professed love for *The Path to Christ* and practiced its spiritual exercises (ep. 61.1, 62.5). There can be no doubt that his writings powerfully attracted his contemporaries, or that devotional writings were avidly read by people of all stations. Furthermore, the Saxons may have considered the traditionally Philippist clergy of Görlitz an unworthy defender of the Lutheran faith; and they may simply have disregarded the aspersions cast by Prof. Hunnius, now combatting heresies in distant Lübeck.

(3) Finally, at the opposite end of the spectrum, it is possible that the officials of the court were hoping against hope that Boehme might be right about the advent of a new reformation. From Dresden, the Lusatian visitor reported that the city was in a victorious mood, as Prague had been years before. He reported that there was talk of a peace agreement between the Emperor and Gabriel Bethlen. But he made it clear that the "tidings" pointed in the opposite direction. He was convinced that the war would go on until the destruction of Babylon. If only the new faith triumphed in Saxony, then at least "the war would have a hole" (*so hätte der Krieg ein Loch*—ep. 62.5). In this same letter, he mentioned having seen or heard of English and Swedish military recruitments in Saxony (ep. 62.10). No other passage in all of his writings is so conscious of specific foreign countries: the Netherlands, Hungary, Sweden, England. A year earlier he had still expected great deeds from the "Oriental beast"; now he is apprehensive about the "enemy" and "destroyer" (*Einreisser*) who will come from many directions, especially from "midnight" (ep. 64.4). It is unlikely that the visitor was privy to tidings unknown to his Saxon hosts. To themselves, if not to him, they may well have acknowledged the grim threat presented by the new war preparations.

In 1624, there were rumors of an emerging great coalition of the north. James I, having formerly abandoned his German son-in-law, was now sending out feelers to the other Protestant states. Potential partners for an alliance with England included Holland, Denmark, Sweden, Brandenburg, and Hungary, with possible backing from France or Russia. Gustavus Adolphus of Sweden was already offering to invade the Empire by way of Poland and Silesia.[10] While the Danielian Kings of the North were hatching their plans, the King of the South, whose cause Johann Georg had well served, was relentlessly pursuing the aims of the Counter-Reformation in neighboring Bohemia. Ferdinand had first expelled the Calvinists and Bohemian Brethren and then the Lutheran pastors. By 1624, even the Lutheran peasants and townspeople were being compelled to convert or flee from the neighboring land.[11] The fruits of the Augsburg system of confessional states were being laid onto the very doorstep of its staunchest defender. Electoral Saxony was a frontline state, between consolidating and increasingly militant confessional camps. It may be an error to assume that the notion of a "new reformation" was not taken seriously by Boehme's Saxon interlocutors, simply because hindsight can see now that no such prospect existed. Twice before, history had proven that a reformation was capable of revolutionizing the political landscape of Middle Europe. Even the least imaginative doctrinarian, if informed about the true prospects in store for Saxony, might have wondered whether a new reformation was not, after all, the lesser evil. Compared to the grapes of wrath ripening slowly in the summer of 1624, the kind of tolerance and love which was propagated by the shoemaker may have appeared not just interesting, but urgently interesting.

During Boehme's stay in Dresden, no action was taken or proposed. It is therefore quite possible that Loß, Hoë, and the officers and clergymen who conversed with him harbored all sorts of thoughts while hearing him out. Their intentions may have been diverse enough to include the diplomatic cultivation of a man who had important contacts in Silesia, a private curiosity about the rare phenomenon of a cobbler who wrote, an eagerness to meet an author whose originality and style were widely esteemed, as well as zeal to assure that Boehme was not an Arian heretic or theorist of witchcraft. They may have been motivated by a wary interest in the potential spiritual leader of a new movement, by fond nostalgia for the bygone Christendom which Boehme evoked—and by fears for the fate of Saxony and for the future of the Lutheran faith. Even without clairvoyance, they could have known that their secure world stood condemned; and they would have had ample grounds to repent for their political sins. If even the practical minded Wallenstein sought the counsels of astrology, it is hardly farfetched to imagine that the Saxon court officials harbored the irrational hope that the prophetic Lusatian might know and tell them some way to avert their own day of reckoning.

Judging by his letters from Dresden, Boehme did not expect the New Reformation to arrive through his sole agency. Arriving in Dresden, he wrote that there were many books of his kind in circulation. In Dresden, books on the "new rebirth and the final age" (of the Spirit) were publicly available in bookstores (ep. 62.8). If the elector decided to declare a reformation (*Will er eine Reformation anfangen* . . .), Johann Georg could take note of the presence of a reformer "in his land" (ep. 63.9). This vague optimism was nourished by Boehme's exhilaration at finding himself in the vanguard of what appeared to be a spreading movement, in a climate of free discussion.

The Inconclusive Duel

Just as the controversy between Gessner and Moller had been resolved by the death of first the accuser and then the accused, the dispute between Richter and Boehme was terminated by the death of the pastor and then of the accused author. The clash was not decisive. However, the mere fact that Boehme adhered to his stance and outlived his opponent provided a kind of triumph, prior to his own death in November 1624. Since his opposition to Richter was by no means purely impersonal, this triumph must have been a source of some satisfaction.

All of his recorded reactions during the spring of 1624 indicate that Boehme adhered to his principles and ideals. Since he planned to publish his reply to Richter, he may well have told the Saxon court officials the same things that he had written in his defense. The *Apologia* is one of Boehme's most eloquent and forceful pieces of writing. "You despise me because I am a layman, and heap contempt on my gifts, which I have received from God . . . ," he writes in answer to Richter's contumelies,

> And ridicule my craft . . . Just look back into the world and see what sort of simple people God has employed for His work. Who were Abel, Seth, Enoch, and Noah? Who were the patriarchs? Shepherds, who were not doctors either. . . . (V *Schutz-Rede* 361–362.4–5)

Boehme goes on to defend the Noble Virgin, to reaffirm the authority of the "Book of Nature," and to argue for the triad of alchemistic principles. He maintains that his inspiration was not an ecstatic transport (*Verzückung*), but rather an illumination of the Spirit. And he rebuffs the pastor's own qualifications as a spiritual guide and corrects the assertion that the Orient fell away from Christianity because of the Arian antitrinitarian heresy: it fell away because the Eastern peoples were sick of the Christian controversies over the Trinity (V *Schutz-Rede* 369.24). If Pastor Richter wants to accuse people of heresy, he should look at himself and look at his fellow theologians. Instead of practicing Christian mildness, every one of them has shouted: "Heresy! Here is Christ, there is Christ, look, He is in the desert, in the tomb, in the field, in the Communion (*Abendmahl*), in the baptism, in the confession . . ." (V *Schutz-Rede* 370.25). "Because of this," he warned Richter, "you are your own prophet, and menace yourself with darkness..."

> and because you call me a prophet, to be sure, with a malicious intent, as a calumny, I shall tell you what the Lord has made known, namely: That the time has been born in which God will settle accounts for your disputes over the chalice of Christ, and punish you for them.... (V *Schutz-Rede* 370.26)

This is the same man who also denied any prophetic gifts, and adhered throughout his life to definite views of the Eucharist. His intent is clear, and the strategy of turning the tables on his adversaries is skillful. However, he could not pursue this intent and strategy without embroiling himself in contradictions.

It is only toward the end of his polemic that the level of this strategy decends to tit-for-tat pettiness. Boehme refutes the charge that he drank foreign wines and brandy: "We poor men have to make do with beer (or with such drinks we can produce)." The pastor himself, however, is notorious in Görlitz for a face livid from drink; he is known to prefer strong drink to serious spiritual discussions (V *Schutz-Rede* 386–387/63–65). In Dresden, Boehme urgently wrote to his friends to send him a copy of this *Apologia* so that he could show it to his Saxon hosts (ep. 63.12).

During the Dresden visit, Richter was inciting the people against him in Görlitz. Boehme sent instructions to his family by way of his friend, Dr. Kober, who was to reassure Katharina and see to her needs. The tone is concerned, but the main point is that he will not leave Dresden until he has concluded his business. His wife is distraught because of the mob threat in Görlitz and because of the exceptional nature of her husband's journey. On June 16, Boehme sends orders by way of Kober that she is not to have new shutters installed in his windows: if the mob smashes his windows, so be it. Everyone can then see the "fruits of the high priest" (ep. 64.12). Two years after the death of her husband, the long-suffering Katharina died of plague in Kober's house, while tending the victims of an epidemic.

By July, Boehme was back in Görlitz. In August, he fell seriously ill. Despite his weakened condition, he undertook another journey to Silesia; apparently he was eager to report to Franckenberg and Schweinich about what he had learned in Dresden. Another illness, a fever, seized him in November. He was transported back to Görlitz, near death upon his arrival.

The dying man and his mortal remains were at the mercy of Richter's pastoral successors, who seized this opportunity to interrogate the failing communicant before giving him the *Abendmahl*. Later, they grotesquely exhibited their unwillingness to perform the burial services ordered by the city council. But they performed his rites all the same. A monument erected by Boehme's friends was destroyed by a populace still incensed by the demagoguery of the pastors of Görlitz.

His death conformed to the style of his life. The cause of death was probably pneumonia and exhaustion. (There is no evidence to substantiate the theory that his heart had been broken by his failure to meet with and convert the Elector Prince of Saxony. If the Lusatians were to enjoy the kind of respect which Boehme had received from their new rulers, this might have been conversion enough.) He had been ill before, and the excitement and danger of his final year could only have weakened his constitution. His great volumes were finished. His hour had come. The Humanists of Görlitz shared the widespread belief of the time that human life was endangered in an advanced age which was a multiple of seven, called a "climacteric." Jacob Boehme—peasant, shoemaker, merchant, philosopher, mystic, and Lusatian envoy—died around the time of his seventh climacteric, most probably at the age of forty-nine. (Since his day of birth is not certain, it is possible that in November of 1624 he was just short of that age.) Could the pattern of seven times seven have induced the numerological mystic to believe that his hour had come round?

Several days after Boehme's death, Kober, who had been at the bedside of the dying man, wrote to the Schweinich brothers that in a nighttime hour the dying man had spoken to his son Tobias of "music." He had asked Tobias to open the doors wide so that the "singing" could be heard. Music often played a role in Boehme's conception of Paradise: the village fiddler summoning guests to the celestial wedding, the angelic hymns echoing in the transparent seas of the "innermost birth," and the clocklike harmonies of the great pipe organ of the world. Two hours after midnight, he told his son that this was not yet his hour. Before six, toward the completion of the seventh hour of the morning, he reportedly took leave of his wife and sons, asked to be turned in bed, and announced: "Now I am travelling thence into Paradise" (*Nun fahre ich hin ins Paradeis!*)—thence departing.[12]

His friends cherished the saying which Boehme customarily inscribed in their guest registries:

> Weme Zeit ist wie Ewigkeit,
> Und Ewigkeit wie die Zeit;
> Der ist befreyt
> Von allem Streit.
>
> For whom time is like eternity
> And eternity is like time
> He is free
> Of all adversity.[13]

We have seen that this saying can stand also as an epitaph for his writings. Boehme's thinking saw "time"—saw all processes, his times, its issues, and his own life experiences—*sub specie aeternitatis*. This accounts both for the difficult and fragmentary aspect of his writings, and for their extraordinary poetic beauty. Time as eternity is the barrier between his thought and our own. His world was both larger and smaller than ours. If time is absorbed into eternity, the causal understanding of the world dissolves with it. This most fundamental aspect of his thinking would only be obscured by any attempt to vindicate him as a prophet of later events, or by any effort to match his views with modern scientific theories. It is wiser to let him be what he was in the confines of his own world, and instead consider the relationship of his vanished universe of fact and belief to our own chimerically defined and truly threatened common existence.

What remains of the philosopher and mystic is above all else his revolving zodiac of symbols, which were intended to mean many things, and can therefore continue meaning even more: the figure of an excruciatingly self-made god, who eternally gives birth to his heart, and expresses it in the outpourings of his spirit; the image of a world, emanating out of the chaos and darkness of the will, in order to return, clarified and rendered transparent unto itself; the figure of the virginal Sophia, bound, but not wedded, to the angry god; and finally the ideal of the pristine seeing of an Adam whose wide open eyes behold the diverse hues and virtues articulating the inchoate divine intention—as an eternal band of stellar reflections in the mirror of darkness.

Notes

Introduction

1. Citations are referenced to the 1730 edition, which has also been published in facsimile: Jacob Böhme, *Sämtliche Schriften* (Stuttgart: Frommanns Verlag, 1955) ed. August Faust and Will-Erich Peuckert. My citations of *Aurora* and of Boehme's letters are sometimes translated from the published autographs: Jacob Böhme, *Die Urschriften* (Stuttgart: Frommanns Verlag, 1963), ed. Werner Buddecke. References are by volume (of the facsimile edition), by page, chapter, and section of the 1730 edition. (The chapter and section numbering as well as the epistle numbers are the same in the *Urschriften* and in several English translations.) For *Aurora*, the volume, page, chapter, and sections pertaining to the illumination are: *I 265ff./19.1ff*. The relevant passage of the letter in which Boehme mentioned that his experience had lasted only "a quarter of an hour" is: *ep. 12.7*. Franckenberg's biography of Boehme is included in vol. 10 of the facsimile edition; the pages pertaining to the illumination are: *X 10–11*.

2. See: Georg Wilhelm Friedrich Hegel, "Jakob Böhme," in *Werke* 20 (*Vorlesungen über die Geschichte der Philosophie* 3) (Frankfurt/M: Suhrkamp, 1971), pp. 91–119.

3. See: Mircea Eliade, *The Two and the One*, trans. J. M. Cohen (Chicago: University of Chicago Press, 1965).

4. Prominent among the philosophical studies is Alexandre Koyré's *La Philosophie de Jacob Boehme* (Paris: Vrin, 1979). Koyré cites the evolving aspect of Boehme's thought; so does Howard H. Brinton's sober-minded work, *The Mystic Will: Based on a Study of the Philosophy of Jacob Boehme* (New York: Macmillan, 1930). Hans Grunsky's valuable *Jacob Böhme* (Stuttgart: Frommann's Verlag, 1956), holds that the "geschlossenes System" of the philosopher Boehme was the outcome of spontaneous illuminations—though not in the ecstatic sense. Among the studies which have focused on Boehme's religious content, Heinrich Bornkamm's *Luther und Böhme* (Bonn: Marcus und Weber Verlag, 1925) and "Jacob Böhme, der Denker," in Bornkamm, *Das Jahrhundert der Reformation* (Göttingen: Vandenhoeck und Ruprecht, 1966), are sensitive to the evolving aspect of his speculation.

5. See: Eberhard H. Pältz, "Zu Jacob Boehmes Sicht der Welt- und Kirchengeschichte," in *Pietismus und Neuzeit* 81 (1980): 133–163; and Ernst Benz, *Der Prophet Jakob Boehme; Eine Studie über den Typus nachreformatorischen Prophetentums* (Wiesbaden: Steiner Verlag, 1959).

6. Scheffler the convert acknowledged the importance of Boehme's writings for his development: "Ich danke Gott dafür, denn sie sind große Ursache gewesen, daß ich zur Erkenntnis der Wahrheit gekommen bin." Cited from: Walter Nigg, *Angelus Silesius; Der Sänger der mystischen Weisheit* (Otten, 1959), p. 14.

7. See: Gershom Scholem, *Die jüdische Mystik in ihren Hauptströmungen* (Frankfurt/M.: Suhrkamp, 1980), p. 260.

8. *Cf.* Ernst Benz, "Zur metaphysischen Begründung der Sprache bei Jacob Böhme," in *Euphorion* (Neue Folge) 37 (1936): 310–57. (Writing in 1936, Benz is especially intent upon uncovering what is specifically German; however, his discussion of the *Natursprache* does recognize its universalistic sense.)

9. *Cf.* II 21/3.6; 83/8.36; V *An Tilke*, 1 84/530. (Franckenberg, whose national sentiments were more developed than Boehme's own, offers, as one of two possible explanations for the designation given his friend by Balthasar Walter: "oder zum Unterscheid der Nationen und wegen der vortreflichen Gabe solcher Hochteutschgesteleten Schriften."—X 15)

10. With regard to the "mediated" character of mystical language, I am in agreement with Steven T. Katz, about "The 'Conservative' Character of Mystical Experience," pp. 3–60, in *Mysticism and Religious Traditions*, ed. Steven T. Katz (New York: Oxford University Press, 1983). *Cf.* Steven T. Katz (ed.), *Mysticism and Philosophical Analysis* (New York: Oxford University Press, 1978).

11. See: Will-Erich Peuckert, *Pansophie; Ein Versuch zur Geschichte der weißen und schwarzen Magie* (Berlin: Schmidt Verlag, 1976), pp. 385ff. (Affecting the attitude of a German professor examining a student in the "pansophic" discipline, Peuckert pronounces that the prerequisites received from Pastor Moller were "ein mystisches Denken von einem recht bescheidenen Format": Boehme's "pansophic" knowledge was thus dilletantish and autodidactic, etc.)

12. *Cf.* Jaroslav Pelikan, *From Luther to Kierkegaard: A Study in the History of Theology* (St. Louis: Concordia Publishing House, 1950), p. 79. ("Curiously, few histories of Lutheran theology do more than mention the Thirty Years' War.... That is indicative of the fact that a large section of Lutheran theology scarcely took notice of the fiery trial through which the people were passing, another index of how completely much of Orthodox theology had lost touch with the people...") Among the poets of Boehme's period, Martin Opitz (born in 1597) was one of the few who displayed a sensitive interest in the effects of the war. Gryphius and Grimmelshausen were products of a later era.

13. Ernst Cassirer, *The Myth of the State* (New Haven: Yale University Press, 1975), pp. 131–132.

14. The best documentary fund of information about Boehme's life and environment is: *Das Neue Lausitzische Magazin*, (henceforth: *NLM*), a cultural

and historical journal published in Görlitz by *die Oberlausitzische Gesellschaft der Wissenschaften*. Some early contributions to the *NLM* provided the standard documentation of Boehme's life and circumstances, notably Hermann Fechner, "Jakob Böhme, sein Leben und seine Schriften," *NLM* 33 (1857): 313–446; 34 (1858): 27–138; and Richard Jecht, "Die Lebensumstände Jakob Böhmes," in: *NLM* 100 (1924): 179–248. A recent study that relies both on the *NLM* and on archival sources of the city of Görlitz, Ernst-Heinz Lemper's, *Jakob Böhme; Leben und Werk* (Berlin: Union Verlag, 1976), draws the balance of previous researches, corrects old errors, and adds some interesting details to the account of Boehme's circumstances and times. Werner Heimbach's monograph also taps the *Oberlausitzische Bibliothek der Wissenschaften* in Görlitz in order to correct and amend the picture of the confessional and intellectual situation in Boehme's time: "Das Urteil des Görlitzer Oberpfarrers Richter über Jakob Böhme," in: *Herbergen der Christenheit* 9 (1973/74): 97–151. In addition, Koyré's *La philosophie de Jacob Boehme* and Stoudt's *From Sunrise to Eternity* begin with useful remarks on the social and religious situation of the region.

15. Emmanuel Le Roy Ladurie, *Montaillou: village occitan de 1294 à 1324* (Paris: Gallimard, 1975); Carlo Ginzburg, *The Cheese and the Worms: The Cosmos of a Sixteenth-Century Miller*, trans. John and Anne Tedeschi (Baltimore: Johns Hopkins University Press, 1980); Frances A. Yates, *The Rosicrucian Enlightenment* (London: Routledge & Kegan Paul, 1972).

Chapter 1

1. See: Gerhard Wehr, *Jakob Böhme in Selbstzeugnissen und Bilddokumenten* (Hamburg: Rowohlt, 1971), p. 59.

2. Boehme's epistolary references distinguish between his own immediate "country" or "fatherland" and its neighbors: Silesia, Bohemia, and Saxony or Meissen. On a journey to Prague, he is "in einem anderen Lande" (ep. 3.3). He writes of the dissemination of his works "in vielen Orten in der Marcke Meissen und Sachsen" (ep. 13.1). In 1622, he reports on "Cosacken," who are galloping toward Poland, but may remain "in Böhmen oder Laußnitz" (ep. 32.4). Instead, they gallop eastward "durch Schlesien bei unsern Nachbarn" (ep. 34.23). In 1624, he writes that his fame has spread "fast durch gantz Europa," meaning as far as Leipzig in Saxony (ep. 50.7). In Dresden, the noble Joachim von Loß is praised for his diplomatic assistance to: "unserm Lande, sowol Schlesien nach dem Falle Frederici" (ep. 63.4). It is also noticeable that Boehme does not use the terms "Vaterland" or "mein Land," to refer to "Teutschland."

3. Hermann Knothe, "Urkundliche Grundlagen zu einer Rechtsgeschichte der Oberlausitz," *NLM* 53 (1877): 11–411, esp. 277–78.

4. See: Richard Jecht, "Die Oberlausitz im Hussitenkrieg und das Land

der Sechsstädte unter Kaiser Sigismund," part 1, in *NLM* 87 (1911): 33–279 (The wars of the *Raubritter* are discussed on pp. 78ff.); part 2, in *NLM* 90 (1914): 31–146 (according to the Humanist Manlius, the songs of the *Raubritter* were still sung 140 years later: pp. 60–62.); part 3, in *NLM* 92 (1916): 72–151. On the papal intervention against the outlaw nobles, and on their execution, see: Willi Boelcke, *Bauer und Gutsherr in der Oberlausitz* (Bautzen: Domowina, 1957).

5. Dr. Schönwälder, "Die hohe Landstraße durch die Oberlausitz im Mittelalter," *NLM* 56 (1880): 342–68, esp. p. 367.

6. Karl Brantl, "Welche Raubburgen wurden im Mittelalter von der Macht der Sechsstädte zerstört?" *NLM* 15 (1837), p. 116.

7. Karl Haupt, "Sagenbuch der Lausitz," *NLM* 40 (1863): 1–475, esp. pp. 121ff.

8. See: Richard Jecht, "Geschichte der Stadt Görlitz," *NLM* 99 (1923): 1–54, pp. 18–20: Görlitz was originally surrounded by Sorb villages, which were gradually germanized.

9. Jecht, "Hussitenkrieg," 1 (1911), pp. 275–276, reports thus of the persecutions of the Lusatian "heretics": "War zunächst die unmittelbare Gefahr beseitigt, so ängstigte eine andere Sorge die führenden Leute der Oberlausitz: Man war der Bewohner des eigenen Landes bei Abwehr der Ketzergefahr nicht mehr ganz sicher und vermutete allenthalben Hinneigung zu den Feinden, ja Verrat.... Noch schlimmer aber, daß man in den Städten selbst Verrat witterte.... Es begann ein bis dahin kaum gekanntes Mißtrauen Platz zu greifen, und die kleinste Unvorsichtigkeit gab Anlaß zur Verhaftung und peinlichen Befragung."

10. Jecht, "Hussitenkrieg," 1 (1911), p. 269.

11. Th. Scheltz, "Gesamtgeschichte der Ober- und Nieder-Lausitz," *NLM* 58 (1882): 1–239, esp. 93–115.

12. W. von Boetticher, "Sculteti e libris rerum gestarum Gorlicensium," *NLM* 91 (1915): 161–97, esp. p. 173.

13. There are two extended accounts of the Reformation in Görlitz: Otto Kämmel's "Johannes Hass, Stadtschreiber und Bürgermeister zu Görlitz," *NLM* 51 (1874): 1–246, esp. pp. 117–41; and Alfred Zobel's "Untersuchungen über die Anfänge der Reformation in der preussischen Oberlausitz," parts 1 and 2, *NLM* 101 (1925): 133–188; 102 (1926): 126–251. Kämmel, a rare Marxist writing in the pages of the *NLM*, and Zobel, a later pastor of Görlitz, agree on the essential points pertaining to the reform in Görlitz. As to the identity of the heretical elements threatened by Hass, Kämmel states that the Slavic rural folk had become Utraquists, and that there were also German Bohemian Brethren around Zittau (pp. 117, 123). However, the first claim is at odds with the assertion of a church historian: that *until* the Lutheran Reformation the local Sorbs

took Communion in one form only. See: Christian Knauthe, *Derer Oberlausitzer Sorbenwenden umständliche Kirchengeschichte* (Cologne, Vienna: Böhlau Verlag, 1980), p. 165 (on the Catholic orthodoxy of the Sorbs).

14. See Hans J. Hillerbrand, *The World of the Reformation* (Grand Rapids: Baker Book House, 1973), pp. 38ff.

15. Zobel, "Untersuchungen," *NLM* 102 (1926), pp. 149–151.

16. Zobel, "Untersuchungen," *NLM* 102 (1926), pp. 145–146.

17. Zobel, "Untersuchungen," *NLM* 102 (1926), pp. 158–159: "[Der Rat] erhoffte von den Innungen für ein Nachgeben auf religiösem Gebiet ein Zurückstellen ihrer kommunalpolitischen Forderungen und damit eine Befriedung der Verhältnisse. Um des Ganzen willen entschloß sich der Rat zur Erfüllung der religiösen Wünsche."

18. See: Authors' Collective (Günter Vogler, Adolf Laube, Max Steinmetz), *Illustrierte Geschichte der deutschen frühbürgerlichen Revolution* (Cologne: Pahl-Rugenstein Verlag, 1982), pp. 322–23.

19. See: Heimbach, "Das Urteil," p. 121.

20. Friedrich Pietsch, "Görlitz im Pönfall," *NLM* 111 (1935): 51–141, esp. p. 53.

21. Pietsch, "Pönfall," pp. 135–136: "Wie sehr sich die politische Stellung der Stadt verändert hatte, zeigt sich auch in dem Verhältnis der Stadt zum Land. Der alte Kampf zwischen Stadt und Landadel beginnt abzuebben.... Der neue Landvogt Christoph von Dohna auf Königsbrück war, wenn man den Anklageschriften der Stände glauben darf, ein sonderbarer Heiliger, mit einer rechten Freude am Foltern, am Brennen, Ziehen und Stäupen und Hinrichten.... Er schob den Adel ebenso beiseite wie die Städte."

22. See: Schönwälder, "Landstraße durch die Oberlausitz," p. 367.

23. Pietsch, *"Pönfall,"* p. 134–136.

24. Walter Gerblich, "Johann Leisentritt und die Administratur des Bistums Meissen in den Lausitzen," *NLM* 107 (1931): 1–78.

25. See: Alexandre Koyré, *La Philosophie de Jacob Boehme* (Paris: Vrin, 1979), p. 2. ("En 1539, en effet, l'anabaptisme avait pris pied dans la Lusace. Un certain Johann Ender prêcha la doctrine de Thomas Müntzer à Görlitz même et dans ses environs. Il eut un grand succès, surtout parmi le bas peuple des campagnes. Malgré le nombre de ses adeptes—peut-être à cause de leur grand nombre—ce n'est qu'en 1549 que le Sénat eut l'occasion d'intervenir. Plusieurs hérétiques furent brûlés, d'autres bannis de pays.")

26. See: Gustav Koffmane, "Die religiösen Bewegungen in der evangelischen Kirche Schlesiens während des 17. Jahrhunderts" (Breslau: Selbstver-

lag des Herausgebers, 1880), p. 3. (Koffmane cites: *Buckische Religionsacte*, vol. IC 12, 1589.)

27. R. Emmet McLaughlin, *Caspar Schwenckfeld: Reluctant Radical* (New Haven: Yale University Press, 1986), p. 215. See also: Horst Weigelt, *The Schwenckfelders in Pennsylvania*, trans. Peter C. Erb (Pennsburg, Pa.: The Schwenckfelder Library, 1985), and Selina Gerhard Schulz, *Caspar Schwenckfeld von Ossig* (Norristown, Pa.: The Schwenckfelder Church, 1946).

28. Lemper, *Jakob Böhme*, pp. 28, 48–49.

29. See: Pastor Johannes Trillmich, "Hoffmann, ein Görlitzer Bürgermeister um 1600," in: *NLM* 90 (1914): 1–30, esp. 28–29.

30. Henry J. Cohn, "The Territorial Princes in Germany's Second Reformation, 1559–1622," in *International Calvinism, 1541–1715*, ed. Menna Prestwich (Oxford: Clarendon Press, 1985), pp. 135–165, esp. p. 141.

31. Cohn, "Second Reformation," p. 138.

32. Reinhold Seeberg, *Textbook of the History of Doctrines*, vol. 1, trans. Charles E. Hay (Grand Rapids: Baker Book House, 1977), p. 381.

33. Ernst Koch, "Moscowiter in der Oberlausitz und M. Bartholomäus Scultetus in Görlitz," in *NLM* 86 (1910), pp. 13–14. This is part of a series of three articles by Koch on Mayor Scultetus, see also under the same title: *NLM* 83 (1907): 1–90; and under the title "Scultetica," *NLM* 92 (1916): 20–58.

34. Thomas Klein, *Der Kampf um die zweite Reformation in Kursachsen, 1586–1591* (Köln, Graz: Böhlau Verlag, 1962).

35. Ilse Hofmann, *Deutschland im Zeitalter des 30-jährigen Krieges. Nach Berichten und Urteilen englischer Augenzeugen.* (Greifswald: Julius Abel, 1927), p. 80.

36. See: "Nikolaus Krell," in *Allgemeine Deutsche Biographie* (Leipzig: Duncker und Humblot, 1883).

37. Max Gondolatsch, "Der Personenkreis um das Görlitzer Convivium Musicum im 16. und 17. Jahrhundert," *NLM* 111 (1935): 76–155.

38. See: *Die Selbstbiographie des Heidelberger Hofpredigers Abraham Scultetus (1566–1624)*, ed. Gustav Adolf Benrath (Karlsruhe: Verlag Evangelischer Presseverband, 1966), p. 22.

39. Koch, "Moscowiter," p. 15.

40. Lemper, *Jakob Böhme*, p. 38 and note 25.

41. Koch, "Moscowiter," pp. 18–20.

42. Karl Vocelka, *Die politische Propaganda Rudolfs II (1576–1612)* (Vienna: Akademie der Wisschenschaften, 1981), p. 150.

43. Gottfried Arnold, *Unparteiische Kirchen- und Ketzergeschichte* (Hildesheim: Olms, 1967), pp. 862–70; *cf.* Schaff, *Creeds*, 1, pp. 345–46; and Thomas Klein, *Zweite Reformation in Kursachsen*, p. 34 (The public execution of Krell was: "ein großes Schauspiel für ganz Dresden.... Die lutherische Geistlichkeit sah ihren Haß auf den besiegten Kanzler Kurfürst Christians aber erst gesättigt, als sie ihm nicht nur das Leben, sondern auch seine Ehre als reformierter Christ und Staatsmann durch eine im Druck verbreitete Leichenpredigt nehmen konnte, in die ein angebliches Schuldbekenntnis und ein Widerruf seiner theologischen Ansichten augenscheinlich hineingelogen waren.")

44. Lemper, *Jakob Böhme*, p. 38.

45. *Aurora* is especially audacious in citing inconsistencies in the Book of Genesis and expressing doubt about its literal truth. Thus, there could be no "morning and evening" before the creation of the sun; and Moses could hardly have observed the world being created, hence the account is hearsay (*cf.* I 245/18.1; 285/20.2; 324/22.26).

46. Koch, "Moscowiter," in *NLM* 83 (1907), pp. 56ff.

47. Koch, "Scultetica," in *NLM* 92 (1916), p. 29.

48 Koch, "Scultetica," in *NLM* 92 (1916): pp. 24, 28. (Koch cites this notation from Scultetus's calendar: "1600 Apr. 15 zu abends ist bei mir gewesen Rabbi Jehuda oder der Löwe." Koch also refers to Scultetus' interest in kabbalistic studies.)

49. Koch, "Scultetica," in *NLM* 92 (1916), p. 28.

50. Ernst Koch, "Scultetica," *NLM* 92 (1916), pp. 29–30. A Görlitzer named Franz Wendler had similar interests; he wrote a treatise on the great comet observed in the winter months of 1618–1619. *Cf.*: Gerhard Eis, "Ein Pesttraktat des Görlitzer Paracelsisten Franz Wendler," in: *Vor und nach Paracelsus; Untersuchungen über Hohenheims Traditionsverbundenheit und Nachrichten über seine Anhänger* (Stuttgart: Gustav Fischer Verlag, 1965), pp. 128–35.

51. See: Robert Kolb, *Caspar Peucer's Library: Portrait of a Wittenberg Professor of the Mid-16th Century* (St. Louis: Center for Reformation Research, 1976), p. 4; *cf.* Koch, "Moscowiter," in *NLM* 83 (1907), pp. 64–65.

52. In fact, this presentation has been maintained in the complete absence of any primary evidence. Heimbach has definitively disproven the image of Richter as a narrow orthodox Lutheran in doctrine, though the suggestion that the image of Moller should also be reversed lacks evidence. See: "Das Urteil," p. 106.

53. Reinhard Zöllner, "Das deutsche Kirchenlied in der Oberlausitz von der Mitte des 16. bis zum Ende des 18. Jahrhunderts," *NLM* 47 (1870): 37–38, 131–35.

54. Gondolatsch, "Convivium Musicum," pp. 76–155.

55. W. Ganzemüller, "Briefe eines Lausitzer Alchemisten aus den Jahren 1496–1506," in: Ganzemüller, *Beiträge zur Geschichte der Technologie und der Alchemie* (Weinheim/Berstraße: Verlag Chemie, 1956), pp. 219–227, esp. 223 ("dan in der zal der 7 tage werden alle ding begriffen....").

56. Heimbach, "Das Urteil," p. 120. *Cf.* Ernst–Heinz Lemper, "Görlitz und der Paracelsismus," in: *Deutsche Zeitschrift für Philosophie* 18: 3 (1970): 347–360.

57. Koch, "Moscowiter," in *NLM* 83 (1907), p. 75., n. 2.

58. Jecht, "Lebensumstände," in *NLM* 100 (1924), p. 203, n. 1.

59. It is worth considering that the Lurian Kabbalah of Safed in Palestine began to acquire fame just before 1600: Walter (and Scultetus), who stood in the Renaissance tradition of Christian Kabbalah, may have been in the avant-garde of the new wave of interest. See: Scholem, *Die jüdische Mystik*, p. 283.

60. Koch, "Scultetica," in *NLM* 92 (1916), p. 24; *cf.* "Moscowiter," in *NLM* 83 (1907), p. 75.

61. See: Wolfgang Behringer, "'Erhob sich das ganze Land zu ihrer Ausrottung...': Hexenprozesse und Verfolgungen in Europa," in: *Hexenwelten; Magie und Imagination vom 16–20. Jahrhundert* (Frankfurt/Main: Fischer, 1987), pp. 131–163.

62. See: Hugh R. Trevor-Roper, "Der europäische Hexenwahn des 16. und 17. Jahrhunderts," in: *Die Hexen der Neuzeit*, ed. Claudia Honegger (Frankfurt/Main: Suhrkamp, 1978), pp. 188–234, esp. 202, 210–11.

63. Eitner, "10 Jahre aus Görlitzens Vergangenheit," *NLM* 70 (1894): 13–20, esp. p. 16.

64. Koch, "Moscowiter," in *NLM* 83 (1907), p. 76.

65. Eitner, "10 Jahre," *NLM* 70 (1894), pp. 17–18.

66. Erich Wentscher, "Die Görlitzer Scharfrichter," *NLM* (1931): 87–101, esp. p. 95.

67. Koch, "Scultetica," *NLM* 92 (1916), pp. 37, 41–42. (With the *Pönfall*, the League Cities had lost their capital jurisdiction over the nobility.)

68. The ghost-riding huntsman is a widespread legend in German folk culture. (The feudal nobility usually enjoyed exclusive hunting rights.) *Cf.* Haupt, "Sagenbuch der Lausitz," pp. 121ff. (wandering ghosts); p. 123 (a restless spirit who is also a *Raubritter*); p. 141 (Junker Hans, who apparently flies through the air, and the village fiddler) pp. 205–231 (legends of treasures buried beneath castle ruins), p. 227 (a "fiery man" who guards a treasure).

69. See: Boelcke, *Bauer und Gutsherr*, p. 5 (executions of outlaw nobles); *cf.* Karl Haupt, "Sagenbuch der Lausitz," p. 227.

70. Richard Jecht, "Pest in Görlitz: 1585/86," *NLM* 109 (1933): 142–48.

71. Martin Luther, *De servo arbitrio*, in *Werke* 18 (Weimar: Böhlau, 1908), pp. 782–83.

Chapter 2

1. The village records indicate that Boehme's mother died sometime prior to 1607, the exact year being unknown. His father settled the inheritance with his children in 1607 and then remarried. The elder Jacob died in 1618. *Cf.* Jecht, "Lebensumstände," in *NLM* 100 (1924): 179–247.

2. As to his education, the mature man and writer, in choosing his metaphors, often recalled the eager faith of a small pupil by allegorizing the spiritual *ABC-Schüler*. The term may betray not only Boehme's early receptiveness to instruction but also the full extent of his schooling. Latin, Greek, and mathematics were not part of his "ABC" tutelage. Even at the renowned *Gymnasium* in Görlitz where Scultetus once taught, mathematics occupied the pupils for only one single hour a week. See: Koch, "Moskowiter," *NLM* 83 (1907), p. 5.

3. Though it is essential for all of his writings, Boehme's characterization of the "historical faith" emerges only gradually. In his second book, a section called "Die Porte zu Babel" construes the Roman apostolic faith as the generalized type of any false, literalistic, and legalistic religion (II 466/26.13ff.). In *The Threefold Life of Man*, the historical and literal contrasts, formulistically, with the inner, eternal, and the spiritual. In Part 1 of *The Human Genesis of Christ* (*Von der Menschwerdung Jesu Christi*), the same contrast reaches fruition when the historical *person* of Christ is eclipsed in favor an omnipresent, eternal, inner, and universally human *process* of Christ (IV I. 3/1.3; 88/11.8).

4. See: *Aurora*, ch. 20. The motives constituting the general context of the nonhistorical faith are taken up in the pivotal sections of Boehme's first work (I 286–87/20.14–15): the "light" of the Prolog to John (I 278/19.88), and the transfigured face of Moses (I 281/19.103), the Platonic interpretation of the *logos* as a higher, eternal order of nature, which sustains the elemental order of the world (I 291/20.48)—and finally, the corollary of a tolerance, resulting from the true understanding of Scripture (I 288/20.22ff).

5. On the broad dissemination of Luther's printed sermons, see: Hillebrand, *The World of the Reformation*, p. 97.

6. Heinrich Bornkamm, *Luther und Böhme* (Bonn: Marcus Weber Verlag, 1925), p. 103.

7. See esp.: "Sermon von dem Sacrament des leibs und bluts Christi, widder die Schwarmgeister," *Werke* 19 (Weimar: Böhlau, 1908), pp. 482–99.

8. Ernst Troeltsch, *Die Soziallehren der christlichen Kirchen*, in *Gesammelte Schriften* I (Tübingen: Mohr, 1923), pp. 863–64, 898. (It is worth remarking that Weigel likewise retained a sense of the importance of the sacraments—it was above all Franck who dropped them.)

9. For the most accomplished discussion of Boehme's Spiritualism, see: Eberhard H. Pältz, "Zum Verständnis von Jacob Boehmes Autorschaft," in *Pietismus und Neuzeit* (1975): 9–21; and his, *Jacob Boehmes Hermeneutik, Geschichtsverständnis und Sozialethik* (University of Jena, Habilitationsschrift, 1961).

10. Behem's letter is reproduced most fully in Fritz Lieb, *Valentin Weigels Kommentar zur Schöpfungsgeschichte und das Schrifttum seines Schülers Benedikt Biedermann* (Zürich: EVZ Verlag, 1962), pp. 38–41, 161–62. n. 90a–91. Behem associated the fallen state with an impure, dark water, which is the subcelestial material nature, said to be an unbecoming vestment for the spirit. The fallen human creature should instead don the pure white garment of the celestial flesh and blood of the reborn soul.

11. *The Formula of Concord, 1576, The Saxon Visitation Articles, 1592*, in: *The Creeds of the Evangelical Protestant Churches, vol. 3*, ed. Philip Schaff (New York: Harper & Brothers, 1899), pp. 93–180, 181–189, cf. 186: ["*Falsche und irrige Lehre der Calvinisten vom heiligen Nachtmahl*"] "Daß Christus allda gegenwärtig sei nur mit seiner Kraft und Wirkung, und nicht mit seinem Leibe; gleichwie die Sonne mit ihrem Scheine und Wirkung hienieden auf Erden gegenwärtig und kräftig ist, aber die Sonne selbst ist droben im Himmel."

12. *Tischreden*, vol. 2 (Weimar: Böhlau, 1912–19), 292, 19–20.

13. See: Seeberg, *The History of Doctrines* 2, pp. 322–328.

14. In *Aurora*, most of Boehme's terms imply divine omnipresence. The luminescence and fecundity of the divine substance is because of God's presence *überall* (I 77/7.25, 29). There is a ubiquity of spirit forces, of the Holy Trinity, and of its eternal "births" (I 98/8.84). The plurality and harmony of the angelic world is due to the ubiquitous immanence of God who "in one place as in another" (I 152/12.41). In *The Three Principles of Divine Being*, the tone is more polemical: the ubiquity of the persons of the Trinity is confirmed (II 404/23.10) and the context of the divine ubiquity is posited as a solution to the disputes over religion (II 454/25.89ff.). It is senseless to list references: the whole of Boehme's vision devolves from the notion that God is everywhere, the source of all that is, and in all things. Instances in subsequent works in which the mysticism of ubiquity is employed to support the ideal of confessional harmony will be discussed in context. However, as we shall see, Boehme's understanding of omnipresence is distinct from the orthodox Lutheran one, and incorporates heterodox terms in an effort at compromise with other confessions.

15. Bornkamm's *Luther und Böhme* acknowledged that Boehme, while spiritualizing the *Abendmahl*, believed in a *real* enjoyment of Christ's spiritual flesh by the communicant (pp. 203–205). However, Bornkamm's treatment is too sketchy to do justice to this pivotal theme of Boehme's mysticism.

16. *Cf. Aurora*, ch. 20, pp. 294ff. ("The Holy Gates," against the eucharistic doctrine of Calvin, and on the "twofold birth through the water"); *The Three Principles of Divine Being*, ch. 23 ("On Christ's most worthy testaments, on Baptism and the Last Supper..."); *The Threefold Life of Man*, ch. 13 ("On Christ's most worthy testaments..."). Boehme insists that the sacraments are not mere "signs." In addition to *The Testaments of Christ*, nearly every other treatise contains significant allusions to the sacraments. In the *Index Rerum* (XI) provided by Boehme's early editors, *Abendmahl* heads up more than three pages of entries.

17. That Boehme, like Luther, proceeded from the premise of divine omnipotence but arrived at the opposite conclusion, is stated, if somewhat obliquely, by Bornkamm in his study of *Luther und Böhme*, p. 119: "Während bei Luther die Ausführung des Allmachtgedankens keinen anderen Sinn hat, als die Tatsache des servum arbitrium zu erweisen, so benutzt Böhme den qualitätslosen Charakter seiner kosmischen Bewegung, um ihr gegenüber die Freiheit in ihrer Herrschaft zu bestätigen." On the distinction of tenor between Lutheranism and Calvinism with respect to predestination, see: Seeberg, *The History of Doctrines* 2, p. 416.

18. (III *Vom dreyfachen Leben des Menschen* 224–227/11.82–91). Similarly, ch. 23 of Boehme's second book begins by alluding to the bloodshed caused by fighting over the "chalice" of Christ.

19. See: Sebastian Franck, *Die Guldin Arch* (Augsburg: Steyner, 1538).

20. Joachim Tanckius, *Promptuarium Alchemiae* (Leipzig, 1610; reprinted in Graz: Akademische Druck- und Verlagsanstalt, 1976), intro. Karl R. H. Frick. (Tanckius's preface begins by stating the complementarity of the Bible and science: "Ob nun wol die heilige Schrift allein meldet/ was Gott und sein Wille sey/ so haben doch die newen Naturkündiger auch aus der Natur/ wie der Apostel Paulus bezeiget/ ein Erkenntnis von Gott schöpfen und fassen können...")

21. The standard work on the pansophic tradition is Will-Erich Peuckert, *Pansophie; Ein Versuch zur Geschichte der weißen und schwarzen Magie* (Berlin: Erich Schmidt Verlag, 1976). (Peuckert stresses philosophical and esoteric aspects of the tradition.) For some more recent discussions of the varieties of syntheis in the arts, sciences, and political thought, see: *Prag um 1600; Kunst und Kultur am Hofe Kaiser Rudolfs II* (two-volume exhibition catalog), (Kunsthistorisches Museum, Vienna: Luca Verlag, 1988); Pietro Redondi, *Galileo Heretic*, (Princeton: Princeton University Press, 1987); Paul Laurence Rose, *Bodin and the Great God of Nature: The Moral and Religious Universe of a Judaiser* (Geneva: Librairie Droz, 1980); Lawrence S. Lerner and Edward A. Gosselin,

"Galileo and the Specter of Bruno," in *Scientific American* 255: 5 (1986): 126–133.; and Allen G. Debus and Robert D. Multhauf, *Alchemy and Chemistry in the Seventeenth Century* (Los Angeles: Clark Memorial Library, 1966).

22. Especially, Pico's *Heptaplus* and *De ente et uno* foreshadow Boehme's mysticism. Since the tropes and themes in question were shared by many other writers, there is no reason to assume a direct influence on the basis of these similarities.

23. The reader of Scholem's *Die jüdische Mystik* is forcefully impressed by what could well have been sources of Boehme's mysticism. In Boehme's second book, this applies to the vision of a divine, world-creating contraction, resembling the Kabbalistic *zimzum*, and to his treatment of the Kabbalistic myth of the first Adam (Adam Kadmon). (However, Cusanus and Bruno are also possible sources for the divine contraction: Jewish and Christian sources were in fact already mixed together centuries earlier.) Scholem was struck by Boehme's affinities with the Kabbalah, most notably by the shoemaker's view of evil as rooted in an aspect of the divine nature. See: Scholem, *Die jüdische Mystik*, p. 259.

24. *Cf.* I 370/25.19: Boehme's "der Locus dieser Welt" is a phrase close to one of Weigel's titles: *Vom Ort der Welt*. In his later writings, Boehme mentioned Paracelsus and Weigel by name (ep. 12.59–60).

25. See: *The Apology for Raymond Sebonde*, trans. and ed. M. A. Screech (London: Penguin, 1987), p. 16.

26. See: Carlo Ginzburg, *The Cheese and the Worms: The Cosmos of a Sixteenth-Century Miller* (Baltimore: Johns Hopkins University Press, 1980).

27. In addressing the closely related question of the origins of evil, Boehme clearly identifies the position that God ignited the fire of evil with the advocates of the "providence- and grace-election," i.e., with the Calvinists (I 216–217/15.57). However, the association of the bound will with the creation *ex nihilo* is also found in Luther's "Biblical anthropology" in the third part of *De servo arbitrio*: a God who created man out of nothing leaves no leeway for human freedom.

28. *Historia von D. Johann Fausten* (Text of the Printing of 1587), ed. Stephan Füssel and Hans Joachim Kreutzer (Stuttgart: Reclam, 1988), see: part 2, ch. 16 ("Die Helle/ der Frawen Bauch/ und die Erden werden nimmer satt."), ch. 18–27, pp. 39, 47, 59.

29. Cf.: Pierre Deghaye, "Dieu et la natur dans *L'Aurore naissante* de Jacob Boehme," in *Epochen der Naturmystik; Hermetische Tradition im wissenschaftlichen Fortschritt*, ed. Antoine Faivre and Rolf Christian Zimmermann (Berlin: Erich Schmidt Verlag, 1979), pp. 125–156.

30. Cited from: Marie Boas, *The Scientific Renaissance, 1450–1630* (New York: Harper & Brothers, 1962), p. 117 (from Tycho de Brahe, *On the Most Recent Phenomena of the Ethereal World*, 1588).

31. Johannes Kepler, *Epitome of Copernican Astronomy,* in The Great Books, vol. 16 (Chicago: Encyclopedia Britannica, Inc., 1952), pp. 854, 856. Like Boehme, Kepler was engaged by theological questions, including the eucharistic controversy and the thesis of divine ubiquity. Leaning toward the Calvinistic doctrine while attempting to remain loyal to the Formula of Concord, Kepler denied physical or local ubiquity but affirmed the effective omnipresence of the divine will. See: Jürgen Hübner, *Die Theologie Johannes Keplers zwischen Orthodoxie und Naturwissenschaft* (Tübingen: Mohr, 1975), pp. 111ff.

32. In order to view pictorial equivalents of Boehme's emblematic concepts, see: *Emblemata; Handbuch zur Sinnbildkunst des XVI. und XVII. Jahrhunderts,* ed. Arthur Henkel and Albrecht Schöne (Stuttgart: Metzlersche Verlagsbuchhandlung, 1967)—note especially the circle of emblems for sun, earth, and the elements. Boehme's influence on the typological tradition finds evidence in Paul J. Korshin, *Typologies in England, 1650–1820* (Princeton: Princeton University Press, 1982).

33. In *Aurora,* the prototype from Ezekiel evolves together with the concept of the heavens. Initially, true to the letter of Ezekiel, there is a model of four wheels, which are compared to the cooperation of forces in the heavens which symbolize the power of God the Father in nature. Here, the *sun* is still said to revolve in its orbit (I 40–41/3.9–11). Later, the model is given seven wheels, mounted in one another. Though this model is of "the true (eternal) birth of God," its language is precisely the same as is employed in *Aurora* in discussing the planets and their orbits: *Rad, Kugel, Umwenden, umdrehen* (I 177–179/13.68–79). In the account of the days of Creation, the eternal model of the spirit forces as wheels coincides with the turning of the *earth* and the planets (I 300/21.5). The eternal model of wheels thus becomes embodied in the created, noneternal solar system.

34. The "crystalline sea" is a leitmotiv in Boehme's writings. It is particularly interwoven with his other emblematic concepts in a passage of *The Threefold Life of Man:* III 82ff./5.11ff.

Chapter 3

1. For the dating of *Aurora,* see: Franckenberg's *Bericht* (X 80); and Hans Grunsky, *Jacob Böhme,* p. 33. Grunsky's considerations supplement Buddecke, *Die Jakob Böhme-Ausgaben,* 2 (Göttingen: Häntzschel, 1957), pp. xvi–xviii.

2. For a brief account of the vicissitudes of *Aurora,* see: Wolfram Buddecke, "Die Jakob-Böhme-Autographen; Ein historischer Bericht," in: *Wolfenbüttler Beiträge* 1 (1970): 61–87.

3. Several sections have an introductory ring: this applies not only to the preface, which must have been composed while the work was in progress, and to chapter one, which begins with fundamental definitions; it applies to

chapter nine as well, where the author provides a resounding apologia for his work and outlines the questions to be discussed in it; and to chapters nineteen and twenty-five, where he recounts his illumination and first efforts to write.

    4. Gershom Scholem, *Die jüdische Mystik*, p. 208; see also: Scholem, *Über einige Grundbegriffe des Judentums* (Frankfurt/Main: Suhrkamp, 1970). The essays, "Das Ringen zwischen dem biblischen Gott und dem Gott Plotins in der alten Kabbalah" and "Schöpfung aus Nichts und Selbsverschränkung Gottes," shed much light on the relations of the monotheistic religions to ancient philosophy.

    5. Plotinus, *The Six Enneads* (I.8), in *The Great Books*, vol. 17 (Chicago: Encyclopedia Britannica, Inc., 1952), p. 4.

    6. In the years 1602 and 1603, Seton was traveling from city to city. His stations included Basel, Frankfurt am Main, Munich, and Dresden. In Dresden, Seton was imprisoned and tortured by Elector Christian II, eager to discover the secrets of gold-making. Arthur Edward Waite, *The Secret Tradition in Alchemy: Its Development and Records* (London: Stuart & Watkins, 1969), pp. 240–43. *Cf.* John Ferguson, *Biblioteca chemica* (Glasgow, 1906), vol. 2, pp. 374–76.

    7. "Creatus homo de terra, ex aere vivit: est enim in aere occultus vitae cibus...." Michael Sendivogius (Alexander Seton), *Novum lumen chymicum*, in *Musaeum hermeticum* (Frankfurt am Main, 1678), p. 579.

    8. Friedrich Helbach, *Olivetum* (Frankfurt am Main, 1605), p. 120. See: Allen G. Debus, "The Paracelsian Aerial Niter," in: *ISIS* 55 (1964): 43–61. *Cf.* Lawrence M. Principe and Andrew Weeks, "Jacob Boehme's Divine Substance *Salitter*: its Nature, Origin, and Relationship to Seventeenth Century Scientific Theories," in *British Journal of the History of Science* 22 (1989): 52–61.

    9. Paracelsus, *De Meteora*, in *Sämtliche Werke* 3, ed. Bernhard Aschner (Jena: Fischer, 1930), pp. 950–954.

    10. The transitional ambiguity between an unreflective view of the cosmos and a mythological, and, finally, a reflective view is evident in chapter three. Employing the astrological analogy that preceded Copernicus, Boehme writes that the sun is the "king and the heart of all things in this world" (I 43/3.19). This is no doubt the kind of knowledge that allowed him to claim that his philosophy did not require the "formula" of the *astrologos*. The ambiguities of Boehme's early heliocentrism are most evident when in one single passage one finds contradictory characterizations of the position of the sun: "Die Sonne Gehed mitten In der Tiffe zwischen den sternen/ und Sie ist das Hertze der sternen...." but only a few lines below this: "Den gleich wie die Sonne mitten zwischen den sternen und Erden stehed/ und gibed allen sternen/ licht und krafft..." (I 43/3.19–20; *Urschriften* I 39). In the first sentence, the words "mitten" and "zwischen" seem to imply an absolutely central position. In the second sentence, the words "mitten zwischen den Sternen und Erden" imply that the sun is positioned between the earth and the stars. I am

inclined to read the two statements as loose and noncontradictory designations of the *metaphysical* significance of the sun. The second expression may be taken just as imprecisely as our own references to the sun's "rising"— which, for us, in no way contradicts the facts of the solar system. At the same time, the first statement is very little concerned with astronomy *per se*. The implications of either statement are ultimately the same: the sun is the symbolic center and the focus of all vital forces.

11. Martin Ruland, *Lexicon Alchemiae* (Hildesheim: Olms, 1964), p. 442.

12. Scholem makes this point with reference to Aquinas and the mystics in his *Die jüdische Mystik*, pp. 4–5. *Cf.* Luther, *The Magnificat*, trans. A. T. W. Steinhaeuser, in Luther, *Works*, vol. 21, ed. Jaroslav Pelikan (St. Louis: Concordia, 1956), p. 302. (Luther cites the psalm in explicating the line "Meine Seele erhebt Gott den Herrn.")

13. See: Isaiah Berlin, "Herder and the Enlightenment," in *Vico and Herder: Two Studies in the History of Ideas* (New York: Vintage, 1977), p. 153.

14. Hermann Knothe, "Die Bemühungen der Oberlausitz um einen Majestätsbrief (1609–1611)," *NLM* 56 (1880): 96–117.

15. The clock on the tower of the Görlitz City Hall was created by Scultetus. The clockface beneath the hands shows a radiant sun. The first concentric circle has thirty digits for the lunar month. This is surrounded by the phases of the moon, and this in turn by the twenty-four hours. The clock on the City Hall in Prague, a city visited by Boehme, shows the signs of the zodiac.

16. Translated from: Andreas Gryphius, *Frühe Sonetten* (Tübingen: Niemeyer, 1964), p. 90:

> Auff Todten! auff! die welt verkracht in letztem brande!
> Der Sternen Heer vergeht! der Mond ist dunckel-rott/
> Die Sonn' ohn allen schein! Auff/ Ihr die grab und kott
> Auff! ihr die Erd und See und Hellen hilt zu pfande!
>
> Ihr die ihr lebt kommt't an: der HERR/ der vor in schande
> Sich richten ließ/ erscheint/ vor Ihm laufft flamm' und noth
> Bey Ihm steht Majestätt/ nach Ihm/ folgt blitz und todt...

17. See "Der Sünden Quell-Ader" (I 185ff.; I 143ff.): here Boehme labors hardest and with the least satisfying results.

18. Human nature in *Aurora* consists of (1) elemental body; (2) soul (called *animalischer Geist*, from *anima*); and (3) astral or sidereal spirit (*siderischer Geist*, from *sidus*). These are the three "births" of the human creature; each is engendered by its own "mother." The flesh is "outermost," the soul "innermost." Later, he simplifies his terminology to *Leib, Seele, Geist*. For a discussion of the background of these concepts, see: Ernst Wilhelm Kämmerer, *Das Leib-Seele-Geist-Problem bei Paracelsus und einigen Autoren des 17. Jahrhunderts* (Wiesbaden: Steiner Verlag, 1971).

19. See: J. N. Findlay, *Hegel: A Re-examination* (New York: Oxford University Press, 1958), p. 160. ("Hegel likes to envisage even such a purely logical situation [as self-identity and difference] in terms of the mystical categories of Jacob Boehme, by whom having a quality is seen as an activity, a *Qualirung* or *Inqualirung* of the qualified object, which must struggle to maintain itself against the swamping environment.")

20. This is defined by Ruland as: *nicht alle mahl hoch über sich steigen/ sondern köstlich gut/ und herrlich werden* ("not necessarily to rise above itself, but rather to become precious, good, and noble").

Chapter 4

1. This is the theory of Grunsky, *Jacob Böhme*, p. 34.

2. Nothing proves this better than the actual contrast between the highly speculative *Aurora* and the prophetic miracles recounted by Peuckert at the beginning of his biography of Boehme, though it was Peuckert's intention to suggest the similarity.

3. Jecht, "Lebensumstände," p. 207.

4. Heimbach, "Das Urteil," pp. 97–150.

5. Karl R. H. Frick, *Die Erleuchteten. Gnostisch-theosophische und alchemistisch-rosenkreutzerische Geheimgesellschaften bis zum Ende des 18. Jahrhunderts—ein Beitrag zur Geistesgeschichte der Neuzeit* (Graz: Akademische Druck- u. Verlagsanstalt, 1973), pp. 158–59.

6. Frick, *Die Erleuchteten*, pp. 145–153.

7. See: Ernst Koch, "Böhmische Edelleute auf dem Görlitzer Gymnasium und Rektor Dornavius," in *NLM* 93 (1917): 1–48, esp. 32–33.

8. Heimbach, "Das Urteil," p. 118.

9. Korschelt, "Kriegsdrangsale von Görlitz und Umgebung," in *NLM* 63 (1888), pp. 325ff.

10. See: Will-Erich Peuckert, "Introduction" to vol. 2 of the facsimile edition, p. 7. Peuckert is surely right in accepting the dating of Boehme's own hand, over against the attempt to arrive at an interval of six years silence, based on dubious arguments.

11. *Cf.* Ruland, *Lexicon Alchemiae* (Facsimile reprint, Hildesheim: Olms, 1964), p. 383.

12. Later Lutheran divines, for example, debated whether the eucharistic presence and divine ubiquity entailed an "illocal omnipresence" or a "multipresence," whether the divine presence was absolute or relative, an

omnipraesentia, a *volipraesentia*, or a *multivolipraesentia*. See: Philip Schaff, *The History of Creeds*, vol. 1 (New York: Harper and Brothers, 1919), pp. 284–90.

13. *Cf.* II 404/23.10–11 ("wesentlich"); 414/23.51 ("das äussere ist Brot und Wein, wie dein äusserer Mensch auch irdisch ist, und das innere in seinem Testament ist sein [Christi] Fleisch und Blut.... nicht als einen Gedanken im Glauben (wiewol der Glaube auch da seyn muß) sondern im Wesen, dem äusseren Menschen unfaßlich). Soon, in *Vom dreyfachen Leben*, this usage becomes more insistent with respect to the "real presence" of flesh and blood, in the dual nature of Christ and in the bread and wine: "ein Wesen ist...ließ zu Fleisch und Blut werden" (III 256–57/13.10–12); at the same time, the German word for "ubiquitous," "allenthalben," is joined by "allwesentlich" in rationalizing the Eucharist (III 259/13.17). The usage is then expanded by the more abstractly tempered word "Wesenheit," which becomes far more frequent in the first part of *Von der Menschwerdung Jesu Christi* (*cf.* IV 8/1.12; 18/3.8, 10; 39/5.15; 71/9.12).

14. See: Luther, *Das Magnificat verdeutscht und ausgelegt* (1521), in *Werke* 7, (Weimar: Böhlau, 1897) pp. 550ff.

15. In *The Three Principles*, "Principium" is thus defined: "ein Principium ist anders nichts als eine neue Geburt, ein neu Leben" (II 49/5.6). *Cf. On the Human Genesis of Christ*: "Denn das ist eigentlich ein Principium, da ein Ding wird, das es nie gewesen ist, da aus dem Nichts ein Qual wird" (IV 140/2.5.1).

16. The following sections pertain to the transition from the fourth to the fifth spirit, from the sulphur-water to the sweet water and *Quinta Essentia*: II 17/12.10; 18/2.11; *cf.* 32/4.18.

17. As with many elements of Boehme's mysticism, one can take one's choice of "origins": the German mysticism of the *Theologia Deutsch*, the Renaissance philosophy of Pico della Mirandola, or Jewish Gnosticism or theosophy (Adam Kadmon).

18. See: W. A. Schulze, "Das Auge Gottes," in *Zeitschrift für Kirchengeschichte* 68 (1947): 149–52.

19. Grunsky, *Jacob Böhme*, pp. 279–80, argues effectively that Eve can only be understood symbolically.

20. Koyré, *La Philosophie de Jacob Boehme*, p. 227.

21. See: Martin Chemnitz, *Ministry, Word, and Sacraments: An Enchiridion*, ed. and trans. Luther Poellot (St. Louis: Concordia, 1981), p. 45 (based on the 1603 edition).

22. Abraham Carlov, *Anti-Böhmius, in quo docetur quid habendum de secta Jacobi Böhmen sartoris Görlicensis* (Wittenberg: Schrödter, 1684) (Among other accusations: Boehme did not adhere to the Scriptures.); Abraham Hinckelmann, *40 Wichtige Fragen betreffende die Lehre so in Jacob Böhmens Schriften*

enthalten (Hamburg: Schulßischen Buchladen, 1693) (Hinckelmann took offense at the supposed denial of the Trinity, the presentation of the origin of evil as in God, the theory of the seven qualities, the Creation *ex se*, and sundry other imprecisions and ambiguities.).

23. The ambiguity arises because of the unclear reference of the pronoun *ihr*: "Ihr Weg ist so subtile wie des Menschen Gedancken, und die Gedancken entstehen auch daraus."

Chapter 5

1. Golo Mann, *Wallenstein* (New York: Holt, Rinehart and Winston, 1971), pp. 112–113, 116.

2. G. Korschelt, "Kriegsdrangsale von Görlitz und Umgegend zur Zeit des dreißigjährigen Krieges," in *NLM* 63 (1888): pp. 332ff.

3. Hermann Knothe, "Die Bemühungen der Oberlausitz um einen Majestätsbrief (1609–1611)," in *NLM* 56 (1880) p. 117.

4. Korschelt, "Kriegsdrangsale," p. 333.

5. See: Arthur Schopenhauer, *Über die vierfache Wurzel des Satzes vom zureichenden Grunde*, in *Werke* 5 (Zürich: Diogenes, 1977), p. 30; *cf.* Rätze's accusation, in Arthur Schopenhauer, *Der handschriftliche Nachlaß*, 1, ed. Arthur Hübscher (Frankfurt am Main: Verlag Waldemar Kramer, 1966), p. 334.

6. Friedrich Baron de la Motte Fouqué, *Jakob Böhme; Ein biographischer Denkstein* (Greiz: Henning, 1831), p. 13.

7. Albert Peip, *Der deutsche Philosoph; Der Vorläufer christlicher Wissenschaft* (Leipzig: Hirschfeld, 1860), p. 157.

8. W. Elert, *Die voluntaristische Mystik Jakob Böhmes; Eine psychologische Studie* (Berlin: Trowitzsch, 1913), p. 2 ("Will man noch zweifeln, ob Böhme deutsch war? Man stelle ihn, wie ihm oft geschah, neben den Juden Spinoza... und man wird nicht länger fragen.")

9. Will-Erich Peuckert, *Das Leben Jacob Böhmes* (Jena: Diedrichs, 1924), p. 91. (*Cf.* X 126) With only minor revisions, Peuckert's invective is maintained in the biography included in volume 10 of the facsimile reprint edition. The standards of Peuckert's own time are applied to Boehme in order to arrive at the judgment: "Wen nötigt es nicht zu einem Lächeln; das laufende, kleine Schuhmacherlein [here Peuckert forces his interpretation onto one of Boehme's letters to claim further cowardice]..." (X 125) The denigrating tone and the unobjective interpretation pose serious questions about the judgement of the publisher which chose to include Peuckert's biography as an integral part of a standard edition.

10. Paul Hankamer, *Jakob Böhme; Gestalt und Gestaltung* (Bonn: Cohen, 1924), p. 70.

11. Herbert Cysarz, "Jacob Böhme und das literarische Barock," in: *Das Jahrbuch des Wiener Goethe-Vereins* 80 (1976): 5–19. (In full, the citation, placed in parentheses in the text, reads: "Böhme ist denn in nachmals Houston Stewart Chamberlains Jahrtausend-Perspektiven ein Vorkämpfer der Reinigung und Reinhaltung des 'arisch-germanischen' Christentums ... ein Widerpart aller fremdbürtigen Verfälschungen des Christentums.")

12. See: Wolfram Buddecke, "Die Jakob-Böhme-Autographen," in *Wolfenbüttler Beiträge* 1 (1972): 61–87. When Rudolf Hess defected to England, the Gestapo attempted to confiscate the still unedited Boehme autographs, which had been rediscovered only a few years earlier, and continued to hold what the officials erroneously considered to be all of the extant originals. It has been said that this action was based on a perception of Boehme's writings as those of an esoteric cultist. During this same time, however, Nazi cultural officials were planning to celebrate Boehme as a great German and man of the people. (*Cf.* Buddecke, "Böhme-Autographen," pp. 79.ff.) It would be worth considering whether the Nazi officials, in holding the autographs against the protests of scholars, acted to keep the "Aryan" canon of German mysticism (signally important because of Rosenberg's theses) pure, by suppressing documentary evidence that Boehme not only adhered to more universal values, but had indeed prophesied doom for the "Antichrist" and "Babylon" in Germany.

13. See: Mirjam Bohatcová, *Irrgarten der Schicksale* (Prague: Artia, 1966), for the reproduced illustrations. The most extensive collections of the "folk songs" are: Emil Weller, ed., *Die Lieder des Dreißigjährigen Krieges* (Basel: H. Georg's Verlag, 1858); and Franz Wilhelm Freiherr von Dithfurth, ed., *Die historisch-politischen Volkslieder des dreißigjährigen Krieges* (Heidelberg: Winter's Universitätsbuchhandlung, 1882).

14. Weller, *Lieder*, pp. 62–73.

15. Weller, *Lieder*, p. 152. ("Ist das nit ein Sünd und Schand/Dass Juden müntzen in Teutschland.")

16. Weller, *Lieder*, p. 34–35.

17. Ditfurth, *Volkslieder*, pp. 23–25.

18. Weller, *Lieder*, pp. 135–140.

19. (Daniel 7:4): "The first [beast] was like a lion, and had eagle's wings: I beheld till the wings thereof were plucked, and it was lifted up from the earth, and made stand upon the feet as a man, and a man's heart was given to it."

20. In ep. 62, as reproduced in vol. 2 of the *Urschriften*, Boehme writes "Bettel Gaber" for the Transylvanian prince; see: II 388.

21. Thus Peuckert: "Zusammenhänge von unten her. Hier kann man, wie selten, erahnen, wie sehr Jakob Böhme dem *Untergründigen* verbunden war." ("Connections from below. Here, as in few other places, one can suspect to what degree Jacob Boehme was linked to the *subterranean*.") From Peuckert's biography of Boehme, in vol. 10 of the facsimile edition, pp. 126–127.

22. *Cf.* Bohatcová, *Irrgarten*, p. 21.

23. From "Das böhmische Jag-Hörnlein" (printed in Prague, 1621), from Ditfurth, *Volkslieder*, pp. 29–36. (*Cf.* pp. 48, 308, 311; and Weller, *Lieder*, pp. XX, 36, 75, 100.)

24. Ditfurth, *Volkslieder*, p. 48.

25. Ditfurth, *Volkslieder*, p. 312.

26. Cited from: W. H. G. Armytage, "The Behmenists," in *The Church Quarterly Review* 160: April–June (1959): 200–209.

27. See: Eberhard H. Pältz, "Zu Jacob Boehmes Sicht der Welt- und Kirchengeschichte," in *Pietismus und Neuzeit* 81 (1980): 133–63. (Pältz emphasizes the Spiritualistic aspect of this prophecy, which, again, distinguishes it from the common conception of the millenarian.)

28. Koch, "Moscowiter," (1907), p. 71. See *Prag um 1600: Kunst und Kultur am Hofe Rudolfs II*, 1, pp. 532–566 (celestial globes, clocks, calendars, and some related artifacts).

29. See: Dietrich Mahnke, *Unendliche Sphäre und Allmittelpunkt; Beiträge zur Genealogie der mathematischen Mystik*, in *Deutsche Vierteljahrsschrift für Literaturwissenschaft und Geistesgeschichte* 23 (Halle/Saale: Niemeyer Verlag, 1937).

30. Koyré, *La Philosophie de Jacob Boehme*, p. 281.

31. See Paracelsus, "Fragment des Buches über die Kraft der Imagination," in *Werke* IV, pp. 265–73. According to Walter Pagel, the Paracelsian "imagination" "has a strong effect on the world of material objects. It alters existing things and generates new things." Through imagination, the human will generates semen in the male and intervenes in the female in the formation of the embryo: by impressing birth marks upon the unborn infant in accordance with the form of imagined objects. Pagel, *Paracelsus: An Introduction to Philosophical Medicine in the Era of the Renaissance* (Basel: Karger, 1958), pp. 121–25.

32. Hermann Knothe, "Der Anteil der Oberlausitz an den Anfängen des Dreißigjährigen Krieges, 1618–1623," in *NLM* 56 (1880), pp. 16ff.

33. "Das böhmische Jag Hörnlein," in Ditfurth, *Volkslieder*, p. 32. (Bohatcová reproduces the accompanying depiction of the "heroic" Saxon assault on Bautzen.)

34. "Ungedruckte Sendbriefe," I, *Urschriften*, 2, pp. 399–402. (The "Urschriften" retain Boehme's own irregular orthography.)

35. Urschriften, 2, *p. 401*.

Chapter 6

1. Lemper, *Jakob Böhme*, p. 74–76.

2. Korschelt, "Kriegsdrangsale," *NLM* 63 (1888): 332–350.

3. *Jacob Böhme: Die Urschriften*, 2, ed. Werner Buddecke (Stuttgart: Frommann, 1966), pp. 402–405.

4. See: III (*Vom dreifachen Leben*) 58/3.90; 227/11.91.

5. *Signatura Rerum* contains a concordance of the instances of trial, seeking, and temptation, which, in Scripture or in the belief of the author, lasted for forty units of time: Adam's forty days of temptation in Paradise, his forty hours of sleep, Israel's forty years in the desert, Christ's forty days in the desert, which made good on Adam's failure, Christ's forty hours in the grave, etc. (VI 160–61/11.80–82).

6. In later works, the counteraction that follows the dry contraction is already called (instead of bitter) *die Scienz* (from Latin *scientia*), and defined as the "root of understanding, as of sensuality," (*die Wurzel zum Verstand, als zur Sinnlichkeit*), this is in keeping with Boehme's tendency to pursue the root of life and awareness ever deeper into the prevital darkness. See: IX *Clavis* 108–09/140–146.

7. See: "Kleines Lexikon von Böhmes Begriffen," in Grunsky, *Jacob Böhme*, pp. 319–339 (individual entries, however, are indexed to the author's full-length discussion of the "system"); and Günther Graf zu Solms-Rödelheim, *Die Grundvorstellungen Jacob Böhmes und ihre Terminologie* (Dissertation, University of Munich, 1962). Solms's presentation has the advantage of grouping terms in accordance with important metaphysical headings (*die klare Gottheit, die ewige Natur, der Mensch*, etc.); in addition, the source material in the second part of the book is most helpful.

8. George Hunston Williams, *The Radical Reformation* (Philadelphia: Westminster, 1962), pp. 48, 79.

9. See: David Walsh, *The Mysticism of Innerworldly Fulfillment: A Study of Jacob Boehme* (Gainesville: University Presses of Florida, 1983).

10. See: *Mysterium Magnum* VII 306–308/33.26–40. (Here, Boehme's speculation is both typological and scientific: the rainbow is a sign of the three principles, a figure of the Final Judgment, *and*, in at least one of its col-

ors, green, the product of water and saltpeter). In a famous painting by Adriaen van de Venne ("I will make you fishers of men," 1614), the rainbow is a symbol of a spiritual unity bridging the opposing Christian camps. The Silesian Humanist, Johannes Fleischer (1539–1593), also theorized about the rainbow in a learned work published in Breslau in 1571. See: Manfred P. Fleischer, *Späthumanismus in Schlesien* (Munich: Delp'sche Verlagsbuchhandlung, 1984), pp. 185–189. Boehme's mystical distinction between fire and light has a "scientific" antecedent in the work of Gerhard Dorn—with a distant parallel in Galileo's early theories. See: Redondi, *Galileo Heretic*.

11. Boehme argued that Schwenckfeld did not properly acknowledge the "creatural" nature of Christ, and that Weigel erred in contesting the human lineage of the Virgin Mary, thereby making her into the Noble Virgin pure and simple (ep. 12.54–59).

12. Gordon E. Pruett, "Will and Freedom: Psychoanalytic Themes in the Work of Jacob Boehme," in *Studies in Religion*, vol. 6, no. 3 (1976–77): 241–251. Pruett observes that Boehme anticipated Freud's view of the complex nature of the human psyche. The dark-world and the light-world parallel the *id* and *ego*. Pruett argues that the mystic's vision of human nature was in certain respects superior to the "reductionism" of Freud.

13. Lemper, *Jakob Böhme*, p. 75.

Chapter 7

1. Johannes Kepler, *Harmonies of the World*, V in vol. 16 of the *Great Books*, (Chicago: Encyclopedia Britannica, 1952), p. 1050.

2. For pertinent examples, see: *Prag um 1600; Kunst und Kultur am Hofe Rudolfs II.* vol. 1, pp. 548–60 (*Wiener Planetenuhr*), p. 565 (*Tischuhr*).

3. Paracelsus' concept of the signature was generally modelled on the marks created by the work of a skilled hand—including the mutilations wrought by the hand of the executioner. Like the deformities of birth, the stigmata of punishment were regarded as signs betraying character. Paracelsus placed physiognomy in the same category. By the same token, the celestial signs made by clouds, comets, and stars prefigured human character, as well as historical events; and geological signs signified hidden mineral deposits. Rust-colored earth, for example, indicated that iron ore was present. The Paracelsian signs and signatures mixed the categories of cause (celestial signs), effect or result (punitive mutilations), and attribute (rust color, physiognomy). See: *De Natura Rerum* ("De Signaturis"), in Paracelsus, *Werke* III, pp. 283–314. The Paracelsian *Liber Azoth* supported this theory of signs with references to Kabbalah. See: *Werke* IV, pp. 841ff.

4. See: Erich Trunz, "Späthumanismus und Manierismus im Kreise

Kaiser Rudolfs II.," in *Prag um 1600; Kunst und Kultur am Hofe Rudolfs II.*, pp. 57–68.

5. See: Ernst Robert Curtius, *European Literature and the Latin Middle Ages*, trans. Willard R. Trask (Princeton: Princeton University Press, 1973), p. 324.

6. Boehme's letter to the Lübecker (ep. 28) praised a work bearing the title *Der Wasserstein der Weisen*. This was the theosophic tract by the Nuremberger Johann Ambrosius Sibmacher, published in 1609, in Frankfurt am Main. Sibmacher's little book—which, incidentally, went through at least one further printing because of Boehme's reference to it—conformed to the time-honored theosophic tradition: it revealed the true philosopher's stone or essence-transforming "hydrolith" as Christ and the Word of God. Sibmacher's book was much nearer to the Christian allegorical pole of alchemy than to its chemical, gold-seeking pole.

7. In his letter of August 15, 1621 to Lindner, Boehme referred to the subtitle of *Signatura Rerum* as: *Von der Bezeichnung der Creation...*" (ep. 12.73). This differs from the actual subtitle (*Von der Geburt und Bezeichnung aller Wesen*); the divergent word "Creation" matches his account of what he now considered the central theme of *Aurora*, i.e., the "creation of all beings" (*die Schöpfung aller Wesen*) (rather than "the root of philosophy, theology, astrology, and the description of nature"). In *Signatura Rerum*, as in *Aurora*, the growth of a stalk of grass and the emergence of its colors are accounted for with reference to the seven forces, here these are identified with the planets. In *Aurora*, the sweet spirit sprang in its upward flight, forming the joints of the stalk (VI 85/8.22).

8. Grunsky, *Jacob Böhme*, p. 311.

9. Walter Pagel, *Paracelsus: An Introduction to Philosophical Medicine in the Era of the Renaissance* (Basel: Karger, 1958), p. 91.

10. See: "The Books of the Secrets of Enoch, 1 and 2" in *The Other Bible*, ed. and intro. Willis Barnstone (New York: Harper & Row, 1984).

11. See: Richard Martin Reinitz, *Symbolism and Freedom: The Use of Biblical Typology as an Argument for Religious Toleration in 17th Century England and America* (Dissertation, University of Rochester, 1967).

12. Note, however, that here as well the typological point applies to all peoples: "Everything that goes out from God's will into its own will belongs in Babylon; you see this in Jews and Heathens, as in all peoples. The heathens clung to their own magic... [Some were devoted to a good, others to an evil magic.] Thus, too, were the Jews: God revealed himself to them, but they were inclined to two wills, a part to the commandment, with their will in accord with God's will, as the patriarchs and all pious expectant ones [*Hoffer*] of Israel. The others performed with their hands the work of the law, and

clung with their will to the poisoned magic, as to greed . . ."—There are always the good and evil variants of his types (IV *Mysterium Pansophicum* 108–09/8.8–12).

13. See: Peter French, *John Dee: The World of an Elizabethan Magus* (London and New York: Ark Paperbacks, 1972), pp. 119ff.

14. Gershom Scholem, *Kabbalah* (New York: Meridian, 1978), pp. 196ff.

15. Significantly, Franckenberg remembered his departed friend as a figure who had recognized the same eternal truths as had a mixed company of heretics and heterodox believers ranging from Cusanus and Pico, to Bruno and Menassa ben Israel, Rembrandt's rabbinnical neighbor in Amsterdam.

16. See: Werner Buddecke, *Die Jakob Böhme-Ausgaben; Ein beschreibendes Verzeichnis*, part 2 (Göttingen: Häntzschel, 1957), pp. xvi–xvii, for the probable dating of these tracts.

17. Ludwig Völker, "'Gelassenheit.' Zur Entstehung des Wortes in der Sprache Meister Eckharts und seiner Überlieferung in der nacheckhartschen Mystik bis Jacob Böhme," in *Getempert und Gemischet* (Festschrift for Wolfgang Mohr), ed. Franz Hundsnurscher and Ulrich Müller (Göttingen: Kümmerle, 1972) pp. 281–312.

Chapter 8

1. A. Kielholz, *Jakob Böhme; ein pathographischer Beitrag zur Psychologie der Mystik. Schriften zur angewandten Seelenkunde*, no. 17. Ed. Sigmund Freud. (Leipzig: Deuticke, 1919), p. 45.

2. Pagel, *Paracelsus*, pp. 315–319.

3. Kämmerer, *Das Leib-Seele-Geist-Problem*, pp. 76–79.

4. Lemper, *Jakob Böhme*, p. 93.

5. For the actual text of Richter's published denunciation, see: *Anhang*, the appendix to Jecht, "Lebensumstände," *NLM* 100 (1924): 242–247.

6. See: Nikolaus Paulus, *Protestantismus und Toleranz im 16. Jahrhundert* (Freiburg/Breisgau: Herdersche Buchhandlung, 1911).

7. See: Lemper, *Jakob Böhme*, pp. 86–97.

8. *Cf.* Lemper, *Jakob Böhme*, pp. 98–99.

9. See: Helmut Obst, "Zum 'Verhör' Jakob Böhmes in Dresden," in *Pietismus und Neuzeit*. (1974): 25–31.

10. See: Golo Mann, *Wallenstein*, p. 291; Georges Pagès, *The Thirty Years' War, 1618–1648* (New York: Harper & Row, 1970), p. 94.

11. Pagès, *The Thirty Years' War*, p. 75.

12. Kober's letter is reproduced as the third part of the *Ausführlicher Bericht von J. Boehmens Leben und Schriften*, in vol. 10, pp. 40–43.

13. See: Franckenberg's *Bericht* (X 20).

Bibliography

Editions of Boehme's Works

The following are the readily available German editions:

Boehme, Jacob. *Die Urschriften*. 2 vols. Edited by Werner Buddecke. Stuttgart: Frommanns Verlag, 1963 and 1966.

———. *Sämtliche Schriften*. 11 vols. Edited by Will-Erich Peuckert and August Faust. Stuttgart: Frommanns Verlag, 1955–61. This is the facsimile reprint of the 1730 edition: *Theosophia Revelata. Das ist: Alle Göttliche Schriften des Gottseligen und Hocherleuchteten Deutschen Theosophi Jacob Böhmens*. Edited by Johann Georg Gichtel and Johann Wilhelm Ueberfeld. Amsterdam, 1730.
   v. 1. *Morgenröthe im Aufgang* (1612).
   v. 2. *Beschreibung der drey Principien Göttliches Wesens* (1619).
   v. 3. *Vom dreyfachen Leben des Menschen* (1620). *Viertzig Fragen von der Seelen* (1620).
   v. 4. *Von der Menschwerdung Jesu Christi* (1620). *Von sechs theosophischen Puncten* (1620). *Kurtze Erklärung von sechs mystischen Puncten* (1620). *Gründlicher Bericht vom irdischenund himmlischen Mysterio* (1620). *Der Weg zu Christo* (1624).
   v. 5. *Schutz-Schriften wieder Balthasar Tilken* (1621). *Bedencken über Esaiä Stiefels Büchlein* (1621/22). *Schutz-Rede wieder Gregorium Richter* (1624). *Unterricht von den letzten Zeiten* (1620).
   v. 6. *De Signatura Rerum* (1622). *Von der Gnaden-Wahl* (1623). *Von Christi Testamenten* (1623).
   v. 7. *Mysterium Magnum* (1623).
   v. 8. *Mysterium Magnum* (1623).
   v. 9. *Betrachtung Göttlicher Offenbarung* (1624). *Tafeln* (1624). *Clavis* (1624). *Theosophische Sendbriefe*, (1618–1624).
   v. 10. *Historischer Bericht von dem Leben und Schriften, Jacob Böhmens. Das Leben Jacob Böhmes*, by Will-Erich Peuckert.
   v. 11. *Register über alle theosophischen Schriften Jacob Böhmens* (1730).

The following is a selection of the English translations:

Jacob Boehme. *The Works of Jacob Behmen, The Teutonic Philosopher*,
   v. 1 *The Aurora, The Three Principles, to which is affixed the Life of the Author*. London: Richardson, 1764.

v. 2 *The Threefold Life of Man; The Answers to Forty Questions Concerning the Soul; The Treatise on the Incarnation, in Three Parts; The Clavis: or an Explanation of Some Principal Points and Expressions of His Writings*. London: Richardson, 1764.

v. 3 *The Mysterium Magnum; Four Tables of Divine Revelation*. London: Robinson, 1772.

v. 4 *Signatura Rerum; Of the Election of Grace; The Way of Christ; A Discourse between a Soul Hungry and Thirsty . . . Of the Four Complexions; Of Christ's Testaments*. London: Robinson, 1781.

_____. *The Aurora*. Translated by John Sparrow. London, 1656. Edited by C. J. Barker and D. S. Hehner. London: John M. Watkins, 1914, reissued 1960.

_____. *Concerning the Three Principles of Divine Essence*. Translated by John Sparrow. London, 1648. Reissued by C. J. Barker. London: John M. Watkins, 1910.

_____. *The High and Deep Searching Out of the Threefold Life of Man*. Translated by John Sparrow. London, 1650. Reissued by C. J. Barker. London: John M. Watkins, 1909.

_____. *The Forty Questions of the Soul* and *The Clavis*. Translated by John Sparrow. London: Matthew Simmons, 1647. Reissued by C. J. Barker, with emendations by D. S. Hehner. London: John M. Watkins, 1911.

_____. *Of the Incarnation of Jesus Christ*. Translated by John Rolleston Earle. London: Constable, 1934.

_____. *De Electionae Gratiae* and *Questiones Theosophicae*. Translated by John Rolleston Earle. London: Constable, 1930.

_____. *The Signature of All Things, With Other Writings*. London and Toronto: J. M. Dent, 1912. Reissued, Cambridge and London: James Clarke, 1969.

_____. *Six Theosophic Points and Other Writings*. Translated by John Rolleston Earle. New York: Knopf, 1920. Reissued with an introductory essay by Nicholas Berdyaev. Ann Arbor: University of Michigan Press, 1958.

_____. *Mysterium Magnum*. Translated by John Sparrow. London, 1654. Edited by C. J. Barker. 2 vols. London: John M. Watkins, 1924; reprinted, 1965.

_____. *The Way to Christ*. Translated by John Joseph Stoudt. New York and London: Harper, 1947.

_____. *The Way to Christ*. Translated by Peter C. Erb. New York: Paulist Press, 1978.

Secondary Literature

The following is neither a complete bibliography of the critical literature on Boehme nor a full list of all works consulted, but rather a selection intended to be representative of the periods and main tendencies of scholarship on Boehme. Of the monographic overviews, the works by Brinton, Stoudt, Tesch,

Walsh, and Wehr combine concise and very intelligible introductions with some significant discussion of Boehme's times and influences upon posterity.

Alleman, George M. *A Critique of Some Philosophical Aspects of the Mysticism of Jacob Boehme.* Philadelphia: University of Pennsylvania Press, 1932.

Andersson, Bo. *"Du solst wissen es ist aus keinem stein gesogen"; Studien zu Jacob Böhmes "Aurora" oder "Morgen Röte im auffgang."* Stockholm: Almqvist & Wiksell International, 1986.

Armytage, Walter H. G. "Behmenists: A History of the Followers of Jacob Boehme in England, 1644–1740." *Church Quarterly Review* 160 (April–June 1959): 200–209.

Aubrey, Bryan. *Watchmen for Eternity: Blake's Debt to Jacob Boehme.* Lanham, Md.: University Press of America, 1986.

Baader, Franz von. *Nachgelassene Werke.* 6 vols. Edited by Franz Hoffman et al. Leipzig: Bethmann, 1850–60.

———. *Sämtliche Werke.* 10 vols. Edited by Franz Hoffman *et al.* Leipzig: Bethmann, 1851–55.

Baden, Hans Jürgen. *Das religiöse Problem der Gegenwart bei Jakob Böhme.* Leipzig: J. C. Heinrich, 1938.

Bailey, Margaret. *Milton and Jakob Böhme.* New York: Oxford University Press, 1914.

Barker, C. J. *Prerequisites to the Study of Jacob Boehme.* London: John Watkins, 1930.

Bartsch, Gerhard. "Jacob Böhme." In *Von Cusanus bis Marx. Deutsche Philosophen aus fünf Jahrhunderten*, edited by R. Gropp and F. Fiedler. Leipzig: Bibliographisches Institut, 1965.

———. "Zur Geschichte der Dialektik im älteren deutschen Pantheismus (Von Cusanus bis Böhme)." *Deutsche Zeitschrift für Philosophie* 16 (1968): 593–604.

Bastian, Albert. *Der Gottesbegriff bei Jakob Böhme.* Kiel: Lüdtke and Martens, 1905.

Benz, Ernst. *Der Prophet Jakob Böhme: Eine Studie über den Typus nachreformatorischen Prophetentums.* Wiesbaden: Steiner Verlag, 1959.

———. *Der vollkommene Mensch nach Jakob Böhme.* Stuttgart: Kohlhammer, 1937.

———. "Die Geschichtsmetaphysik Jakob Böhmes." *Deutsche Vierteljahresschrift für Literaturwissenschaft und Geistesgeschichte* 13 (1935): 421–55.

———. "Die schöpferische Bedeutung des Wortes bei Jakob Böhme." *Eranos Jahrbuch* 39 (1970): 1–40.

———. "Zur metaphysichen Begründung der Sprache bei Jakob Böhme." *Euphorion* 37 (1936): 340–57.

Berdyaev, Nicholas. "Unground and Freedom." *Six Theosophic Points*, translated by John Rolleston Earle, pp. v–xxxvii. Ann Arbor: University of Michigan Press, 1958.

Bommersheim, Paul. "Die Welt Jakob Böhmes." *Deutsche Vierteljahrsschrift für Literaturwissenschaft und Geistes-geschichte* 20 (1942): 340–58.

Bornkamm, Heinrich. "Jacob Böhme, der Denker." Bornkamm, *Das Jahrhundert der Reformation*, pp. 332–45. Göttingen: Vandenhoeck and Ruprecht, 1966.

———. *Luther und Böhme*. Bonn: Marcus and Weber, 1925.

———. "Renaissancemystik, Luther und Böhme." *Jahrbuch der Luther-Gesellschaft* 9 (1927): 156–97.

Brinton, Howard H. *The Mystic Will: Based on a Study of the Philosophy of Jacob Boehme*. New York: Macmillan, 1930.

Brown, Robert. *The Later Philosophy of Schelling: The Influence of Boehme on the Works of 1809–1815*. Lewisburg, Pa.: Bucknell University Press, 1977.

Buddecke, Werner. "Die Böhme-Handschriften und ihr Schicksal." *The Jacob Boehme Society Quarterly* 1 (1953): 17–22.

———. "Die Handschrift Jakob Böhmes." *Nachrichtungen von der Gesellschaft der Wissenschaften zu Göttingen*. Berlin, 1933.

———. *Die Jakob Böhme-Ausgaben. Ein beschreibendes Verzeichnis*. (2 parts: 1. Originals, 2. Translations) Göttingen: Häntzschel, 1937 and 1957.

———. "Zur Textgeschichte der Werke Jacob Böhmes." *Kant-Studien* 42 (1942/43): 238–44.

Buddecke, Wolfram. "Die Jakob-Böhme-Autographen, Ein historischer Bericht." *Wolfenbüttler Beiträge* 1 (1972): 61–87.

Colloque Jacob Boehme. Centre de Recherche sur l'Histoire des Idées de l'Université dePicardie. (Contributions by H. Schmitz, P. Deghaye, J. L. Vieillard-Baron, J.-F. Marquet, M. Vetö, M. de Gandillac, B. Rousset, A. Faivre, P. Trotignon, with a valuable bibliography) Paris: Vrin, 1979.

Channing-Pearce, Melville. "Boehme and the Ungrund." *Church Quarterly Review* 149 (1949): 15–26.

Čizevškij, Dmitrij. "Deutsche Mystik in Russland." *Aus zwei Welten. Beiträge zur Geschichte der slawisch-westlichen literarischen Beziehungen*. S'-Gravenhage: Mouton, 1956.

Cysarz, Herbert. "Jacob Böhme und das literarische Barock." *Jahrbuch des Wiener Goethe-Vereins* 80 (1976): 5–19.

David, Zdenek V. "The Influence of Jacob Boehme on Russian Religious Thought." *American Slavic Review* 21 (1962): 43–64.

Deghaye, Pierre. "Jacob Boehme: Ou la difficulté du discours sur Dieu." *Recherches de sciences religieuses* 67 (1979): 5–30. See also: *Colloque Jacob Boehme*. Paris: Vrin, 1979: 31–60.

———. "Psychologia Sacra." In Deghaye and Gerhard Wehr, *Jacob Böhme*, pp. 201–24. With translations of Boehme by L. C. de Saint-Martin. Paris: Michel, 1977.

———. "Dieu et la Nature dans *l'Aurore naissante de Jacob Boehme*." *Epochen der Naturmystik*, edited by Faivre and Zimmermann, pp. 125–56. Berlin: Schmidt Verlag, 1979.

Deinert, Herbert. "Die Entfaltung des Bösen im Böhmes *Mysterium Magnum*." *PMLA* 79 (1964): 401–10.

Deussen, Paul. *Jakob Böhme*. 3d ed. Leipzig: Brockhaus, 1922.

Ederheimer, Edgar. *Jakob Böhme und die Romantiker*. Heidelberg: Winter, 1904.

Elert, Werner. *Die voluntarische Mystik Jakob Böhmes*. Berlin: Trowitzsch, 1913.

———. *Jakob Böhmes deutsches Christentum*. Berlin: Runge, 1914.

Faivre, Antoine. "La critique boehmienne de Franz von Baader." In *Colloque Jacob Boehme*. Paris: Vrin, 1979: 135–154.
Faust, August. *Die Handschrift Jakob Böhmes: Ein Hinweis*. Breslau: Historiche Kommision für Schlesien, 1940.
_____. "Die weltanschauliche Grundhaltung Jakob Böhmes." *Zeitschrift für deutsche Kulturphilosophie* 6 (1940): 89–111.
_____. "Jacob Böhme als 'Philosophus Teutonicus.' Ein Beitrag zur Unterscheidung deutschen und westeuropäischen Denkens." *Das Deutsche in der deutschen Philosophie*, edited by Theodor Haering. 2d ed. Berlin/Stuttgart: Kohlhammer, 1942.
Fechner, Hermann. "Jakob Böhme, sein Leben und seine Schriften." *Neues Lausitzisches Magazin* 33 (1857): 313–446; 34 (1858): 27–138.
Feilchenfeld, Walter. *Der Einfluß Jacob Böhmes auf Novalis*. Berlin: Ebering, 1922.
Feuerbach, Ludwig. *Geschichte der neueren Philosophie von Bacon von Verulam bis Benedikt Spinoza*. Leipzig: Wigand, 1844.
_____. *Vorlesungen über die Geschichte der neueren Philosophie*. Darmstadt: Wissenschaftliche Buchgesellschaft, 1956.
Fouqué, Friedrich Baron de la Motte. *Jakob Böhme; Ein biographischer Denkstein*. Greiz: Henning, 1831.
Franckenberg, Abraham. *Gründlicher und wahrhafter Bericht von dem Leben und dem Abschied des in Gott selig ruhenden Jacob Boehmes*. In Jacob Böhme, *Sämtliche Schriften*, vol. 10.
Franz, Inge. "Jakob Böhme und der Konservatismus." *Deutsche Zeitschrift für Philosophie* 36 (1988): 836–39.
de Gandillac, Maurice. "Le Jacob Boehme de Nicolas Berdiaeff." *Colloque Jacob Boehme*. Paris: Vrin: 1979: 115–124.
Gorceix, Bernard. "L'ange en Allemagne au XVIIe siècle, Jacob Böhme et Johannes Scheffler." *Recherches Germaniques* 7 (1977): 3–28.
_____. "La mélancholie aux XVIe et XVIIe siécles, Paracelse et Jacob Böhme." *Recherches Germaniques* 9 (1979): 18–29.
_____. "Jacob Boehme." *Deutsche Dichter des 17. Jahrhunderts*. Ed. Harald Steinhagen and Benno von Wiese. Berlin: Erich Schmidt Verlag, 1984: 49–73.
Grunsky, Hans. *Jacob Böhme*. Stuttgart: Frommanns Verlag, 1956.
_____. *Jacob Böhme als Schöpfer einer germanischen Philosophie des Willens*. Hamburg: Hanseatische Verlagsanstalt, 1940.
Haensch, Gerd. "Gesellschaftskritik und Reformationsgedanken im Werk Jakob Böhmes; Zur Geschichte der Ideologie des Kleinbürgertums im 17. Jahrhundert. *Mühlhäuser Beiträge zur Geschichte und Kulturgeschichte*. 2: 38–51.
_____. "Jakob Böhme und die Dialektik der Erkenntnis." In *Deutsche Zeitschrift für Philologie* 26 (1978): 191–208.
Hamberger, Julius. *Die Lehre des deutschen Philosophen Jakob Böhmes*. Munich, 1844; reissued: Hildesheim: Gerstenberg, 1975.
Hankamer, Paul. *Jakob Böhme: Gestalt und Gestaltung*. Bonn: Cohen, 1924.
Hansen, Jan-Erik. *Jacob Böhme: Liv—lenkning—Idehistoriske forutsetninger*. Oslo: Solum, 1985.
Harless, G. C. Adolf von. *Jakob Böhme und die Alchimisten*. Berlin, Schlawitz, 1870.

Hartmann, Franz. *Personal Christianity, a Science: The Doctrines of Jacob Boehme, the God-Taught Philosopher*. New York, 1919; reissued: New York: Ungar, 1957.
Hauck, Wilhelm August. "Oetinger und Jakob Böhme." In *Das Geheimnis des Lebens. Naturanschauung und Gottesauffassung F. Chr. Oetingers*, pp. 159–79. Heidelberg: Winter, 1947.
Hegel, G. W. F. "Jakob Böhme." (*Vorlesungen über die Geschichte der Philosophie* 3) Werk 20. pp. 91–119. Frankfurt am Main: Suhrkamp, 1971.
Heimbach, Werner. "Das Urteil des Görlitzer Oberpfarrers Richter über Jakob Böhme; eine kultur- und geistesgeschichtliche Untersuchung 'Mit Poltern, Pantoffeln und Pasquillen.' *Herbergen der Christenheit; Jahrbuch für Kirchengeschichte* 9 (1973–74): 97–151.
Heinrich, Gerda. "Aspekte Frühromantischer Böhme-Rezeption." *Deutsche Zeitschrift für Philosophie* 23 (1975): 427–39.
Heinze, Reiner. *Das Verhältnis von Mystik und Spekulation bei Jakob Böhme*. Inaugural dissertation, University of Münster, 1972.
Heller, Arno. *Die Sprachwelt in Jacob Böhmes "Morgenröthe im Aufgang."* Inaugural Dissertation, University of Innsbruck, 1965.
Hirsch, Emanuel. "Jakob Böhme und seine Einwirkung auf die Seitenbewegung der pietistischen Zeit." *Geschichte der neueren evangelischen Theologie*, vol. 2, pp. 208–55. Gütersloh: Mohn, 1951.
Hobhouse, Stephen. *Selected Mystical Writings of William Law. Edited with Notes and Twenty-four Studies in the Mystical Theology of William Law and Jacob Boehme and an Inquiry into the Influence of Jacob Boehme on Isaac Newton*. 2d ed. New York and London: Harper, 1948.
Hoffmeister, Joachim. *Der ketzerische Schuster; Leben und Denken des Görlitzer Meisters Jakob Böhme*. Berlin: Evangelische Verlagsanstalt, 1975.
Huber, Wolfgang "Die Kabbala als Quelle zur Anthropologie Jakob Böhmes." *Kairos* 13 (1971): 131–50.
Hutin, Serge. *Les Disciples anglais de Jacob Boehme aux XVIIe et XVIIIe siècles*. Paris: Editions Denoël, 1960.
Hvolbek, Russell H., *Seventeenth-Century Dialogues: Jacob Boehme and the New Sciences*. Dissertation. Chicago: University of Chicago, 1984.
Jecht, Richard. "Die Lebensumstände Jakob Böhmes." *Neues Lausitzisches Magazin* 100 (1924): 179–248.
———. *Jakob Böhme: Gedenkausgabe der Stadt Görlitz zu seinem 300-jährigen Todestage*. Görlitz: Selbstverlag der Stadt, 1924.
Jones, Rufus M. *Spiritual Reformers in the 16th and 17th Century*. London: Macmillan and Co., 1914.
Jung, C. G. *Mysterium Conjunctionis: An Inquiry into the Separation and Synthesis of Psychic Opposites in Alchemy*. Translated by R. F. C. Hull. Princeton: Princeton University Press, 1963.
Jungheinrich, Hans-Georg. *Das Seinsproblem bei Jakob Böhme*. Hamburg: Hansischer Gildenverlag, 1940.
Kämmerer, Ernst Wilhelm. *Das Leib-Seele-Geist-Problem bei Paracelsus und einigen Autoren des 17. Jahrhunderts*. Wiesbaden: Steiner Verlag, 1971.

Kayser, Wolfgang. "Böhmes Natursprachenlehre und ihre Grundlagen." *Euphorion* 31 (1930): 521–62.

Kielholz, A. *Jakob Böhme; Ein pathographischer Beitrag zur Psychologie der Mystik.* Leipzig and Vienna: Deuticke, 1919.

Knevels, Wilhelm. "Der große Mythos des Theosophus silesius vom Grund und Sinn der Welt oder Deutung des Bösen und des Übels." *Jahrbuch der Schlesischen Friedrich-Wilhelms Universität* 7 (1962): 29–59.

Koenker, Ernest. "Potentiality in God: Jacob Boehme." *Philosophy Today* 15 (1971): 44–51.

Konopacki, Steven. *The Descent into Words: Jacob Boehme's Transcendental Linguistics.* Ann Arbor: Karoma, 1979.

Korn, E. R. "Sur le premier 'Philosophus Teutonicus'." *Revue Thomiste* 73 (1973): 47–62.

Koyré, Alexandre. "Die Gotteslehre Jakob Boehmes." *Husserl-Festschrift. Ergänzungsband zum Jahrbuch für philosophische und phänomenologische Forschung* (1929): 225–81.

_____. *La Philosophie de Jacob Boehme.* New York: Franklin, 1968; originally published Paris: Vrin, 1929; reissued 1979.

Lasson, Adolf. *Jacob Böhme.* Berlin: Gaertner, 1897.

Leese, Kurt. *Von Jakob Böhme zu Schelling.* Erfurt: Stenger, 1927.

Lemper, Ernst-Heinz. *Jakob Böhme: Leben und Werk.* Berlin: Union Verlag, 1976.

Llewellyn, R. T. "Jakob Boehmes Kosmogonie in ihrer Beziehung zur Kabbala." *Antaios* 5 (1963): 237–50.

Malekin, Peter. "Jacob Boehme's Influence on William Law." *Studia Neophilologica* 36 (1964): 245–60.

Marquet, Jean-François. "Désir et imagination chez Jacob Boehme." *Colloque Jacob Boehme.* Paris: Vrin, 1979: 77–98.

Martensen, Hans L. *Jacob Boehme: Studies in His Life and Teaching.* Translated by T. Rhys Evans. Revised edition with notes by Stephen Hobhouse. New York: Harper, 1949.

Miller (Guinsberg), Arlene A. *Jacob Boehme: From Orthodoxy to Enlightenment.* Ph.D. dissertation, Stanford University, 1971.

_____. "Theologies of Luther and Boehme in the Light of Their Genesis Commentaries." *Harvard Theological Review* 63 (1970): 261–303.

Muses, Charles A. *Illumination on Jakob Boehme: The Work of Dionysus Andreas Freher.* New York: King's Crown Press, 1951.

Nicolescu, Basarab. "Wheels Within Wheels: Jacob Boehme's Inseparable Cosmos." *Parabola* 14: 3 (August 1989): 4–10.

Nigg, Walter. *Heimliche Weisheit. Mystisches Leben in der evangelischen Christenheit.* Zürich: Artemis Verlag, 1959.

Obst, Helmut. "Zum 'Verhör' Jakob Böhmes in Dresden." *Pietismus und Neuzeit.* (Yearbook) (1974): 25–31.

Oetinger, Friedrich Christoph. *Sämtliche Schriften. Zweite Abtheilung: Theosophische Werke.* 6 vols. Edited by Karl C. E. Ehmann. Stuttgart: Steinkopf, 1858–64.

Pältz, Eberhard H. "Jacob Böhmes Hermeneutik. Geschichtsverständnis und Sozialethik." Habilitationsschrift, University of Jena, 1961.

———. "Zum Problem von Glaube und Geschichte bei Jacob Böhme." *Evangelische Theologie* 22 (1962): 156–60.

———. "Zum pneumatischen Schriftverständnis Jacob Böhmes." *Kirche, Theologie, Frömmigkeit. Festschrift für G. Holtz*, pp. 119–27. Berlin: Evangelische Verlagsanstalt, 1965.

———. "Zur Eigenart des Spiritualismus Jacob Böhmes." *Wort und Welt. Festgabe für Eric Hertzsch*, pp. 251–61. Berlin, 1968.

———. "Jakob Böhmes Gedanken über die Erneuerung des wahren Christentums." In *Pietismus und Neuzeit* 79 (1977/78): 83–118.

———. "Zu Jakob Böhmes Sicht der Welt- und Kirchengeschichte." In *Pietismus und Neuzeit* 81 (1980): 133–63.

Paschek, Carl. *Der Einfluß Jacob Böhmes auf das Werk Friedrich von Hardenbergs (Novalis)*. Inaugural dissertation, University of Bonn, 1967.

Peip, Albert. *Jakob Böhme; der Vorläufer christlicher Wissenschaft*. Leipzig: Hirschfeld, 1860.

Penny, Anne J. *Studies in Jakob Boehme*. London: John M. Watkins, 1912.

Peuckert, Will-Erich, ed. *Das Leben Jacob Böhmes*, vol. 10, *Sämtliche Schriften*, edited by W. E. Peuckert. Stuttgart: Fr. Frommanns Verlag, 1961.

———. "Einleitung," vols. 1–9, *Sämtliche Schriften*. Stuttgart: Frommanns Verlag, 1955–61.

Pietsch, Roland. *Die Dialektik von Gut und Böse in der Morgenröthe Böhmes*. Inaugural dissertation, University of Innsbruck, 1975.

Piorczynski, Jozef. "Jakob Böhme als Vorläufer der Hegelschen Absoluteslehre." *Reports on Philosophy* 9 (1985): 33–39.

Popp, Karl R. *Jakob Böhme und Isaac Newton*. Leipzig: Hirzel, 1935.

Poppe, Kurt. "Über den Ursprung der Gravitationslehre. J. Böhme, H. More, I. Newton." *Die Drei* 23 (1964): 313–40.

Popper, Hans. "Schöpfung und Gnade. (I) Betrachtungen über Jacob Böhmes Gnaden-Wahl. (I) Das Wort in der Großen und kleinen Welt; (II) Freiheit und Vorsehung." *Antaios* 3 (1962): 458–75, 544–59.

Pruett, Gordon E. "Will and Freedom: Psychoanalytic Themes in the Work of Jacob Boehme." In *Studies in Religion*. 6:3 (1976–77): 241–51.

Rätze, J. G. *Blumenlese aus Jacob Böhmes Schriften, Nebst einer Darstellung seines Lebens und seiner Schicksale*. Leipzig: Hartmann, 1819.

Reguera, Isidoro. *Objetos de melancolia (Jacob Böhme)*. Madrid: Ediciones Libertarias, 1984.

Richards, Philip Clayton. *Visionary Mysticism: A Study of Visionary Mystical Experience as it Informs the Works of Jacob Boehme and William Blake, and its Importance for the Philosophy of Religion*. Claremont Graduate School, Dissertation, 1987.

Richter, Julius. "Jakob Böhme and Goethe." *Jahrbuch des freien deutschen Hochstifts*. (Yearbook) (1934/35): 3–55.

Richter, Liselotte. *Jakob Böhme. Mystiche Schau*. Hamburg: Hoffman and Campe, 1943.

Roos, Jacques. *Les Aspects littéraires du mysticisme philosophique et l'influence de Boehme et de Swedenborg au début du romantisme: William Blake, Novalis, Balanche*. Strasbourg: Heitz, 1953.

Rousset, Bernard. "En quel sens Boehme peut-il intéresser un marxiste?" *Colloque Jacob Boehme*. Paris: Vrin, 1979: 125–134.
Schäublin, Peter. *Zur Sprache Jakob Böhmes*. Winterthur: Keller, 1963.
Schering, Ernst. "Adam und die Schlange. Androgyner Mythos und Moralismus bei Antoinette Bourignon." *Zeitschrift für Religions- und Geisteschichte* 10 (1958): 97–124.
Schmidt, Josef. *Die Figur des ägyptischen Joseph bei Jakob Biedermann (1578–1624) und bei Jakob Böhme (1575–1624)*. Zurich: Keller, 1967.
Schmitz, H. R. "L'option de Boehme." *Revue Thomiste* 74 (1974): 35–81.
_____."L'âme et l'Ungrund." *Revue Thomiste* 76 (1976): 208–42.
_____."L'expérience mystique chez Jacob Boehme et son projet philosophique." In *Colloque Jacob Boehme*. Paris: Vrin, 1979: 9–30.
Schreyer, Lothar. *Die Lehre des Jacob Böhme*. Hamburg: Hanseatische Verlagsanstalt, 1924.
Schulitz, John Robert. *Einheit in Differenz: Die kabbalistische Metamorphose bei Jakob Böhme*. Dissertation, University of Michigan, 1990.
Schulze, Wilhelm A. "Der Einfluß Boehmes und Oetingers auf Schelling." *Blätter für württembergische Kirchengeschichte* 56 (1956): 171–80.
_____. "Jacob Boehme und die Kabbala." *Judaica* 11 (1955): 12–29.
_____. "Das Auge Gottes." *Zeitschrift für Kirchengeschichte* 68 (1947): 149–52.
Schüssler, Ingrid. "Boehme und Hegel." *Jahrbuch der schlesischen Friedrich-Wilhelms-Universität* 10 (1965): 45–58.
Schwarz, Peter Paul. *Aurora; Zur romantischen Zeitstruktur bei Eichendorff*. Bad Homburg: Verlag Gehlen, 1970. (See index under "Böhme," "Runge.")
Schwarz, Wolfgang. "Pico della Mirandola und Jakob Böhme oder der spielende Gott." *Deutsches Pfarrerblatt* 69 (1969): 755–57.
Solms-Rödelheim, Gunter. *Die Grundvorstellungen Jacob Böhmes und ihre Terminologie*. Inaugural dissertation, University of Munich, 1960.
Sparrow, John. "The Englisher's Preface." To: *Of Christ's Testaments, viz.: Baptisme and the Supper*. Translated by John Sparrow. London: Simmons, 1652.
_____. "To the English Reader." Preface to *Concerning the Election of Grace, Or God's Will Towards Man*. London: Streater, 1655.
Steinacker, Peter. "Gott, der Grund und Ungrund der Welt: Reflexionen zum Verhältnis von Welterfahrung und Gottesbild am Beispiel der Mystik Jakob Böhmes." *Neue Zeitschrift für Systematische Theologie* 25, 2 (1983): 95–111.
Stewing, Christine. *Böhmes Lehre vom "inneren Wort" in ihrer Beziehung zu Franckenbergs Anschauung vom Wort*. Inaugural dissertation, University of Munich, 1953.
Stoudt, John Joseph. *From Sunrise to Eternity: A Study in Jacob Boehme's Life and Thought*. (Preface by Paul Tillich) Philadelphia: University of Pennsylvania Press, 1957.
Struck, Wilhelm. *Der Einfluß Jakob Böhmes auf die englische Literatur des 17. Jahrhunderts*. Berlin: Junker and Dünnhaupt, 1936.
Tesch, Hans. *Jakob Böhme; Mystiker und Philosoph*. Munich: Delp, 1976.
Thune, Nils. *The Behemenists and the Philadelphians: A Contribution to the Study*

of English Mysticism in the 17th and 18th Centuries. Uppsala: Almquist and Wiksells, 1948.

Trotignon, Pierre. "Méditation sur la nuit, en hommage à Jacob Boehme." *Colloque Jacob Boehme.* Paris: Vrin, 1979: 155–158.

Vetö, Miklos. "La Idea del mal en la metafísica de Jacob Boehme." *Dialogos* 7 (1971): 63–74.

———. "Le mal selon Boehme." *Colloque Jacob Boehme.* Paris: Vrin: 1979: 99–114.

Vetterling, Hermann. *The Illuminate of Görlitz.* Leipzig: Markert & Peters, 1923.

Vieillard-Baron, Jean-Louis. "Le problèm du dualisme dans la pensée de Jacob Boehme." In *Colloque Jacob Boehme.* Paris: Vrin, 1979: 61–76.

Voigt, Felix. "Das Böhme-Bild der Gegenwart." *Neues Lausitzisches Magazin* 102 (1962): 252–312.

Völker, Ludwig. "'Gelassenheit.' Zur Entstehung des Wortes in der Sprache Meister Eckharts und seiner Überlieferung in der nacheckhartschen Mystik bis Jacob Böhme." *Getempert und Gemischet* (Festschrift for Wolfgang Mohr) Edited by Franz Hundsnurscher and Ulrich Müller. Göttingen: Kümmerle, 1972: 281–312.

Walsh, David. *The Mysticism of Innerworldly Fulfillment: A Study of Jacob Boehme.* Gainesville: University Presses of Florida, 1983.

———. "The Historical Dialectic of Spirit: Jacob Boehme's Influence on Hegel." (Comment by Eric von der Luft) *History as System.* 1984: 15–46.

Wehr, Gerhard. *Jakob Böhme in Selbstzeugnissen und Bilddokumenten.* Reinbeck bei Hamburg: Rowohlt, 1971.

Weiss, Victor. *Die Gnosis Jakob Böhmes.* Zurich: Origo, 1955.

Wentzlaff-Eggebert, Friedrich-Wilhelm. "Naturmystik und Naturspekulation im 16. und beginnenden 17. Jahrhundert." *Deutsche Mystik zwischen Mittelalter und Neuzeit.* Berlin: de Gruyter, 1969.

Windfuhr, Manfred. "Jakob Böhme." *Die barocke Bildlichkeit und ihre Kritiker.* Stuttgart: Metzlersche Verlagsbuchhandlung, 1966.

Wollgast, Siegfried. "Jakob Böhme—Werk und Wirkung." *Philosophie in Deutschland zwischen Reformation und Aufklärung, 1550–1650.* Berlin: Akademie-Verlag, 1988.

Worbs, Erich. "Johann Wilhelm Ritter, der romantische Physiker, und Jakob Böhme." *Aurora; Jahrbuch der Eichendorff-Gesellschaft* 33 (1973): 63–76.

———. "Jakob Böhme—ein geistiger Ahne des englischen Frühromantikers William Blake." *Aurora* 34 (1974): 75–86.

Index

Abendmahl. See Doctrines, Eucharist
Adam, first or angelic, 85, 114–121, 141, 143, 150, 153, 167, 206. *See also* Scripture, Adam
Africa, 142
Albertus Magnus, 48
Alchemy, 29, 30, 41, 48, 67–68, 70, 73–74, 82–83, 106, 122–123, 152–153, 165, 182, 186, 187, 192, 193, 201, 216
Alt-Seidenberg, 35, 43
Anabaptists, 21, 45
Androgyny. *See* Symbols
Angels, 61, 64, 75, 78–81, 88, 90, 115, 120, 142, 143, 189, 195, 198
Anger of God. *See* God
Animism, 68, 76
Antinomianism, 162–163
Antisemitism, 131, 134, 202
Antitrinitarians, 45
Apocalypse. *See* Scripture
Aquastric. *See* Nature, water
Aquinas, Pseudo-, 29
Aquinas, Thomas, 48, 76
Arcimboldo, Giuseppe, 89
Arian heresy, 211, 215, 216
Aristotle, 31, 48, 54, 62–63
Arndt, Johann, 95
Arnold, Gottfried, 25
Arnold of Villanova, 48
Asia, 142
Astronomy. *See* Sciences
Augsburg Confession, 21, 23, 212
Augsburg, Peace of, 21, 22, 215
August, Elector Prince of Saxony, 24
Augustine, Saint, 28
Aurora. See Boehme, works
Aurora consurgens (Pseudo-Aquinas), 29

Avicenna, 29

Baader, Franz Xaver von, 2
Bacon, Francis, 70
Baroque Age, 209
Baroque literature of Germany, 4
Bautzen, 14, 16, 20, 24, 25, 26; siege of, 154–156, 159
Behem, Abraham, 30, 39, 42–43, 62
Benz, Ernst, 4
Berlin, Isaiah, 78
Bernhard, Christian, 128, 139, 157, 159, 169, 184, 187, 210
Bernhard, Saint, 28
Bethlen, Gabriel, 129, 131, 132, 136–137, 214
Bible. *See* Scripture
Blake, William, 2
Boccalini, Trajano, 95
Boehme, Jacob, reception by contemporaries, 2, 43, 93–95, 159, 161–162, 165, 169–174, 182–184; 185–187, 205–206, 210–216; reception by posterity, 2–3, 4, 5, 139, 174, 207
Boehme, Jacob, life: general context of his times, 6, 7, 9–10, 23–26; childhood and youth, 9, 20, 35, 40–43; as a shoemaker, 13, 183; *1600–1612*, 42–59, 61–62, 76–77, 80–81; *1613–1619*, 93–102, 125–126; *1619–1620*, 127–130, 132–135, 138–156; *1621–1623*, 136–139, 157–184 (chapter 6), 185–208 (chapter 7); *1624*, 209–219 (chapter 8)
Boehme, works: general pattern of, 146, 160, 165–175, 177–180, 195–196; narrative elements in, 36;

language and style of, 13, 98–102, 143, 165–175, 206; *Aurora*, 2, 14–15, 16, 23, 29, 33–35, 37, 43, 47, 51–52, 54–59, 61–92, 93, 95, 98, 100, 101, 104, 106, 109, 110, 112, 138, 140, 143–145, 146, 165, 166, 167, 169, 178, 189, 191, 196; *Aurora* autograph, 61; *Aurora*, title and outline, 61–62; *Clavis*, 171, 210; *Election of Grace*, 162, 166, 177; *Forty Questions On the Soul*, 120, 142, 146–149, 167, 170, 171, 172–173; *Four Complexions* (including treatise *On Melancholy*), 32, 166, 207; *Human Genesis of Christ*, 142, 149–154, 166, 173; *Letters*, 97–99, 138, 154–156, 159–161, 162, 166, 176, 210, 214–216; *Mysterium Magnum*, 29, 78, 135, 166, 167, 168, 169, 195–204, 210; *Mysterium Pansophicum*, 203; pamphlets, 142, 204–205; *Path to Christ*, 205–208, 214; Replies to Kaym (*On the Last of Days*), 139–140, 163; to Richter, 210–211, 216–217; to Stiefel, 134, 162; to Tilke, 161–162, 180; *Signatura Rerum*, 166, 167, 168, 187–195; *Six Mystical Points*, 203; *Six Theosophical Points*, 69, 166, 167, 168, 175–182; *Table of Principles*, 168; *Testaments of Christ*, 208, 166; *Three Principles of Divine Being*, 97–126 (chapter 4), 132, 141, 143, 146, 166, 167, 169, 182, 192; *Threefold Life of Man*, 69, 78, 132, 136–137, 140–146, 147, 161, 166, 167, 169, 172, 201

Boehme, Jacob and Ursula (parents of the mystic), 35

Boehme, Katharina (neé Kuntzschmann), 42, 160, 169, 217

Boehme, Tobias, 218

Bohemia, Kingdom of, 14, 19, 20, 35, 80, 96, 125, 127–128, 215

Bohemian Brethren, 215

Bohemian Confederation, 128, 131–133, 142, 153–154, 157–158, 163, 184

Brandenburg, 14, 23, 25, 157, 214

Breslau, 157

Bruno, Giordano, 5, 24, 49

Brunswick, 95

Buchholzer, Abraham, 28

Buchholzer, Gottfried, 28

Burghers, 16, 18, 20, 22, 32, 42, 119, 184, 199, 215

Calvin, John, 23, 47

Calvinists, Calvinism, 21, 22–26, 31, 46, 47, 125, 128, 131, 133, 162–164, 187, 213, 215

Capistrano, Saint John, 131–132

Carlov, Abraham, 121

Cassirer, Ernst, 8

Catholics, Roman Catholicism, 14, 21, 24, 45, 47, 83, 84, 131, 145, 201

Celestial Eve or Celestial Virgin. *See* Symbols, Sophia

Celibacy, 117

Censorship, prerogative of, 212

Charles II, King of England, 139

Charles V (Habsburg Holy Roman Emperor), 19

Cheese and the Worms, The (Carlo Ginzburg), 10

Chemical Wedding, The, 95

Chemnitz, Martin, 121

Christendom and the church, notions of, 21–22, 48, 80, 84, 119–120, 125–126, 132–135, 142, 152, 163–165, 176, 188–189, 200–202, 204, 206, 208, 210–211

Christian I, Elector Prince of Saxony, 24, 40

Christian II, Elector Prince of Saxony, 24

Church properties confiscated, 22

City, urban patrician oligarchy, 18; city council, 29, 32, 93–95, 128, 196, 211, 212, 218. *See also* Görlitz

Comenius, Jan Amos (*The Labyrinth of the World and the Paradise of the Heart*), 101–102, 132

Communion. *See* Doctrines, Eucharist
Complexions (four humors), 32, 73, 107, 207
Concord, Formula or Book of, 24, 25, 44–45, 46
Consistorium (Lutheran church consistory), 20, 21
Conversion. *See* Doctrines
Convivium Musicum, 28–29, 94, 169
Copernicus, 48
Cossacks (Polish cavalry), 158
Counter-Reformation, 5, 20–21, 96, 128, 133, 215; in Silesia, 4
Craftsmen, 21, 32, 40, 42, 43, 44, 94, 96, 183, 216; guilds, 18–19, 43–44, 94
Creation. *See* God; Doctrine; Scripture
Croll, Oswald, 67, 191
Crypto-Calvinism, 23–26, 28, 29, 40, 42, 45
Cuius regio, eius religio, 20, 23
Culture of everyday experience, 32–34; class differences, 32, 173; darkness and light, 31–33; town-country conflicts, 34, 43.
See also City
Curtius, Ernst Robert, 191
Cusanus (Nicholas of Cusa), 147
Cysarz, Herbert, 130

Dee, John, 203
Defenestration of Prague (1419), 15; (1618), 17
Deism, 189
Denmark, 138, 214
Descartes, René, 3, 95, 127
Devil, Lucifer, Satan, 15–16, 31, 33, 37, 77, 80, 81, 82, 85, 87–88, 115, 116, 119, 120, 126, 134, 143, 144, 198–199, 206, 210, 211; discourse with, 34; primal rebellion of, 33, 52–54, 104–105, 109, 111, 112, 119, 120, 131. *See also* Evil
Dies Irae (hymn), 28, 131
Doctrinal conflicts, 40, 43–48, 63–64, 83, 94, 133, 150, 161–165, 177, 184, 186, 188–189, 208, 210
Doctrinal pluralism, 20, 26–31, 33, 210
Doctrines: general significance for Boehme, 6, 7, 208; baptism, 101, 160, 178, 208, 210; the bound will, 31, 45, 47; Christology, 150–154, 163, 176–178, 188; *communicatio idiomatum*, 55, 87; conversion, 38, 45; creation *ex nihilo*, 34, 37, 45, 51–52, 54, 63–64, 104, 112, 123, 179; Eucharist, 15, 19, 22, 23, 26, 37–38, 44–46, 47, 49, 55–59, 63–64, 86, 88–89, 100, 101, 133, 143, 146, 151, 160, 164, 171, 187, 203, 204, 208, 217; faith from hearing, 38; good works, 18, 174; grace, 36, 45, 101, 149, 160, 175, 202, 204, 210; predestination and election, 52, 63–64, 134, 145, 149, 162–164, 177, 207; purgatory, 174, 201; real presence, 21, 140; salvation by faith alone, 18, 44, 141, 146, 151, 174; synergism, 31; Trinity, 216; the two kingdoms, 33, 45; ubiquity, 22, 44, 46, 47, 49, 51, 55–59, 62, 69, 88–89, 90, 140, 152–154, 165, 171; the Virgin Mary, 122, 152, 174, 177. *See also* Dualism; Evil; God; Scripture, authority of
Donne, John, 127, 172, 209
Dornavius (rector of the Görlitz *Gymnasium*), 96
Dresden, 24, 159, 199, 209–210, 212–216, 217
Dualism, 39, 50–52, 59, 62, 64–65, 66, 72–73, 76–77, 82–83, 88, 89, 120, 170, 175–181, 204, 208
du Chesne, Joseph, 67

Earth (as planet), *See* Nature
Eckhart, Meister, 208
Elements, *See* Nature, matter
Elert, Werner, 129
Eliade, Mircea, 3
Emmerich (mayor of Görlitz), 96
Emperor, Holy Roman, 19, 21, 22, 25, 137, 142, 155, 214

Ender, Carl von, 21, 93, 94, 97, 161, 187, 197, 208
England, 128, 139, 163, 203, 214
Enthusiasm (as a religious tendency), 37
Epistemology, 69, 113
Erasmus of Rotterdam, 45, 48
Erastus, Thomas, 211
Erigena, Johannes Scotus, 50
Eschatology. *See* Prophecy
Esotericism, magic, 48
Eternity and time, 36, 38–39
Europe, 133, 142
Evil, Boehme's understanding of, 16, 37, 62, 87–88, 104, 107, 109, 121, 175–181; common notions of, 31; fall from grace, 37, 91, 143; problem of evil and the divine goodness, 82, 91, 100, 109, 110, 115, 116, 118, 121, 126, 175–181, 190, 199
Evil spirit. *See* Devil
Existentialism, 174

Faith. *See* Doctrines, salvation by faith
Fall from grace. *See* Evil
Faust, Dr. Johann (chapbook protagonist), 51–54
Fechner, Hermann, 12
Ferdinand I (King of Bohemia, Holy Roman Emperor), 19
Ferdinand II (King of Bohemia, Holy Roman Emperor), 96, 127–128, 133, 137, 154, 158, 215. *See also* Counter-Reformation
Fichte, Johann Gottlieb, 207
Ficino, Marsilio, 49
Flacian (doctrinal adherent of Flacius Illyricus), 162
Fludd, Robert, 49 (author of *Utriusque Cosmi Historia*), 99
Folk piety. *See* Mysticism
Fouqué, Baron de la Motte, 129
France, 214
Franck, Sebastian, 38, 48
Franckenberg, Abraham von, 1–2, 9, 30, 35, 40, 42, 61, 137, 146, 168–169, 182–184, 185, 210, 217
Frankfurt an der Oder, University of, 94
Free will, problems of freedom and order, of freedom and divine omnipotence, etc., 31, 37, 43–44, 45–46, 47, 52, 62, 70, 109, 110, 114, 124, 143–144, 149, 152, 167–168, 175, 178, 179, 189, 190, 194
Freud, Sigmund, 181, 211
Freudenhammer von Freudenheim, Gottfried, 186
Friedrich I (Barbarossa), 132
Friedrich, Caspar David, 116
Friedrich V, Elector Palatine, King of Bohemia ("Winter King"), 25, 125, 127–128, 131, 132, 137, 155, 157–158, 163, 199, 214
Frisius, Pastor, 211–212
Fürstenau, von, 187, 193, 212

Galileo, 191
Geber, 29
Genesis. *See* Scripture
Geocentrism. *See* Sciences
German Baroque poets, 2, 84
German Idealism, 148
German language, 76; Boehme's defense of, 4
German mysticism. *See* Mysticism, German
German national traits of Boehme, 4–5, 137–138, 140
German nationalism, 129–138, 139, 163
German philosophers, 2–3, 174
German Romantics, German Romanticism, 2, 129
Germany, 128–129, 131, 133, 134, 137, 158, 163, 174
Gersdorf, Rudolf von, 184
Gessner, Salomon (Wittenberg professor), 26, 216
Gestapo, 130
Ghosts, Boehme's references to, 8, 32
Gichtel, Johann Georg, 171
Gilbert, William, 5

Index 261

Ginzburg, Carlo (*The Cheese and the Wurms*), 10, 198
Gnosticism. *See* Mysticism
God: Godhead (clear or pure divinity), 74, 79, 90, 91, 104, 109, 110, 112, 123, 124, 153, 168, 173, 188, 193, 205, 207; anger of God, 38, 81, 85, 97, 98, 104, 114, 122, 132, 144, 153, 159, 163, 176, 178, 182; contrasting views of God, 63–64; creation *ex Deo*, 74, 88, 106, 109, 145, 151, 192, 197–198; divine light, 114, 172; divine nature, 114, 123–124; divine self-revelation, 179–180, 189–192, 196–197; Father, 36, 42, 68–69, 79, 89, 107, 109, 122, 168, 170, 172, 178, 179, 181; First Mover, 106; hidden God, 5, 101, 109, 111, 114, 144, 147–149, 150, 170, 208; Holy Spirit, 38, 75, 82, 90, 153, 188, 189 (*See also* Spirit); image and likeness, 106, 112, 124, 150–154, 171, 176; Judge, 146; Passion of God, 107, 109, 178; Resurrection, 109, 178; Ruler, 53, 80, 125, 182, 198, 204; Son (Christ, Heart), 33, 36, 38, 74–75, 82, 89, 106, 107, 109, 116, 119, 121, 122, 126, 132, 142–143, 150–154, 162, 163, 169, 171, 172, 173, 176–178, 181, 186, 189, 193; virgin birth, 109; theodicy, 114; Trinity, 42, 51–52, 68–69, 71, 86, 89, 98, 109, 113, 121–126, 143, 153, 172, 179, 188–189, 201; Word, 111, 115, 119, 143, 145, 152, 171, 188, 192, 193, 197, 198. *See also* Symbols, love; Spirit, in God
Goer, Georg, 29
Görlitz, 13, 14, 15, 16, 18–21, 24–31, 33, 35, 42–43, 93, 147, 154–155, 157, 183–184, 186, 205, 211–212, 217–218
Grace. *See* Doctrines
Grießmann, Valentin, 211
Grunsky, Hans, 6, 136, 171, 197
Gryphius, Andreas, 84
Guilds. *See* Craftsmen
Gunpowder, 66

Gustavus Adolphus, King of Sweden, 138, 214

Hankamer, Paul, 130
Hass, Johann (scribe and mayor of Görlitz), 18
Haug, Georg, 174
Heathens, 134, 163–164, 202–204
Hebrew language, 76
Hegel, Georg Wilhelm Friedrich, 2–3, 90, 129
Heidelberg, 127–128
Heimbach, Werner, 10
Helbach (*Olivetum*), 67
Heliocentrism. *See* Sciences
Hell and damnation, 54, 62, 85, 142, 153, 176
Herder, Johann Gottfried, 78
Heretics, persecution of, 16–17, 18, 21, 23, 31, 32, 40, 42, 45, 47, 144–145, 182, 201, 210, 211, 212, 214, 216, 217; blasphemy as heresy, 211
Hermes Trismegistos, 95, 101
Hermetism, 48, 68, 82, 106, 152
Hidden treasure. *See* Irrationalism
Hildegard of Bingen, Saint (*Scivias*), 46
Hill, Christopher, 139
Hinckelmann, Abraham, 121
Hinckelmann, Benedikt, 212, 214
Historical faith, 36, 38, 74, 109, 114, 118, 150–152, 165, 176, 197, 199
Hoë, Dr. (Matthias Hoë von Hoënegg, court chaplain to Elector Johann Georg), 213–215
Holland, 138, 214
Holy Roman Empire, 14, 128–129, 132, 133, 136, 158, 174
Holy Spirit. *See* God and Spirit
Huizinga, Johan, 32, 173
Human nature and condition, 88, 110, 113–121, 126, 143–144, 145, 146, 151–152, 170, 172, 175–182, 190, 194; eternal human form, 79; body, 88, 89, 114, 144; light of awareness, 102, 105–106, 115–116, 123, 124, 145; soul, 32, 59, 88,

109–110, 143, 167, 168, 172. See also Complexions; Spirit
Humanists, Humanism, 23, 27–28, 29, 31, 48, 49, 147, 218
Humors. See Complexions
Hungary, 25, 32, 158, 214
Hunnius, Nikolaus (Wittenberg professor), 211, 214
Hus, Jan, 15, 163
Hussites, Hussite faith, 127, 128
Hussite Wars, 15–17, 19, 25
Hutterites, 21
Hylozoism, 64–66

Illuminations ascribed to Boehme, illumination of 1600, 1–2, 3, 7, 42, 43–44, 72, 82, 111, 124–125, 160–161, 196; while a journeyman, 40–42
Illuminism, 127, 165, 183; theories of, 3, 166, 172–173
Imagination. See Symbols, concepts, etc.
Indians, American, 133
Irrationalism in Boehme's work and thought, 8, 186–187, 216; of hidden treasure, 9, 15–16, 40–41; of *Familiar-Geist*, 183. See also Magic

Jägerndorf, von, 155, 157, 213
James I of England, 128, 163, 214
Jecht, Richard, 10, 16
Jesuits, 131, 132, 158
Jews, 130, 131, 134, 201, 202
Johann Georg, Elector Prince of Saxony, 128, 154–156, 157–158, 210, 212
John, Gospel of. See Scripture, biblical books
Jung, Carl G., 117
Jupiter. See Nature
Justice system, influence on Boehme, 35; his legal language, 36

Kabbalah. See Mysticism
Karlstadt, Andreas Bodenstein von, 208

Katz, Steven, 6
Kaym, Paul, 139, 140, 160, 162, 163, 166, 169
Kepler, Johannes, 5, 49, 188–189
Khlesl, Melchior Cardinal, 131, 133
Kingdoms, doctrine of the two. See Doctrines
Kleist, Heinrich von, 116
Kober, Dr. Tobias, 217–218
Kotter, Christian, 132, 140
Koyré, Alexandre, 6, 148
Krell, Nikolaus, 25
Kuhlmann, Quirinus, 4, 84

Laborers, agricultural, 22
Ladurie, Emmanuel Le Roy (*Montaillou*), 10
Landowning gentry, 21–22, 169
Latin language, 76
League of Six Cities (*Sechsstädtebund*), 14–17, 18–19, 27, 35, 158, 199
Leipzig, 27, 48, 210, 211
Leisentritt, Johann, 20
Lemper, Ernst-Heinz, 10, 21
Letter of Majesty, 20, 80, 96, 127
Liegnitz, 211, 212
Lindner, Caspar, 160–161, 166, 169, 176, 187, 196
Loß, Joachim von, 213–215
Louis II, King of Bohemia and Hungary, 19
Löw, Rabbi Jehudah, 43
Lower Lusatia, 14
Lübeck, 138, 214
Lucifer. See Devil
Ludovicus (rector of Görlitz *Gymnasium*), 25, 77
Lull, Ramon, 29
Lusatia, 80, 93, 96, 128, 133, 142, 154–156, 157–161, 184, 199, 210, 213. See also Lower Lusatia; Upper Lusatia
Luther, Martin, 15, 18, 23, 33, 36, 37, 38, 45–46, 47, 48, 76, 110, 129, 133, 135, 163, 211; *On the Bondage of the Will*, 45, 100

Lutheran Evangelical faith, 135, 187
Lutheran orthodoxy, 23, 31, 39, 47, 55, 133, 163, 176–177, 214; tenets of, 102, 174
Lutheran sermons, 36, 37–38

Magic, 30, 31, 52–53, 86, 151–152, 177, 192–195, 203, 208, 211
Maier, Michael (*Atalanta fugiens*), 99
Mainz, 29
Mann, Golo (*Wallenstein*), 127
Matthias, King of Bohemia, Holy Roman Emperor, 80, 96
Medical doctors, 29–30, 169, 186
Medicine, 29, 42, 48, 101
Meditationes sanctorum patrum (Martin Moller), 28
Meissen, 14, 20, 184
Melanchthon, Philipp, 19, 23–24, 27, 31, 62
Menocchio. *See* Ginzburg, Carlo
Merchants, 43
Meth, Ezechiel, 134, 140, 160, 162, 163, 166, 211
Michael (Archangel), 16, 80
Middle Europe, 10, 14, 27, 102, 127, 157; definition of, 10
Millenarianism. *See* Prophecy, chiliasm
Mohács, Battle of, 19
Moller, Martin, 26, 28, 38–39, 43, 94, 216
Montaigne (*Apology for Raymond Sebond*), 49
Montaillou (Emmanuel Le Roy Ladurie), 10
Moravia, 21, 96, 128, 158
Moravian church, 101
Morgenröthe im Aufgang. See Boehme, works, *Aurora*
Mühlberg, Battle of, 19
Müntzer, Thomas, 174, 208
Muslims, Islam, 202, 211
Mysterium Magnum (work by Martin Moller), 26
Mysticism; applicability of general definitions, 5, 6, 8, 31–32, 35–39, 46–47, 85, 86, 100–101, 104, 136, 138–142, 147, 160–161, 162, 164–175, 178, 182, 185, 196, 200, 207, 216; bridal (*Brautmystik*), 83, 168, 195; currents of, 30; folk piety, 173; German mysticism, 14, 129; Gnosticism, 7, 88, 115, 148, 200, 204; Kabbalah, 7, 30, 43, 106, 116, 130, 147, 200, 204–205; medieval, 206, 208; natural magic, 203; traditions of mysticism, 48; *Pansophia*, 6, 48, 173, 203. *See also* Hermetism; Magic; Panvitalism

Nassau, House of, 23
National Socialism, 130, 134, 135, 138
Nature, nature philosophy and nature mysticism, 33, 38–39, 44, 47, 82–83, 188, 200; air, 89, 112; animals, 110, 115, 190; aqua fortis, 67; aqua regia, 68; cause of all things, 112; comets, 109; cosmogony, 112, 206; cosmology, 69–75, 175, 189, 199, 209; darkness, 112, 113, 145, 206; earth, 89, 110; fire, 87, 89, 112, 144–145, 151, 153, 167–168, 174, 178, 179, 181, 182, 201, 206; force(s), 65–69, 89, 173, 178, 193; germination of plant life, 75–76; heavens, 51, 53–54, 55–59, 65, 89–90, 112; *Herbigkeit* (primal dryness), 64, 66, 77–78, 86–87, 105–106, 112, 173; life's origin, 69, 75, 168, 179, 180–181; light, 144–145, 153, 167–168, 175, 179–181; *Limbus*, 110, 111, 115; macrocosm-microcosm, 50, 64, 69–70, 82, 89–90, 112, 113–114, 151; magnet, 168, 175; matrix or womb, 65, 112; matter (elements, palpability, *Begreiflichkeit*), 49, 51, 53, 55–59, 64, 66, 70, 81, 82, 85, 87, 89, 98, 102, 110, 111, 144–146, 151, 164, 208; mercury, 66, 188; metals, 75, 123; natural order, 59; plants, 110, 190; qualities in general, 64–65, 70, 71–76, 87, 104, 106, 107,

164, 167, 178; quintessence, 67, 89, 110, 115, 167; rainbow, 175; *Salitter* (*sal niter*, niter), 64, 65–68, 88, 198; saltpeter, 66–67; salt(s), 75; sevenfold nature of all things, 70–75, 86, 166–168; solar system with planets, 72–73, 75, 90, 179, 198–199, 209; stars (sidereal force or spirit), 33, 69, 72, 89, 103, 111, 124, 164, 198, 209; sulphur, 106, 108; *Tria Prima* (triad of principles), 50; water (*aquastrisch*), 73, 87–88, 89, 103, 111, 112, 206, 208

Nature language, 4, 34, 76, 119, 147, 188, 189–190

Nature mysticism. *See* Nature

Nature philosophy. *See* Nature

Neisse River, 14

Neoplatonism, 7, 39, 49, 62, 88, 147, 204

New Harmony (Indiana), 117

New World, 5, 203; impact of its discovery on Boehme, 1, 201–202

Noble Virgin. *See* Symbols, Sophia

Nobles, 22, 32, 131, 183–184, 186–187, 193, 199, 204

Novalis, 2

Numerology, 86, 146, 147, 167, 173–174, 188, 218

Ockham, William of, 46

On the Bondage of the Will (*De servo arbitrio*). *See* Luther

On the Lodestone (William Gilbert), 5

One and many, speculative problem of, 124

Origen, 50

Osiander, Andreas, 48, 211

Pagel, Walter, 151

Pältz, Eberhard, 4, 146

Pansophia. *See* Mysticism, *Pansophia*

Pantheism, 69

Panvitalism, 49

Papists. *See* Catholics, Roman Catholicism

Paracelsus, 34, 49–50, 82–83, 88, 191, 211; followers of, 29–31, 42, 48, 193, 197, 211; writings of, 30, 95, 151–152

Paradise. *See* Scripture

Paris, 30, 95

Parmenides, 147

Pascal, Blaise, 3

Pastors, 131, 145, 153–155, 169, 215; Lutheran, 22, 24, 25, 27, 28, 31, 44, 121, 155, 187, 199, 211, 212, 217, 218

Peasant Wars, 21

Peasants, 21, 31, 32, 33–34, 35, 75, 119, 174, 199, 215

Peip, Albert, 129, 135

Pembroke, Lord, 139

Peucer, Caspar, 24, 25, 27

Peuckert, Will-Erich, 6, 130, 135, 136

Philippists, Philippism, 23–24, 28, 45, 94, 214

Philosophia ad Athenienses (Pseudo-Paracelsus), 29, 197–198

Philosophus der Einfältigen, Boehme's designation as, 3, 26, 34

Philosophus Teutonicus, Boehme's designation as, 3, 4–5, 127–130

Philosophy in general, its influence on Boehme, 5, 48, 82, 86–87

Pico della Mirandola, Giovanni, 49, 205

Pietism, 117, 169

Plague, 18, 33, 42–43, 49, 65, 217

Planets. *See* Nature, solar system

Plato, Platonism, 48, 49, 62

Plotinus, 63

Poděbrad, George, 17, 19

Poland, 14, 163, 214

Pönfall, 19, 22, 25, 32

Pope, Roman Catholic, 21, 131, 132, 133

Prague, 15, 25, 49, 83, 89, 96–97, 127–128, 157–158, 173, 191, 199, 203, 214

Prayer and meditation, 41, 206–207, 214

Preischwitz, Peter, 17

Prophecy, Boehme as prophet, 4, 136–142, 146, 167–169, 173, 184,

186, 214–215, 217; chiliasm, 38, 96, 132, 139–141, 147, 159, 162, 174, 200, 214–215; eschatology, 75, 81–85, 109, 140–142, 146, 147, 208; Judgment, 135, 172, 199; prophesies concerning the Antichrist and the Whore of Babylon, 97, 125, 142, 186, 211, 214. *See also* Scripture, Paradise; Symbols, lily
Protestant tradition, 4; worldview, 43–48, 70, 174
Protestant Union, 128
Pseudo-Dionysius (Dionysius the Areopagite), 8, 50, 148
Psychoanalysis, 181–182
Ptolemaic astronomy, 53
Punishments, 31, 32

Quakers, 38
Qualities. *See* Nature, qualities in general

Rappites, 117
Raubburg (outlaw castle). *See* Robber knights
Raubritter. *See* Robber knights
Raubschloß (outlaw castle). *See* Robber knights
Rebirth. *See* Symbols, birth and rebirth
Reformation, German, 15, 18–19, 21, 27, 83, 119, 120, 163, 173–174. *See also* Luther
Renaissance, 27, 48, 49–50, 119, 120, 174
Reuchlin, Johannes, 205
Richter, Gregor, 28, 209–212
Robber knights, 15–16, 19
Rosenberg, Alfred, 130
Rosicrucian Enlightenment, The (Frances A. Yates), 10
Rosicrucians, 131, 138, 211
Rotbart, Franz, 18–19
Rudolf II, Habsburg Holy Roman Emperor, King of Bohemia, 25, 49
Ruland, Martin, 73, 82, 122
Russia, 214

Sacrament. *See* Doctrines
Sagan, 128, 159
Saints, 122
Sal indicum, 29
Salpetersieder, 66
Satan. *See* Devil
Saxon Articles of Visitation, 44, 50–51, 125, 211
Saxony, 14, 18, 23, 24, 25, 44, 128, 131, 133, 154, 184, 209–210, 212–216
Scheer, Conrad, 30
Scheffler, Johannes (Angelus Silesius), 4, 14, 84
Schellendorf, Hans von, 186, 187
Schelling, Friedrich Wilhelm Joseph von, 2, 129
Schmalkaldic League, 19
Scholars, 34, 216
Scholasticism, 48
Scholem, Gershom, 62
Schopenhauer, Arthur, 2, 129
Schweinich, David von, 183–184, 212, 218
Schweinich, Hans Siegmund von, 168, 184, 196, 206, 217, 218
Schwenckfeld, Caspar, 14, 38; followers of, 21–22, 28, 45, 94, 120, 133, 177, 186, 211
Sciences, influence on Boehme, 44, 48, 49, 50–54, 62, 86; astronomy and astrology, 1, 27, 49, 52, 55–59, 70, 147, 209, 215; geocentrism and heliocentrism, 8, 44, 45, 53–54, 55–59, 69–70, 89–90, 109, 114; mathematics, 147, 209; technology, 96
Scivias. *See* Hildegard of Bingen
Scripture, authority of, 26, 36, 44, 45, 49, 50–54, 62, 83–85, 86–87, 114–115, 117–118, 121, 139, 140, 141, 143, 150, 165, 177–178, 188, 191, 197, 199–200, 211; biblical books and figures: *Acts*, 148; Adam, 37, 76, 110, 153, 207; Antichrist (*See* Prophecy, prophesies concerning Antichrist); Arc of the Covenant, 101; Armageddon, 84; *Apocalypse* (*Revelation*), 39, 67,

97, 153; Cain and Abel, 97; crystalline sea, 39, 83, 123; *Daniel*, 136; Dinah, 201; Enoch, 200; Eve, 116, 207; *Ezekiel*, 74; *Fiat* ("Let there be"), 115, 197; *Genesis*, 34, 36, 39, 55–59, 63, 67, 74, 114, 115, 118, 169, 188, 197, 199–204; *Isaiah*, 199; *John*, 36, 38, 74, 104, 115, 118, 169, 174, 197, 199; Joseph and his brothers, 47, 200; Mammon, 120; *Matthew*, 83; Moses, 48, 118, 197; New Man, 159; parable of the faithful servants, 160; Paradise, 35, 84, 85, 98, 112, 114, 115–121, 144, 200, 207, 218; Paul, 148; Prodigal Son, 35, 133; *Proverbs*, 121, 122; waters above and below the firmament, 39, 63, 67, 107; Whore of Babylon (*See* Prophecy, prophecies concerning the Antichrist); woman on the moon, 122. *See also* God; Hell and damnation; Prophecy; Symbols

Scultetus, Abraham (court chaplain to the King of Bohemia), 25, 131, 133

Scultetus, Bartholomäus (mayor of Görlitz), 15, 17, 27, 30, 31, 32, 33, 43, 146, 169

Second Reformation. *See* Calvinists

Seeberg, Erich, 23

Sefirot, 147

Seidenberg, 40

Self-knowledge, 109–110, 121, 123, 149, 159, 171, 177–178, 180–181, 192, 196–197, 206

Sendivogius, Michael, 67

Serfdom, 204

Sermon on Preparing to Die, A (Luther), 38

Seton, Alexander, 67

Sexuality, attitudes toward, 54, 111, 113, 115–118

Shakespeare, William, 195

Sibmacher, Ambrosius, 193

Sigismund (King of Bohemia, Holy Roman Emperor), 15

Silesia, 13–14, 21, 23, 30, 93, 96, 128, 135, 154–155, 157–159, 161, 184, 210–214, 217

Silesius, Angelus. *See* Scheffler

Simultankirche, 20

Solms-Rödelheim, Gunter von, 171

Sommerfeld, Abraham von, 196

Sorbs (Slavic population of Lusatia), 14, 17

Source-spirits. *See* Spirit, in nature; Symbols

Spaeth, Johann Jakob, 4

Spinoza, 129

Spirit, in God, 74, 110, 152–153, 174, 188, 189, 192; in nature, 55–59, 63–64, 69–78; 86, 88, 90, 91, 111, 113–114, 190, 199, 208; and in human nature, 39, 44, 51, 88, 118; illuminative spirit, 54–59; world-soul, 63, 64, 71; *Spiritus Mundi* (*Geist maioris Mundi*), 97, 119, 121, 199

Spiritualism, 37, 38–39, 47, 62, 118, 173, 176, 200, 203

Staritius, Dr., 162, 185, 196

Steinberg, Christian, 138

Stiefel, Esaiä, 134, 160, 162, 163, 166

Strauch, Ägidus, 213

Styria, 96

Süleyman the Magnificent, 19

Sun. *See* Nature, solar system

Sweden, 138, 214

Symbols, concepts, and themes: abstinence, 192–195; androgyny, 115–121, 206; aurora, 52; birth and rebirth, 39, 55, 71, 72, 82, 91, 106, 107, 109, 110, 111, 114, 118–119, 121, 123–124, 134, 145, 153–154, 165, 167, 188, 192, 193, 206; Book of Nature (*Liber Mundi*), 119, 188, 191, 216; center, 100, 118, 198; chaos, 113, 173, 196, 198; circle, 147; circle of life, 91, 111; clock, 189–190; coagulation, 171; compaction, 171; darkness, 32, 147, 150, 168, 175–181, 199; Egyptians, 203–204; elixir, 170–171; essence, 100, 106,

110, 125, 171, 177, 178, 199; eternal band, 103, 110, 124; eye, 122, 123–124; *Gelassenheit*, 208; golden age, 159; harmony (temperature, equality), 71, 90, 189, 192, 195; heraldic symbols, 137; *Ichheit*, 171; imagination, 102, 119, 121, 149–153, 176, 179, 206; impression, 171; light, 82, 102, 104, 106, 109, 112, 123, 125, 141, 145–147, 150, 153, 159, 167, 175–181, 190, 208; lily, 95, 122, 125, 126; love, 71, 88, 108, 146, 175, 186; magic, 150–152; meaning, expression, 77–78, 190, 198; mirror, 83, 122, 123, 147, 149, 171, 179, 180, 182, 192; music (sound), 71, 72, 146, 188, 189, 190, 218; *mysterium*, 197–198; new reformation, 209, 214–216; nothingness, 104, 110, 123, 175, 192–195; opposition, 87, 110, 111, 112, 124, 184, 192, 194, 207; particular, 171; pearl, 159; philosopher's stone, 193; philosophical globe, 147; principles, 90, 101, 109, 113, 117–120, 175–181, 216; reason or logic, 104, 168, 173, 205, 208; root, 110; rose, 95, 122; *Schrack* (flash or "fright"), 71, 87, 106–108, 112, 124, 168, 177, 180, 198; selfhood, 171; sevenfold pattern, 167–168; separation, 82–83, 84, 103; signature, 143, 167, 188–192; Sophia (Noble Virgin of Divine Wisdom), 5, 83, 113, 116–120, 121–126, 146, 149–151, 168, 169, 174, 177, 178, 180, 192, 194–195, 206, 207, 216; source-spirits, 5, 70–71, 73–74, 88, 110, 141, 143–146, 167, 168, 207; speaking word/spoken word, 78, 199; star, 98, 103, 199; star within, 98, 102; *Szienz*, 146; *Ternarius Sanctus*, 101; tincture, 101, 103, 122, 123, 145, 151, 153, 170; *Ungrund*, 147–149, 171, 192; universal, 170–171; wave, 90; *Wesen, wesentlich*, 100, 146, 171, 179; wheel, 5, 74, 106, 109, 123–124, 144–145, 173; will (metaphysical voluntarism), 90, 110, 111–114, 117, 123, 140, 141, 143–145, 149, 151, 168, 172, 174, 178, 189, 190, 192, 194, 205, 207; worlds, 109, 178–179, 192; yes and no, 205. *See also* God; Nature; Spirit; Trichotomy

Tanckius, Joachim, 48
Tanners. *See* Craftsmen, guilds
Tauler, Johannes, 208
Technology. *See* Sciences
Textile industry, 29
Theodicy. *See* God
Theologia Deutsch, 50, 208
Theosophy. *See* Mysticism
Thirty Years' War, 2, 7, 17, 84, 125–126, 127–129, 163–164, 167–168, 173, 204, 214–215; war propaganda, 130–132, 140, 154–156, 157–161, 163
Thuringia, 211
Thurn, Matthias Count, 127–128
Tieck, Ludwig, 2
Tilke, Balthasar, 160, 161–164, 185, 196
Timaeus (Plato), 63
Tolerance. *See* Universalism and tolerance
Trichotomy, triad, 50, 51, 88, 99–100, 147, 206, 211, 216
Troeltsch, Ernst, 38
Turba Philosophorum (Pseudo-Aquinas), 29
Turks, 19, 24, 25, 32, 136, 158, 211
Typology, 74, 203, 204
Typotius, Jakob, 191

Universalism and tolerance, 4, 47, 83–85, 96, 133–135, 141–142, 163–165, 188, 200, 202–204, 205, 206, 210, 215
Upper Lusatia, history and culture, 13–34 (chapter 1), 42, 44, 46–47, 174, 201
Utraquism, 15, 17, 20, 47

Vienna, 131

Wallenstein, 157, 215
Walsh, David, 174
Walter, Dr. Balthasar, 30, 43, 146, 154, 210
War, aggression, tyranny, 141, 144–145, 153, 154–156
Waters above and below the firmament. *See* Scripture
Weber, Max, 120
Weigel, M., 159
Weigel, Valentin, 24, 30, 38, 39, 162, 177, 186, 207, 208, 211

Wheel. *See* Symbols
White Mountain, Battle of, 157
Widmann, Peter, 211
Winter King. *See* Friedrich V
Wisdom. *See* Symbols, Sophia
Witchcraft, 30–31, 183, 211, 215
Wittenberg, 24, 26, 27, 28, 211
Woman, 110, 111; creation of, 110, 116
Women, role of, 169

Yates, Frances A., 10

Žiška, 131, 163
Zittau, 27, 159, 212